The Politics of Public Budgeting

Eighth Edition

CQ Press, an imprint of SAGE, is the leading publisher of books, periodicals, and electronic products on American government and international affairs. CQ Press consistently ranks among the top commercial publishers in terms of quality, as evidenced by the numerous awards its products have won over the years. CQ Press owes its existence to Nelson Poynter, former publisher of the *St. Petersburg Times,* and his wife Henrietta, with whom he founded Congressional Quarterly in 1945. Poynter established CQ with the mission of promoting democracy through education and in 1975 founded the Modern Media Institute, renamed The Poynter Institute for Media Studies after his death. The Poynter Institute (*www.poynter.org*) is a nonprofit organization dedicated to training journalists and media leaders.

In 2008, CQ Press was acquired by SAGE, a leading international publisher of journals, books, and electronic media for academic, educational, and professional markets. Since 1965, SAGE has helped inform and educate a global community of scholars, practitioners, researchers, and students spanning a wide range of subject areas, including business, humanities, social sciences, and science, technology, and medicine. A privately owned corporation, SAGE has offices in Los Angeles, London, New Delhi, and Singapore, in addition to the Washington DC office of CQ Press.

SAGE was founded in 1965 by Sara Miller McCune to support the dissemination of usable knowledge by publishing innovative and high-quality research and teaching content. Today, we publish over 900 journals, including those of more than 400 learned societies, more than 800 new books per year, and a growing range of library products including archives, data, case studies, reports, and video. SAGE remains majority-owned by our founder, and after Sara's lifetime will become owned by a charitable trust that secures our continued independence.

Los Angeles | London | New Delhi | Singapore | Washington DC | Melbourne

The Politics of Public Budgeting

Getting and Spending, Borrowing and Balancing

Eighth Edition

Irene S. Rubin
Northern Illinois University

FOR INFORMATION:

CQ Press

An Imprint of SAGE Publications, Inc.

2455 Teller Road

Thousand Oaks, California 91320

E-mail: order@sagepub.com

SAGE Publications Ltd.

1 Oliver's Yard

55 City Road

London, EC1Y 1SP

United Kingdom

SAGE Publications India Pvt. Ltd.

B 1/I 1 Mohan Cooperative Industrial Area

Mathura Road, New Delhi 110 044

India

SAGE Publications Asia-Pacific Pte. Ltd.

3 Church Street

#10-04 Samsung Hub

Singapore 049483

Printed in the United States of America

Library of Congress Cataloging-in-Publication Data

Names: Rubin, Irene, author.

Title: The politics of public budgeting : getting and spending, borrowing and balancing / Irene S. Rubin.

Description: Eighth edition. | Los Angeles : Sage/CQ Press, 2016. | Includes bibliographical references and index.

Identifiers: LCCN 2016016509 | ISBN 9781506354804 (pbk. : alk. paper)

Subjects: LCSH: Local budgets—Political aspects—United States. | Budget—Political aspects—United States.

Classification: LCC HJ9147 .R83 2016 | DDC 352.4/80973—dc23 LC record available at https://lccn.loc.gov/2016016509

This book is printed on acid-free paper.

Acquisitions Editor: Carrie Brandon

Editorial Assistants: Zachary Hoskins and Duncan Marchbank

Production Editor: Veronica Stapleton Hooper

Copy Editor: Karin Rathert

Typesetter: C&M Digitals (P) Ltd.

Proofreader: Sally Jaskold

Indexer: Sheila Bodell

Cover Designer: Anupama Krishnan

Marketing Manager: Amy Whitaker

SFI label applies to text stock

16 17 18 19 20 10 9 8 7 6 5 4 3 2 1

Contents

Tables, Figures, and Minicases

Tables

Figures

Minicases

Foreword

In this edition of *The Politics of Public Budgeting,* as in prior editions, I argue that public budgeting is necessarily and appropriately political, in the sense of reflecting public priorities. The process of tapping into public needs and desires and incorporating them into the public budget is complicated and not necessarily smooth. In recent years, that process has become tumultuous, much more partisan, and ideological. The work of government budgeters has become more difficult, sometimes nightmarish. Courts mandate spending while ideologues prohibit tax increases; bridges collapse from lack of sufficient money and maintenance, taking lives and property and cutting off transit routes. Social service providers don't get their contractual payments and as a result shrink services and lay off staff. States run out of unemployment funds and have to borrow, at above market rates, from the federal government or tighten eligibility, shorten the time that the unemployed can receive benefits, and/or reduce the amount of money they can receive.

While the practical problems are often overwhelming, for those who study public budgeting and seek to understand it, it has become more exciting. Many years ago, there was a movie serial called *The Perils of Pauline,* where the heroine experienced a series of dramatic, life threatening events that were resolved just before the end of each episode. Budgeting has become a bit like that, only sometimes the budget does not escape in time, and government partly or completely shuts down.

Example: Illinois

Illinois has a Republican governor and a Democrat-dominated legislature. The governor's budgetary powers are very strong: He can reject legislative decisions, rewrite portions of legislation, and reduce budget lines. His policies stand unless a supermajority of the legislature votes to overturn his decisions. The state is in severe fiscal stress, the origins of which stretch back in time.

The governor's solution is to radically change the government. His policies include cutting social services for the poor, elderly, and handicapped, while allowing a tax increase to lapse, making the financial stress more severe, and from the governor's perspective, strengthening his argument that services needed to be cut, public pensions reformed, property taxes frozen, and public unions disempowered. The Democratic legislature has not been willing to go along with the governor's radical program, which also contains term limits for themselves. While they have not been able to overrule the governor, they don't have to pass a budget that the governor feels he can sign. One result has been a long running budget stalemate.

Back in June of 2015, the governor drastically reduced eligibility for day care subsidies for poor people. He also increased the amount that parents had to pay as their share of the costs. One result was that 90 percent of new applicants had to be rejected. The governor argued that such cuts were necessary, because the state was in financial trouble and could not afford the payments. He ignored the consequence that low income families might be unable to afford day care and hence might be unable to work and become or remain dependent on the public sector. He did not mention the possibility that poor parents might have to leave their children in unsafe conditions. Under prior rules, when family members took care of the children while the parents worked, the care providers were eligible for some pay, which may have helped lift the family out of poverty. The governor's supporters argued that family members would continue to provide day care even if they were not paid.

The governor urged the legislature not to restore the childcare eligibility levels. The legislature responded by trying to restore the program and protect it in the future, designing new legislation that would make the day care subsidy an entitlement rather than a discretionary program. That means that the program would become a legal requirement for the state to pay, regardless of the levels of appropriations, which were largely controlled by the governor with his strong amendatory veto powers. The legislative proposal would have protected the program from future cuts by the governor, making future changes up to the legislature. But legislators had to pass their proposal with a supermajority or the governor would exercise his veto and in all probability, they would unable to muster enough votes to override. Earlier in the year, the legislative Joint Committee on Rules (JCAR), which could have rejected the governor's restricted eligibility rule, had been unable to achieve a supermajority to overturn the governor's program changes. Reflecting the trend in the state toward increased political polarization, JCAR had begun to vote along party lines, even though in the past it had acted in a bipartisan fashion.

If the Democrats could get some Republican votes, they would have a chance to pass their legislation. The governor needed to prevent that possibility. The evening before the key vote in the House, some Republicans along with some Democrats met with the governor to argue in favor of restoring the cuts. Confronting the possibility that the legislation reversing his cuts might pass, the governor offered a compromise, raising the income level for eligibility to about 88 percent of what it had been before his cuts but maintaining his increase in the fees that parents would have to pay. Before the governor's cuts, the income eligibility level was set at 185 percent of the federal poverty level; after his cuts it was 50 percent of the federal poverty level. The governor's compromise proposal was for 162 percent of the poverty level. At 50 percent of the federal poverty level, even a family working full time for the federal minimum wage ($15,080 per year) would not be eligible for assistance. (The average annual cost of childcare at a day care center is over $11,000.) Some categories of formerly eligible parents were still excluded under the governor's new proposal but his offer suggested he would restore categories of eligibility pending further review. He also indicated that he would restore eligibility to 100 percent of its former level when the budget was passed. If the legislators really wanted day care assistance at former levels, they had to agree not only to disempower public unions but also themselves and freeze a major revenue source for local governments.

After the compromise was reached between the governor and the bipartisan group arguing for restoration of former program levels, there was insufficient support in the House to pass the legislation for full restoration and a more secure basis for funding. In the short term, more poor people would be eligible for help than under the governor's original cuts, but poor families might not be able to afford the new higher fees. Most important, under the compromise proposal, the governor retained complete control over the program and could change eligibility or fees in the future almost at will.

Themes of the Illinois Child Care Subsidy Case and This Edition of the Politics of Public Budgeting

The story has a number of themes that are emphasized in this edition. One is the increased intensity of partisanship in budgeting and the implications for democracy. A second is that budget stories develop over time—over years and sometimes decades. A third theme is that to understand the politics of public budgeting in the United States, one needs to understand our federal system, the legal, judicial, and behavioral relationships between the national government, the states, and the local governments. Although the national government and the states are in many ways independent of each other, they participate in joint programs, such as the day care subsidy program. Fourth, despite a history of distrust of overly powerful chief executives, the president, governors, and mayors have a great deal of budget power. At the state level, power between the executive and legislative branches is often one sided in favor of the executive, even when the opposition party controls both houses of the legislature. Supermajority voting requirements to override the governor reinforce this outcome.

Partisanship and Ideology

The long-term trend toward more intense partisanship was apparent in the Illinois case, where a Democratic majority in the legislature confronted a Republican governor and the Joint Committee on Administrative Rules voted along party lines. This intensified partisanship has been visible at the federal and state levels of government in recent years. Party lines have been more clearly drawn, not only where there is divided government—executive and legislative of the opposite parties—but where there is alternation between parties over time. One party wants to maintain publicly funded health and income support programs while the other wants to reduce them; one is willing to raise taxes especially on the rich, while the other seeks to reduce taxes, especially for the rich.

Along with the rise in voting according to party lines has come an increase in ideology with fixed goals and an unwillingness to bargain or compromise. Reinforcing this ideology, outside groups with particular points of view, like the American Legislative Exchange Council (ALEC), composed of conservative legislators and corporate lobbyists, have written, circulated, and in some cases dictated what they consider model legislation. Some wealthy individuals, such as John Arnold, have funded supposedly neutral think tanks to present research results that support their policy goals. Some conservative groups, such as Americans for Tax Reform, threaten to and in some cases actually campaign against those in their own party who have not been firm enough in adhering to the political positions they espouse. On the left, unions and some advocacy groups try to counter business-backed legislative proposals and what they consider biased studies. Unions often support candidates who have been loyal to their cause and take states to court when policies hurt their constituencies. One result is more budgeting rigidity, fewer options, and less adaptability. A second is a loss of quality of information in budget policy debates, because information that is sometimes touted as nonpartisan is actually biased on one side or another. A third consequence is an increased frequency of hostage taking, to force compliance with ideological policy demands, ignoring the damage that may be done in the process.

Intensified Partisanship: Rhetoric Versus Analysis

Political rhetoric has thoroughly penetrated budget stories to the point that readers need to be able to recognize rhetoric and distinguish it from analysis. Program advocates and detractors put out stories that are picked up by the press, stories that are intended less to inform and more to persuade. They often look like factual stories but on further examination, turn out to be misleading or distortionary.

One common technique is to make some proposal look bigger or smaller in order to rouse supporters or opponents. If a particular revenue source generates only a small amount of revenue, opponents to increasing it may report only the proposed percent increase, which looks very large on a small base, and omit the actual dollar increase, which may be both modest and affordable. Those who want to cut spending might cite a huge number of dollars of increased spending in recent years without reporting that the amount is only a tiny portion of the whole. The latter technique is magnified by giving figures that cover many years—much larger than the figure for any one year.

An example of a correct but misleading result occurred recently when the federal Government Accountability Office released a report saying that from 2005 to 2014, the Social Security Disability Insurance program overpaid $11 billion to beneficiaries who were not qualified to receive them.[1]

Such reports on overpayments are often used by program opponents to demonstrate waste and thereby justify spending reductions. They typically do not report or subtract out *underpayments* or describe those who were eligible for payments who did not receive them. They multiply the sums involved by the number of years they pick, which could be any number. Many studies reporting overpayments fail to subtract out the amount of money that the government eventually collects back from recipients who received the money in error.

In the case of disability insurance, although it was not the focus of the report, the GAO did note that the federal government wrote off only $1.4 billion over a ten-year period. When looked at as a percent of program outlays over that decade, the overpayments are extraordinarily small. The accuracy rate is 99.88 percent.[2] The response to such a report ought to be, what an amazingly efficient organization, but the takeaway from the GAO report was $11 billion of wasteful spending.

Some of the Illinois governor's supporters have argued that cuts in day care subsidies are justified because much of the money is wasted. There has been no evidence to that effect, however; it appears that cutting programs for the poor is an item of ideology rather than analysis. Because the day care program is a joint federal-state program, the federal government has an interest in assuring that the programs are tightly run. In line with this concern, the Government Accountability Office did a study in 2010 of five state-subsidized day care programs. It noted that in Illinois the fake applications that the GAO tried to submit were examined and rejected while other states accepted them.[3] Moreover, the state inspector general for Healthcare and Family Services in an annual report in 2010 described the number of cases of abuse investigated in the day care program as twenty-six, of which five were unfounded and which resulted in six convictions.[4] In a typical year, the program serves 150,000 children. The twenty-one cases thus represent .01 percent—one one hundredth of a percent—of youngsters in the program. The six convictions represent an even smaller proportion of the total, .004 percent of the children. In 2014, the inspector general did not even mention childcare fraud or abuse in the annual report. In the Illinois case, there was no effort to either document cheating or provide evidence that cheating was widespread.

Political rhetoric, intended to persuade, often includes extreme examples implying that they are common. Thus public pensions are attacked, because some people have six-figure pensions; conclusion? Pensions are overly generous. Some people gain benefits to which they are not entitled, giving rise to the conclusion that income support programs are riddled with fraud and waste. Given this rhetorical spin on budget discussions, readers need to get into the habit of asking themselves whether the information they are reading is intended to persuade, if there is missing information that might change the interpretation, how many years are included in a study and added up, whether a number is exaggerated or minimized, whether a case is exceptional or common, and the direction of recent trends. Who requested or financed a study may have to become part of the interpretation, and that information is not always easy to find.

Intense Partisanship and Hostage Taking

The childcare subsidy example helps to describe recent trends in budgeting. Those trends not only indicate a sharper partisan divide with its accompanying conflicts, rhetorical heat, and distortions, but also an increased willingness to hold government—and in this case children—hostage to satisfy demands of political minorities when majorities won't go along.

The Republican governor in Illinois was willing to cut off children from day care, making it more difficult for poor parents to work, in order to pressure the legislature to accept his policy agenda, which was not related to the budget and which he knew they did not support. The governor would not approve a budget without legislative acceptance of his unrelated policy agenda, and so the state was without a budget—the stalemate lasted the entire fiscal year 2015–2016. The governor required state employees to continue working and get paid, even without a budget, and he approved the portion of the budget that funded the public schools, while leaving the public universities and contractually provided social services without their funding. Since these constituencies matter to the Democrats who are in the majority in both houses, the governor's strategy was to force them to agree to his policies by hurting the poor, the elderly, the mentally and physically disabled, and college students who are dependent on government grants and services. If the legislature will agree to the governor's policy agenda, he will stop hurting those most dependent on state aid—and restore the childcare subsidies to their prior level.

Hostage taking and various forms of extortion have become common in public budgeting. Sometimes the budget as a whole is held up, even to the point of closing down the government until the desired policies are approved. At the federal level, Tea Party Republicans have threatened to not raise the debt ceiling, risking the credit quality of the federal government, in order to get their preferred policies accepted. The budget stalemates typically occur when there is divided government, an executive of one party and one or both houses of the legislature dominated by the other party. It doesn't matter whether the executive is a Democrat or a Republican. While in Illinois the governor was a Republican and the legislature Democratic, a budget standoff in Pennsylvania also lasted for months, in that case resulting from policy differences between a Democratic governor and Republican legislature. Back in 2011, the Democratic governor in Minnesota tried to use a government shutdown to pressure the Republican-dominated legislature to pass a tax increase on the top earners. In that case, the strategy did not work.

In 1991, Maine, Connecticut, and Pennsylvania shut down; and Pennsylvania had a one-day shutdown in 2007 (Pennsylvania's recent shutdown has been much longer); Tennessee had a partial shutdown in 2002; Minnesota experienced its first shutdown in 2005; New Jersey experienced its first shutdown in 2006. Michigan had a brief shutdown in 2009. While late budgets have been relatively common over the years, actual shutdowns used to be averted, but in recent years, as partisan differences on policy have intensified, shutdowns have become a little more common and last longer. These shutdowns, even when partial or brief, cause service disruptions and increased costs as well as loss of productivity.

The strategy is to use actual harm and the threat of harm—such as threatening to shut down the government—to force compliance with a given policy rather than bargaining and compromise. The more ideological the participants, the less likely they are to be willing to compromise. In the Illinois case, the governor backed down somewhat and negotiated over specific cuts that he had unilaterally imposed only because there was a real possibility that a coalition of Democrats and Republicans might overturn his decision. And despite the negotiations on this one issue, he maintained his stance against passing any budget if the legislature did not go along with his policy demands.

Implications for Democracy

The intensity of partisanship has led to a search for pressure points, such as using the increase in the debt ceiling at the federal level, which used to be automatic, allowing bills to be paid that had already been approved, to force compliance with minority policy proposals. There has been an increased use of supermajority requirements to make it more difficult to pass tax increases. No-tax-increase pledges have also added ideological rigidity to budgeting, so that cutting spending seems like the only option to balance or rebalance budgets, regardless of the will or needs of the citizens.

In the Illinois case, supermajorities were required to override the governor's rule changes, and supermajorities were required to pass legislation that would restore program cuts and create funding stability. Supermajority requirements empower minorities, allowing them to block the will of the majority. Forcing a legislature to pass laws of which members disapprove by holding the poor, the elderly, and the disabled hostage is neither democratic nor just. One may agree or disagree with the policies being pressed, such as smaller government or better funding for the public schools, without agreeing that forcing compliance through hostage taking is a good way to achieve those policies.

The increase in partisanship seems to legitimate tactics such as the use of shell bills, the content of which is determined at the end of a legislative session without sufficient time for opponents to read and react to them. Increased shopping around for studies that support a predetermined policy preference and supposedly neutral policy shops that tilt one way or another depending on who asks for a study or who funds it also delegitimize the policy debate.

The seemingly irreconcilable positions of two political parties unwilling to compromise leads to budget solutions such as pretending to follow the rules without actually doing so. Having passed an across-the-board cut in federal spending after a period of hostage taking, conservatives then argued that the cuts should not apply to defense. Those who opposed the reductions wanted to keep the ceilings on defense to create pressure to lift the ceilings for nondefense spending as well. While this pressure and counter pressure were ongoing, portions of defense spending were taken off budget, taken out of the rules, so they didn't have to be offset with revenues and did not have to come under the ceiling. This was an Alice in Wonderland kind of budget approach, to make some expenditure disappear.

Budget Stories Develop Over Time

Many of the cases described in this edition took years to reach fruition. In Illinois, the story of the day care subsidy cutback began well before the current governor was elected, as prior governors and legislators continued to spend more than the state was taking in in revenue. The dire fiscal stress created a supportive environment for an increase in the state income tax, which is modest in level and not progressive—that is, rich people do not pay a higher proportion of their income for this tax than poorer people. The tax increase was temporary, but when it came time for it to lapse, it was clear that doing so would dig the state into a deeper hole. The new governor supported the return of the tax to its lower level, exacerbating the financial problems of the state. Then the governor acted on his own initiative to change the rules to kick people out of the subsidized childcare program, arguing that it was necessary because the state was in such bad financial condition.

Only if the researcher's time span is long enough can he or she see trends or sequences of actions and reactions over time. As described in a later chapter, one city reluctantly agreed to set up an inspector general office to root out corruption but then stalled for years in actually setting up and funding the office. In one state, citizens voted to require a supermajority of legislators to pass a tax increase; that public vote was binding only for several years. As soon as it was legally possible, the legislature rescinded the requirement and, desperate for additional revenue, passed a tax increase. At the federal level, an agreement to cut spending worked out in one year set spending ceilings for the next several years. The amount of money given out in tax breaks is usually available several years later, when credits are finally used. State commissions have been appointed to look at unfunded mandates to see if any can be eliminated to save local governments money. Such commissions may take years to make recommendations, and then it takes time for legislatures to act—or fail to act—on the recommendations. Sometimes the commissions are then disbanded. Some events only occur episodically, as when a state takes over a local government revenue source, or the opposite, when a state takes over and funds what had been a local government responsibility. The balance of budgetary power between executives and legislators is not fixed and shifts more toward one or the other over a period of years. All these stories develop over time.

Whether a program grows from one year to the next is much less interesting or important than whether it continues to grow faster than other programs year after year and similarly if cuts occur year after year in particular programs, such as state funding for higher education. Are decreases in state aid to local governments during a recession restored after the recession ends? The stories lie less at a given point in time than in the trends over time.

Federalism

Federalism is emphasized more in this edition than in prior editions. The structure of federalism is a key to understanding the politics of budgeting at all levels of government. Federalism is not just about grants from the federal government to the states or from the states to the local governments, the conditions attached to those grants, or mandates that are or are not adequately funded. It is also about taxes, the assignment of responsibilities or preemption of some revenue source, and about jointly provided programs, where the federal government and the states share costs and the states determine program rules, such as eligibility, scope, and the size of payments. The day care subsidy program in Illinois was one illustration of a shared program, but the really big one is Medicaid. In recent years, Medicaid has become very expensive and a topic of partisan contestation. President Obama has sought to expand the program, with the federal government paying for most of the costs, but some states have resisted, despite the offer of money.

The federal government can persuade, offer incentives to the states, and mandate some behaviors as conditions of grants. It can preempt some areas of responsibility but at a fundamental level, the states and the national government are *both* sovereign and independent. The states are not subordinate units of the federal government. The monetary relationship is thus key to cooperation and policy implementation. The states, by contrast, have direct authority over the local government as well as responsibility for them. They don't have to persuade; they can order. They can determine the scope of services, taxing powers, and budget processes. They can help their local governments when they encounter fiscal stress, or they can hang them out to dry, metaphorically. In the Illinois case, the governor wanted the state legislature to pass a law that would freeze property taxes for local governments.

Because the local governments are subordinates of the state government, the states are responsible for their local governments. In the past, this has meant that states have taken measures to assure the fiscal health of their local governments and have helped them out when they got into trouble. However, the number of municipal bankruptcies of large cities and counties has increased in recent years. Some states have taken over the finances of their local governments, others have allowed or encouraged them to declare bankruptcy under federal law. There has thus been a marked change in the relationship between some states and their local governments, shifting from prevention and help to overruling the local elected officials and taking over budgeting, deciding which creditors lose how much money. This shift may reflect the increase in partisanship and ideology noted above, as some governors, intent on keeping taxes down, cut aid to local governments, deny them additional revenue sources, and refuse to spend much money to bail them out.

Executive Versus Legislative Budget Power

The Illinois case illustrates one extreme of executive budget power compared to the legislature. The governor was able to change the eligibility criteria and the fees charged to parents in the day care program on his own initiative. The legislative committee charged with overseeing the rules issued by the executive branch was unable to muster a supermajority to overturn the governor's rule change. The governor maintains the ability to reduce any appropriation the legislature passes, on a line-by-line basis, for this and any other program. That is why the legislature sought to change the structure of the day care program and turn it into an entitlement, which would give the legislature more and the governor less power over the program's design. In that, they did not succeed.

While Illinois is on the extreme end of executive budgeting power, the cases related later in the book illustrate that the general direction of change is toward stronger and more unified executives with more authority over budgeting, even in states that have historically had strong legislatures.

At the national level, the president has weaker veto powers than many governors, but his power over the budget is still considerable. Nevertheless, it is continually being contested, as Congress works to control the way money is spent and "handcuffs" agencies that diverge from congressional intent and instructions. The president can order the agencies to refuse to implement legislative earmarks or issue signing statements indicating that he won't carry out some portion of a law that he thinks violates the constitution or other legitimate responsibilities. Congress can limit the amount of discretion executive agencies have in spending money, can use inspectors general to criticize agencies and the president, and can threaten to not raise the debt ceiling (for more on the politics of the debt ceiling see p. 23), among other tactics.

At all levels of government, the balance between the executive and legislative branches with regard to budgeting is somewhat fluid, depending as much on personality and skills as formal powers. It is one area where informal relations may be as important as formal powers. Thus, when the governor in Illinois sensed that he might be facing a coalition of Democrats and Republicans who could overturn his policies, he backed off and negotiated a settlement with a group of legislators.

Conclusion

To understand the politics of budgeting today, one has to know not only what happened yesterday and the rules of the game but also that the rules continue to change or may be suspended entirely from time to time. The laws guiding the congressional budget process have changed over the years, but even if one understood all the arcane details, one might not be prepared for the *ad hoc* nature of the decision-making that sometimes overtakes the formal rules.

This book should help explain the politics of budgeting in two ways. First, it sets out the separate clusters of budgetary decision-making—revenue, budget process, spending, balance, and implementation—and describes the politics that characterize each one. Second, the book emphasizes the direction of change, patterns of adaptation, and chains of action and reaction, over time. That the politics of budgeting keeps changing creates some challenges but also rewards curiosity and invites new editions of the book.

Acknowledgments

I would like to thank all those who provided the information on which this book revision is based, including legislative budget offices, investigative journalists, those who design and maintain openness websites, and staff who respond to my queries. I also want to acknowledge the struggles of those in the budgeting trenches, as they wrestle with tax and expenditure limits, with shrinking tax bases, with unfunded and underfunded mandates, and with contradictory demands from rigid partisans. Finally I need to mention the terrific team at CQ Press, who have always been supportive of this project, and the gentle reviewers of the last edition who offered guidance and suggestions for this one.

Publisher's Acknowledgments

SAGE wishes to acknowledge the valuable contributions of the following reviewers.

Whitney Afonso, University of North Carolina at Chapel Hill

Leann Beaty, Eastern Kentucky University

James Jimenez, University of New Mexico

Mark Nagel, Metropolitan State University

Paul Pope, Montana State University

Lonce Sandy-Bailey, Shippensburg University of Pennsylvania

Notes

1. Government Accountability Office, "Disability Insurance: SSA Could Do More to Prevent Overpayments or Incorrect Waivers to Beneficiaries," Report to the Subcommittee on Social Security, Committee on Ways and Means, House of Representatives, October 2015, http://www.gao.gov/assets/680/673426.pdf.
2. David Dayen, "Why $11 Billion in Government Overpayments Is Actually an Insignificant Amount," *The Washington Post,* November 4, 2015, https://www.washingtonpost.com/news/federal-eye/wp/2015/11/04/why-11-billion-in-government-overpayments-is-actually-an-insignificant-amount/.
3. GAO, "Child Care and Development Fund: Undercover Tests Show Five State Programs Are Vulnerable to Fraud and Abuse," Washington, DC: GAO, 2010.
4. http://www.state.il.us/agency/oig/docs/2010%200ig%20annual%20report%20final%20062011.pdf.

1 The Politics of Public Budgets

A public budget links tasks to be performed with the amount of resources required to accomplish those tasks, ensuring that money will be available to wage war, provide housing, or maintain streets. Most of the work in drawing up a budget is technical, such as estimating how much it will cost to feed a thousand shut-ins with a Meals-on-Wheels program or how much revenue a 1 percent tax on retail sales will produce. But public budgeting is not only a technical, managerial process, it is also necessarily and appropriately political.

- Budgets reflect choices about what government will and will not do. They reflect the public consensus about what kinds of services governments should provide and what citizens are entitled to as members of society. Should government provide services that the private sector could provide, such as water, electricity, transportation, and housing? Do all citizens have a guarantee of health care, regardless of ability to pay? Is everyone entitled to some kind of housing? Should government intervene when market failures threaten people's savings and investments?
- Budgets reflect priorities—between police and flood control, day care and defense, the Northeast and the Southwest. The budget process mediates among groups and individuals who want different things from government and determines who gets what. These decisions may influence whether the poor get job training or the police get riot training—either one a response to an increased number of unemployed.
- Budgets reflect the degree of importance that legislators place on satisfying their constituents and responding to interest group demands. For example, legislators may decide to spend more money to keep a military base open

1

because the local economy depends on it and to spend less money to improve combat readiness.

- Budgets provide accountability for citizens who want to know how the government is spending their money and whether government has generally followed their preferences. Budgeting links citizen preferences and governmental outcomes; it is a powerful tool for implementing democracy.
- Budgets reflect citizens' preferences for different forms and levels of taxation as well as the ability of some taxpayer groups to shift tax burdens to others. The budget indicates the degree to which the government redistributes wealth upward or downward through the tax system.
- At the national level, the budget influences the economy, and so fiscal policy influences how many people are out of work at any time.
- Budgetary decision-making provides a picture of the relative power of budget actors within and between branches of government as well as of the importance of citizens, interest groups, and political parties.

Budgeting is both an important and a unique arena of politics. It is important because of the specific policy decisions it reflects: decisions about the scope of government, the distribution of wealth, the openness of government to interest groups, and the accountability of government to the public at large. It is unique because these decisions take place in the context of budgeting, with its need for balance, its openness to the environment, and its requirement for timely decisions so that government can carry on without interruption.

Public budgets clearly have political implications, but what does it mean to say that key political decisions are made in the context of budgeting? The answer has several parts: First, what is budgeting? Second, what is public budgeting, as opposed to individual or family budgeting or the budgeting of private organizations? Third, what does *political* mean in the context of public budgeting?

What Is Budgeting?

The essence of budgeting is that it allocates scarce resources, implying choices among potential expenditures. Budgeting implies balance between revenues and expenditures, and it requires some kind of decision-making process.

Making Budgetary Choices

All budgeting, whether public or private, individual or organizational, involves choices between possible expenditures. Since no one has unlimited resources, people budget all the time. A child makes a budget (a plan for spending, balancing revenues and expenditures) when she decides to spend money on a marshmallow rather than a chocolate rabbit, assuming she has money for only one. The Air Force may choose between two different airplanes to replace current bombers. These examples illustrate the simplest form of budgeting, because they involve only one actor, one resource, one time, and two straightforward and comparable choices.

Budgeting is usually more complicated, with many possible options that are not always easily comparable. To simplify this complexity, budgeters usually group together similar things that can be reasonably compared. When I go to the supermarket, I compare main dishes with main dishes, beverages with beverages, desserts with desserts. This gives me a common denominator for comparison. For example, I may look at the main course and ask about the amount of protein for the dollar. I may compare the desserts in terms of the amount of cholesterol or the calories. Governmental budgeters also try to make comparisons within categories of similar things. For example, weapons are compared with weapons and computers with computers. They could be compared in terms of speed, reliability, and operating costs, and the one that did the most of what you wanted it to do at the least cost would be the best choice. As long as there is agreement on the goals to be achieved, the choice should be straightforward.

Sometimes, however, budgeting requires comparison of different, seemingly incomparable things. How do I compare the benefits of providing shelters for the homeless with buying more helicopters for the navy? I may move to more general comparisons, such as how clearly the need was described or who received the benefits last time and whose turn it is this time. Are there any specific contingencies that make one choice more likely than the other? For example, will the country be embarrassed to show our treatment of the homeless in front of a visiting dignitary? Or are disarmament negotiations coming up, in which we need to display strength or make a symbolic gesture of restraint? Comparing dissimilar items may require agreement on priorities. Such priorities may be highly controversial.

Not only does budgeting have to deal with a large number of sometimes incomparable possible expenditures, it also involves multiple resources, resulting in multiple and sometimes unrelated budgets. Budgeting often allocates money, but it can allocate any scarce resource—for example, time. A student may choose between studying for an exam or playing softball and drinking beer afterward. In this example, it is time that is at a premium, not money. It could be medical skills that are in short supply, or expensive equipment, or apartment space, or water.

Government programs often involve a choice of resources and sometimes involve combinations of resources, each of which has different characteristics. For example, some federal farm programs involve direct cash payments plus loans at below-market interest rates, and welfare programs often involve dollar payments plus food stamps, which allow recipients to pay less for food. Federal budgets often assign agencies money, personnel, and sometimes borrowing authority, three different kinds of resources. Some programs offer tax breaks, while others offer direct payments and still others offer insurance that is unavailable or extraordinarily expensive in the private sector.

Balancing and Borrowing

Budgets have to balance. A plan for expenditures that pays no attention to ensuring that revenues cover expenditures is not a budget. That may sound odd in view of huge federal deficits, but a budget may technically be balanced by borrowing. Balance means only that outgo is matched or exceeded by income. Borrowing means spending more now and paying more in the future, when the debt has to be paid off. It is a balance over time.

To illustrate the nature of budget balance, consider me as shopper again. Suppose I spend all my weekly shopping money before I buy dessert. I have the option of treating my dollar limit as if it were more flexible, by adding the dimension of time. I can buy the dessert and everything else in the basket, going over my budget, and then eat less at the end of the month. Or I can pay the bill with a credit card, assuming I will have more money in the future with which to pay off the bill when it comes due. The possibility of borrowing against the future is part of most budget choices.

A budget is not balanced if there is no plan for and reasonable expectation of paying back the loan over time. Similarly, a budget is not balanced if insufficient money is set aside each year to pay for future expenses. For example, a number of years ago, San Diego approved an increase in pension benefits for its employees but did not increase its annual contributions to the pension system to cover the increased costs, because pension board members hoped a strong stock market would reduce the need for city contributions. When the market faltered, the city was stuck with a huge deficit in the pension fund.

Process

Budgeting cannot proceed without some kind of decision process. The process determines who will have a say at what point in the decision-making and structures the comparisons among alternatives. A successful budget process assures that decisions are made in proper order and in a timely way.

Returning to the shopping example, if I shop for the main course first and spend more money than I intended on it because I found some fresh fish, there will be less money left for purchasing the dessert. Hence, unless I set a firm limit on the amount of money to spend for each segment of the meal, the order in which I do the purchasing counts. Of course, if I get to the end of my shopping and do not have enough money left for dessert, I can put back some of the items already in the cart and squeeze out enough money for dessert.

Governmental budgeting is also concerned with procedures for managing trade-offs between large categories of spending. Budgeters may determine the relative importance of each category first, attaching a dollar level in proportion to the assigned importance, or they may allow purchasing in each area to go on independently, later reworking the choices until the balance between the parts is acceptable.

The order of decisions is important in another sense. I can first determine how much money I am likely to have, and then set that as an absolute limit on expenditures, or I can determine what I must have, what I wish to have, and what I need to set aside for emergencies and then go out and try to find enough money to cover some or all of those expenditures. Especially in emergencies, such as accidents or illnesses, people are likely to obligate the money first and worry about where it will come from later. Governmental budgeting, too, may concentrate first on revenues and later on expenditures or first on expenditures and later on income. Like individuals or families, during emergencies governments commit expenditures first and worry about where the money will come from later.

Governmental Budgeting

Public budgeting shares many of the characteristics of budgeting in general but differs from personal and business budgeting in some key ways:

1. In public budgeting there are a variety of participants, who have different priorities and different levels of power over the outcome. In family and business budgeting there may be only one key actor or a few, and they may have similar views of what they want the budget to achieve.
2. Individuals and small business owners spend their own money. By contrast, in governmental budgeting, elected officials spend citizens' money, not their own. Public officials can force expenditures on citizens that they do not want, but citizens can vote the politicians out of office. Consequently, public officials try not to stray too far from what they think the public wants. Because of the variety of budgetary actors and demands, there is no single set of demands to follow. To create enough coherence to guide decisions, budget processes in the public sector involve the negotiation of consent among representatives of competing groups and interests.
3. Because elected officials make spending decisions for citizens, accountability is an important part of public budgeting. The budget document helps explain to the public how its money was spent. That document is necessarily public, unlike business budgets, and may be the focus of public controversy, if citizens do not like what they see or do not fully understand it.

4. Public budgets are planned well in advance of the beginning of the fiscal year and are intended to last a whole year or even two years. Many changes can occur over that period of time—in the economy, in public opinion, in political coalitions, in the weather. Public budgets need to be able to respond to such events during the year without major policy changes. If the deals that were necessary to prepare the budget come undone during budget implementation, budget actors will lose their trust in the process. Private sector budgets are more flexible: They can be remade from week to week or month-to-month, and policy changes can be adopted at any time. Private sector budgets are not designed to last unchanged for eighteen months or more. Moreover, private sector budgets are less open to pressures from the outside, from public opinion, or frequent changes in elected officials.

5. Public budgets are incredibly constrained compared with those in the private sector. There are often rules about the purposes for which revenue can be spent and the time frame in which it can be spent as well as requirements for balance and limits on borrowing. Capital projects may require public referendums for approval, and taxation growth may be limited to the inflation rate unless citizens approve higher rates in a referendum. Other levels of government may mandate some activity or expenditure or limit the amount or form of taxation. Past agreements may bind current decision makers. Courts may play a role in budgeting, sometimes telling jurisdictions that they must spend more money on education or prisons or that a proposed program is illegal or that officials cannot cut spending in some area because such reductions violate the constitution. Rather than one bottom line, which is the business model, government agencies may have multiple bottom lines, in each of several funds or accounts, each of which must balance.

The minicase concerning the DeKalb budget (see box on p. 8) should give the reader a feel for governmental budgeting and some of the ways it differs from personal or business budgeting. One key feature of public budgeting is an ongoing, not always courteous, dialogue between opponents and supporters, because no matter how many interests are served by a budget, some claimants will feel they did not get all they wanted or expected. Sometimes politicians and professional staff ignore and at other times respond to the constant stream of criticism and lack of understanding of the issues opponents demonstrate.

The venue of the Dekalb debate was the local newspaper. Accountability does not happen by itself; budgets do not wade into crowds and attract circles of admiring readers. Budgets have to be interpreted; someone has to tell a good story to get the readers involved. This is where newspapers come in, but reporters are not necessarily knowledgeable, and newspapers are not necessarily neutral. Public officials often think they are giving clear signals on the budget and are puzzled by citizen responses. The budget can be harder to explain than elected officials imagine. Public budgeting is complex and rule bound, whereas political dialogue is simple, simplifying, and sometimes biased.

Another theme that emerges from the DeKalb minicase is that nearly all new administrations have to run against their predecessors. They come into office and find a mess and try to clean it up. If they get started without a process of reckoning, they are likely to be blamed for the financial mistakes of their predecessors, who, as in this case, may have run down fund balances and put off expenditures until the next administration. The inherited budget may be booby-trapped in a variety of ways, because time is an element in budgeting and expenditures can be put off or revenue moved up.

Prior administrations may still be around to find fault, hoping to return to office. Other potential electoral rivals can play a similar role, picking the budget apart, making normal decisions look odd, emphasizing projects that have not been completed or that came in over estimated costs. Taxpayer groups may criticize the budget from their own point of view. Politics thus infiltrates budgeting whenever the budget goes public. Budgeters have to stay alert to the political implications of their actions and the implications of politics for their actions. Keeping governmental finances afloat can be difficult when others are intentionally rocking the boat. There can be great temptation to keep parts of the budget obscure to prevent massive criticism from political opponents.

The attack and defense of the DeKalb budget made clear that there is policy in the budget, not just technical decisions about the timing of debt issuance or increases in the property tax rate. The editorial was wrong in some of its charges, but it was right in noting the increase in fees for developers. These fees were not just a way of balancing the budget; they reflected a judgment about who should pay for government and who should benefit from public spending. In this case, the former mayor had implemented a policy whereby all residents paid for growth. He claimed that everyone benefited, but it seemed likely that developers and new businesses benefited disproportionately compared with existing residents and businesses. In many cities, growth is highly subsidized, often by citizens who do not benefit directly from it and who might prefer that additional growth not take place. In DeKalb, the citizens were asked in a political campaign precisely whether they wanted to continue to subsidize growth, and they said no, voting to change mayors in order to change the existing policy. If politicians drift too far in their policies from what citizens wish, they are likely to be turned out of office at the next opportunity.

The manager's letter to the editor made clear that public budgeting is constrained—by other levels of government, through prior agreements to earmark tax increases and by state-mandated expenditures and by competition with surrounding jurisdictions. The manager defended the charging of fees to developers by noting that surrounding towns were doing the same thing, so the community would not lose development by charging a fee.

The point of the minicase is that public officials must not only do the right thing for the community and follow the public will, as best they understand what that is, but also figure out a way to explain and justify their choices. They are engaged in a dialogue in which there are always other arguments, whose advocates represent legitimate interests. Equally important, engaging in this dialogue is a way of getting the public involved and getting across information about budgetary decisions in a way that people can understand.

In sum, public budgeting is necessarily and legitimately different from personal and business budgeting. It is not only that the budget is fought out in public but that it involves a variety of actors with different perspectives and interests. Moreover, those who make the decisions about spending are not the ones who actually pay the bills, and that fact introduces problems of responsiveness of elected officials and accountability to the public. More than personal or business budgets, public budgets are highly constrained, surrounded by rules, and hence somewhat rigid, while at the same time open to and necessarily influenced by changes in the environment.

Minicase: City Manager Replies to Scathing Budget Critique

DeKalb, Illinois, has a council-manager form of government with an active, policy-oriented mayor. One mayor, who favored business development and expansion, was defeated by a candidate who advocated a different balance between new development and existing neighborhoods. Not long after the new mayor and a new manager took office, the local newspaper ran an editorial criticizing the new manager for his fiscal practices.

Filled with innuendo, exaggeration, and outright mistakes, the editorial was a thinly disguised effort to discredit the new administration and its policies of balanced growth. It argued that taxes and fees were growing, that the city was trying to build too large a fund balance (demonstrating unnecessary taxation), and that it was unclear where the increased revenues were going. The editorial further charged that the former administration had run a tight ship and that the city was in good financial shape when the new mayor took over, but that now staff were resigning and were not being replaced, reportedly to save money. The implication was that the new manager and mayor were fouling things up.

The new manager responded with a letter to the editor. In his reply, he documented the problems he had inherited from the prior administration. The city finances had not been so fine when he began his term. Property taxes increased due to state-mandated expenditures; the increase in sales taxes was obligated to the Tax Increment Financing District, a district formed a number of years earlier to fund economic development, and to other units of government through existing intergovernmental agreements. The actual amount of sales tax revenue going into the general fund was decreasing, not increasing, so there was no puzzle about where the increased revenue was going, contrary to what the newspaper editorial had said.

Finally, the editorial had correctly pointed out that the city had increased the fees levied on developers to pay the present and future costs of growth. The new administration's goal was for growth to fund itself, rather than be subsidized by the existing community residents. The manager argued that such policies were common, not only elsewhere in the country, but in the neighboring cities with which DeKalb was competing. This fee policy symbolized the policy difference between the current and previous administrations.

A Variety of Actors

The actors involved in budgeting have different and often clashing motivations and goals. In the executive branch, bureau chiefs, budget officers, and chief executives are involved in the budget process; in the legislative branch, legislators and their staff members make proposals and react to proposals given to them. Interest groups may be involved at intervals, and sometimes citizens get into the act or the press gets involved in budget issues. At times, courts play a role in budgets. What are these actors trying to achieve?

Bureau Chiefs. Many students of budgeting assume that agency heads always want to expand their agencies for reasons of personal aggrandizement, but many bureaucrats are more motivated by the opportunity to do good for people—to house the homeless, feed the hungry, find jobs for the unemployed, and send out checks to the disabled.[1] In the Office of Personnel Management survey of federal employee attitudes in 2014, 95.3 percent of executives responding to the survey indicated that they agreed or strongly agreed that the work they do is important. Not only are the motivations for growth often less selfish than the traditional model suggests, but agency heads sometimes refuse to expand when given the opportunity.[2] Administrators may prefer to hire fewer but more qualified employees and refuse to add employees if doing so would not add to the agency's capacity to get things done.[3] Expansion may be seen as undesirable if a new mission swamps the existing mission, if it appears contradictory to the existing mission, or if the program requires more money to carry out than is provided, forcing the agency to spend money designated for existing programs on new ones or do a poor job. Moreover, most bureaucrats, if not all, believe that their role is to carry out the policies of the chief executive and the legislature. If that means cutting back budgets, agency heads cut back the agencies. Agency heads may be appointed precisely because they are willing to make cuts in their agencies.[4]

Bureaucrats, then, do not always try to expand their agencies' budgets. They have other, competing goals, which sometimes dominate. Also, their achievements can be measured in other ways than by expanded budgets. They may try to attain some specific items in the budget, without raising totals, or may try for changes in the wording of legislation. They may strive to obtain a statutory basis for the agency and security of funding. They may take as a goal providing more efficient and effective service rather than expanded or more expensive service.

The Executive Budget Office. The traditional role of the budget office has been to scrutinize requests coming up from the agencies, to find waste and eliminate it, and to discourage most requests for new money. The executive budget office has been perceived as the naysayer, the protector of the public purse. Most staff members in the budget office are very conscious of the need to balance the budget, avoid deficits, and manage cash flow so that there is money on hand to pay bills. Hence they tend to be skeptical of requests for new money.

At the national level, under President Ronald Reagan, budgeting became much more top-down, with the director of the Office of Management and Budget (OMB) proposing specific cuts and negotiating them directly with Congress, without much scrutiny of requests coming up from departments or bureaus. OMB became—and remains—more involved in trying to accomplish the policy goals of the president through the budget.[5] At the state level, too, there has been an evolution of budget offices concerned primarily with technical goals toward more attention to political and policy-related goals. When the governor is looking for new spending proposals, these may come from the budget office.

Chief Executive Officers. The goal of the chief executive officer (the mayor or city manager, the governor, the president) cannot be predicted without knowledge of the individuals. Some chief executives have been expansive, proposing new programs; others have been economy minded, cutting back proposals generated by the legislatures, reorganizing staffs, and trying to maintain service levels without increasing taxes or expenditures. Whatever the policy preferences of the chief executives, they generally want more power to impose those preferences on the budget. In most states, the governor frames the budget proposal, has a powerful veto, and often has the ability to make cuts during the year to rebalance a budget if revenues fall short of projections. As the Missouri minicase, which follows, demonstrates, those powers can be used to override the legislature's preferences. Similarly, in Wisconsin in 2008, voters passed a constitutional amendment to curtail the governor's so called Frankenstein veto, which allowed the governor to cross out words and numbers from different sentences creating a new sentence that altered legislative decisions. Governor Doyle had been using that power to increase spending on schools and to allow local governments to increase property taxes more than the legislature wished. The Wisconsin governor's budget powers are still extremely strong, despite the amendment, as he or she can still eliminate words within a sentence of the budget, delete sentences, and omit digits from a number.

Minicase: Missouri Constitutional Amendment Reduces Governor's Powers

In Missouri in November 2014, voters passed a constitutional amendment permitting the legislature with a two-thirds majority to overturn the governor's decisions to withhold funds during the year. The amendment also prevents the governor from proposing a budget with revenues the legislature has not already approved.

According to some observers, the Democratic governor, Jay Nixon, was using budget holdbacks as leverage to prevent the legislature from passing additional tax breaks. The governor wanted the legislature to pass comprehensive tax credit reform; he also wanted the legislature to approve using federal dollars to improve and expand Medicaid. He vetoed or withheld spending additions to his budget request. He argued against legislative program spending increases that were likely to balloon in future years. The governor maintained that the finances of the state could not depend on vetoes that might be overridden, presumably his justification for cutting funds during the year in a way that the legislature could not overturn.

(Continued)

(Continued)

Governor Nixon blocked billions of dollars in spending during his administration. In 2011, he cut funding for forty-five programs during the year. He claimed that much of the money was going to storm relief, but a later audit showed that of $172 million withheld that year, only $7.8 million was spent on disaster relief, giving rise to the belief that he was imposing his goals over the legislature's by remaking portions of the budget during the year. Through the constitutional amendment, the Republican-dominated legislature handcuffed the Democratic governor and gave considerable power over budget implementation back to the legislature.

Sources: Associated Press, "Voters Approve Amendment Limiting Governor's Budget Powers," November 4, 2014, http://www.abc17news.com/news/voters -approve-amendment-limiting-governors-budget-powers/29540868; Marshall Griffin, "Schweich Releases Audit Critical of Nixon's Withholding of Money from the Budget," St. Louis Public Radio, September 8, 2014, http://news.stlpublicradio .org/post/schweich-releases-audit-critical-nixons-withholding-money-budget. See also Jay Nixon, Office of the Governor, "Governor Nixon Restricts $400 Million From Fiscal Year 2014 Budget, Citing Costs of House Bill 253, June 28, 2013," online at https://governor.mo.gov/news/archive/gov-nixon-restricts-400-million-fiscal -year-2014-budget-citing-costs-house-bill-253.

Legislators. Just as executives sometimes have been mischaracterized as always being fiscally conservative, legislators have sometimes been depicted as always trying to increase spending.[6] The argument runs that their success in getting reelected depends on their ability to provide constituent services and deliver "pork"—jobs and capital projects—to their districts. Legislators are reluctant to cut one another's pork, lest their own be cut in return. As a city council member described this norm of reciprocity, "There is an unwritten rule that if something is in a councilman's district, we'll go along and scratch each other's back."[7]

While there is some truth to this picture, the budgetary importance of pork— more properly called legislative earmarks—has been exaggerated. Earmarks are directions in legislation for spending money on particular companies, contracts, locations, or projects or for granting tax breaks to particular companies or individuals. At their peak, earmarks never accounted for more than 1 percent of the federal budget.

Earmarks came under fire at the national level, not because the dollar amounts were so huge, but because the number and costs were growing seemingly out of control and because some of them were embarrassingly wasteful. Even more important, they permit or even invite corruption: Some legislators have rewarded campaign contributions or other favors and gifts with earmarked contracts or tax breaks that benefit specific firms or individuals. The resulting scandals fueled a drive for reform that resulted initially in greater transparency and later in party-wide pledges to abstain from earmarks. In 2007, President Bush instructed the agencies to ignore any legislative earmarks that were not written into law. President Obama stated in his state of the union address in 2011 that he would veto any bill with earmarks in it.

While some legislators have found ways around the controls, evidence suggests a dramatic drop in spending for legislative earmarks. This decline is illustrated in Figure 1.1. Figure 1.2 shows the decline in number of earmarks.

These days, legislators seem more likely to favor small government and tax reductions than expanded programs. Predicting the policy goals of legislators in general is as difficult as predicting the policy goals of executives. They have to be examined case by case.

Interest Groups. Interest groups, too, have often been singled out as the driving force behind spending increases. They are said to want more benefits for their members and to be undeterred by concerns for overall budget balance or the

FIGURE 1.1 Pork-Barrel Spending, 1991 to 2015

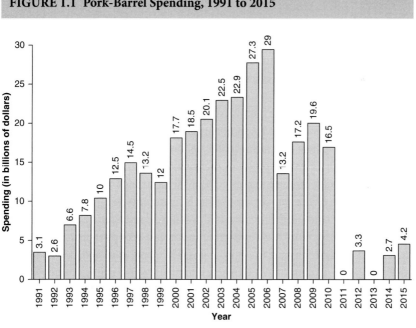

Source: Reproduced with permission from Citizens Against Government Waste, 2015 Congressional Pig Book, online at http://cagw.org/reporting/2015-pig-book#historical_trends

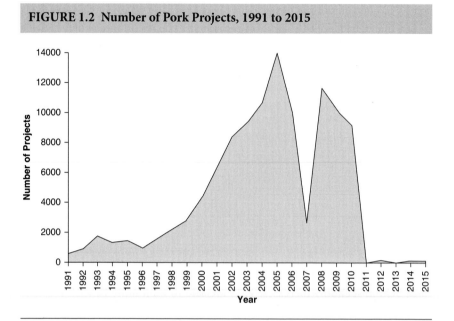

FIGURE 1.2 Number of Pork Projects, 1991 to 2015

Source: Reproduced with permission from Citizens Against Government Waste, *2015 Congressional Pig Book*, online at http://cagw.org/reporting/2015-pig-book#historical_trends

negative effects of tax increases. Well-funded interest groups reportedly wine and dine legislators and provide campaign money for candidates who agree with their positions.

This picture is partly true but oversimplified. Interest groups have other policy goals besides budget levels. Most probably deal with the budget only when a crisis occurs, such as a threat to funding levels. Because they can be counted on to come to the defense of a threatened program, they reduce the flexibility of budget decision-makers, who find it difficult to cut programs with strong interest group backing. But many areas of the budget do not have strong interest group backing. For example, foreign aid programs have few domestic constituencies. Agencies may even have negative constituencies—that is, interest groups that want to reduce their funding and terminate their programs. The American Medical Association sought for years to eliminate the Health Planning Program. Often when interest groups are involved, there are many of them rather than one, and the groups may have conflicting styles or conflicting goals, canceling one another out or absorbing energy in battles among themselves. A coalition of interest groups representing broad geographic areas and a variety of constituencies is likely to be more effective at lobbying. To that end, coalitions may form, but some members of the coalition may not go along with measures supported by others, so the range of items for which the unified group can lobby may be narrow. Extensive negotiations and continual efforts are required to get two or more independent groups together for a lobbying effort, and the arrangement can then fall apart. Interest groups are sometimes more interested in maintaining their autonomy than joining an effective lobbying coalition that may not press their issues enthusiastically. Moreover, some interest groups are interested in lowering taxes rather than maintaining or increasing spending.

Citizens. Citizens play a role in budgeting when they vote on referendums to limit revenues, forbid some forms of taxation, require budgetary balance, or amend the constitution to limit executive budget power. They may initiate legislation that requires some given percent of revenues to be spent on education or otherwise lock in their budget priorities. They sometimes voice their opinions at budget hearings, reply to public opinion polls, and call or write their elected representatives. Their knowledge of the budget usually is not detailed, but their feelings about the acceptability of taxation and priorities for spending constrain public budgeting. The public's preferences for less-visible taxes and for taxes earmarked for specific expenditures have been especially important in shaping tax structures. Citizens have reacted to reports of corruption by voting affirmatively on referenda to create offices of the Inspector General to oversee spending and uncover fraud and abuse.

In twenty-four states, citizens can put a proposal on the ballot. Many of these proposals have budgetary implications, sometimes mandating the expenditure of funds without any source of revenue or cutting taxes without any parallel cuts in spending or offsetting tax increases. In Washington state, for example, a citizens' initiative to increase class sizes was estimated to cost the state about $2 billion for fiscal years 2016 and 2017; the cost was projected to increase to $2.7 billion for the following two years. There was no mention of where this money was supposed to come from.[8]

The Courts. The courts play an intermittent role in budgeting.[9] They become involved when some budget actors, often interest groups, bring suit against the government. Suits that affect the budget may involve service levels or the legality of particular forms of taxation. If a particular tax is judged unconstitutional, the result is usually lost revenues. If there is a suit concerning levels of service, a government may be forced to spend more money on that service.

Constitutional requirements to provide adequate funding for public schools or to avoid cruel and unusual punishments have often gotten courts involved in mandating spending. For example, after years of underfunding the public schools, the state supreme court in Washington fined the state $100,000 per day for each day that it continued to defy the court mandate to provide adequate spending for education, reducing class sizes, and improving teacher pay. The court had mandated improvements in 2012, but according to the court, the state had done too little to comply. In September of 2015, the court ruled the state in contempt but agreed to wait until the end of the 2015 legislative session before imposing sanctions. When the governor and legislature failed to come up with a plan, the penalty was imposed. Other states have also had battles with courts over school funding that resulted in threatened sanctions. The New Jersey Supreme Court once shut down the schools for eight days, and in 2016, the supreme court in Kansas threatened to shut down the schools if adequate funding was not provided.[10]

Damage suits against governments can also affect expenditures. These are usually settled without regard to the government's ability to pay. The result may be forced cuts in other areas of the budget, tax increases, or even bankruptcy. When the courts get involved, they may impose budget priorities. They introduce a kind of rigidity into the budget that says do this or pay this first.

The courts also may intervene in decisions about which actors have more power over budget decisions. In New York, the courts decided in favor of the governor over the legislature; in Maryland, the courts decided that the governor had to fund programs that the legislature had passed and he had approved in prior years. In Chicago, the courts have gotten involved in determining the degree of independence of the inspector general.

Courts sometimes judge whether programs are legal and whether rights have been violated. At the national level, the Supreme Court judged the constitutionality of the Obama administration's health reform law, which contains both revenue increases and spending cuts. Typical areas in which courts have mandated expenditures by state and local governments, besides school funding, are prison overcrowding (declared cruel and unusual punishment) and the deinstitutionalization of mentally ill and mentally handicapped patients. From the perspective of the courts, the priority of rights outweighs immediate concerns over balanced budgets, autonomy of governmental units, and local priorities.

The courts have increasingly gotten involved in both bankruptcy cases and pension funding issues. In both these situations, one key concern is the circumstances under which a government can go back on prior legal and sometimes constitutionally protected commitments. (See the minicase of New Jersey on p. 17 for one example.)

Minicase: The Courts and New Jersey Pension Reform

In New Jersey in 2011, the governor engineered a pension reform to begin to remedy years of state failure to contribute the annually required contributions to the state pension system. The agreement required additional contributions from both the workers and the state to make up for prior underfunding. The reform included a binding promise from the state to discontinue its practice of failing to make its whole payment. The workers were granted an enforceable contractual right to the increased contributions from the state.

Violating his own reform law, the governor then failed to put in the whole state share. The resulting lawsuits reached the state supreme court. The judges decided 5–2 that the governor and legislature could not legally require an increased payment to the pension system, because the state's constitution prohibits lawmakers from binding the state to financial obligations greater than 1 percent of the budget without citizen approval in a referendum. Under the reform law, the state payment would be closer to 7 percent of the budget.

The employee unions questioned whether the 2011 deal created any new debt or only required the payment of existing debt, but the judges argued that it didn't matter and invalidated the 2011 reform that prevented the state from shortchanging the pensions. The court argued that although the governor and legislature intended to create a contract, they did not have the legal authority to do so and hence could later violate that illegal contract.

Source: Andrew Seidman and Maddie Hanna, "N.J. Supreme Court Sides With Christie in Pension Case," *Inquirer Trenton Bureau,* June 9, 2015 online at http://www.philly.com/philly/news/politics/20150610_N_J__Supreme_Court_sides_with_Christie_in_pension_case.html#IUpA1ttsFLpkJwfE.99

The Press. The press plays several roles in budgeting. First, it helps spread the word about budgetary decisions, explaining the significance of those decisions in more understandable terms than those in the budget document. They frame the issues for the public. Second, reporters tend to look for conflicts, for scandals, or for abuses that make good stories. Third, editorials may call for spending decreases and tax reductions or argue against particular proposed spending cuts. They advise the public on whether to vote for or against referenda and inform citizens of the likely consequence of passage or failure to pass such measures.

Not only do these various budget actors have different and potentially clashing budgetary goals, they wield different levels of power at different times. The courts, the press, and the public are not routinely involved in decision-making, they episodically influence and sometimes determine budgetary decisions. For the routine actors, the combination of different preferences and different levels of power has to be orchestrated by the budget process in such a way that agreement is reached and the players stay in the game, continuing to abide by the rules. If some actors lose on important issues during the creation or approval of budget proposals, they may try later to influence budget implementation to favor themselves. Or the actors with less budget power may try to change the budget process so that they have a better chance of influencing the outcome next time. If some actors feel too powerless over the budget, they may cease to participate or become obstructionist. Why participate in negotiations if the decision will go against you regardless of what you do?

Separation of Payer and Decider

One of the major characteristics of public budgeting is that those who pay the bills are not the ones who make the decisions on how the money is to be spent. The possibility exists that elected officials will spend the money differently than taxpayers wish. This problem and its solution over time have been clearly visible at the local level.

In some cities in the later 1800s, the problem was solved by having taxpayer groups elect their own members as mayors and council or board members.[11] Payer and decider were, if not the same individuals, then of the same social class with the same interests. At that time, nearly all local taxation was based on property taxes, and only those who owned property could vote or run for office in many places. Under the control of these taxpayers, local officials spent money on projects that would benefit those paying the taxes—projects such as public markets, ports, roads, and bridges.

Over the years, as more poor people moved into the cities and were permitted to vote without property ownership, a gap began to open between the wealthy people who were paying the bills and poorer people who benefited from government services and elected people who would provide them those benefits. Those who made the taxing and spending decisions were no longer under the thumb of the major taxpayers. What the wealthy wished to spend their tax money on and what elected officials actually spent the money on began to diverge. When tax money was not being spent on the wealthy, they opposed taxation. Antitax revolts subsequently became widespread.

During the twentieth century, property ownership broadened as immigrants and blue-collar workers bought their own homes. Also, over the last generation taxation at the local level has shifted away from dependence on property taxes and toward sales taxes. The result is that there is not now a class of taxpayers and a class of tax users or consumers of government services. Everyone pays local taxes, including the relatively poor in many cities. The result has been to shift the focus of concern to whether everyone benefits from public taxation or only a few. For those services that benefit only a few, the question arises, why should everyone have to pay for them?

At the national level and in some states, the tension between those who pay the taxes and those who benefit from them remains, because the graduated income tax exempts the very poor and taxes the very rich more heavily than the middle class. The result has been an ongoing effort to shift the burden of taxation up or down in a moderated form of class warfare.

At all levels of government, those who demand services that benefit only a narrow group and want others to pay for those benefits have to be strategic. They may form a coalition with others who also want narrow benefits; they tolerate some projects that others want, in exchange for support on their favored projects. Still, there are expenditures in many budgets that benefit one group or interest that are not balanced by benefits to other groups or interests. Such expenditures can be politically contentious and may be disguised or obscured.

Sometimes whether there will be political stress depends on perception or presentation, not on the characteristics of the actual program. Taxpayers who earn regular incomes often bridle at paying for welfare for those who do not work, seeing it as an outlay from which they do not and will not benefit. Viewed differently, anyone could end up needing unemployment benefits or even welfare, when the economy performs poorly or downsizing throws older workers out of their jobs. If taxpayers see themselves as possible future beneficiaries of a safety net, they may be willing to support it; to the extent that they see such expenditures as only for others and believe that they will never need such services, they are more likely to oppose it. The separation between taxpayer and budgetary decision-maker highlights the importance of symbolic politics—that is, the way expenditures are presented and viewed. Expenditures that benefit some narrow group may survive if they are represented as being for the collective good, whether they are in fact or not.

Sometimes it is difficult to make a convincing argument that everyone benefits from an expenditure aimed at a few or from a tax break that benefits a narrow group. Elected officials may try to obscure such costs or make them seem smaller than they are in order to avoid controversy or quiet opposition. Because some budgetary decisions will not be acceptable to everyone, budgets have not always been clear about the decisions that underlie them.

In a democracy, the budget document is an important means of public accountability, reporting to the payers what the deciders have done with tax money. The clarity and openness of the document is critical. Did the public's representatives spend tax revenue as the majority of citizens wished, or did they spend it on some project, program, or tax break demanded by a few who had political influence? Citizens do not typically watch the decision-making, but they and the press have access to the budget document and can look for the answers. They can see whether officials kept their promises if the budget is clear enough.

In recent years, there has been progress in making budgets more readable, inclusive, and informative. To achieve more transparency, budgeters have tried grouping expenditures by program and establishing performance goals and measurements for each program. At the national level, the Government Performance and Results Act of 1993 (GPRA), updated in 2011 by the GPRA Modernization Act, required that all federal agencies create program plans and performance measures. The goal of performance budgeting at all levels of government has been to broaden the notion of accountability from a record of where the money was spent to how well the money was spent and to hold public officials accountable for program outcomes and impacts. The movement toward improved accountability, better reporting, and more readable budgets suggests that public officials should be free from prior constraints and should be allowed to use their training and best judgment but should be held accountable for their choices after the fact. Accurate reporting of what they have done and the consequences of those decisions is absolutely necessary for this model to work. But if elected officials have made choices that some members of the public disapprove of, officials may be reluctant to report the details of their decisions, lest they open themselves to attack. Political opponents can use performance data to attack an agency, program, or administration. The vulnerability to attack contributes to ambivalence about collecting possibly damaging data and making it public. If officials have made mistakes, they may be reluctant to reveal them (see the minicase "Doctoring Audit Reports" on p. 21).

Every budget is selective to some degree about what it will present and how. The art of selective revelation is part of public budgeting. The amount of secrecy in budgets goes up and down with different administrations and requires constant monitoring.

Minicase: Doctoring Audit Reports

Audit reports are essential to after-the-fact accountability. They must be honest and open beyond question. But the temptation to hide wrongdoing or the suggestion of cronyism, ineptitude, laxness of supervision, or outright corruption sometimes leads to refusal to make audit reports public or to editing out (called *redacting*) the suggestive portions. In one recent case, the inspector general for USAID was accused by whistle-blowers of removing critical portions of reports from 2011 to 2013. He was only in an acting capacity and had applied for the permanent position; reportedly, as a result he tried to avoid controversy and downplayed criticism of the agency to win support for his application. The *Washington Post* noted that one report from his office was edited down from 20 pages to 9.

Source: Scott Higham and Steven Rich, "Whistleblowers say USAID's IG removed critical details from public reports," *Washington Post*, October 22, 2014. http://www .washingtonpost.com/investigations/whistleblowers-say-usaids-ig-removed-critical -details-from-public-reports/2014/10/22/68fbc1a0–4031–11e4-b03f-de718edeb92f_ story.html?hpid=z2.

Openness to the Environment

The need for accountability means that the budget passed in public should be the budget actually implemented and that the budget should reasonably reflect public desires and the deals that were struck between actors with different goals. But public budgets are open to the environment, which means that they also have to be reasonably flexible and adaptive.

Openness to the environment includes a number of different factors, such as the overall level of resources available (changes in the amount of taxable wealth or in current economic conditions) and a variety of emergencies, such as heavy snowfall, tornadoes, wars, bridge collapses, drought or floods, chemical explosions, terrorist attacks, or water pollution. Changes in public opinion may bring about changes in budget priorities.

The federal system and the resulting intergovernmental relations between national, state, and local governments are also a key part of the changing environment for budget actors. A state government can—as California has done—take over a local revenue source, leaving the local governments with shortfalls, or—as New York State has done—put caps on local property taxes while keeping in place expensive state mandates on local governments. The federal government may offer state or local governments grants, the size of which may vary from year to year. The requirement that some grants be spent on particular items or that a recipient match grant amounts may result in a pattern of spending different from what the state or local government would have preferred.

Budgeting is open to the environment not only in the sense of changing amounts of revenue, emergency demands on spending, and the changing intergovernmental system that frames responsibilities and revenue sources but also in the sense that decision-making itself is public. Committee hearings on the budget are public. Revenue and expenditure proposals are public. They are reported in newspapers and debated in editorials, blogs, and letters to the editor. The budget as proposed and as adopted is available for public inspection as are reported comparisons of plans and actual spending. The whole budget process takes place under public scrutiny. Potentially embarrassing mistakes are harder to hide than in the private sector, which may lead to a kind of caution. Public officials adapt to working in a room with glass walls and no window blinds.

The openness of public budgets to the environment means that budgets have to be adaptable when unexpected events occur. At the national level, supplemental appropriations legislation may help the government deal with emergencies, such as wars, hurricanes, or earthquakes. At the state and local levels, there may be contingency accounts to provide for unexpected events. Budget makers aim to build in enough flexibility to manage the problems that arise without changing the underlying policies that have emerged from complex public negotiations among multiple actors with different points of view.

Constraints

Public budgeting is much more constrained than private sector or family budgeting. The federal government can mandate unrelated state expenditures as conditions of receiving grants; states can tell their local government what to do and how to do it. Some state governments tell local governments what format to use for a budget and what information has to be included. States may limit borrowing by local governments or even require that the state government approves all local borrowing. The reason for the current emphasis on after-the-fact reporting rather than prior controls is that there were so many prior controls that government managers had a difficult time getting anything done. Despite the recent emphasis on after-the-fact reporting, few prior constraints have actually been removed.

One of the constraints in the public sector is the fund structure. Public budgeting is based on "funds"—that is, separate accounts for separate purposes. Money can be spent only through those accounts and cannot be freely swapped between accounts. Such transfers normally require justification and explicit permission. Each account or fund must balance; that is, revenue must equal or exceed expenditures. The result is not one bottom line, as in a family or business, but multiple bottom lines. Creating some flexibility within these constraints requires continuing effort.

Tax and borrowing limits provide major constraints on budgeting. For state and local governments, revenue limits spending, because balance is required by law. If levels of borrowing and total accumulated debt are also limited, it is more difficult to circumvent the requirement for balance by borrowing. Tax limits are a common feature of state laws and constitutions. Procedural requirements for legislative supermajorities to pass tax increases have made it more difficult to raise taxes in some states, regardless of the actual spending level.

At the national level, much of the politics of constraint has been concerned with the level of borrowing. (See the minicase on the federal debt limit below for how this particular constraint has worked.) At the state level, the focus in recent years has been more on limiting taxes. One of the most drastic of the constraints on revenue is Colorado's Taxpayers' Bill of Rights (TABOR), a constitutional amendment passed in 1992. It has been seen as a model for other states, but its tight constraints have caused many problems in Colorado and eroded its popularity. (See the minicase "Highly Constrained Budgeting—Colorado's TABOR Amendment" on p. 25.)

Minicase: The Federal Debt Limit as a Constraint

Unlike the state and local governments, the federal government is not required to balance its budget every year; it may borrow to cover gaps between revenue and spending. Since 1917, the federal government has had a debt limit. Historically, the debt limit has been increased in sufficient time to permit required borrowing. Federal borrowing reflects spending commitments already made, so that a failure to raise the debt limit would result in failure to pay bills on time, with major consequences to the perceived creditworthiness of the nation. In a highly controversial move in 2011, Republicans withheld their support for raising the debt limit unless the Democrats and the president accepted their terms for cutting future spending.

The consequences of failure to raise the debt limit and subsequent default were considered so severe that Democrats in Congress and the president yielded to Republican demands for billions of dollars of spending cuts as the price for Republican votes for an increased debt ceiling. In February of 2014, with the president adamant about not yielding to Republican threats a second

(Continued)

(Continued)

time, Congress suspended the debt ceiling for a year. By March 2015, the country had again reached its debt limit, forcing the treasury department to take extraordinary measures to assure there was enough cash on hand to pay bills. By late fall of 2015, when these measures would have been exhausted, Congress agreed to suspend the debt ceiling until early 2017.

Sources: Mindy R. Levit, Clinton T. Brass, Thomas J. Nicola, Dawn Nuschler, and Alison M. Shelton, *Reaching the Debt Limit: Background and Potential Effects on Government Operations,* Congressional Research Service, July 27, 2011. Peter Schroeder, "Debt Limit Deadline Now Seen at End of 2015," *The Hill,* May 18, 2015 http://thehill.com/policy/finance/242404-debt-limit-deadline-now-seen-at -end-of-2015. Chad Stone, "Four Things to Like in the Budget Deal," *U.S. News and World Report,* November 6, 2015, http://www.usnews.com/opinion/economic -intelligence/2015/11/06/4-things-to-like-in-the-debt-ceiling-budget-deal.

Efforts to control borrowing have resulted in one set of constraints. A second set results from efforts to stop perceived abuses of discretion. Once in place, these controls sometimes become rigid, even constitutional, remaining in place for years, sometimes long after the problem that generated the constraint has disappeared. A third reason for budget constraints is to facilitate supervision. States cannot easily monitor local budgeting and financial conditions if each jurisdiction puts its budget in a different format or includes different information and uses a different definition of balance. Because the states are ultimately responsible for the finances of local governments, they have an interest in keeping local governments financially healthy and identifying those that might be headed for trouble.

Prior constraints in public budgeting include the fund or account structure and constraints on transfers, tax limits, borrowing limits, requirements that tax increases or general obligation bond issues be approved by the public in a referendum, uniform budget formats, and uniform accounting rules. There may be separate rules limiting the number of employees and their rank or requiring the comparative bidding of contracts or purchases over a given dollar amount.

Reforms in recent years have reduced some of these prior controls—such as separate limits on total spending and on the number of personnel. Proposals for reducing constraints sometimes run into the reason for the constraint in the first place. Weakening controls may remove some political or policy tool that is still cherished. Thus in 1993 and 1994 the Clinton administration urged greater discretion for executive branch officials, including discretion over staffing levels. Soon thereafter, the administration and Congress proceeded to pass the Workforce Restructuring Act, reducing federal employment levels by some 270,000. Despite the plea for more agency autonomy, each agency still had an assigned personnel ceiling.

Minicase: Highly Constrained Budgeting—Colorado's TABOR Amendment

The Colorado Taxpayers' Bill of Rights (TABOR) limited the revenue the state could collect in any given year to the previous year's level, plus a factor for population growth and inflation. In 2000, to protect education from the resulting cuts, opponents of TABOR successfully passed Amendment 23, which required the state to increase spending on K–12 education by the inflation rate plus 1 percent every year through 2010.

Beginning in 2001, an economic slowdown affected many states, including Colorado. However, Colorado's problem was compounded by the combination of these two prior constraints, one holding down revenues, the other mandating increases in spending.

Rather than keeping the size of the government budget stable, TABOR had a notorious ratchet effect: The base on which maximum allowable tax revenue is calculated drops with recessions, and the provisions in the constitution make it impossible for the state either to recover former revenue levels or to provide a substantial rainy-day fund to buffer against recession revenue losses. With declining revenues and mandated increases in a major portion of the budget, state officials were forced to cut other areas of the budget deeply. What made this vise so difficult to escape is that TABOR had strong Republican support while Amendment 23 had strong Democratic support, and neither party was willing to compromise.

In November 2005, a new referendum was held. Referendum C eliminated the infamous downward ratcheting effect permanently, while TABOR's spending limits were suspended for five years, with the constraint that revenues over the TABOR ceiling had to be spent on public K–12 education, higher education, health care, and transportation.[1]

The suspension of TABOR ended in 2010, but as a result of the recession and spending limits modified upward by Referendum C, revenues for the state were less than the ceiling in TABOR for years, so TABOR had no immediate effect. Nevertheless, the battle against TABOR continued. In 2011,

(Continued)

(Continued)

opponents brought a federal suit against TABOR, arguing that the amendment violated the federal Constitution, because it removes the power to tax from the legislature. In 2015, The Supreme Court of the United States kicked the case back to the circuit court, asking the lower court to reconsider its decision that legislators had standing to bring the suit. The court's decision regarding the TABOR challenge was related to a recent case in Arizona in which the court ruled that the people were the originating source of all governmental powers and defined legislative powers as belonging to the people. The people could thus pass laws, even when powers were explicitly granted to the legislature. It looks as if TABOR survived the constitutional challenge.

Coloradans have had to live with the law, but when its constraints became too tight, they voted to lift the limits. Douglas Bruce was the person who brought the TABOR amendment to Colorado; overriding the limitations in the law through local referenda is thus called de-Brucing. Cities and counties have made de-Brucing or asking for overrides of the TABOR law from voters commonplace in Colorado. Out of a total of 543 municipal referenda for de-Brucing from 1993 to 2015, 86.4 percent passed.[2]

In 2012, Denver, experiencing fiscal stress, de-Bruced its sales tax permanently and also de-Bruced its property tax, so that the city could keep any growth in revenue that exceeded the narrow limits of TABOR. Recently at the state level, the governor proposed a workaround to TABOR that required treating some earmarked funds as something other than revenue, so the TABOR excess revenue trigger for tax rebates would not be reached. The Senate rejected the proposal.

The rules for what would happen to any excess revenue past the TABOR limits have changed over the years. In 2015, the first use of any excess would go to pay for an earned income tax credit (EITC), which helps poor working people. The amount of the rebate would be 10 percent of the federal EITC. Once triggered, it would become a permanent tax credit. If there was enough revenue left after that amount, it would be used for a temporary reduction in the income tax rate. If there was not enough money left over to pay for that reduction or if there was money left over after that reduction, it would go to tax payers according to their incomes, with richer people getting more money. In 2015, for the first time in fifteen years, the state was expecting enough revenue to trigger the rebate. However, the amount of rebate could shrink if the legislature passed and the governor signed other tax breaks that would reduce the amount of revenue.

In an ironic twist, the rebate was scheduled for 2016, despite a looming deficit, because the rebate is triggered by an increase in revenue that is greater than the growth in population and inflation, not by the existence or size of a budgetary surplus. Revenue growth exceeded TABOR limits but was insufficient to pay the bills, creating a budget gap that would probably require spending cuts at the same time that citizens were getting a tax rebate. And since the state EITC will be funded, the tax rebate will create an ongoing obligation to keep up this tax break for the working poor.

1. Colorado Fiscal Policy Institute, Issue Brief, November 9, 2005.
2. Colorado Municipal League, "Municipal Elections, Revenue and Spending Changes," 1993–Fall 2014, pdf, online at www.cml.org.

Other sources: "Lawsuit Seeking to Overturn TABOR Faces Federal Ruling on Justiciability," *Huffington Post,* February 15, 2012, www.huffingtonpost .com/2012/02/15/colorado-lawsuit-against-tabor_n_1279854.html. Megan Verlee, "How TABOR works: Tracking the Fate of Your 2015 Refund," *Colorado Public Radio,* May 7, 2015, http://www.cpr.org/news/story/how-tabor-works-tracking-fate -your-2015-refund.

The Meaning of Politics in Public Budgeting

Public budgets, unlike personal or family budgets, are necessarily political. The literature suggests at least five major ways of viewing politics in the budget: reformism, incrementalist bargaining, interest group determinism, process, and policymaking.

- The first is a *reform orientation,* which argues that politics and budgeting are or should be antithetical, that budgeting should be primarily or exclusively technical, and that comparisons among items should be based on efficiency and effectiveness. Politics—in the sense of the opinions and priorities of elected officials, interest groups, and voters—is an unwanted intrusion that reduces efficiency and makes decision-making less rational. The politics of reform involves a clash of views between professional staff and elected officials over the boundary between technical budget decisions and properly political ones.
- The second perspective is the *incrementalist* view, which sees budgeting as negotiations among a group of routine actors—bureaucrats, budget officers, chief executives, and legislators—who meet each year (or biennium) and bargain to resolution. To the extent that interest groups are included at all in this view, they are conceived of in the pluralist model. The process is open, anyone can play and win, and the overall outcome is good; conflict is held down because everyone wins something and no one wins too much.

- The third view, *determinism,* is that interest groups are dominant in the budget process. In its extreme form, this argument posits that richer and more powerful interest groups determine the budget. Some interests are represented by interest groups, and others either are not or are represented by weaker interest groups; the outcome does not approximate democracy. There may be big winners and big losers in this model. Conflict is more extensive than in the incrementalist model. This view of politics in budgeting raises the question of whether the interest groups represent narrow or broad coalitions or possibly even class interests. To what extent do these interest groups represent the oil or banking industries or the homeless, and to what extent do they represent business and labor more broadly?

- The fourth view, *the politics of process,* is that the budget process itself is the center and focus of budget politics. Those with particular budget goals try to change the budget process to favor their policy preferences. Branches of government struggle with one another over budgetary power through the budget process; the budget process becomes the means of achieving or denying separation and balance between the branches of government. The degree of examination of budget requests and the degree to which review is technical or political, cursory or detailed, are regulated by the budget process. The ability of interest groups to influence the budget, the role of the public in budget decisions, the openness of budget decision-making—all these are part of the politics of process. In this view of politics, the individual actors and their strategies and goals may or may not be important, depending on the role assigned to individual actors in the budget process and depending on whether the external environment allows any flexibility.

- The fifth view, *policymaking,* is that the politics of budgeting centers in policy debates, including debates about the role of the budget. Spending levels, taxing policies, and willingness to borrow to sustain spending during recessions are all major policy issues that have to be resolved one way or another during budget deliberations. Budgets may reflect a policy of moderating economic cycles, or they may express a policy of allowing the economy to run its course. Similarly, budgets must allocate funding to particular programs and, in the course of doing so, decide priorities for federal, state, and local governments. This view of politics in the budget emphasizes trade-offs, especially those that occur between major areas of the budget, such as social services and defense or police. This view also emphasizes the role of the budget office in making policy and the format of the budget in encouraging comparisons between programs.

These five views of politics have been developed over time and often contradict each other. However, parts of each may be true, and one definition or another may describe different parts of budgetary decision-making or be true of budgetary decision-making at different times or at different levels of government.

Budgetary Decision-Making

This book explores the kind of politics that occurs in budgetary decision-making. What is budgetary decision-making like? We have already discovered that public budgeting is open to environmental changes and that it deals with policy conflicts. Policy conflicts can delay particular decisions or prevent them from being made at all; other budget decisions must be independent enough to be made without the missing pieces. They can be corrected later when missing pieces fall into place. Environmental emergencies can reorder priorities and alter targets that have already been determined. As a result, public budgeting must be segmentable and interruptible. The need for segmentation and interruptibility is satisfied by dividing budgeting into separate but linked decision clusters: revenues, process, expenditures, balance, and implementation.

Decision-making in each cluster proceeds somewhat separately from, but with reference to, decisions made or anticipated in other decision streams. Decisions on spending are made with an eye on revenue totals, even though revenue estimates may not yet be firm. Decisions in different streams may be made iteratively, with tentative revenue estimates followed by tentative spending estimates, followed by updated revenue estimates and fine-tuning of spending estimates. The order of decision-making may vary from year to year. In one year, there may be no change in the definition of balance, so that prior years' definitions frame the current year's deliberations. In another year, the definition of balance may change during the deliberations, requiring adjustments in spending or revenue plans. Sometimes the decision-making moves faster in one cluster than in another and decision makers in the cluster that is ahead may have to guess or anticipate what the decisions will be in other clusters and revise later if necessary.

Each cluster attracts a different characteristic set of actors and generates its own typical pattern of politics. Some clusters attract heavy interest group activity, while others have virtually none. Some clusters are marked by intense competition and negotiations and efforts to bind future decisions to restrict open competition. Some are marked by deep ideological splits, while others seem not to be ideological at all. In some, a technical perspective prevails, while others are clearly determined by the priorities of elected officials and the public, and still others represent a blend of the two.

The Revenue Cluster

Revenue decisions include technical estimates of how much income will be available for the following year, assuming no change in tax structures, and policy decisions about changes in the level or type of taxation. Will taxes be raised or lowered? Will tax breaks be granted, and if so, to whom and for what purpose? Which tax sources will be emphasized, and which deemphasized, with what effect on regions, economic classes, or age groups? How visible will the tax burden be? Interest groups are intensely involved in the revenue cluster. The revenue cluster emphasizes the scarcity of resources that is an essential element in budgeting and illustrates the tension between accountability and acceptability that is a characteristic of public budgets. Revenues are also extremely sensitive to the environment because changes in the economy influence revenue levels and because the perception of public opinion influences the public officials' willingness to increase taxes.

The Budget Process

The process cluster concerns how to make budget decisions. Who should participate in the budget deliberations? Should the agency heads have power independent of the central budget office? How influential should interest groups be? How much power should the legislature or the chief executive have? How should the work be divided, and when should particular decisions be made? Interest groups play a minor role, if any at all. The politics of process may revolve around individuals or groups trying to maximize their power through rearranging the budget process. This jockeying for power rises to importance when the competing parties represent the executive and legislative branches and try to influence the separation and balance between the branches of government. The politics of process may revolve around the policy issues of the level of spending and the ability of government to balance its budget.

The Expenditure Cluster

The expenditure cluster involves some technical estimates of likely expenditures, such as those for grants that are dependent on formulas and benefit programs whose costs depend on the level of unemployment. But many expenditure decisions are policy relevant—which programs will be funded at what level, who will benefit from public programs and who will not, where and how cuts will be made, and whose interests will be protected. Agency heads are more involved in these decisions than in taxation or process decisions, and interest groups are also often active. The expenditure portion of the budget emphasizes competition for limited resources and the resulting trade-offs—choices between specific sets of alternatives. If we want more money spent on streets, does that translate into less money spent on day care? Does more money spent on hurricane relief translate into less money for defense or housing for the poor?

The Balance Cluster

The balance cluster concerns the basic budgetary question of whether the budget has to be balanced each year with each year's revenues or whether borrowing is allowed to balance the budget, and if so, how much, for how long, and for what purposes. The politics of balance deals with questions of whether balance should be achieved by increasing revenues, decreasing expenditures, or both, and hence it reflects policies about the desirable scope of government. Sometimes the politics of balance emphasizes definitions, as the group in power seeks to make its deficits look smaller by defining them away. The balance cluster also deals with questions of how deficits should be eliminated once they occur. At the national level, because deficits may be incurred during recessions in an effort to help the economy recover, the ability to run a deficit is linked to policies favoring or opposing use of the budget to influence the economy, and in particular to moderate unemployment. These issues—whether budgets should balance, the proper scope of government and level of taxation, and the role of government in moderating unemployment—are issues of public concern. Citizens care about which programs and services may be cut back as well as which taxes or fees may be raised. Businesses and investors care about which bills or bonds may not be repaid on time or in full. They may participate in this decision cluster through referendums and opinion polls. Further, broad groups of taxpayers and interest group coalitions representing broad segments of society may lobby on this issue. Political parties may include their policies toward deficits in their election platforms.

Budget Implementation

Finally, there is a cluster of decisions around budget implementation. How close should actual expenditures be to the ones planned in the budget? How can one justify variation from the budget plan? Can the budget be remade after it is approved, during the budget year? The key issues here revolve around the need to implement decisions exactly as made and the need to make changes during the year because of changes in the environment. The potential conflict is usually resolved by treating implementation as technical rather than policy related. Executive branch staff play the major role in implementation, with much smaller and more occasional roles for the legislature. Interest groups play virtually no role in implementation. The allowance for technical changes does open the door to policy changes during the year, but these are normally carefully monitored and may cause open conflict when they occur. The implementation cluster deals not only with how close actual spending is to planned spending, but also to how well, how honestly, and how transparently the money was spent.

Microbudgeting and Macrobudgeting

The five clusters of decision-making outline the nature of the decisions being made, but they tell little about how and why they are made. On the one hand there are a number of budget actors, all of whom have individual motivations, who strategize to get what they want from the budget. The focus on the actors and their strategies is called *microbudgeting*. But the actors do not simply bargain with one another or with whomever they meet in the corridor. The actors are assigned budget roles by the budget process; the budget process also often regulates the issues they examine and the timing and coordination of their decisions. There are choices that they are not free to make because they are against the law or because the courts have decreed it or because previous decision makers have bound their hands. The total amount of revenue available is a kind of constraint, as are popular demands for some programs and popular dislike of others. Budgetary decision-making has to account not just for budgetary actors and their strategies but also for budget processes and the environment. This more top-down and systemic perspective on budgeting is called *macrobudgeting*. Contemporary budgeting gives attention to both macrobudgeting and microbudgeting.

One way of viewing the determinants of budgetary outcomes is as a causal model, depicted in Figure 1.3. In this schema, the environment, budget processes, and individuals' strategies all affect outcomes. The environment influences budgetary outcomes both directly and indirectly through process and through individual strategies. It influences outcomes directly, without going through either

FIGURE 1.3 Decision-Making: Environment, Process, and Strategies

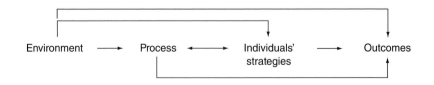

budget process or individual strategies, when it imposes emergencies that reorder priorities. Thus a war or a natural disaster preempts normal budgetary decision-making.

The environment influences the budget process in several ways. The level of resources available—both the actual level of wealth and the willingness of the citizens to pay their taxes—influences the degree of centralization of budgeting. When resources are especially scarce and there is apparent need either to cut back according to a given set of policies or to make each dollar count toward specific economic goals, there is no room for bottom-up demands that result in compromises and a little bit of gain for everyone regardless of need. When resources are abundant, a more decentralized model of process may hold, with less emphasis on comparing policies and less competition between supporters of different policies.

The environment may influence the format of the budget as well. When revenues are growing, there may be more emphasis on planning and on linking the budget to future community goals to stimulate public demands for new spending. When there is little new money, planning may seem superfluous. Changing direction or setting new goals may seem impossible in the face of declining revenues that make current goals difficult to sustain.

Environment, in the sense of the results of prior decisions, may also influence process. If there is a huge accumulation of debt and little apparent way to control it or if the budget has been growing rapidly for reasons other than war, there may be attempts to change the budget process in an effort to control spending and debt. In contrast, if the environment suggests a need for additional spending and the current budget process is delivering very slow growth, the process may be changed to make spending decisions quicker and easier.

The environment influences not only the budget process but also the strategies of the budget actors. The level of resources available determines whether actors press for new programs and expansion of existing ones or strive to prevent cuts and protect their revenue sources from encroachment by other programs. The certainty of funding influences strategies as well. If whatever an agency was promised may never arrive, agency heads are likely to engage in continuous lobbying for their money. Long-term or future agreements will be perceived as worthless; the possibility of toning down conflict by stretching out budget allocation times will disappear. Attention will focus on going after what is available now, whether it is what you want or not, inasmuch as what you really want may never show up and hence is not worth waiting for.

The intergovernmental grant structure is part of the environment that may influence strategies. Because some grant money may seem free, state and local governments may focus their energies on getting grants instead of raising local revenues. Or they may seek to decrease the amount of match required for a grant or increase their authority over how the money can be spent. Intergovernmental grants may make some expenditures relatively cheap and some cutbacks relatively expensive and, hence, frame choices for state and local budget officials.

The legal environment also influences strategies. For example, if public school teachers want tax rises to fund education and there is a provision in the state constitution forbidding income taxes, the teachers must either campaign for a constitutional revision (a time-consuming and difficult task) or support a tax they know to be more burdensome to the poor. Thus the environment can frame choices and influence strategies.

In Figure 1.3, the budget process influences strategies and to a lesser extent outcomes, directly. But there is a double-headed arrow on the link between budget processes and strategies, suggesting that individuals' strategies also influence budget processes.

Budget processes influence strategies in some obvious ways. If the budget process includes detailed budget hearings that are open to the public and interest groups and that actually influence decisions, then various actors are likely to concentrate their efforts on making a good impression at those hearings. If the chief executive prepares the budget, which is subject to only superficial scrutiny and pro forma hearings before being approved by the legislature, anyone who wants to influence the budget—including the legislators themselves—must make his or her opinions heard earlier in the process, before the final executive proposal is put together. Informal discussion with department heads or even telephone calls to the budget office may be the route to influence. If the budget is made two or three times, with only the last time being effective, then actors may grandstand initially, taking extreme positions to attract media attention, and adopt more reasoned and moderate positions later when the final decisions are made. The budget process orders the decisions in such a way that some of them are critical; budget actors focus their strategies on those key decisions no matter where they are located or when they occur.

When budget outcomes contradict some group's preference, the group may try to change the budget process to help it obtain the outcomes it prefers. When coalitions of the dissatisfied can agree on particular changes, fairly substantial changes in process may result. A change in process will bring about a change in outcome, if the change in process shifts power from one group of individuals who want to accomplish one goal to another group with different goals.

The final link in the figure is between the strategies of budget actors and outcomes. The effect of different strategies on the outcomes is hard to gauge, but strategies that ignore the process or the environment are likely to fail. Budget actors have to figure out where the flexibility is before they can influence how that flexibility will be used. Strategies that try to bypass superiors or fool legislators generally do not work; strategies that involve careful documentation of need and appear to save money are generally more successful.[12]

Summary and Conclusions

Public budgeting shares the characteristics of all budgeting. It makes choices between possible expenditures, it has to balance, and it includes a decision-making process. But public budgeting has a number of additional features peculiar to itself, such as its openness to the environment; the variety of actors involved, all of whom come to it with different goals; the separation of taxpayers from budget decision makers; the use of the budget document as a means of public accountability; and numerous constraints.

Public budgeting is both technical and political. "Politics" takes on some special meanings in the context of budgetary decision-making. Budgetary decision-making must be flexible, adaptive, and interruptible, which leads to a structure of five semi-independent strands of decision-making: revenues, process, expenditures, balance, and implementation. Each strand generates its own political characteristics.

Budget outcomes are not solely the result of budget actors' negotiating with one another in a free-for-all; outcomes depend on the environment and on the budget process as well as individual strategies. Budgetary decision-making changes over time: Interest group power waxes and wanes, competition in the budget increases and decreases, and the budget process itself varies. Changes in process take place in response to individuals, committees, and branches of government jockeying for power; to changes in the environment from rich to lean or vice versa; to changes in the power of interest groups; and to scandals or excesses of various kinds.

Chapters 2 to 8 describe the patterns of politics associated with each of the decision streams and the sources and patterns of change over time. The final chapter integrates the decision streams into one model of budgetary decision-making and points out the commonalities and differences among the decision streams.

Useful Websites

The **Congressional Research Service** is an agency of Congress that issues reports to members of Congress, helping members understand issues and past history of particular bills. A number of their studies deal with budget topics. While not issued to the general public, many of these studies are reprinted on various websites. For example, a discussion of the 2013 Department of Defense budget request is posted on the Department of State website (http://fpc.state.gov/documents/organization/189140.pdf). Also on that website is a CRS report analyzing the constitutional issues with the Patient Protection and Affordable Health Care act (Pub. L. no. 111-148, as amended), sometimes called Obamacare (http://fpc.state.gov/documents/organization/189134.pdf). **Open CRS** (www.opencrs.com) is a wiki where individuals can post CRS studies they have obtained. These sometimes include budgeting topics, such as "Reducing the Budget Deficit: The President's Fiscal Commission and Other Initiatives" (http://assets.opencrs.com/rpts/R41784_20110429.pdf). The **University of North Texas digital library** (http://digital.library.unt.edu/explore/collections/CRSR/) makes an effort to find CRS studies posted by individuals on various websites.

The **National Council of State Legislatures** (www.ncsl.org) is a good general source for information on state budgeting and policy issues.

For discussion of many budget issues including the impact of proposed legislation on economic classes, especially on the poor, see the **Center on Budget and Policy Priorities** (www.cbpp.org). The website includes material on state budgeting issues with a similar focus. The **Tax Foundation** (www.taxfoundation.org), with a somewhat different focus, tracks tax burdens and distributional effects of taxes, including those on businesses, at the federal and state level. Though each of these organizations has a point of view, both provide basic explanations of many key issues in clear language.

For data on earmarks, the federal **Office of Management and Budget** has posted a list of earmarks from 2005 to 2010 on its website (http://earmarks.omb.gov/earmarks-public/). The White House does not include in its database executive based earmarks, that is, sole source or noncompetitive contracts. For a different perspective on earmarks, see **Citizens Against Government Waste** and its congressional PIG book (www.cagw.org/reports/pig-book/#trends). This website documents the rise of what it derogatorily calls pork and its recent decline.

Ballotpedia (http://ballotpedia.org/wiki/index.php/Main_Page) is a good source for explaining one technique for citizen input in taxation and budget issues. The website describes individual citizen referenda and initiative measures that have been proposed and their status.

The federal **Office of Personnel Management** does an annual survey of employee attitudes toward their work and workplace. The surveys are posted online from 2004 to 2014. Called the Federal employee viewpoint survey, it is available at http://www.fedview.opm.gov/.

2 Revenue Politics

> But if you really want to raise taxes, I do want to have an argument.
>
> —Grover Norquist

> And I don't think you can have a rule that you're never going to raise taxes or that you're never going to lower taxes. I don't want to rule anything out.
>
> —Rep. Peter K. King

In public budgeting, the tax payers and the decision makers who determine tax and spending levels are separated. This separation sets up the possibility of some radical disagreements. Citizens would undoubtedly be happier about paying taxes if they could choose the services they wanted and pay only what they felt those services were worth. They might be even happier if they could get others to pay the taxes while they received the services. Individual taxpayers usually do not control the mix of services and may have to pay for some programs they do not want. Moreover, many citizens are convinced that they are paying for waste and mismanagement and that others are getting away with paying less than they pay. They resent being forced to pay what they consider to be more than their share.

Elected officials often have legal power to raise taxes, but they cannot do so willy-nilly. The ability to raise taxes is highly constrained, by legislative or constitutional tax limits, by politicians' campaign promises and written pledges not to increase taxes, and by the often justified belief that the public will throw out of office any elected officials who raise taxes. Active lobby groups continually push for reductions in taxes and oppose increases. Further, many elected officials express the need to avoid putting an undue burden on businesses that would make it difficult for them to compete. Given all these constraints on raising taxes, the puzzle is not why—as some have asked—government grows in a democracy, but rather how government can ever raise taxes to pay the bills.[1]

This chapter describes the difficulty of raising taxes and the variety of strategies employed. It then discusses the various tax breaks granted to offset inequitable tax burdens and to respond to interest group demands and the resulting complexity of tax codes at all levels of government. Finally, the chapter addresses efforts to reform the tax system, to make it simpler, more productive, and more equitable.

Raising Taxes

Raising taxes is problematic, not only because citizens get angry when their taxes are raised, but also because some states have passed laws making it intentionally difficult to raise taxes. States sometimes limit the permissible rate of growth of tax revenue (see the minicase of TABOR in Colorado for one example, in Chapter 1) or require public referendums for tax increases. Some states require difficult-to-obtain supermajorities in the legislature to pass tax increases. These constraints on revenues can be more or less restrictive and easier or harder to change. Some are written into state constitutions, a particularly inflexible constraint.

In our federal system, the states have power over the local governments. States have found it tempting to impose limits on taxes at the local level. By limiting local taxes, state elected officials get the credit for tax relief without unbalancing the state budget. As a result, local officials may find it difficult to raise sufficient revenue to pay for basic services. Sometimes the states replace the lost revenue for the local governments, but when times get tough, as during recessions, this assistance may be reduced or disappear.

Raising taxes is not only unpopular; it can be embarrassing. In order to force elected officials to keep their campaign promises not to raise taxes, Grover Norquist of the Americans for Tax Reform has asked those running for office to sign a written pledge that they will not raise taxes. If they fail to keep their word at any time after they sign and while they are still in office, Norquist publicizes and criticizes their defection, threatening them with electoral defeat. The written agreement, called a *taxpayer protection pledge,* is a promise to oppose *any* tax increase. Norquist makes no exceptions for emergencies. Elimination of tax breaks is treated as a tax increase and hence prohibited. Some of Norquist's Republican supporters complained that they did not think when they signed his document that it would be binding perpetually, regardless of the circumstances or the amount of time passing. One, Representative Frank Wolf, R-VA, charged that the pledge made it more difficult to tackle the deficit problem at the federal level.[2]

Despite the occasional complaint, signing the pledge is almost a prerequisite for running for statewide or national office among Republicans and among Democrats running in Republican districts. Though there has been a noticeable drop in the past few years, the numbers of those bound by the no-tax-increase pledge are still impressive. According to the Americans for Tax Reform database, the 2015 numbers are 221 House members and 49 Senators.[3] At least eleven of those listed as incumbent pledgers on the Americans for Tax Reform website had repudiated part or all of the pledge (Coburn, McCain, Graham, Corker, Alexander, and Crapo in the Senate, and Rigell, Fortenberry, Cole, Desjarlais, and King in the House). One of the retired senators who repudiated the pledge, Saxby Chambliss, was still listed as an incumbent; one of the defeated representatives, Cantor, was also still listed as a pledger, though no longer as an incumbent. A corrected total for 2015 is 216 in the House and 42 in the Senate.

There were thirteen Republican governors in office in 2015 who had taken the pledge, with few surprises: Alabama, Florida, Georgia, Louisiana, Maine, Mississippi, North Carolina, Ohio, Oklahoma, Pennsylvania, South Carolina, Texas, and Wisconsin. In addition to the governors, over a thousand state legislators had taken the pledge. However, some of the newer congresspersons and two of the seventeen Republican presidential candidates expressed reluctance to sign the pledge: Jeb Bush and Donald Trump. Even if the pledge has lost some of its obligatory nature, the large number of signers has made it more difficult to raise taxes, especially where Republicans are in the majority or where supermajorities are required to raise taxes.

Never raising taxes is a difficult promise to keep. During recessions, revenue levels fall and need increases simultaneously, creating budget gaps. States that have sharply reduced tax rates have often created budget gaps for themselves as well. Continual deep spending cuts have put pressure on these states to raise revenues in some manner. Even without recessions or tax cuts, without service expansion or new programs, the costs for state and local governments may grow more quickly than revenues, opening budget gaps that need to be closed.

Minicase: Louisiana—Getting Around the No Tax Increase Pledge

Never raising taxes is indeed a difficult promise to keep. Louisiana's governor, Bobby Jindal, was one of the governors who took the no-tax-increase pledge. He threatened to veto any legislatively approved tax increases.

(Continued)

(Continued)

Louisiana had a budget surplus of $1.1 billion when Jindal took office in 2007. In the ensuing years, the surplus was spent and there were major tax reductions, amounting to half of the 2002 voter-approved income tax increase and half the corporate income taxes. In an effort to balance the budget, the state made spending cuts, but not enough to offset the tax reductions. For 2016, the budget shortfall was predicted to be $1.6 billion. Facing the largest budget gap in decades and after severe spending cuts in prior years, the state needed more revenue.

Jindal, caught between the need for additional revenue and fear of violating his oath to never raise taxes, devised an odd scheme that would allow him to raise taxes while appearing to be keeping the pledge. Part of his proposal was to change reimbursable to non-reimbursable tax credits, meaning that taxpayers could no longer collect more in tax breaks than they owed in taxes. That would save the state money, and Norquist agreed to treat that change as a cut in spending rather than an increase in taxation. But there were also increases in fees and in cigarette taxes, which Jindal needed to offset with tax reductions elsewhere or at least create the appearance of tax reductions elsewhere. So Jindal proposed and the legislature reluctantly approved a fee on public college students in the state, while giving them a tax credit to compensate them, and then the students were to give the tax credit to the state board of regents, which in turn would collect the money from the state. Though there is no way that this scheme could actually offset anything, Jindal claimed that he had not raised taxes and obtained Norquist's consent to the plan. Presumably, Jindal did not count the assessment on the students (which they did not pay) as a tax but counted the tax credit as a tax reduction, helping to offset the new revenue from the cigarette tax increase.

In 2016, facing huge deficits and with Jindal out of office, the legislature repealed Jindal's SAVE tax credit and raised taxes. One legislator called the SAVE program no more than an accounting gimmick. Conclusion: Constraints that are too tight encourage evasions, unfathomable complexity, and sometimes, downright silliness.

Sources: Campbell Robertson and Jeremy Alford, "Louisiana Lawmakers Hold Their Noses as They Balance the Budget," *The New York Times*, June 11, 2015, http://www .nytimes.com/2015/06/12/us/louisiana-lawmakers-arrive-at-11th-hour-compromise -on-funding.html?ref=us&_r=1; Stephen Winham, "Louisiana Budget Practices: A Brief 30-Year History and One Scenario for Closing the $1.6 Billion Gap for Fiscal Year 2016," *Louisiana Voice*, March 31, 2015, http://louisianavoice.com/?s=budget+practices. "House Votes to Repeal Much-Maligned Jindal Tax Credit," *Biz New Orleans*, February 19, 2016, House%20Votes%20To%20Repeal%20Much-Maligned%20Jindal%20Tax%20 Credit%20-%20Biz%20New%20Orleans%20-%20February%202016.html.

Given the seriousness of these constraints, when politicians feel taxes must be raised, they try to do so very carefully. The fear of being thrown out of office by angry taxpayers is based on cases where this has occurred, but taxpayers do not uniformly reject tax increases or the politicians who propose them. One study pointed out, for example, that even among Republican voters, there was considerable sentiment for combining spending cuts and tax increases in order to reduce the federal deficit.[4] In surveys, two-thirds of the U.S. public and half of Republicans agreed to support higher taxes as part of deficit reduction.

Research has generally supported the position that those who advocate tax increases are more likely to face defeat, but the relationship is not airtight, and many other factors besides tax increases influence reelection chances, including the public dislike of deficit spending and the impacts of deep service cuts absent a tax increase. In fact, raising taxes is not impossible, just difficult.

Looking at tax increases that have failed and those that have succeeded suggests a number of principles for a successful tax increase that doesn't result in (metaphorical) slaughter of incumbents at the next election:

1. Make the extent of the revenue problem clear and credible.
2. Spell out clearly and realistically the consequences of cuts in spending if taxes are not increased.
3. If need be, make the tax increase temporary to make it more palatable.
4. If necessary, go to the public for a referendum; if it passes, there can be little blame for the politicians.
5. Make it as clear as possible that the money will not be wasted. Describe how the revenue will be spent. Show a collective benefit from the tax increase or tie it to specific benefits for several groups. A tax increase to prevent a further reduction in spending for education may be more acceptable than a vague proposal to balance the budget.
6. Demonstrate that prior inefficiencies have already been wrung out of the budget.
7. Design the increase so that it is fair and not overly burdensome to any particular group. One approach is to raise a variety of revenue sources that affect different groups just a little bit each; another is to raise taxes for groups that have not been paying taxes proportional to their incomes.
8. Explain all of the above to the public.

Any given campaign may emphasize some of these over others, depending on the problems being confronted. The minicase of Philadelphia, Pennsylvania, illustrates that taxes can be increased if these principles are followed (see p. 42).

Many states have tried the referendum option, testing the public level of willingness to accept a tax increase. Sometimes, the public is convinced there is nothing left to cut and that more deep cuts are on the way if they don't pass a tax increase. However, Oregon did not intentionally put a tax increase before the public for approval. Rather, Oregon legislators took a chance on public reaction by passing tax increases in 2009. The decision was challenged in a public veto referendum, a direct democracy device that allows citizens to vote on legislation of which they disapprove. (Twenty-three states have such a procedure.) Several citizen and business groups organized a petition drive to get the tax increase on the ballot, with the hope that the public would vote it down. These opponents of the tax increase were probably surprised by the result: In January of 2010, voters supported the legislatively approved tax increases, including a historic increase in corporate minimum taxes, which had been set at $10 since 1931, an increase in business taxes, and an increase in the income tax for top earners.

Proposed cuts if the taxes were not approved included those to education, public safety, and services to the elderly. The public was informed that these cuts would be necessary without a tax increase. Campaigns organized by unions to approve the taxes tapped resentment against the highest earners.[5] In addition, the state had already cut $2 billion from the budget before the legislature passed the tax increases. Under Oregon law, any surpluses have to be returned to the taxpayers, making it impossible to create a rainy-day fund to see the state through recessions, deepening the level of necessary cuts. The state had no buffer, so the choice was between deep additional cuts or a tax increase.

Minicase: A Recent Tax Increase in Philadelphia

Property taxes are highly unpopular, but Philadelphia successfully raised its property taxes in 2011, for the second year in a row. How did the city do it?

The answer involves all three levels of government—national, state, and local. During the recession that began at the end of 2007, the national government passed an antirecession package including aid to school districts to prevent teacher layoffs. The federal assistance ended in 2011. The governor then proposed and the legislature accepted drastic reductions in aid to education for 2012. The school district for Philadelphia was in a deep hole and pleaded with the city of Philadelphia for help.

The city had just increased the property tax the previous year, and doing it again seemed impossible, so the sympathetic mayor proposed a tax on sweet bottled drinks instead. The soft drink manufacturers engaged in a full court press of lobbying to block the mayor's proposal. The soft drink industry had contributed heavily to the campaigns of the council members, which made them vulnerable to such pressure.[1] As a result, the mayor was unable to maintain a majority of the council to vote for the soft drink tax. In addition, some council members voiced concern that the school district would misspend the money. They argued that the school district knew about the future loss of funding and had not done enough to prepare for it.

Mayor Nutter had no alternative but to advocate a second property tax increase. To gain council members' support, he negotiated a deal that required the school district to outline in detail how the money would be spent and what the consequences of failure to pass the tax would be. Another requirement was that the school district had to submit to the city a five-year financial plan, forcing it to plan ahead. A third feature of the tax increase was that it was temporary. While there was some grumbling that the deal had no enforcement mechanism to see that the school district was following through on the agreement and that standards of financial soundness were met, it was clear to all that there was a need and that the consequences of failure to bail out the school district would be severe. A narrow majority of council members reluctantly voted to increase the property tax, because, as they said, sometimes you have to do what you have to do.[2]

---

1. Jeff Shields, "Soft-Drink Industry Has Given Heavily in Council Races," *Philly .com*, June 5, 2011, http://articles.philly.com/2011−06−05/news/29623332_1_ danny-grace-council-races-soda-tax.
2. Marcia Gelbart and Jeff Shields, "How Philadelphia's City Council Decided on a Property-Tax Boost," *Philly.com*, June 19, 2011, http://articles.philly.com/2011 -06−19/news/29676981_1_property-tax-hike-soda-tax-tax-on-sugary-drinks.

The referendum on taxes split labor and business, creating a kind of budgetary class warfare. A major campaign supported by broad coalitions on each side educated and, sometimes, miseducated the public. Supporters claimed that families earning less than $250,000 a year would not be affected. Further, the supporters argued that business and the wealthy should pay their fair share. Most business groups opposed the increases. Opponents of the tax increases called them job killing and a threat to small businesses. A key to the success of this tax increase in a low-tax, low-service state is that ordinary voters understood that these increases would not affect them directly and would stave off deep cuts in necessary services.

While tax increases can be successful, they sometimes fail because they are either poorly timed or ignore some of the principles of a successful tax increase. The failure of the governor in Minnesota to raise taxes in 2011 suggests the importance of educating the public and the difficulty of raising taxes when there is a Republican majority in the legislature. Governor Dayton, a Democrat, faced Republican majorities in both houses. The state faced a gap of $5–6 billion over the biennium. The governor proposed a tax increase on the top 1 percent of earners, which the legislature refused to pass. The governor's main strategy seemed to be to allow a long government shutdown to pressure the Republicans to compromise—to force some cuts but allow some tax increase. The Republicans did not yield. Twelve of Minnesota's thirty-seven Republican state senators and twenty-five of the seventy-two Republican state representatives had signed Norquist's no-tax-increase pledge; even more important, three of the four top leaders of the Republican caucuses had signed the pledge.[6] Several Democrats had also signed. Many Republican legislators who had not signed the pledge also believed that government should not raise taxes.

During the shutdown, Governor Dayton began to travel the state and make speeches explaining what would be cut and with what consequences under the Republican plan, but his effort was too late and too little. The governor gave in but did not give up.

The next session of the Minnesota legislature was dominated by the governor's own party, and in 2013, the governor just managed to get his tax increase through. The vote was nearly completely along party lines in the senate. One argument Governor Dayton used was the unfairness of the state income tax, in which higher earners paid a smaller share of their income than middle class and lower income people. Although initially opposed to a cigarette tax because the burden would fall on poorer people, the governor included an increase in cigarette taxes when a coalition of health advocates convinced him that higher taxes on cigarettes would reduce use and improve public health. His tax package also included several business-to-business sales taxes. He used the new money to plug a $1.1 billion budget gap, boost school funding, and provide property tax relief. Less than a year later, Governor Dayton signed off on more than $400 million of tax cuts.

Defying traditional political wisdom, despite the tax increases, Dayton got reelected by a wide margin in 2014. He had taken time to educate the public, there was clearly a need, and there were many beneficiaries and few losers. The income tax increase affected only the top 2 percent of earners. After the tax increase and tax cuts, people with higher incomes still paid a smaller proportion of their income for state and local taxes than poorer people did, but the gap was not so great. (See Figure 2.1 on p. 45.)

The Politics of Protection

The politics of raising revenues has a mirror image, that of protecting the specific groups or the population in general from taxation or lowering tax levels for individuals or groups. Just as raising taxes necessarily brings a certain

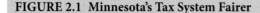

FIGURE 2.1 Minnesota's Tax System Fairer

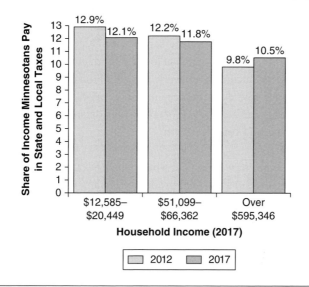

Source: Nan Madden, "Minnesota's Tax System Fairer; Proposed Legislation Would Take Us Backward," *Minnesota Budget Bites,* March 18, 2015, http://minnesotabudgetbites .org/2015/03/18/minnesotas-tax-system-fairer-proposed-legislation-would-take-us -backward/#.VYMtgflViko. Reprinted with the permission of the Minnesota Budget Project.

amount of blame, the lowering of taxes brings, if not praise, at least a measure of gratitude. Interest groups may hire lobbyists to help deflect taxation onto others, or they may contribute to election campaigns to promote candidates who will protect them from tax increases. Groups seeking protection from taxation try to influence the choice of which taxes to use and the definition of taxable wealth; they also try to secure exceptions for themselves from broad-based taxes.

The acceptability of taxation is at least in part a function of where the burden falls. The choices revolve around which taxes to rely on more heavily and what exceptions to broad-based taxes are granted.

Different Revenue Sources Hit Different Groups Differently

Part of revenue politics involves pressure to adopt or increase reliance on tax sources that burden others more than oneself. The major sources of revenue currently in use are income and wage taxes, sales taxes of various sorts, tariffs, property taxes, and user fees. Each works differently and affects the population differently.

Income and Wage Taxes. Income taxes are taxes paid on different forms of income, including wages and income from investments. They are paid by almost everyone who lives in a jurisdiction regardless of where they work or how they derive their income. Income taxes may burden the rich more heavily than the poor, or they can tax everyone the same percentage regardless of income. Sometimes they actually tax the rich at lower rates than the poor. Wage taxes are taxes only on *earned* income from work, not on all income regardless of source, and they tax those who earn their income in a jurisdiction, whether they live there or not. Wage taxes are one way of taxing outsiders: commuters to a city who work there but live and vote elsewhere.

Sales Taxes. Sales taxes are taxes paid when people or businesses buy something, usually (but not always) a finished product. Retailers who collect the tax have extra work to do, and because the price with tax is higher than without tax or with lower taxes, they may lose some customers. Consumers are the most directly affected, but they pay sales taxes in small, almost invisible amounts during the year, so they tend not to mind them too much. Sales taxes are not closely linked to ability to pay; they often fall more heavily on the poor than the wealthy because the poor spend a larger proportion of their incomes on taxable items.

Tariffs. Tariffs are fees that foreign producers pay to be allowed to market their goods in this country. Tariffs protect domestic industries from foreign competition by raising the price of imported products, but they also raise prices for consumers. Tariffs are ultimately paid by the consumer, without regard to ability to pay. Tariffs are levied only by the national government.

Property Taxes. Property taxes are levied on a proportion of the worth or sales value of property people own. This may be personal property (for example, cars or horses) or real estate (land and buildings). Property taxes on real estate are loosely related to ability to pay, because wealthier persons are likely to own more expensive homes, but the relationship is not tight. Older people on fixed incomes may find property taxes rising because the value of their homes is increasing over time. A business may own expensive property and equipment but not be making much income on it proportional to the value of the property. Owners of rental property typically pass the tax on to their tenants, who usually have less income than the owners.

User Fees. User fees produce revenue when citizens pay in proportion to how much they use a service. For example, you may pay a fee each time you use a public golf course or swimming pool, and you typically pay per gallon for water you use. User fees have the advantage of allowing those who pay to select only the services they want and not to use them and not pay if the cost is too high. But they have several disadvantages as well. First, they often have little to do with ability to pay. And second, others who are not currently using the services directly, and hence not paying for them, may benefit indirectly. Because indirect users are not sharing the cost with the direct users, the direct users have to pay the entire price. As a result, the price may be too high to be affordable by many would-be service users.

Business groups often prefer sales taxes on consumers and oppose income taxes, especially those levied on corporate income. Labor groups usually favor income taxes, but as wages have risen, labor rank and file have become more reluctant to support high individual income taxes and are more supportive of higher corporate income taxes. Many groups support user fees, because they seem to be both fair and voluntaristic. Those who favor smaller government tend to favor user fees.

Because different forms of taxation affect different kinds of wealth, and the regions of the United States depend on different kinds of wealth, the politics of taxation has historically had a strong regional cast. Until the late 1930s, "the Northeast favored first tariffs (which protected their industrial goods) and excise, license and land taxes if needed; the South and West resisted all these taxes, whose impact fell disproportionately on them, and favored taxes on income and wealth, of which they had little."[7]

When they have power and face budget gaps, many Democrats favor increasing taxes rather than cutting services; when they raise taxes, they prefer to increase the burden on the rich and businesses. When Republicans are in power, many prefer to reduce taxes, especially for high earners and businesses, and close budget gaps primarily by cutting services and programs.

As a result of these partisan preferences, sometimes elected officials shift the burden of taxation up or down by raising or lowering income taxes, which typically fall more on the wealthy, and by raising and lowering sales taxes, which fall more on the poor. As described above, Governor Dayton in Minnesota, a Democrat, raised the income tax on top earners when he had Democratic majorities in both houses; Bobby Jindal, a Republican governor in Louisiana, cut the income tax, benefiting the wealthy, and raised the sales tax on cigarettes, which burdens the poor disproportionately. In the past few years, other states have also experienced major shifts in the burden of taxation. Ohio, North Carolina, and Kansas fall into the camp of reducing burdens on richer people and businesses; Delaware and California fall in the opposite camp, increasing the tax burden on the wealthy.

Ohio reduced personal income taxes while increasing the sales tax. North Carolina changed from a graduated income tax, which asks richer people to pay a larger proportion of their income than the poor, to a proportional income tax that asks everyone, rich or poor, to pay the same percentage of their income; the state also increased the sales tax on electricity and is phasing in a dramatic reduction in corporate income tax rates. Until forced to raise taxes by persistent failure of revenue to meet expectations and pressed by a long running dispute with the courts over school funding, Kansas continued to reduce its income tax rate. When the state had to raise revenue, the governor and legislators raised the sales tax rate. On the other side of the ledger, Delaware increased the top rate of its personal income tax. California in 2012 raised its income tax substantially for upper income earners. Proposition 30 was a citizen initiative passed by the voters, to amend the constitution. The purpose was to fund education and local public safety. It was also a temporary tax, to last seven years. At the same time, the voters passed an increase in the sales tax .25 percent, for four years.

Tax Breaks

Tax breaks are exceptions from the structure of a tax. If a sales tax applies to all goods purchased (the structure), but a law is passed that exempts bull semen (the example is real), that omission is an example of a tax break. In addition to exemptions, some tax breaks are phrased as tax credits, amounts deducted from taxes otherwise owed. Preferential rates for some purposes may also be classified as a tax break, though some consider such preferences part of the tax structure rather than an exception to it. What counts as a tax break is controversial; estimates of losses because of tax breaks vary widely.

At the federal level, the Department of Treasury and the Office of Management and Budget keep track of tax breaks for the executive branch; the Joint Committee on Taxation does the same for Congress. Different states use different definitions of tax breaks, though most now have some kind of reporting. By contrast, until recently, local governments seldom reported their tax breaks. New accounting standards may make local tax breaks more visible going forward. Although estimates of revenue losses due to tax breaks are rough, the amounts are substantial. For the federal level, estimates for 2015 range from $1.3 to 1.5 trillion annually.[8] Studies using data from 2004 estimated the cost of state and local tax incentives to stimulate business growth at fifty billion a year, with another twenty billion in tax breaks not related to economic development.[9] A more recent estimate put the figure for business subsidies alone from state and local governments at more than $80 billion, and that was considered a low estimate.[10]

Tax breaks may be granted for policy purposes, to gain some public benefit—in the same way that direct expenditures are aimed at achieving some policy goal—or they may be granted because groups or individuals ask for them and elected officials want their support at election time. In the extreme case, an elected official may grant a tax break and expect (and receive) a campaign contribution in return. Such transactions are a form of corruption.

Tax breaks, sometimes called *tax expenditures* to emphasize the parallels to direct expenditures, often work like entitlement spending, that is, anyone who qualifies and applies for the tax break can get it. The cost to government is indeterminate, difficult to budget for, and may grow over time. Other tax breaks are either capped at a certain budgetary total or may be project specific. Project-specific tax breaks more often occur at the state and local level, though states and cities may also offer entitlement type tax breaks. The budgetary costs and implications vary depending on the mix—from all entitlement on one end to all project based on the other.

Narrow tax breaks, for a specific industry or even a single company, tend to broaden over time, as others use the same justification to make their claim to a tax break. A generous tax break for the oil industry was gradually extended to include other raw materials that, like oil, can be used up (this break is called a *depletion allowance*). Because of the way the tax break was worded, it came to include gravel, which is not in short supply and not a pillar of the economy, but the gravel in any individual quarry might be used up, and so gravel qualifies for a generous tax break. The process of expanding a tax break over time from the original purpose, which may have made sense, to others that seem to serve no public purpose, is also illustrated in a tax deferral called *like-kind exchange*. There is a special federal tax break that allows art collectors to defer some of their tax payments. This break was initially aimed at farmers in the 1920s who wanted to swap property and then was expanded to real estate investors selling one property and buying another. Now it is used by high-end art collectors who want to sell one expensive work of art and buy a different one.

Tax breaks have some positive characteristics. First, they gain credit for elected officials, without the political risk of raising taxes. They function like direct expenditures for specific constituencies or supporters and hence are extremely tempting.

Second, tax breaks may be more efficient than lowering overall business taxes (to improve business climate), because they can be targeted to specific industries, businesses, or projects that may have higher payoff and can be designed to ensure the creation of public benefits. For example, a tax break may be given over a period of years, as new jobs are created. If the jobs are not forthcoming, the government may withdraw the tax break. Or tax breaks may be given to companies that pay employees a living wage and provide health insurance, which lowers the costs to the public of provision of Medicaid to the poor. By contrast, a broadly lower business tax benefits those who create jobs as well as those who do not, those who pay a living wage and those who do not. Its ability to serve as an incentive for providing a public benefit is therefore close to zero.

Third, tax expenditures of various sorts can be used to offset inequitable burdens imposed by the tax structure. *Regressive* taxes, like sales taxes, which fall more heavily on the poor, are often easier to pass than taxes that are more *progressive,* that fall disproportionately on the rich. Sales taxes can be made less burdensome on the poor by exempting food and medicine. Property taxes, also somewhat regressive, can be modified by adopting so-called circuit breakers, which grant people with low incomes a break on their property tax bills.

Tax breaks also have some less desirable characteristics. Money that is not collected is less visible than money that is collected, counted, reported, and budgeted. The names of recipients of tax breaks are sometimes withheld from public scrutiny, allowing breaks for political supporters or campaign donors and making it impossible to see if the public has received promised benefits. Tax breaks typically do not get the same level of scrutiny as direct expenditures (see the minicases on Wisconsin and Illinois for examples of wasteful tax breaks) and, equally serious, normally are not compared with direct expenditures in budget deliberations. Budget deliberations on direct expenditures take place after tax breaks have been subtracted from the available revenue totals. They thus weaken one of the major functions of good budgeting, prioritization according to need or urgency and public purpose. They take some spending out of competition and protect it. Sometimes tax breaks are not only given priority in the budget but are not offset by any revenue source, forcing cuts in other programs or increases in borrowing.

Minicase: Wisconsin and Unexamined Tax Breaks

Wisconsin subsidized Kohl's department stores, a local company, with the goal of retaining existing jobs, creating new ones, and encouraging investment. In 2012, tax credits were granted for up to $62.5 million, in exchange for Kohl's promise that it would create three thousand new jobs and invest $250 million to construct a new headquarters building. The deal included financial incentives for retaining existing jobs as well as tax reductions for the creation of new jobs. Only a small proportion of the promised jobs had been created by 2015, and instead of building a new headquarters, the company refurbished a purchased building.

The incentives were worded in such a way that even if the company did not comply with expectations, it would still receive tax breaks. Thus the company was required to retain at least 3,783 jobs, while its current level of employment was reported at 4,500. The company could thus fire employees or outsource jobs and still get a tax reduction for retention of jobs. Also, the company got tax credits for creating new jobs, even if those jobs disappeared after a year. While theoretically the state could "claw back" tax credits that had not been earned, there was no procedure for doing so. The agency giving out these tax credits, created by governor Scott Walker in 2011, awarded such breaks to Kohl's and twenty-three other companies without formal scrutiny. The requirements for tax credits have been tightened up since these original benefits were awarded.

Source: Dee J. Hall and Tara Golshan, "Scott Walker's Untold Story: Jobs Lacking After Big State Subsidy of Kohl's Stores," *Wisconsin Watch.Org*, September 20, 2015, http://wisconsinwatch.org/2015/09/scott-walkers-untold-story-jobs-lacking-after-big-state-subsidy-of-kohls-stores/.

Minicase: Illinois and the Role of the Press

Like Wisconsin, Illinois had a large tax break program for businesses. The depth of Illinois's fiscal problems and long-running budget stalemate focused new attention on this tax incentive program. Designed to ensure that the state retained and added jobs and investment, the program had a number of serious weaknesses, but no action was taken to redesign the program until the *Chicago Tribune* did an investigative report on the recipients of tax breaks and the outcomes of these incentives. The report discovered that not only did the program pay for job retention as well as job creation, but companies that added jobs in one location and cut even more in another location still got tax breaks for the ones they added. To make matters worse, the program was not transparent, providing public information on job creation only for several years, after which, if the company reduced employment, the public could not find out.

When the extent of the corporate welfare (a term the governor used) was revealed, the governor changed the program to eliminate tax breaks for companies that increased jobs in one place and reduced them elsewhere and to eliminate the breaks for job retention and keep them only for job creation and investment. He had frozen new applications when he first took office, but with these changes he reopened the program to new applications and unfroze existing applications.

(Continued)

(Continued)

The governor planned to restore the film subsidy, one of the most expensive and least effective subsidy programs. Thus he seemed to be responding only to the specifics of the Tribune's investigative report rather than trying to make the tax break program more cost effective for the state. It was only the relative invisibility of the corporate tax breaks that allowed these expensive subsidies to continue; once brought to light, they were curtailed.

The governor then proposed a public private partnership to award tax breaks to businesses. The new organization would not be subject to freedom of information requirements, allowing it to operate more or less in the dark. When the speaker of the house proposed that the arrangement be evaluated after three years to assure that tax dollars were spent wisely, the governor opposed the legislation.

Source: Ray Long and Michael J. Berens, "Gov. Rauner Ends Tax Break for Firms That Add Jobs in One Place, Cut in Another," *Chicago Tribune*, November 11, 2015, http://www.chicagotribune.com/news/watchdog/ct-rauner-edge-changes-met -20151111-story.html." Rich Miller, "Madigan Forms New Committee to 'Study'" Rauner's New Economic Development Agency, *Capitol Fax*, February 24, 2016, http://capitolfax.com/2016/02/24/madigan-forms-new-committee-to-study -rauners-new-economic-development-agency/.

Tax breaks erode the tax base, meaning that rates for everyone have to rise to obtain the same amount of revenue on a narrower base. Another problem is these tax breaks often result in two similar taxpayers paying different amounts of taxes, which not only makes the tax system famously complicated (and has created an industry of accountants to help people minimize their tax bills) but also inequitable, as those with accountants to show them the possibilities pay less than those who do not know about tax breaks. Tax breaks for a new business coming into a city or state may put the existing businesses at a disadvantage.

At the national level, tax breaks for the federal income tax are often skewed toward the wealthy. Because the federal income tax is progressive, with higher rates on higher incomes, tax breaks are worth more to those who have greater incomes. Fifty-one percent of the benefits of the tax expenditures go to the top 20 percent of earners.[11]

While some tax breaks are aimed at encouraging desired behavior, such as owning a home or carrying health insurance, some have few if any benefits for the public at large. The minicase on hedge fund managers on p. 53 illustrates both the bias toward the rich and the lack of policy thrust of some federal tax breaks.

Minicase: Tax Breaks for Hedge Fund Managers

The carried interest tax break is a federal tax expenditure for hedge fund managers who run particular types of investment funds, often including risky investments and investment strategies for sophisticated and wealthy investors. For 2014, the income of hedge fund managers over $406,750 was taxed at 20 percent instead of the 39.6 percent they would have had to pay if they earned the same amount in a different job. The top twenty-five hedge fund managers earned $11.62 billion in 2014. They saved $2.2 billion on their tax bills because of this break. The social or economic good to be achieved by this break is unclear. Some have argued that the carried interest tax deduction has no economic rationale. "With most other tax breaks there is at least an argument as to how it serves some socially useful purpose. That is not the case with the hedge fund managers' tax break."[1] Commentators speculate that one reason for this tax break is that the hedge fund managers have good lobbyists. Another possibility is that these wealthy investment managers contribute heavily to political campaigns and so win legislators' support for their requests. In 2014 campaigns, the hedge fund industry contributed over $50 million to congressional candidates.[2] (See Table 2.1 on p. 54.)

1. Dean Baker, "The Hedge Fund Managers Tax Break: Because Wall Streeters Want Your Money," *Center for Economic Policy and Research*, April 14, 2014, http://www.cepr.net/publications/op-eds-columns/the-hedge-fund-managers-tax-break-because-wall-streeters-want-your-money.
2. Scott Klinger, "Meet the 25 Hedge Fund Managers Whose $2.2 Billion Tax Break Could Pay for 50,000 Highway Construction Jobs," *Center for Effective Government,* May 21, 2015, http://foreffectivegov.org/blog/meet-25-hedge-fund-managers-whose-22-billion-tax-break-could-pay-50000-highway-construction-job.

Tax breaks are difficult to eliminate, in part because, like entitlements, they are built into people's lives and businesses and people are unwilling to give them up. The no-tax-increase pledgers define the reduction or elimination of tax breaks as a tax increase, which makes it even more difficult to rescind them. Tax breaks are also hard to remove because many of them were demanded by lobby groups, who continue to defend them. Even when tax breaks are shown to be ineffective and budget gaps threaten, it is difficult to reduce or eliminate them. Efforts to eliminate even the most ineffective of tax breaks may take years, as the minicase on California and its enterprise zones on p. 55 indicates.

TABLE 2.1 Hedge Funds: Long-Term Contribution Trends

Election Cycle	Total Contributions	Contributions From Individuals	Contributions From PACs	Soft/Outside Money	Donations to Democrats	Donations to Republicans	% to Dems	% to Repubs
2016	$220,500	$168,500	$0	$52,000	$250	$168,250	0%	100%
2014	$50,833,908	$13,959,307	$312,500	$36,562,101	$4,398,245	$9,862,162	31%	69%
2012	$45,432,676	$17,581,101	$281,500	$27,570,075	$4,220,813	$13,617,288	24%	76%
2010	$14,031,544	$12,425,044	$407,500	$1,199,000	$5,992,462	$6,784,882	47%	53%
2008	$20,159,156	$19,932,156	$227,000	$0	$13,436,062	$6,675,117	67%	33%
2006	$6,047,951	$5,879,851	$168,100		$4,334,656	$1,461,845	72%	24%
2004	$5,097,706	$5,029,406	$68,300		$3,142,255	$1,953,951	62%	38%
2002	$4,650,364	$1,140,604	$6,500	$3,503,260	$3,124,653	$1,524,711	67%	33%
2000	$3,160,490	$1,213,298	$14,000	$1,933,192	$2,182,138	$976,102	69%	31%
1998	$1,908,892	$598,392	$7,500	$1,303,000	$1,101,242	$765,150	58%	40%
1996	$2,185,454	$744,854	$0	$1,440,600	$1,112,974	$1,072,480	51%	49%
1994	$811,799	$329,929	$0	$481,870	$273,600	$537,199	34%	66%
1992	$742,390	$382,900	$0	$359,490	$636,300	$106,090	86%	14%
1990	$128,450	$128,450	$0	$0	$107,950	$20,500	84%	16%
Total	$155,411,280	$79,513,792	$1,492,900	$74,404,588	$44,063,600	$45,525,727	49%	51%

Source: Center for Responsive Politics, https://www.opensecrets.org/industries/totals.php?cycle=2014&ind=F2700.

Minicase: California and Enterprise Zone Tax Breaks

California had an Enterprise Zone (EZ) Tax Credit Program, providing tax breaks for businesses that located in designated places with concentrations of the poor and unemployed. To lure companies to those less-than-desirable locations and encourage them to hire the poor and unemployed, the state granted the companies tax breaks, including state income tax credits, property tax abatements, utility tax exemptions, sales and use tax credits, and interest deductions. The state also offered a tax credit for new jobs created.

Many analysts viewed California's program as badly designed and ineffective. The success of Enterprise Zones varied from zone to zone, but little selectivity was used in awarding areas EZ status, and ineffective zones were allowed to persist. Two major studies years apart concluded that the zones did not have a significant effect on business creation or employment growth rates, shifting jobs around the state rather than creating new ones.[1] Even program advocates acknowledged that only a small proportion of businesses locating in enterprise zones even applied for the tax credit, suggesting that the credit played little role in encouraging businesses to locate in poverty areas.[2] The program was not only ineffective, it was also expensive, costing hundreds of millions of dollars a year.[3]

The governor called for the elimination the ineffective tax break program in an effort to save money during a severe budget crunch. In the face of opposition to elimination of the zones, he revised his proposals to retain the zones but required evidence of new job creation rather than rewarding businesses for decisions they had already made. However, the budget passed in June of 2011 without a vote up or down on the Enterprise Zone Program. As a substantive tax change, it would have required a two-thirds majority to pass. The supermajority requirement was intended to make it more difficult for the state to increase taxes, but in this case, made it more difficult to eliminate wasteful spending.

In response to legislative inaction, the governor proposed a study of regulatory changes that could be made to the program in the executive branch and in the interim, stonewalled the granting of EZ status for new applications. Those that had been conditionally approved were frozen at that level.

It took another two years before the legislature terminated the program and then only with the creation of some new tax expenditures.[4] The case of the California Enterprise Zones provides testimony to the difficulty of eliminating tax breaks.

---

1. Jed Kolko and David Newmark, "Do California's Zones Create Jobs?" *Public Policy Institute of California,* June 2009, 14–15; Legislative Analyst's Office, *An*

(Continued)

(Continued)

Overview of California's Enterprise Zone Hiring Credit, December 2003, www.lao
.ca.gov/2003/ent_zones/ezones_1203.pdf.
2. CLC Tax Credits, "CA Enterprise Zone," www.clctaxcredits.com/ca-enterprise
-zone.
3. Alissa Anderson, "California's Enterprise Zone Program: No Bang for the Buck,"
California Budget Project, February 2011, 3, www.cbp.org/pdfs/2011/110207_
Enterprise_%20Zones.pdf.
4. "Out With California Enterprise Zones, In With the New California Hiring
Credit and Sales Tax Exemption," *A&M,* October 23, 2013, http://www
.alvarezandmarsal.com/out-california-enterprise-zones-new-california-hiring
-credit-and-sales-tax-exemption.

State and Local Business Tax Incentives

No one knows exactly how much state and local governments spend on incentives for business location and growth. The Accounting Standards Board for state and local governments recently added a requirement that state and local governments report their tax abatements, but data are not yet available. No one knows whether business tax incentives are effective, because no one can tell you what would have happened in the absence of the tax breaks. Some of the projects subsidized by state and local governments probably would have succeeded without taxpayer help, but no one knows what portion of the positive outcomes to attribute to the break. The fact that no one knows—or can know—how well the incentives work makes the frequent use of business tax incentives puzzling.

Tax incentives to new or existing businesses seldom pay for themselves, forcing deeper cuts in basic services or tax shifting to individuals and homeowners. Moreover, they attract footloose industries that are likely to pick up and move when they get a better offer. Nevertheless, even in hard times, states have continued to grant such incentives. Supporters of these transfers argue that if we don't offer them, the businesses will go to other states that do offer them. Politicians running for office would be vulnerable to attacks from opponents if they failed to win bidding wars. One result has been a proliferation of incentives.

These tax incentives can take a variety of forms, including tax sharing, in which a unit of government lures a commercial site to the state or community, promising to share any new taxes generated by the business with the business itself. This arrangement seems free to the elected officials, because if the business did not locate there, there would be no taxes at all. Of course the business should have good economic reasons to locate there anyway, in which case the government would be entitled to all the revenue, not just a part of it, but this counterargument is often ineffective.

One of the oddest and least well-known subsidies to business occurs when states allow particular businesses to keep some of the state taxes they withhold from employee paychecks. The employees pay their taxes, records are kept indicating they have paid this total, but the business gets to keep some or all of the taxes—it never goes to the government to pay for roads or education or police or unpaid bills. The employees are generally unaware that part of their paycheck is going to subsidize the company. Sometimes states offer businesses their employees' tax withholding funds against future tax liabilities. The businesses' employees are thus paying the businesses' taxes due to the state.

Illinois is one of the states that passed such legislation (Pub. L. No. 97-0002). Originally intended to help the automotive industry (Ford in 2007, and Chrysler and Mitsubishi in the depths of the recession in 2009), the law was later expanded to other businesses that threatened to leave the state or promised major new capital investment. Such businesses could keep up to half the amount of withheld taxes for retained jobs and up to 100 percent for new jobs created. All these companies had to do to reduce their tax liability was threaten to leave the state and take jobs with them. One of the companies that received the special tax incentive was Motorola, which proceeded to lay off 1,400 employees, but the company was still "eligible to keep $22.6 million of its employees' taxes."[12]

Seventeen states had such programs as of August 2015. A 2012 estimate of the costs based on sixteen states (Oklahoma was not included in these estimates; its program cost $11 million in 2014) was $685 million a year.[13] The recession and state financial problems seemed to encourage this form of subsidy to businesses, in the desperate hope of retaining or creating new jobs. The state that used this tool the most, New Jersey, as of December 2014, had diverted $1.5 billion from employee withholding, and the diversion program still had many obligations for the future, though the program was no longer accepting new applications.[14] Many of these programs do not result in new jobs but either subsidize a move from one state to another or pay (bribe?) a company not to move out of state.[15] The minicase of North Carolina (p. 58) explains why the state offered businesses large tax breaks and makes the point that businesses that need to close or leave a state for economic reasons will do so regardless of any subsidy they have received.

Why do public officials offer business tax breaks rather than allowing the market to determine the location of firms? One possibility is that elected officials believe these incentives are effective, even without evidence. Perhaps they accept the results of studies that exaggerate the benefits. Or perhaps they believe that such tax breaks will pay for themselves, that they are in essence free. Elected officials also seem to respond to threats to leave the state or city if particular businesses do not get the tax break they demand. For some elected officials, such tax breaks may be a way of giving something to a constituent who asks for it, while the actual costs are often obscured or at least kept out of the public eye. Finally, the excitement of deal making and the occasional big wins create experiential learning that is hard to challenge.

Minicase: North Carolina and Business Tax Breaks

North Carolina has good transportation, good schools, universities, and research centers, and an attractive location on the East Coast. The state has no reason to offer tax breaks to overcome locational disadvantages. But then BMW built its plant in South Carolina and Mercedes Benz chose Alabama, largely on the basis of hundreds of millions of dollars of state incentives. North Carolina officials, frustrated, bought into the policy of competing by granting bigger subsidies. They offered tax breaks to FedEx, which decided to locate in the state, cementing the association between tax incentives and success.

State officials offered a huge tax incentive package to Dell Corporation, which subsequently located in North Carolina, but the company closed its facilities within a few years, laying off its staff. While the local governments were able to claw back much of their investment, the governor had given the legislature a non-negotiable package to vote up or down, which omitted major claw-back features. As a result, the state simply lost its investment.

Companies respond to market forces and will open, close, expand, or move in response to those forces, regardless of state tax breaks. Lack of claw-back provisions or reluctance to invoke them exacerbates public losses.

Source: Paul B. Johnson, "NC Becomes Reluctant Player in Incentives Game," *High Point Enterprise*, October 16, 2011, www.hpe.com/view/full_story/16069769/article -NC-becomes-reluctant-player-in-incentives-game?

There is another possible explanation. In the face of stagnating economies because of recession and globalization, some decision makers have become desperate. They are unwilling to give up policies of subsidizing business, because these policies create the *appearance* of doing something to help. As an illustration, cities in North Carolina during the Great Recession began to change the way they used incentives, adding small business and retail outlets to the list of candidates eligible for public funds. Small businesses have minimal impact on the economy, and retail outlets choose their locations on the basis of market demand. The fact that location decisions for retail outlets seldom depend on government incentives was apparently beside the point. At least they were doing something, even if that something wasn't likely to be effective.[16]

Business tax incentives may have some positive impact, but the increase in revenue to government from successful incentives does not typically cover the outlays to pay for business tax incentives. While one can argue that the overall social good to come from them outweighs these losses, one ought not argue that tax breaks to business are a good way to get out of a deficit situation. Because state budgets have to balance, expenditures for business tax breaks have to be offset by additional service reductions or increased taxes somewhere else.

A study of Michigan's MEGA program to subsidize businesses found an overall positive benefit but noted that the subsidy accounted for the success in something like 8 percent of the cases where it was used. Most of the business successes that occurred would have occurred without the tax break. And MEGA did not pay for itself, as the projects tended to pay for only about two-thirds of the cost; the rest had to be picked up by deeper service cuts or increased taxation. Finally, the cost per job created was $4,000 per job year. That means for a new job that lasted ten years, the cost of the subsidy would be $40,000.[17]

When companies get states or local governments to bid against each other to see who can offer the largest subsidy and lure a business away from another state or city, the costs to the winner can outstrip the benefits. In a recent case, Tesla cost Nevada up to $200,000 per job created.[18] If the number of jobs created or retained increases, the cost per job goes down to a more reasonable level, and if the quality of the job goes up—that is, if it carries health insurance and provides enough money to live on—the benefits to the society increase. The number and the quality of jobs produced are critical to ensuring that such programs on balance produce more benefit than costs. In fact, many states in recent years have improved their programs to monitor the number of jobs produced or designed their programs so that subsidies are paid only if the promised jobs are actually produced. Some states have added requirements that the jobs produce what is called a *living wage*, that is, good jobs with benefits, jobs that will keep people out of poverty and off welfare and Medicaid rolls. In addition, some have added claw-back provisions, requiring that companies that fail to meet the requirements of the aid give back the benefits they have received.

Against this logical set of requirements is the logic or illogic that says, we have to offer this tax break, because others do, and if we don't, we will lose the business.

When nearly all states offer the same benefits so that no state gets an advantage from them, the logic shifts to offering larger targeted tax breaks and doing so more quickly than rivals. The prime example of this logic in recent years has been subsidies for making movies in a given city or state. In 2002, only five states offered movie tax incentives; by 2010, forty-four states did.[19]

The movie industry produces few new jobs, and those that are created last at most a year or two. The cost per job created is often high. According to the Massachusetts Department of Revenue, the cost to the state per film industry job created during 2006 through 2009 was $133,055. Louisiana reported in 2005 that it would earn back only 16 to 19 percent of its costs through new revenue, while Massachusetts reported that every dollar of tax credit earned back only fourteen cents.[20] These figures suggest that the social benefit from this particular industry subsidy does not outweigh the costs to the public sector, and yet these programs have increased and become more expensive from year to year.[21]

Minicase: Michigan—Terminating Its Film Subsidy

In 2010, Michigan faced an anticipated budget gap of over $1 billion. Hoping to stimulate an industry other than the struggling automobile industry, it appropriated about $50 million a year in subsidies to film companies like Disney. The city of Pontiac built a state of the art film studio, hoping to lure the companies subsidized by the state. Acting on reports that film subsidies were not cost effective (the state reportedly got back only eleven cents for each dollar of subsidy, and the program did not create a single permanent job in 2013), Governor Rick Snyder cut back the film subsidy. The film business dried up, and the studio was unable to make the payments on its loans. To complicate matters, former governor Jennifer Granholm had required the state pension fund to guarantee the loan to build the studio, so when the studio failed, the severely underfunded pensions were on the hook to make the payments instead. For the 2015 through 2016 fiscal year budget, the state appropriation for the film credit was to be used mainly to pay off the bond obligation and free the pension fund. In July 2015, the state terminated the subsidy.

Predictably, film industry advocates vociferously protested the cuts, but there was also support for terminating this tax subsidy. A spokesperson from the national federation of independent businesses argued that such programs meant that other businesses had to bear the burden of paying for the film subsidy. Also against the subsidy were legislators hearing from constituents that the top priority was roads and transportation. The subsidy was draining funds from badly needed projects.

Industries like the film industry that respond to incentives are "footloose," that is, they do not have sunk costs in any geographic location and will move to seek the highest bidder, playing off one state against another and pushing up the costs of this subsidy from year to year. Someone has to pay for such subsidies, which is especially difficult when states are in fiscal stress and do not have the funds to pay the costs of basic services.

Sources: Kathleen Gray and Julie Hinds, "Senate Panel Votes to Kill Mich. Film Office, Incentives," *Detroit Free Press*, June 10, 2015, http://www.freep.com/story/ news/politics/2015/06/09/bill-end-film-incentives-funding-film-office -oct/28742183/; Kathleen Gray, "House Panel Votes to End Michigan Film Incentives," *Detroit Free Press*, March 4, 2015, http://www.freep.com/story/ news/politics/2015/03/04/film-incentives-end-oct-bill-house/24360757/; Joseph Henchman, "Michigan-Subsidized Film Studio Fails; State Pension Fund Had Guaranteed Loan," *The Tax Foundation*, January 27, 2012, http://taxfoundation.org/ blog/michigan-subsidized-film-studio-fails-state-pension-fund-had-guaranteed -loan; *The Wall Street Journal*, "Film Subsidies: Exit Stage Right," March 17, 2015, http://www.wsj.com/articles/film-subsidies-exit-stage-right-1426634855.

During the Great Recession that began in late 2007, many states encountered financial problems. One response was to begin to review their tax expenditures. A number of states singled out their film subsidy for reduction or elimination, because of the subsidy's lack of effectiveness and expense. Arizona, Kansas, Iowa, and New Jersey suspended theirs. Washington state failed to renew its film tax reduction program. Idaho, Arkansas, and Maine appropriated no money for the program for 2011. New Mexico capped its program. Governor Doyle in Wisconsin was able to cut back this break after a negative evaluation of its costs and benefits.

While state and local governments may compete with each other with new or expanded tax breaks, during times of economic hardship, there is also pressure to review existing tax breaks because of the high costs and sometimes dubious public purpose behind them. As of January 2015, seventeen states plus the District of Columbia required some evaluation.[22]

It is easier to evaluate tax breaks if you know what they are, how much they cost, and what the purpose is. At the state level, reporting on the number and cost of tax expenditures has become widespread in recent years. By 2014, forty-seven states plus the District of Columbia had some kind of tax expenditure report. Some are published yearly, cover most tax sources, and include realistic estimates of costs, the legislative basis for the tax break, and its purpose and success. Some even include recommendations for further action. Others are issued only episodically or cover only some tax sources and do not refer to actual tax forms to see how much revenue was lost.

Recent years have witnessed an additional push to adopt and improve regular reporting on tax expenditures, to make them more visible, make their public purposes clearer, and make the effectiveness of the tax breaks clearer. Such reports seem to be a good government reform with few drawbacks, other than the cost of preparation. However, because tax breaks for new businesses may disadvantage existing businesses, they may be controversial within the business community, and because some ineffective tax breaks persist because of interest group support or campaign contributions, they may be embarrassing to elected officials. When expenditures would not be acceptable to the public if known, they are often not clearly presented or easily available. Tax expenditure reporting can become a political hot potato, as illustrated in the case of New Mexico (see the minicase "New Mexico and Tax Expenditure Reporting" below).

Minicase: New Mexico and Tax Expenditure Reporting

In an eye-catching set of events, the New Mexico legislature passed a bill for the third time in 2013 to require the state to prepare a tax expenditure report, only to have the governor veto it. In 2007, Governor Richardson vetoed the measure, arguing that tax expenditure reporting was not an executive responsibility. More recently, governor Susana Martinez vetoed the second attempt to mandate tax expenditure reporting, saying that it was exclusively an executive responsibility. She went on to issue an executive order to list and evaluate tax expenditures in the state on a yearly basis. Some legislators were not content with her mandated report, as it lacked evaluation of the effectiveness of the tax breaks, and so was not a sufficient basis for decision-making. When the legislature passed a requirement for more extensive tax expenditure reporting, Martinez vetoed that too, saying her executive order was sufficient. Legislators in 2014 tried to get some traction for a constitutional amendment, but the proposal died in committee. The governor took complete control of the process, selecting what to reveal and what to deemphasize and was not bound by an evaluation of effectiveness.

Source: Matthew Reichbach, "Gov. Vetoes Tax Expenditure Budget Again," *New Mexico Telegram*, April 5, 2013, http://www.nmtelegram.com/2013/04/05/gov-vetoes-tax-expenditure-budget-again/.

Policy analysts have argued that net losses to government revenues in the short run must be outweighed by overall societal benefits of these incentives in the mid- and longer term. Toward this end, states have increasingly been building into their economic development incentives requirements for jobs above minimum wage and with health benefits, maintenance of those jobs over time, and termination and claw-back requirements in cases of failure to deliver on promised results. Transparency has increased, with some states posting online detailed descriptions of who received how much benefit from what state program and who promised to deliver what results. Despite these improvements, much still remains to be done. Of state economic development programs, "fewer than half provide any kind of wage standard for the workers at subsidized companies, and fewer than a fourth require any sort of healthcare coverage."[23] Some have few requirements for job creation. For the programs that have few requirements and weak enforcement, the social benefits from the tax expenditures may not justify the revenue losses.

Tax Reform

Not every change in the tax structure or every addition or subtraction of a tax break can be called a reform. To be a real tax reform, the proposals have to solve or at least address some basic problems with the tax structure.

Tax structures may become outdated and unproductive, as when they rely on bricks and mortar stores and bypass Internet sales or when they tax only physical things and ignore services. Sometimes taxes are earmarked in order to gain political support. When this is done to an excess, there can be a mismatch between the amount of revenue from an earmarked source and the amount needed, resulting in too much revenue in some places and too little elsewhere, overwhelming attempts at rational prioritization. Programs with earmarked funds are difficult or impossible to cut back during recessions, so that those without earmarked funds take the full brunt of cuts.

Tax structures may not be well designed to deal with recessions, especially if those recessions are long lasting. Revenues may grow rapidly when the economy is strong but shrink too much when the economy slows down. They may depend overly much on a single industry that waxes and wanes. Taxes may be higher than in surrounding cities, states, or countries, putting businesses at a disadvantage. They may be unfair, burdening one class of people or businesses and advantaging others. Tax breaks may worsen problems of equity, make the tax system overly complex, and reduce transparency and accountability. Tax breaks exempt some individuals or businesses, forcing increases in tax burdens on others who are not eligible for breaks, angering taxpayers and feeding tax limitation movements. The perception that taxes are unfair encourages legal and illegal forms of evasion, pushing up the costs of tax collection and putting added burdens on those who do pay their full taxes.

Mismatch of Economy to Tax System

Sometimes a tax structure is devised during one period of time when the economy has particular characteristics and does not adjust when the economy changes, making it less and less productive. For example, as the economy in the United States has changed from heavy manufacturing to more service industries, some states have found their sales taxes, levied on manufactured goods, capture less and less of the actual economy. Online purchases have also been excluded from taxation, except when the company has a physical presence in a given state or has a relationship with a company in the state. The resulting loss of revenue to state and local governments has been substantial and growing, leading to a variety of reform proposals, including taxation of Internet sales and sales taxes on services.

Tax Unfairness

Many large and profitable corporations pay either no taxes or considerably less than the stated rate for corporate income taxes. A recent study of 265 Fortune 500 companies looked at the amount of state taxes they actually paid compared to what they would have owed if they had paid the full corporate rate. The average rate in the states for corporate income taxes was 6.2 percent in 2008 through 2010, but these companies paid about half that rate. Even more telling, sixty-eight of the companies paid no corporate income taxes at all during that period, despite telling shareholders that they had made $117 billion in pretax profits during those years.[24]

The story is similar but even more dramatic at the national level. In 2014, Citizens for Tax Justice looked at Fortune 500 companies that had been consistently profitable between 2008 and 2012. Although the statutory rate was 35 percent, these 288 companies paid an average rate of 19.4 over the five-year period. Twenty-six paid no taxes at all over the five-year period. One hundred eleven of the 288 companies paid zero or less than zero in at least one of the five years, despite earning $227 billion in the years they paid no taxes. Most startling, twenty-six of the companies paid less than nothing over the five years—they used so many tax credits they more than offset their tax obligations, so that the federal government owed them money.[25]

Some inequities are built into the tax structure. The basic federal income tax rates are progressive: People with greater incomes are supposed to pay a higher percentage of their income than poorer people. This feature adds an important element of equity to the U.S. tax system, because taxes at the state and local level tend to burden the poor more than the wealthy. However, Social Security taxes are regressive, because Social Security taxes are paid only up to a given dollar limit of income. Dollar limits change from year to year, but in 2015 it was $118,500. If you earn $1 million a year, you pay a much smaller percentage of your income for Social Security than someone earning much less.

Moreover, a key feature of the federal income tax has offset the progressivity of the federal income tax for the highest earners, with the result that some wealthy people have paid a lower rate of taxation than people earning much less. The billionaire investor Warren Buffett called attention to this problem by noting that he paid a lower proportion of his income in taxes than his secretary. The reason is that there is a differential rate of taxation depending on the source of people's income: The federal income tax imposes a higher rate of taxation on income from wages than on income from investments. A lower rate applies to both capital gains and dividends, that is, on profits gained from the sale of an investment and on income from shares of the profits of a company. Richer people have a much larger share of their income from investments than poorer people, with the result that the very rich have paid a lower rate of taxation than people with more moderate incomes—such as Warren Buffett's secretary.

The IRS reports on the taxes paid by the country's four hundred top-earning families. In 2012, the top four hundred earners averaged $336 million income each. Their average tax rate was 16.72%. To put that figure in context, first, the percentage of their income that the superrich paid in taxes dropped from an average of 29.35 percent in 1993 to 16.72 percent in 2012. Second, in 2012, because much of their income comes from investments that were taxed at a lower rate than ordinary income from wages and because many tax breaks applied to them, the top four hundred earners paid a lower rate than ordinary workers. A person earning $100,000 in 2012 would pay almost 20 percent of his or her income in federal taxes, while the person earning an average of $336 million would pay less than 17 percent. Generally, the more you earn, the higher percent of your income you pay, but in 2012, that rule did not apply to the very wealthy.

In January of 2013, the income tax rate for those earning more than $464,850 per year for dividends and long-term capital gains was increased from 15 percent to 20 percent but remained 15 percent for those earning less than $464,850. In addition, some itemized deductions had less value for higher-income earners. A surcharge on Medicare for high earners added to the taxes paid by the highest earners. These changes pushed through by the Obama administration resulted in an increase in the percentage of their income that the very, very wealthy paid, to 22.89 percent. That is a substantial increase but still considerably below the rate the very, very wealthy had paid in 1993. Had all the income of the very wealthy been taxed at the rate of ordinary income, they would have paid 39.6 percent of their income in federal income taxes.

The basic structure of the federal income tax remains that income from investments is taxed at lower rates than income from wages, but at present, the very well off are paying more than they had been. How long this will last is unclear, as the very wealthy wield a disproportionate amount of political power, especially after the Supreme Court decision in Citizens United in 2010, which has permitted a small number of extremely wealthy individuals to make unlimited contributions to single-candidate super PACs (political action committees). In the future, a Republican majority Congress and a Republican president might well reverse these increases on the very wealthy.

State and local taxes, including excise, sales, income, and property taxes, are regressive; that is, middle income and the poor people pay a higher percent of their income on these taxes than the rich. Data for 2015, from Citizens for Tax Justice, demonstrate the extent to which state and local taxes take a bigger bite from poorer than from richer taxpayers. Those with the lowest incomes paid 12.1 percent of their income on state and local taxes, while those with the highest incomes paid only 8.3 percent of their incomes.[26] A second study came up with even more extreme results, concluding that those with the lowest incomes paid on average double what those with the highest incomes paid, 10.9 percent for the lowest income group compared to 5.4 percent for those in the highest income class.[27]

The Institute on Taxation and Economic Policy updates its study on who pays state and local taxes at regular intervals, so it is possible to see trends. There have been five studies, beginning in 1996. What do these numbers suggest about trends in equity of state and local tax burdens? First, state and local tax burdens remain regressive, burdening the poor more than the well-to-do. Second, the overall burden for *all* taxpayers of state and local governments has been *decreasing*. The rate of decrease has been steeper for the very rich than for the poor or middle income groups. The rich experienced about 31 percent reduction; the poor a bit over 12 percent reduction; the middle about 4 percent. One result is to make an already regressive tax system even more regressive. In 1996, the share of income the bottom 20 percent of earners spent for state and local taxes was 1.63 times larger than the share of income spent by the top 1 percent of earners; in 2015, the poorest paid 1.85 times as much of their income as the top 1 percent.

While state and local taxes are regressive, the federal income tax is generally progressive. Because federal taxes are greater than state and local taxes, when added up, the U.S. tax system is mildly progressive. However, it is not progressive enough to offset the increasing inequality created by the free market. The United States does less to offset market-based inequality than other developed countries.[28]

The Congressional Budget Office does an annual study on the distribution of income and federal taxes. Based on tax data for the most recent year available, 2011, CBO estimated that federal taxes made income distribution *slightly* more equal. The lowest 20 percent received 5 percent of all income, including transfer payments as income, before taxes and 6 percent after taxes; the 20 percent of the population with the highest incomes received 52 percent of all income before

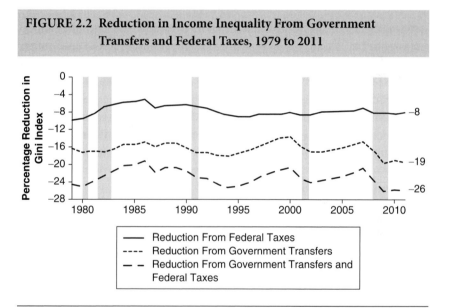

FIGURE 2.2 Reduction in Income Inequality From Government Transfers and Federal Taxes, 1979 to 2011

Source: Congressional Budget Office, "The Distribution of Household Income and Federal Taxes, 2011," November 2014, https://www.cbo.gov/publication/49440, p. 27.

Notes: The Gini index is a measure of income inequality that ranges from zero (the most equal distribution) to one (the least equal distribution). Gini indexes are calculated using income measures adjusted for household size.

Government transfers are cash payments and in-kind benefits from social insurance and other government assistance programs. Those transfers include payments and benefits from federal, state, and local governments.

Federal taxes include individual income taxes, payroll taxes, corporate income taxes, and excise taxes.

taxes and 48 percent after federal taxes. CBO notes that between 1979 and 2011, transfer programs reduced inequality more than taxation did. Transfers accounted for two-thirds of the reduction in inequality observed between market income and after tax income.[29]

The CBO graphic shows the reduction in inequality due to taxes, due to transfers, and due to both together, over the period of the study. The graph shows clearly that taxes reduced inequality considerably less than transfer payments did but also shows that during the 2008 to 2009 deep recession, transfer payments played an increased role in reducing inequality, while tax policy maintained a constant role. This is what one might expect given the nature of entitlements that increase automatically as need increases.

Tax Complexity

The difficulty of raising taxes and the desire to protect particular groups from increased taxation lead to a multiplicity of revenue sources and a variety of tax breaks, sometimes hundreds of them. Efforts to get support for tax increases often lead to earmarked taxes, which further increase the complexity of the tax system. Richer and more determined individuals and companies hire accountants to get them through the thicket of changing rules. The costs of doing so in time, money, and aggravation create pressure to simplify the tax code, reviewing and eliminating the most wasteful of the tax breaks.

Taxes and the Economy

Ideally, a tax system yields revenue growth when the economy is booming but doesn't fall too far when the economy is shrinking or growing only slowly. To achieve this golden mean requires some more elastic and some less elastic revenue sources—*highly elastic* means grows quickly and drops quickly, *less elastic* is more stable and doesn't change much when the economy changes. States that have highly elastic revenue systems, with income taxes that are dependent on the higher earners, fared poorly during the Great Recession because the stock market fell and these earners suddenly paid much less tax. When tax systems do not respond to cycles of the economy in the optimal fashion, there may be pressure to reform the tax system and increase or decrease the degree of elasticity.

Dynamics of Tax Reform

In general, tax reforms are difficult to achieve. They are relatively easier to accomplish if they are revenue neutral; that is, they do not increase or decrease the overall tax burden. They are also easier to pass if they do not result in a *major* shift from one group to another, burdening some at the expense of others. Those who would be negatively affected by the reforms are often organized and represented by dogged lobby groups. Tax reforms do sometimes succeed, but often they do not (see the following minicases of Georgia and Michigan).

Minicase: Georgia Tax Reform Left Hanging

The story of Georgia's failed tax reform effort in 2011 reveals some of the dynamics of tax reforms and how difficult they are to adopt. It is not only that each tax break proposed for elimination has an organized constituency and experienced lobbyists to defend it, but also that the tax overhaul needs to leave the burden of most of the taxpayers as is or reduced in order to gain sufficient public and political support.

In 2011, Georgia was coming off several years of poor growth and deep spending cuts. The state was determined to redesign its tax system to encourage growth and be more reliable during economic downturns. Taxing food for home consumption would provide a more dependable (inelastic) source of revenue during economic downturns, as people need to eat during good times and bad. The state sales tax had many exemptions and included few services. Many of the exemptions in the sales tax were ineffective. No one had shown that the exemptions in the corporate income tax were effective either. A number of state officials, along with the panel of experts assigned to recommend a new tax system, assumed that income taxes were bad for business growth and therefore had to be reduced or eliminated.[1] The major thrust of reform proposals was to shift the burden of taxation away from income taxes onto consumption (sales) taxes. At the same time, any tax reform had to be revenue neutral—the state could not afford further cuts in spending after years of deep cuts, and opposition to any tax increase was intense.

A panel of experts convened to examine the tax system and make recommendations to a joint legislative committee that held public hearings on the proposals. The public, including interest groups, was alerted to the possible elimination of specific tax breaks before legislation was prepared and presented to the legislature.

The panel recommended a broad set of reforms, first flattening the graduated income tax and reducing the rate and then eliminating the tax completely. The reforms would pay for the initial changes by eliminating nearly all exemptions and deductions, including that for food for home consumption, but offsetting the effect with a tax credit for the poor. Both personal and corporate income taxes were to be eliminated. The sales tax was to be extended to many services. Several new tax exemptions were proposed to make the state

(Continued)

(Continued)

more competitive with its neighbors, including the elimination of a tax on energy for manufacturing. The proposals included a shift in the burden of taxation from wealthier to less wealthy people, but also included at least some consideration for equity, including a temporary tax credit for the poor.

The proposals ran into difficulty because the governor opposed taxing food for home consumption, which hit the poor most severely. Difficulty also arose because interest groups actively lobbied to prevent the extension of the sales tax to their services. In the end, only two survived, the private sale of cars outside of dealerships and automobile repair services, neither of which had strong lobbies. But ultimately, the reason that the reform failed was that, although the proposals were almost revenue neutral, some providing a little more or a little less revenue than before, some groups of taxpayers were negatively affected. Studies showed that the very well-to-do would benefit greatly, but that the majority of middle-class taxpayers would pay more under the reforms than before. Republicans who sponsored the tax reforms were unwilling to be seen as responsible for this increase of tax burden before an election.

Many of the same proposals have resurfaced and will be eligible for reconsideration in 2016.

1. It is not clear that this assumption is correct. A recent study comparing high income tax states with no income tax states found that economic growth rates were higher in the high income tax states and that those states generally weathered the recession better than the no income tax states. Institute on Taxation and Economic Policy, "High Rate Income Tax States Are Outperforming No Tax States: Don't Be Fooled by Junk Economics," February 2012, www.itepnet.org/pdf/junkeconomics.pdf.

Source: This case relies heavily on "Revenue and Taxation HB 385 388," *Georgia State University Law Review* 28, no. 1, Article 13, http://digitalarchive.gsu.edu/gsulr/v0128/iss1/13. See also, Kelly McCutchen, "Issue Analysis: Analyzing Georgia's Tax Reform Proposal," *Georgia Public Policy Foundation*, March 29, 2011, www.gppf.org/pub/Taxes/IAGATaxreform110328.pdf.

Minicase: Michigan Tax Reform or Class Warfare?

Michigan reduced its taxes on businesses by eliminating tax breaks for the poor and retirees, despite public opposition. Some argued that this was a tax reform, aimed at stimulating the economy of a financially strapped state, but others saw it as class warfare that deepened inequities in the state tax system.

The changes in Michigan were not fully revenue neutral: The reductions in business taxes and the continuation of the credits already granted resulted in over a billion dollars in losses each year, while the increases in income taxes did not cover all the losses. A portion of the Michigan Business Tax revenues that the reforms repealed had been earmarked for education; the education fund losses were not replaced.

The court made the tax reform more regressive. The court ruled taxing pensions legal, but declared the phase-out of tax breaks for the wealthy illegal. The phase-out of the tax break to the wealthy had been necessary to get enough votes to pass the legislation, but that feature was removed after the fact.

Michigan changed its tax structure for the purpose of stimulating business in a state hard hit by recession. However, the specific changes led to charges of class warfare as the government cut funding for public education (K–12 cut by 6 percent, higher education by 15 percent), increased taxes on the elderly and on the poor, reduced welfare payments, cut taxes for businesses, and maintained tax breaks for the wealthy.

Source: Charles Crumm, "Gov. Snyder Signs Tax Changes into Law," The *Oakland Press*, May 25, 2011, www.theoaklandpress.com/articles/2011/05/25/news/doc4ddd35a684a04708490852.txt.

Not all changes to a tax system should be thought of as reforms. Just cutting taxes is not necessarily a reform and may in fact increase fiscal stress as well as encourage excessive borrowing or odd adaptations to balance the budget. Reducing the burden of taxes may be a reform if a government realistically is concerned that its level or type of tax puts it at a competitive disadvantage with respect to neighbors or rivals. Raising or lowering the burden on one class or another may be a reform if the burden was excessive to start with or if there were major disincentives in the tax structure to engage in socially desired behavior. Just claiming the existence of a disincentive should not be sufficient to warrant the term "reform." For example, some have claimed that relatively higher taxes on the well-to-do discourage them from working or encourage them to leave the state or country. The evidence for either of those claims is weak. The idea that lower taxes on income and higher taxes on sales stimulates business has not been demonstrated convincingly either, but such shifts may be considered reforms if high reliance on income taxes has resulted in high volatility of revenue, deepening the impact of recessions. The minicases suggest that what is claimed as tax reform sometimes just means passing the tax burden from one class to another when the party in power can protect its own constituents from taxation.

Real tax reforms are not impossible, just difficult and often take years. California, for example, succeeded in collecting sales taxes on Internet sales, helping to rematch the economy and the tax system. Minnesota, as described earlier in the chapter, made its tax system more equitable. Maine broadened its sales tax base to include more services in 2009. Oregon, Minnesota, and the District of Columbia publish informative and transparent tax expenditure reports. New York State changed its business taxes, not only lowering them, but combining banks and other financial institutions into one category, so that those engaged in the same kind of enterprise are not working with different laws. Some states, like Michigan, have terminated their film subsidies. Utah increased the amount of money it could put into its rainy day funds, helping to manage revenue volatility over the business cycle. Washington, D.C., also broadened its sales tax base, while lowering the overall rate. Several states increased their Earned Income Tax Credit, which is a way of helping the lowest earners through the tax system. Washington state, though it failed in an effort to eliminate some outdated tax breaks, managed to include in budget legislation a ten-year sunset for any new tax exemptions and a requirement for any new exemption that the legislature specify the purpose and include measurements to see whether those purposes were being achieved.[30]

This list of examples is only meant to demonstrate possibility; it is not a complete list of all recent tax reforms.

Summary and Conclusions

The politics of taxation has a number of special features. One is the tendency of one group or political party, when it is in the majority, to shift taxes to another group and protect itself, either by specifying that taxes will be levied on the income sources of another group or economic class or by changing rates up or down on particular groups, often making exceptions in the taxes for particular industries or groups of people with effective lobbyists. These exceptions make the tax system more complicated, less transparent, and often unfair. They also erode the tax base, either reducing revenue or increasing the rates paid by those who do pay the taxes, increasing resentment against the public sector and energizing tax reduction movements.

Increasing taxes is fraught with danger for politicians and consequently is done carefully. Temporary taxes and earmarked taxes are easier to pass, relatively speaking, with the result that taxes may not be sufficiently flexible to deal with changing priorities or fluctuations in revenue caused by recessions. Sometimes tax changes that need to be made are not, leading to a mismatch between the economy and the revenue system.

Narrow tax bases that do not match a changing economy or deliver sufficient revenues, complicated tax structures that frustrate taxpayers and result in unequal burdens as some taxpayers manage to pay much less than others with similar incomes, ineffective and hard to track tax breaks—all feed into a need for periodic review and revamping of tax structures. Sometimes more popular taxes and less visible taxes fall more heavily on the poor, raising serious questions of equity, which also suggest the need for tax reform.

Tax reforms are even more difficult to achieve than tax increases. Many fail. The ones most likely to succeed are those that are revenue neutral and do not hurt large numbers of taxpayers. Alerting those who might lose by a proposed tax reform is likely to trigger an army of lobbyists to defend their relatively advantaged positions. Symbolic politics becomes the norm, as political candidates support or decry a millionaire's tax or call attention to wealthy corporations that pay no taxes at all or claim that wealthy people are paying too large a share of government costs.

Useful Websites

A site that has useful information on state and local finance is the **Rockefeller Institute of Government** (www.rockinst.org/government_finance/) in Albany, New York. The institute monitors revenue trends such as the impact of recession on property taxes.

The **Pew Charitable Trusts' Subsidyscope** (www.subsidyscope.org) is a good source for information about tax breaks from the Federal Income Tax. This source compares estimates of revenue losses between the Treasury (executive branch) and the Joint Committee on Taxation (legislative branch). Data go back to 2001, allowing some examination of trends. This data archive provides totals by functional areas as well, which is particularly handy. Data can be downloaded and manipulated by the user.

Citizens for Tax Justice (www.ctj.org) on the left and **Americans for Tax Reform** on the right (Grover Norquist's group, www.atr.org) present many of the political arguments for increasing or decreasing taxes or shifting the burden from one economic class to another. Closer to the center is the **Urban-Brookings Institute Joint Center on Taxation** (www.taxpolicycenter.org/). This site presents the results of economic simulations to describe the impact of tax proposals on different groups and income levels; it also presents extensive information about taxes and social policy more generally.

A website that focuses on business incentives is **Good Jobs First** (www.good jobsfirst.org). This website offers a database called **Subsidy Tracker** (http://good jobsfirst.org/subsidy-tracker), along with some eye-opening studies of who does or does not pay taxes.

3 The Politics of Process

It is tempting to believe that if only we could come up with some clever budget rules, fiscal prudence would follow. Unfortunately, it does not work that way. The desire for fiscal responsibility must come first. Then rules can be important in strengthening the efforts of those supporting fiscally responsible policies.

—Rudy Penner, former director of the
Congressional Budget Office, in
testimony before the House of
Representatives Budget Committee, 2011

The budget process divides up the work of budgetary decision-making, assigns particular decisions to particular actors or groups of actors, and coordinates the decision-making among them. The budget process sets the rules for deliberations, selects the options that will be compared, and controls the level of competition for governmental resources.

The budget process is important because it influences policy outcomes and the distribution of political power. In terms of policy, process can make it easier or harder to spend public money, to balance the budget, to make long-term investments, or to borrow money. The budget process may tilt toward lower taxes and a smaller scope of government or toward higher taxes and more publicly provided goods and services. The budget process influences who benefits from taxation and spending decisions. In terms of the distribution of power, budget process can give one group of actors a veto over the decisions of other actors; it can be inclusive of new groups or reinforce the power of long-entrenched groups; it can facilitate democratic participation or strengthen top-down decision-making. Budget process affects the distribution of power between and within the executive and legislative branches of government.

74

The budget process is often a key instrument of democratic accountability. The openness of the decision-making, the responsiveness of the process to democratically determined priorities, and the quality of reporting on how much money has been spent for what programs all reflect the degree of democratic control. Because the budget process is such an important part of governance, if there is public participation in and control over the budget, there is likely to be public control over government more broadly.

Budget Process and the Characteristics of Public Budgeting

The characteristics of public budgeting described in Chapter 1 help to explain the functions and design of the budget process. Budget processes are not just a list of decision makers and a set of steps to coordinate timely decision-making. They help the decision makers adapt to changes in the environment, facilitate the resolution of competing claims, create a smooth flow of information between payers and deciders, and constrain decisions about taxation and allocations.

Adaptation

Budget processes facilitate adaptation to the environment. The process may allow a variety of changes during the year to accommodate revenue declines or emergencies. The routines of decision-making normally offer ways of handling conflict when it spills over and threatens to derail the budget. And the process itself can change as needed. If the economy is weak, process rules may change to allow higher spending levels and permit deficits. On the other hand, if deficits and debts have become a problem, the budget process may shift to emphasize balance. If public support for government is low, elected officials may change the budget process to give the public more information and more control over budget decisions.

Competition

Public budgets involve claimants who want different things from the budget and a variety of political actors who want to exercise control over budgetary decision-making. The budget process has to regulate competition among these claimants.

The budget process may make it equally easy for all funding applicants to make their pleas or may make it difficult for some and easier for others. For example, nonprofits applying for grants from cities may be required to fill out lengthy questionnaires, including indicators of their financial solvency and descriptions of their client base, while small businesses applying for assistance may have only to ask for the money.

The budget process also regulates the level of competition among claimants by determining which programs compete most directly with which other programs for how much money. For example, process rules may designate a group of claimants and assign them a particular pool of funds. Those claimants must then compete among themselves, sometimes intensely, for that limited pool of resources. At the other end of the continuum, some programs may be given their own source of revenue, with no other programs allowed to compete for those funds.

The budget process may favor some requests over others. For example, the process may assign decisions on funding of particular programs to decision makers who favor or oppose those programs. Budget rules often determine the order in which requests will be considered, giving money first to items such as debt repayment or entitlements, programs that are structured in such a way that all those eligible for benefits are paid before any other requests can be considered. In Colorado, voters who found the cuts to education under TABOR unacceptable put forth a successful constitutional amendment to require that education be fully funded. California's constitution requires payment of debt service, just behind school funding and before other expenditures. When times are tough and huge budget gaps need to be closed, these constitutional protections for some expenditures force others to be cut disproportionately. In California in the recent recession, vendors were paid with promissory notes, so-called IOUs, while bondholders were paid their interest in full and on time. The city of Stockton, California, entered bankruptcy proceedings in 2012, which normally requires negotiations with *all* creditors, but state law provides that pensions not be diminished. The contradiction between two sets of rules caused havoc. The minicase of Harrisburg, Pennsylvania, below, illustrates the kind of controversy that can happen over who should get paid how much when a city does not have enough money to pay its bills.

Minicase: Harrisburg—Whose Priorities Dominate?

Some states allow their local governments to declare bankruptcy under Chapter 9 of the federal bankruptcy law. This law allows a city or county to negotiate with vendors and creditors and agree to pay a certain percentage of the bills owed. Chapter 9 does not give automatic priority to bondholders; if loans are considered unsecured, their payments may be cut along with other obligations. In recent years, controversy has developed about whether states should allow their local governments to declare bankruptcy, or whether the troubled local governments should instead give up their autonomy to a state appointed financial crisis administrator who could make decisions on which bills would be paid in full. One reason for the state control option would be to protect bondholders and, by implication, the ability of the state and its other governmental units to borrow at inexpensive rates. A default on bond repayment in one city would push up perceived risks and hence borrowing costs for other jurisdictions in the state.

When Harrisburg, Pennsylvania, experienced severe financial problems, city officials wanted all the city's major creditors, including the bondholders, to take some losses, as would likely occur under a bankruptcy proceeding, but without state permission, the city could not successfully declare bankruptcy. The state denied the city permission to declare bankruptcy and instead appointed a receiver for the city with unprecedented powers to control the city's finances.

Separation of Payer and Decider

The separation of payer and decision maker also has important implications for the budget process. To facilitate communication between government and the taxpaying public, the budget process often mandates open hearings before allocations are cast in law. Extensive reporting after the fact is also required to assure citizens that their money was spent in the fashion agreed to in the budget.

Constraints

Of all the characteristics of public budgeting, the budget process most clearly represents constraints. Guidelines often set limits to expenditures, revenues, borrowing, or debt. The process may begin with goals for reallocation or productivity savings or targets for cutting back capital or staff. The budget process can include prior controls (such as ceilings on the number of personnel that may be hired) and/or post controls, based on after-the-fact reporting of costs and accomplishments. The budget process can require that revenues exceed expenditures by particular margins. It can even put constraints on subparts of the budget, setting ceilings on revenue by fund and purpose (e.g., no more than ten mills of property tax rate may be levied for roads and bridges) or on expenditure (e.g., no more than $10 billion can be spent on the State Department).

One example of the kind of constraints that can be built into a budget process occurred in 2011 at the federal level when Republicans withheld support for increasing the debt limit unless their preferred level of cuts became law. The result was the Budget Control Act of 2011 that reduced spending by $1.2 trillion over ten years, with a cap on discretionary spending each year. If the caps are exceeded, then an across-the-board, automatic cut (called a *sequester*) is automatically evoked.

Constraints on decision-making narrow the range of policy choices. For example, once general obligation borrowing has reached its legal limit in a city, decision makers can no longer consider the option of borrowing in that inexpensive, federally subsidized way to pay for capital projects.

Macro- and Micropolitics

Because the budget process influences policy outcomes and political power, political actors continually try to reshape it. Some seek macrochanges, in an effort to bring about major policy shifts and lock them in over time. Others seek microchanges, short-term deviations or alterations in the rules addressed to specific beneficiaries, often for partisan gain.

Macropolicy goals can include stimulating the economy during a recession, reducing the gap in wealth between the rich and the poor, balancing the budget, or shrinking the size and intrusiveness of government. One example of political actors' trying to achieve macropolicy change through the budget process occurred when some conservative Republicans in Washington proposed restructuring the budget process to encourage tax reduction. Presumably they hoped not only to reduce the level of taxation but also to reduce the scope of government services. By contrast, when political actors are seeking micropolitical goals, they try to influence particular decisions that may affect only one company or interest group. This second group may ignore, bend, or change the rules without regard for long-term or broader policy consequences. For example, one group of senators and representatives raised the caps on discretionary spending to increase outlays for highways and pork-type projects. These members of Congress did not argue that the caps themselves were wrong. They wanted to influence the outcome of a specific decision, not the rules that structure the outcomes more broadly. The rules were simply in the way.

The two minicases that follow illustrate macro- and microstrategies with respect to the budget process. The first, an illustration of macrostrategies, describes efforts of Republicans in Congress to change the process to achieve broad policy goals. The second is an example of microstrategies, the way rules can be used and abused for short-term political gain, without regard to broader policy issues. The chief Democratic counsel for the Senate Budget Committee in Washington, Bill Dauster, gave a partisan speech in 1996, pointing out a number of rule changes or evasions that the Republicans had devised for short-term advantage or to benefit a single constituent. It is not only Republicans who do such things when they are in the majority, but in this example, a Democrat was commenting on Republican behavior (see the minicases on pages 79 and 82).

Minicase: Republican Macrolevel Reform Proposals

In 2013, the House Budget Committee passed a budget reform proposal called Budget and Accounting Transparency Act of 2014 (H.R. 1872). The goal was to make expenditures for loan programs more transparent and reflect actual cost, by requiring a shift to using "fair value" accounting for loan programs, as is used in the private sector. Fair value accounting includes an estimate of risk in the cost. Thus federal loans and loan guarantees would be recorded in terms of the worth to the recipients, closer to what they would have to pay to the private sector for a similar loan or guarantee. The techniques in actual use in 2013 calculate costs in terms of expected value over time, which, based on historical data, includes the estimated rates of default, a measure of risk to the government. Commercial lenders would charge a higher rate for riskier loans than the government does, and the committee members felt that this higher number was a better reflection of actual government costs. This change would make loan and loan guarantee programs seem more expensive. However, the committee envisioned the president's budget would contain cost estimates with and without the estimate of the cost of risk. The proposal required such cost estimates to be made clear at the time when programs are adopted, presumably discouraging their adoption. The reform also requested CBO and OMB to look into using fair value accounting for insurance programs. The committee voted to bring Fannie Mae and Freddie Mac on budget, and thus make it clearer that at present these are governmental programs and responsibilities. (For more on Fannie and Freddie, see p. 167.) The committee wanted OMB and CBO to review, update, and make consistent the many terms the government uses with regard to budgeting. Finally, the proposal would require agency budget justifications to be made public. The thrust of these reform proposals was to make spending more transparent and to increase cost estimates, in the hope of controlling new spending.

A second and likely more important Republican reform proposal was to include "dynamic scoring" for major changes in taxing or spending policy, that is, estimating and including secondary impacts on the economy of proposed or altered revenue and expenditure legislation. Both the House and the Senate adopted rules instructing CBO and the Joint Committee on Taxation to use dynamic scoring. Dynamic scoring is controversial, because there is no accepted methodology for estimating the size or even the direction of those impacts. The rule could allow legislators to assume sufficient positive effects on the economy to make tax cuts seem to pay for themselves.

Both these sets of reforms were aimed at traditional Republican policy goals, controlling or reducing spending and cutting taxes.

Designing Process to Achieve Policy and Political Goals

Budget actors try to design and alter budget processes to produce the results they hope for, whether on a broad scale or in specific cases. Participants' efforts to change the process help make clear how particular parts of the budget process are intended or expected to work to achieve particular policy and power outcomes. What follows is a discussion of the parts of budget processes that political actors can change and the goals they hope to achieve through those changes.

Budget Process and Policy

A variety of features in budget processes may be used to achieve particular policy goals. For example, if elected officials feel the need to build public trust, then the budgeters can solicit public opinion and demonstrate that public priorities have been followed and that the programs are well managed and effective. Budget documents can be laid out in programs, each of which has performance measures to show what was planned and what was actually accomplished.

If the goal of the budget process is to reduce spending, then the process can build in constraints, such as spending caps and incentives for end-of-year savings. Budget rules may create lockboxes or prohibitions on transfers between funds or accounts, so that savings in one area are not used to increase spending somewhere else. Budget actors may change the assumptions on which future budgets are built, reducing or eliminating baselines that include inflation costs. They may build in automatic cuts if various actions are not taken. Target-based or zero-based budgets set targets for spending and systematically compare options to facilitate tradeoffs and stay within ceilings.

Target-based and zero-based budgets are incorporated into the budget format. The format of the budget proposal influences the information that is presented to decision makers, posing particular questions and providing data for particular analyses. Budget format also influences the way government explains its budgetary decisions to the public.

Frequently used budget formats are the line-item budget, performance budgets, and program budgets. Zero-based and target-based budgets are also used, but although they may influence the layout of the budget and frame budgetary decision-making, they are more descriptive of process than of layout. Each is intended to accomplish a different set of policy and political goals.

A line-item budget lists each department and assigns a sum of money to the department or other administrative unit. The money is not granted in a lump sum, to be spent as needed, but is divided into categories for specific purposes—travel, payroll, commodities, and the like. Each category of expenditure is listed on a separate line in the budget document. The department then has to spend its allocation in accordance with the requirements of each line. If the budget is broken into many detailed lines, such as paper supplies, pencils, desks and chairs, computers, and stamps, the department head has very little discretion about how the money can be spent. This kind of budget emphasizes financial control. A line-item budget plays down competition, because it does not compare programs and makes it difficult to introduce new programs. Its orientation is to maintain the status quo in the distribution of funds and spending power.

A performance budget lists what each administrative unit is trying to accomplish, how much it is planning to do, and with what resources. The documents report on how well administrators did with the resources they had in the prior year. A performance budget emphasizes getting the most service for the dollar. This form of budget is high on accountability and may be used especially when public skepticism of government is high. The goal is to show elected officials and the public what government agencies are doing, how much work they are doing, and how well they are doing it, with the goals of demonstrating effectiveness and encouraging program administrators to improve compared to a series of well-chosen benchmarks.

A program budget divides expenditures by activities so that, for example, the costs for juvenile counseling are broken out from traffic patrol, and both of those are separated from crime detection. Sometimes program budgets are formally linked to a planning process, wherein public goals are stated and expenditures allocated to reach those goals. The emphasis in this format is on the appropriateness of current spending priorities and the possible need for trade-offs between programs. Program budgets have the most potential for allowing legislators to review the policy implications of spending decisions.

Zero-based budgeting is a particular kind of program budget. It associates service levels in each program with costs, and then it prioritizes all the options, treating high and low service levels as different program options. All those at the top of the priority list are funded. If there are more items than money, the ones on the bottom of the list are not funded. Zero-based budgeting formally allows for and creates a mechanism for reallocation: One department may suggest a higher level of service or a new program that is ranked high on the priority list, while another department's programs are ranked low. The new proposal may be funded at the expense of the older. The potential for generating competition and conflict is so great in this budget format that it is seldom used; but a less-extreme version, called "target budgeting," typically puts only 5 percent to 10 percent of departments' budgets at risk for reallocation. Target budgeting is common.

The information presented in each budget format allows different kinds of analyses to be made. The line-item budget forces attention to changes in accounting categories. Why are office supplies more expensive this year than last? These are technical questions of limited policy interest. When a budget is presented in line items, it can be very difficult to examine proposed expenditures for sound management practice or appropriateness. The program budget, especially with its zero-based budget component, forces comparisons between programs on the basis of stated priorities. These priorities are usually statements of policy—for example, a program that benefits the poor should have a higher priority than one that benefits the rich, or programs that emphasize prevention should receive funding before programs that emphasize suppression. Performance budgets lay out not only what programs cost and roughly what they achieve but also the (implied) criteria of productivity for the choices between programs.

Because the different budget formats have different strengths and weaknesses, many actual budgets combine formats. Everyone has to be concerned about financial control, so there is often a line-item budget conforming to administrative units; but sometimes program budgets are added to line-item budgets and, less often, performance budgets are added to the program budget. In times of financial stress or in response to demands to reduce spending, governments may adopt zero-based or target-based budgets and put them on top of program budgets.

Minicase: Micropolitics—Bending the Rules to Win Individual Decisions

Bill Dauster, then chief Democratic counsel of the Senate Budget Committee, argued in a speech that the Republican majority in Congress showed a willful disregard for rules and laws when it served their legislative purposes.[1] In one case, to approve some unrelated legislation favoring the Federal Express Corporation, the Senate Republicans changed a century-old, standing rule that limited conference committees to the subject of the legislation that was sent to the conference.

Dauster charged that the Senate overturned another century-old rule, this one limiting legislation in appropriations bills. At the national level, there is a difference between appropriations bills, which provide money, and bills that design and modify programs. Appropriations bills are supposed to contain money approved for each program; they are not supposed to contain new legislation modifying programs or creating new ones. New or modifying legislation can take years to hammer out, as compromises between interests are negotiated. By contrast, appropriations bills are "must-pass"—the government will shut down unless there is money appropriated to pay for its programs and services. Allowing legislation in appropriations bills empowers a simple majority of the Senate to add unrelated provisions to a fast-track budget vehicle that is likely to pass.

The reason for such an important change in the rules, according to Dauster, was to adopt an unrelated amendment sponsored by Sen. Kay Bailey Hutchison, R-Tex. Hutchison's amendment to an emergency supplemental appropriation bill was a rescission (withdrawal of funding) for the rest of the year, so that no new endangered species could be declared while an authorizing committee was working on revisions in the law to make it more difficult to declare a species endangered. Hutchinson thus accomplished quickly and for the short term, without a reauthorization bill, what she hoped to accomplish with reauthorization legislation later in a broader, more deliberative setting.

Dauster also charged the Republicans with abusing their scorekeeping powers. He argued that on October 27, 1995, during consideration of an amendment by chair William Roth, R-Del., of the Finance Committee, Budget Committee chairman Pete Domenici, R-N.Mex., misrepresented off-budget Social Security savings as if they were on-budget savings and thus paved the way for adoption of Roth's amendment. Under the Budget Enforcement Act, Social Security was supposed to be off-budget, so counting savings in Social Security was a violation of the Budget Act. One senator raised a point of order noting the violation, but rather than recognize the point of order, which would have required 60 votes to waive, Domenici chose to ignore it. Domenici did not disapprove of the rule; it was just in the way.[2]

---

1. Bill Dauster, "Stupid Budget Laws: Remarks Before the American Association of Law Schools," January 5, 1996, and *Congressional Record,* October 27, 1995.
2. Ibid.

Budget Process and Power

Elected officials in the executive and legislative branches, budget office staff, and interest groups try to change the budget process to enhance their power over policy, and politicians also try to use it to ensure their reelection and the dominance of their party. Budget processes summarize the outcomes of those contests at any given moment. Sometimes the actors manage to make changes that are relatively long-lived, building them into constitutions that are hard to change; at other times, they make rule changes that do not have the force of law, let alone constitutional backing. The latter changes are much easier to overturn or modify. The longer-term changes are sometimes considered structural, though their effects are not determinative and may be modified by actual practice.

In normal budgetary decision-making, someone makes a budget request, someone reviews that request, and someone has to approve or cut or disallow that spending. But within that overall framework, there is variation in who makes which decisions and who can overrule whose decisions.

One of the key contests of power has been between the legislative and executive branches of government. In some cases, the executive branch dominates the decision-making, and in others, the legislative branch has an equal or even larger role. In the model of executive dominance, the chief executive is responsible for formulating the budget proposal, which reflects his or her priorities and policy agenda. The chief executive may keep the executive branch agencies completely away from the legislature, other than to present the chief executive's approved version of the proposal. The legislature may rubber-stamp the executive

In most states, the governor dominates the budget process; like puppets, legislators sometimes go through the motions but do not have much independent power.

budget—that is, approve it without detailed examination or emendation. Should the legislature make any changes that the chief executive opposes, the chief executive can veto the changes and sometimes even rewrite the legislation. In the legislatively dominated budget process, the bureau chiefs write up their requests for spending with the assistance of legislators who want some particular expenditure. The requests are not scrutinized by the chief executive but are handed directly to the legislature for review and approval.

Budget processes normally fall between the extremes of total dominance by either the executive or the legislature. Formally and legally, legislatures often have the power to approve taxation and proposals for spending, but they may delegate much of that power to the executive. One reason for delegating that authority is the belief that expenditures are out of control and that the legislature cannot discipline itself, especially on capital projects and jobs for constituents. The chief executive is expected to be able to cut out proposals that legislators make to please constituents and impose discipline on the legislature. The belief that legislatures are more vulnerable to interest group and constituent demands than the chief executive leads to pressure to shift budget power from the legislature to the chief executive. One way that the executive is supposed to exercise control is to veto any increases the legislature adds to the executive's proposed budget (for how this actually works, as opposed to the ideal, see the minicase "How the Governor's Veto Is Used," on p. 87).

Although the allocation of budget power between the executive and legislative branches of government is a major and highly visible area of contested power, it is not the only one. A second politically significant characteristic of budget processes is their degree of centralization. Centralization refers to two related concepts: (1) the degree to which the budget process is bottom-up or top-down; and (2) the degree to which power is scattered among independent committees, commissions, and elected officials.

Bottom-up procedures begin with the budget requests of bureau chiefs. These requests are scrutinized either by the chief executive and his or her budget staff or by the legislature or by both, but the requests form the framework of decision-making and set the agenda. There is little or no prioritizing of programs in this model; each request is judged on its merits, independently of other requests. A loose coordination is achieved by setting revenue or spending limits at the beginning of the process; cost increases are kept within rough limits by giving no agency an increase much higher than the total percentage increase in revenues.

Top-down budgeting virtually ignores bureau chiefs. The chief executive may not even ask bureau chiefs for their budget requests or may give them detailed instructions on how to formulate their requests. The proposal can be made from whole cloth at the top of the executive branch by taking last year's actual budget and making changes in it in accordance with policy preferences, giving more to one and less to another, regardless of what those running the bureaus would have asked for. A more moderate top-down procedure takes the bureaus' requests and gives a bit more to one and somewhat less to another based on policy choices.

In the legislature, too, budget processes can be more top-down or more bottom-up, depending on whether spending and revenue committees receive budget and revenue targets to work with or do their own work and give the totals to the body as a whole.

Budgeting processes normally combine some top-down elements and some bottom-up elements. Budgeting tends to become more top-down when there is a revenue problem or a defined budget crisis that requires reduction in expenditures. Top-down budgeting is associated with spending control and a policy orientation in the budget. That is, if the chief executive has a marked preference for achieving some goal, he or she is more likely to use a top-down process to select some programs and reject others as a means to achieve that goal.

The second dimension of centralization is the extent to which power is scattered among relatively independent actors. For example, the chief executive may have to share power with other elected executive branch officers or with independent commissions. When power is widely shared, the effect may be to immobilize decision-making. No one has responsibility or can tell anyone else what to do; approval for any action has to go through a number of different actors. The purpose of a highly fragmented and decentralized budget process may be precisely to limit spending and curtail activist government.

One aspect of decentralization is the degree to which the public has access to the process, through participation in planning, direct access and access through the media to useful information, and the chance to testify at hearings. The most open processes are those that make all decisions in plain public view, before the press, the public, and interest groups. Meetings are held at convenient times for visitors and are announced well in advance. Representatives of various interests are invited to share their views during budget hearings and on advisory boards. The process is closed if the public, the press, and interest groups are not permitted to watch the decision-making or to express their views during the budget process. Or their views may be solicited but routinely disregarded. Budget processes may be more or less open.

Open budget processes are more accountable to the public, but they are also more vulnerable to interest group pressure. Closing the budget process may help control increases in expenditures; opening it is usually a way of increasing expenditures. Closing the process is also a way of helping to pass tax increases, because those who would object have a less direct role in the decisions. A more closed process should make it easier to balance the budget.

Minicase: How the Governor's Veto Is Used

One of the major arguments for strong veto powers for the executive is that they enable the executive to remove "pork" that legislatures irresponsibly slip into the budget. According to this view, the executives are financially responsible—they seek the public policy goal of balanced budgets, with a minimum of waste. Legislators presumably are interested in narrower, more partisan issues, such as bringing projects home to their districts so as to be reelected. Because of this view, most governors were granted powerful vetoes over the state legislatures.

How is this veto power actually used? Is it used to maintain fiscal discipline or to remove projects and appropriations added by members of the opposite political party, making their reelection more difficult?

The question of how governors use their veto power was addressed in a now-classic article by Glenn Abney and Thomas P. Lauth. They argued, on the basis of a survey of state officials, that governors were no more likely to use line-item vetoes in states where the legislature was heavily inclined toward pork projects than in states where the legislature was more fiscally responsible or less wasteful. What these authors found instead was that governors were more likely to use the line-item veto when they faced legislative majorities of the opposite party. Line-item vetoes, at the time of the study, were used as a tool of partisan contestation.[1] James Gosling refined this finding to include policy issues as well as partisan ones; he confirmed that for the state of Wisconsin saving money did not seem to be a major reason for the use of line-item vetoes.[2]

Is the line-item veto still used in a partisan fashion or to enforce the governor's policies as opposed to those of the legislature? For some governors, the answer is yes. For example, in 2015, Governor Chris Christie of New Jersey, a Republican governor facing a Democratic legislature, line item vetoed $1.6 billion from the legislative budget. The Democrats in the legislature had increased taxes on the rich to pay for increased contribution into the severely underfunded pension system; the governor vetoed both the tax increase and the additional funding for the pensions.[3]

In Illinois, when the governor faces opposition control of the legislature, he or she is likely to use the line-item veto extensively to impose personal policy preferences; when the governor controls both houses by comfortable margins, proposals can move through easily and the governor does not need to use the veto. But when there is a relatively even split, with shifting majorities in each house from one election to the next, the governor negotiates with the legislative leadership, (usually) coming to agreement before the budget is formally submitted to the legislature. The leadership of the legislature has to

(Continued)

(Continued)

control the rank and file sufficiently to ensure that the agreement with the governor is approved.

The major means of winning over the rank and file is what Illinoisans call *member initiative grants,* providing funds for legislators to spend in their districts. The leadership has allocated the funds in return for votes on the budget deal. The governor has also been able to award funds from various state grant-in-aid programs and capital development funds. These, too, could be used to reward the faithful. Voting against the leadership's negotiated budget could mean the loss of access to funds beneficial to a legislator's district and would endanger his or her chances of reelection.

Rather than using the line-item veto to eliminate pork—in this case, member initiative grants—the governor actually increased the use of the grants. In Illinois, the governor has not been interested in eliminating pork; it is too powerful a tool for gaining legislative support for the budget.[4] The current very wealthy governor has changed the pattern a bit, encouraging legislators to vote for his policies by giving them donations from his private funds, but presumably not all future governors will be multimillionaires willing to spend their own money to win policy fights.

---

1. Glenn Abney and Thomas P. Lauth, "The Line-Item Veto in the States: An Instrument for Fiscal Restraint or an Instrument for Partisanship?" *Public Administration Review* 45, no. 3 (1985): 372–377.
2. James Gosling, "Wisconsin Item-Veto Lessons," *Public Administration Review* 46, no. 4 (1986): 292–300.
3. John Reitmeyer, "Budget Business as Usual: Christie Line-Item Vetoes $1.6b From Dems' Plan," *NJSpotlight*, June 27, 2015, http://www.njspotlight.com/stories/15/06/26/budget-business-as-usual-christie-uses-line-item-veto-to-cut-1–6b-from-dem-s-spending-plan/.
4. Douglas Snow and Irene Rubin, "Budgeting by Negotiation in Illinois," in *Budgeting in the States, Institutions, Processes, and Politics,* ed. Ed Clynch and Thomas P. Lauth (Westport, CT: Praeger, 2006).

Variation Between and Among Federal, State, and Local Governments

Because there is so much contestation for control, and because the outcomes of that contestation depend on existing structures, party dominance, the economic and political environment, and public opinion—as well as skill in using existing resources, laws, and rules—there is considerable difference in budget process between federal, state, and local levels of government as well as among state and among local governments.

For years, scholars used the federal budget process as a model against which other processes could be compared and understood. But in recent years, the federal budget has been put together in a different way almost every year. The advent of ad hoc budgeting at the federal level shifted attention to the states and to local governments in the search for a pattern that would convey the idea of a budget process. However, a survey of state and local budget processes reveals enormous variation. To come up with an idea of budget process based on this survey requires a description of that variation and the mechanisms that generate it. This chapter illustrates some of the key ways that budget processes differ from one another. The next chapter describes how and, to some extent, why federal, state, and local budget processes have changed and discusses some common themes in their evolution.

Variation Between Levels of Government

Federal, state, and local budget processes differ in the distribution of power over the budget between the legislative and executive branches of government; they differ in the degree of dispersion or coordination of power within the executive and legislative branches; and they differ in terms of the composition of the budget and the integration or separation of budget processes for different kinds of resources and programs.

Executive and Legislative Budget Powers. One way of describing budget processes is according to the balance between the executive and the legislature in drawing up and reviewing the budget. At the state level, the executive is usually stronger than the legislature, but the legislatures have made some gains toward more equal powers.[1] At the local level, for all but the smallest cities, the model of executive dominance generally holds. Mayors often hold powerful vetoes, and city councils may be prohibited from increasing the mayor's estimates. Councils typically have little or no budget staff. However, councils must approve the budget in most cities, and in some, they play a substantial role in budget review.

Minicase: Maine—The Governor Versus the Legislature

Maine has an executive budget process. The governor proposes the budget, the legislature can make changes to it as long as the budget remains balanced, but the governor can veto line items or funding for entire programs. He or she can reduce legislatively approved amounts and can replace a vetoed amount, so long as he or she does not increase the total budget by

(Continued)

(Continued)

doing so. The governor has considerable power in this situation but Governor LePage wanted to impose his policies on tax reform on a reluctant legislature and ended up demonstrating the relatively balanced powers of the governor and legislature.

In a battle that took place over six months, the governor insisted that the legislature pass a constitutional amendment to eliminate the income tax, which required a supermajority of legislators and a vote of the electorate. In the interim, the governor proposed to increase the sales tax and decrease the income tax. He also had other policy initiatives in his budget proposal that were not accepted by the legislature. Because his policy initiatives were rejected, Governor Lepage first used line-item vetoes, which require only a simple majority to overturn, and then vetoed the entire budget passed by the legislature, which required a two-thirds vote to overturn. That veto would have resulted in a government shutdown at the beginning of the fiscal year, had the legislature not overridden his veto with two-thirds majorities in both houses.

Sources: Steve Mistler, "After Long, Fierce Fight, Maine Gets a Budget and Avoids a Shutdown," *Portland Herald Press*, June 30, 2015. http://www.pressherald .com/2015/06/30/house-overrides-lepage-budget-veto/; Steve Mistler, "Maine House Votes to Override All 64 LePage Vetoes on Budget," *Kennebunk Journal/Morning Sentinel, Central Main.com*, June 18, 2015, http://www.centralmaine.com/2015/06/18/ lepage-vetoes-64-lines-worth-60-million-in-6–7b-budget/.

Governors generally have broader veto powers than the president. Constitutionally, the president of the United States has to veto all of a bill or none of it, which permits Congress to package bills to discourage vetoes. Forty-five governors can veto a line item. Twenty-four governors can veto the wording in a line of the budget bill. That means only five governors have the limited veto power that the president exercises.[2] While governors have stronger and more detailed veto powers than the president, those powers are not unlimited. The minicase about vetoes in New Mexico, following, illustrates the limits of these broader gubernatorial powers.

Minicase: Limits of Governor's Vetoes in New Mexico

While most governors can veto parts of legislation, the extent of those powers varies considerably, from being able to veto a single line in a budget to being able to wipe out entire programs and rewrite language or change numbers in an appropriation bill. The scope of these gubernatorial powers is often contested in court; the court in this sense is a player in budget process conflicts. In New Mexico, in 2011, Governor Susana Martinez vetoed legislation that increased the contribution by employers to the state's unemployment insurance fund. The legislature was trying to prevent depletion of the fund due to high unemployment in the recent recession. The court found for the legislature, arguing that the governor's veto contradicted existing law concerning the unemployment insurance program and made the rest of the law unworkable. The court had earlier ruled that the governor's "partial veto" or reduction of the legislature's appropriation for low income housing was also illegal. The governor concluded (threatened?) that without a reduction veto she would have to eliminate the entire line or total appropriation for the low income housing program.

Sources: "Susana Martinez Overstepped Authority With Line-Item Veto: New Mexico State Supreme Court," *Huffington Post,* June, 23, 2011, www.huffingtonpost .com/2011/06/22/susana-martinez-veto-new-mexico-supreme-court_n_882719 .html; Steve Terrell, "Supreme Court Rules Against Martinez." Roundhouse Roundup: The Blog, December 14, 2011, roundhouseroundup.blogspot.com/ 2011/12/supreme-court-rules-against-Martinez.html.

At the national level, since the president can veto only an entire bill, not parts of it, Congress sometimes puts a number of measures together, including some that the president wants badly, to make it difficult for the president to veto the entire bill. One type of budget legislation that often combines different pieces of legislation into one bill is a continuing resolution (called a *CR*). A CR is passed when one or more of the annual appropriations bills required to fund the federal government's operations are not passed on time. Congress funds the departments and programs whose appropriations have not yet passed with one (usually temporary) continuing resolution. If two or more appropriations have not yet passed, they are combined into one piece of legislation. The large scope makes it difficult to veto without harming some absolutely essential spending. Supplemental appropriations, passed during the year, also generally lump a number of separate items together, including some must-pass legislation, of such urgency that a veto seems unthinkable. Other, lower priority items often get mixed in.

A budget reconciliation bill also puts a number of separate pieces together into one bill. Reconciliation is a part of the congressional budget process, in which separate committees take action to comply with the budget resolution. The budget resolution is a kind of plan or road map for spending and taxing that is supposed to be approved by both houses of Congress, ideally before the budget deliberations begin. Based on this overall plan, the budget committees give instructions to the committees on tax and spending legislation. After the committees have carried out their assignments, making whatever changes they wish within the targets, Congress gathers up the committees' work and passes it as one omnibus piece of legislation. Unrelated legislation has often been put in the omnibus reconciliations because their broad scope makes them more difficult to veto.

At the state level, because the governor can generally veto parts of bills, omnibus legislation provides no protection against a veto. However, if the governor can only veto part of an appropriation if it appears in a line in the budget, the legislature can avoid putting one item in a line by itself. Or the legislature can combine many budget lines into one, so the governor has to accept the whole section of the budget or reject it all. For example, in Texas, the legislature responded to the governor's political use of the line-item veto by creating a lump sum appropriation for higher education rather than appropriating expenditures line by line.[3]

At the local level, most budgets are passed as a single ordinance, without unrelated provisions. The mayor and council often work out agreement on the budget in advance,[4] so the council approves the mayor's or manager's proposed budget and the need for a veto is slight. City staff typically monitor council statements throughout the previous year, weigh the spending and tax proposals embodied in such discussions, and incorporate the ones that make sense to them into the budget. By the time the council gets the budget, the things they wish to see are usually already incorporated. The mayor or budget office sometimes lays aside a small amount of money for a limited number of addbacks in case council members insist on adding some project the mayor, manager, or budget office intentionally deleted.

Whether the mayor has a budget veto depends largely on the powers of the mayor and the form of government at the local level. The two most common structures are the mayor-council form of government and the council-manager form. In the first, the mayor often has broader executive powers, including budget veto power; in the second, a manager hired by the council exerts more budget control than the mayor. There are also hybrids of these forms, in which mayors may have more or less power than the legal form of government suggests. Tables 3.1 and 3.2 give an idea of the relationship between the form of local government and the veto powers of the mayor (see also the minicase on San Diego changing its form of government, p. 95).

Sometimes negotiations between the mayor and council break down and the mayor threatens to use or actually does use his or her veto. Because municipal politics, unlike state and national politics, is normally not linked directly to

TABLE 3.1 Mayoral Veto Power in Large U.S. Cities

City	Government Structure	Mayoral Veto	Votes to Override
New York	Strong mayor-council	yes	2/3
Los Angeles	Strong mayor-council	yes	2/3, some 3/4
Chicago	Strong mayor-council	yes	2/3
Houston	Mayor-council	no	n/a
Philadelphia	Strong mayor	yes	2/3
Phoenix	Council manager, weak mayor	no	n/a
San Diego	Strong mayor-council	yes	5/8
San Antonio	Council-manager	no	n/a
Dallas	Council-manager	no	n/a
San Jose	Council-manager, weak mayor	no	n/a
Detroit	Strong mayor	yes	2/3
Indianapolis	Strong mayor, city or county council	yes	2/3
Jacksonville	Strong mayor	yes	depends
San Francisco	Strong mayor	yes	2/3

Source: Appendix 3 of the "San Diego Charter Review Committee Report," 2007.

Note: Chicago legally has a weak mayor form, but mayors have been strong by dint of the personality.

Democratic or Republican Party politics, the use of the veto is less clearly linked with partisanship and may be more closely related to fiscal policy. Although party loyalty is seldom an issue at the local level, relations between the mayor and council over the budget can become confrontational if a council member is a potential rival for mayor; even then, the lack of a budget staff for the council makes it difficult for council members to pull the budget apart and make their own proposals. Council members can become a noisy opposition and in some cases can prevent the passage of the budget or force compromises as the price for their support.

To summarize, there are major differences in the formal powers and patterns of negotiation between the executive and legislative branches at the federal, state,

TABLE 3.2 Mayoral Veto Power in California Cities

City	City Government Form	Mayoral Veto	Votes to Overturn
Los Angeles	Strong mayor-council	yes	2/3, some 3/4
San Diego	Strong mayor-council	yes	5/8
San Jose	Council manager, weak mayor	no	n/a
San Francisco	Strong mayor, county board	yes	2/3, some 3/4
Long Beach	Mayor-council, weak mayor	yes	2/3 for budget
Fresno	Strong mayor	yes	5/7
Sacramento	Council manager, weak mayor	no	n/a
Oakland	Strong mayor-council	no	n/a
Santa Ana	Council manager, weak mayor	no	n/a
Anaheim	Council manager, weak mayor	no	n/a
Bakersfield	Council manager, weak mayor	no	n/a
Riverside	Council manager, weak mayor	no	n/a
Stockton	Council manager, weak mayor	no	n/a

Source: Appendix 3 of the "San Diego Charter Review Committee Report," 2007.

and local levels. At the federal level, where the balance is relatively even, executive and legislative members must engage in extensive formal or informal bargaining. The results of these negotiations tend to frame the budget and set limits for departments. While bottom-up budget requests continue to be generated and examined, they may play a small role in determining outcomes, because the agreements reached by the executive and legislative branches take priority over the expressed needs of the departments and agencies.[5] The result has been a considerable shift to top-down budgeting.

At the state level, governors generally have more powerful vetoes than the president. There is little occasion or use for omnibus legislation. Instead, particular budget lines may be merged or obscured to evade the governor's line-item veto pen.

At the local level, the budget is typically a single piece of legislation. Budgeting may be dominated by the mayor or the manager and the council, depending on the form of government. There may be some contestation between the legislative and executive branches, especially over fiscal policy, such as which programs should be cut by how much to balance the budget. But bottom-up budgeting is more common, in which requests coming up from the departments and programs are accommodated as much as possible within revenue constraints. There is little or no political party influence and generally less policy conflict between the executive and legislative branches.

Minicase: San Diego—Fiscal Problems, Strong Mayor, and Veto Powers

Up until 2004, San Diego had a council-manager form of government, which is supposed to provide honest and efficient government. When the city ran into financial difficulties and shorted its pension funds, the public lost confidence in the council–manager form and opted for a five-year experimental period of strong-mayor government.

When San Diego changed to the strong-mayor form, not surprisingly, the mayor wanted to increase his budgetary power vis-à-vis the council, including strong veto powers. He proposed requiring a majority of eight of the eleven council members to override his veto, a requirement notably more difficult to achieve than the override requirements of other cities. The council granted the mayor other budgetary powers—he can transfer funds between departments and cut up to 15 percent of the total budget without council approval. When the mayor presents a budget, the council has little time or ability to react to it and so routinely votes for passage. But the council balked at giving the mayor a real veto over its decisions, requiring only the same majority to overturn a veto as to pass legislation initially. A ballot measure in 2010 on whether to retain the strong mayor form and increase the size of the majority required to override a veto to two-thirds passed easily.

Sources: P. Erie and Norma Damashek, "San Diego's Backroom Reform: A Push to Revise the City's Charter Is Little More than a Power Grab by the Mayor," *Los Angeles Times*, October 7, 2007; "The Mayor's Veto: City Council Retreats on Critical Charter Reform," editorial, *San Diego Union Tribune*, February 10, 2008, www.signonsandiego.com/uniontrib/ 20080210/ news_lz1ed10top.html; Gene Cubbison, "'Strong Mayor' to Stay," *NBC San Diego*, June 9, 2010, www.nbcsandiego .com/news/politics/Strong-Mayor-Prop-95934794.html.

Dispersion of Power. Despite the policy orientation of the federal budget and its relatively top-down process, budgetary power is most dispersed and fragmented at the national level, partly because the decisions are so important that everyone wants a piece of the action. Before 1974, Congress divided budget responsibility among legislative committees that designed and authorized programs, revenue committees, and appropriation committees. In 1974, it added budget committees to set spending and revenue targets and coordinate the other committees. The summit agreements between the executive branch and Congress that occurred from time to time added an additional level of fragmentation, because they performed some of the functions of the budget committees, they occurred at unpredictable intervals, and they were negotiated by a shifting set of actors. The congressional "supercommittee" in fall of 2011, which was supposed to come up with a plan to cut the federal budget but failed to do so, was a further illustration of power fragmentation at the national level, as it too bypassed completely existing committee structure.

By contrast, state and local governments have simpler and less fragmented decision-making, in part because the executive branch tends to dominate budgeting. Responsibility for budgeting in state legislatures tends to be more concentrated in appropriations and revenue committees, although, as at the federal level, sometimes the leadership of each house overrides committee decisions. In the cities, the structure is even simpler. At the local level, legislative consideration of the budget may be confined to a single finance committee that is responsible for both revenue and spending approval.

Entitlements, Grants, Loans, and Operating and Capital Budgets. Federal budgeting is really two processes that are only loosely linked. Some expenditures are approved annually by the appropriations committees, but a substantial portion of the federal budget is composed of entitlements, which do not go through the appropriations process and are approved for long periods of time rather than annually. Entitlements are special programs, the spending for which is determined by how many people or organizations meet eligibility requirements.

One budget process applies to entitlements and one applies to other spending. Among the other spending, however, are some that don't conform to normal operating budget characteristics. The federal government deals in loans and loan guarantees and insurance. Figuring out how much these loans, guarantees, and insurance actually cost the government has been difficult and controversial, but estimates are included in the budget. These estimates are not equivalent to budget estimates for, say, employee salaries in the Office of Personnel Management, so they are not merged and added to each other in a direct way.

Both state and local governments budget separately for capital and operating expenses, which the federal government does not do. The process for formulating and approving the capital budget is often distinct from the process for formulating the operating budget, though they may be considered at the same time. Capital budgets have a different time frame from the operating budget, as the projects they fund often drag out over several years. While the operating budget may look the same (or nearly so) from year to year, the capital budget does not. Items in the capital budget come and go as projects are completed. States also have entitlement programs, some in cooperation with the federal government and some of their own. State governments are also the recipients of federal grants both for themselves and as agents for the local governments. Such grants are now generally appropriated by the legislature, but they used to form a kind of second budget that was handled differently from normal appropriations. State budgets are thus complicated mixes based on different kinds of resources that can remain segregated or be merged in different ways into the budget. States often have different processes of decision-making for each of these different categories of programs.

Local governments generally do not have entitlements and appropriate all or nearly all their budgets every year. Grant revenue from the federal government or from the state may be incorporated into the budget, or it may be budgeted separately. Tax breaks, which operate as entitlements at the federal level and often at the state level as well, are usually handled on a case-by-case basis at the local level, so the costs are known in advance on a yearly basis. There are few open-ended responsibilities that originate at the local level, but the states sometimes pass through mandates for services to their local governments. Nevertheless, most local government expenditures do not go up at the same time that revenues go down, as they do for the states and the national government.

Variation in Budget Processes Among States and Among Cities

Not only do federal, state, and local governments differ from one another in their budget processes, but states differ from states, and cities differ from cities. Two examples at the state level illustrate the range of possibilities. The legislature dominates the budget process in Texas; the executive dominates in Georgia.

In Texas, the governor and the Legislative Budget Board (LBB) prepare a broad policy statement that informs the agencies' planning process. The LBB is composed of the lieutenant governor; the speaker of the house; the chairs of the Senate Committee on Finance, Senate Committee on State Affairs, House Committee on Appropriations, and House Committee on Ways and Means; two additional members of the senate appointed by the lieutenant governor; and two additional members of the house of representatives appointed by the speaker.

The governor also creates some goals and performance standards for the agencies. The agencies use this guidance to draw up plans, which have to be approved by the governor's budget office and the LBB. Later, the LBB sends out instructions to the agencies for the preparation of their budget requests, which must include the performance measures they described earlier in the process. Then the budget office and the LBB together hold hearings on the agencies' strategic plans and budget requests. Based on feedback the agencies receive during the hearings, they revise their plans and requests. The revised submissions form the basis for the LBB to put together the appropriations legislation. The governor makes budget recommendations, but the legislature can recommend different amounts of money than the agencies request or than the governor recommends. The approved budget goes to the governor for signature, though he or she has a line-item veto. The LBB and legislators oversee budget implementation. Oversight is reportedly detailed and forceful, to ensure that the agencies are doing what they promised to do and are taking the performance monitoring system seriously.

The Texas governor actually has little formal budget power, except at the conclusion of the process through the line-item veto. The governor's power is based more on indirect influence. Both the governor's policy guidance and detailed instructions to the departments from the budget office are blended with instructions from the Legislative Budget Board to the departments before they prepare their strategic plans and budget requests. The legislature is unusually active and powerful throughout the budgeting process.[6]

The picture is reversed in Georgia, where the legislature has had very little influence over the budget process. As one scholar described it, legislators have virtually no role in discussing budget reforms. The legislative session is extremely short, only forty days, during which the legislators see only the parts of the budget that the governor has proposed to change. Legislators discuss a few politicized programs and pay attention to pork-barrel-type spending for their districts.

> The legislative institutions available to provide oversight have atrophied from over a hundred years of single party dominance. The legislative budget office consists of few staff, many of whom are political appointees rather than professional budget analysts, and the residuum of an early effort to create some audit and evaluation capacity, the Budget Research and Oversight Committee has been underfunded and understaffed. Institutionally, the legislature is hardly prepared to consider a regular budget much less make use of increased information that would result from a budgetary reform.[7]

The budget requests are prepared by the agencies and submitted to the executive budget office. Then the governor has hearings with the agencies to discuss their budgets and work out differences. The governor makes his recommendations to the legislature that are subject to hearings by the house and senate appropriations committees. The house votes first and then the senate votes on its version. From there, the budget goes to a committee appointed by both houses to work out differences.[8] The budget then goes back to the governor, who can make changes with a powerful veto.

If the legislative budget office were fully staffed by budget professionals and if there were time during the session for legislators to examine the budget proposal and make their own recommendations, power would be more nearly equal, even with the governor's powerful veto. In the past few years, one-party dominance has ended, with the result that there is some pressure from the legislature to play a more active role in reviewing the budget, but change has been slow.

Most states fall between the extremes of executive and legislative dominance, but they lean more toward executive budgeting. In some states, such as Kentucky and Florida, agencies submit budget proposals to the legislature either before or at the same time as to the executive budget office.[9] The legislature can choose between the governor's proposals and the agencies', where the proposals differ. This arrangement dilutes executive power over the agencies. If the legislature is of the opposite party to the governor, members may spend more time and energy examining the governor's requests or coming up with their own.[10]

The major systematic source of variation in municipal budget processes is the form of government. In the town meeting, citizens vote directly on the budget, providing the maximum imaginable level of accountability. This structural form is necessarily limited to small towns and relatively simple issues. In the commissioner form, which was widely adopted in the early 1900s, the department heads sit as the council and jointly make budget decisions. This form makes no distinction between the executive and legislative branches. It has become rare in recent years, in part because it created problems of accountability.

Most cities today have either a mayor-council form or a council-manager form of government. In mayor-council forms, the mayor may be chosen by the council and may have little more authority than other council members or the mayor may be chosen by the citizens directly and have considerably more power than other council members. Although small cities may still budget legislatively, with spending recommendations coming from the departments to the council finance committee for review, in medium- and large-sized cities the mayor and members of his staff generally prepare the budget and the council has limited ability to make changes in or even review the budget. In council-manager cities, the executive-legislative distinction is blurred because the city manager, who prepares the budget, is hired and fired by the council. If the manager insists on a budget that departs from council priorities, he or she can be fired. Councils tend to play a more active role in budgeting in council-manager cities, at least to the point of making their policy preferences known and ensuring that their interests are represented in the budget. The council-manager form is more common in middle-sized cities, whereas strong, independently elected mayors are typical of larger cities.

Summary and Conclusions

Budget processes are partly technical, coordinating decision-making and keeping the flow of resources to the agencies timely and partly political. Because budget power is perceived as such an important component of overall political power, there is considerable jockeying for decision-making power within the budget process. More broadly, many budget actors try to change the budget process to help achieve the goals they value, whether those be public policy goals, such as growth or decline in the scope and size of government, or short-term partisan and electoral goals, such as the distribution of pork or deregulation that benefits specific constituents or contributors.

A decentralized, legislative budgeting process is very open to interest groups and short-term issues and not as open to longer-term policy concerns. A more top-down, executive-dominated process can be more responsive to policy concerns. Budget formats that make comparisons among programs also encourage a policy orientation. The process can rein in interest groups to some extent; it can exaggerate or tone down competition and can encourage or discourage budget trade-offs.

Budget processes differ at the federal, state, and local levels as well as across states and between cities. The differences depend in part on the structure. For example, in our federal system of government, state and local governments receive grants from the national government but not the other way around. The separation between the executive and legislative branches is more marked at the national and state levels than at the local level. Budget processes also vary among states and among local governments, partly as a result of structural differences, such as those between strong mayor and council-manager forms of municipal government but also as a result of divided government: In states where the executive and legislature are of different parties, budget processes differ from those in states where they are of the same party. But above all, budget processes differ depending on how particular actors have changed the process to match their needs, values, and problems.

Useful Websites

NASBO, the National Association of State Budget Officials, periodically updates a handy report on state budget processes, called Budget Processes in the States. http://www.nasbo.org/sites/default/files/2015%20Budget%20Processes%20 -%20S.pdf.

The Congressional Research Service (CRS) has a number of publications that describe the federal budget process. Technically not open to the public, many are available at Open CRS. A nice summary is *The Congressional Budget Process: A Brief Overview*, by James V. Saturno, 2011 (http://assets.opencrs.com/rpts/ RS20095_20110303.pdf). See also Jessica Tollestrup, *The Congressional Appropriations Process: An Introduction*, CRS, November 14, 2014, http://www .senate.gov/CRSReports/crs-publish.cfm?pid=%260BL%2BP%3C%3B3%0A. Other CRS reports to Congress on federal budget process are posted on www .Senate.gov. Use the search engine on the website to find them. A new website, CRSreports.com, boasts it has found and posted the largest number of CRS reports, many of which deal with budget process. Just put the word "budget" in the keyword search to bring up hundreds of reports.

4 The Dynamics of Changing Budget Processes

> We developed during the 1990s a series of budget process rules that helped us bring to heel these deficits. . . . [T]wo of the rules that we adopted were of signal success. One was a rule called PAYGO. . . . The other was a rule called discretionary spending caps.
>
> —John Spratt, former representative,
> *Congressional Record,* 2004

Budget processes are not cast in concrete—they change. When and how do budget processes unravel? What does a budget process failure look like? Does process failure stimulate process reform, or does process reform occur for other reasons? How do process changes influence outcomes? What features of budget process have what kinds of effects on outcomes? Does better budgeting result from shifting more power to the executive? Do budget rules, like PAYGO or spending caps, make a difference, as former representative John Spratt, D-S.C., argued?

Examining budget process changes makes it possible to see a chain of events, a set of causes and consequences followed by further changes. An increase in executive power (and abuse of that power) generates blowback from the legislature; an imbalance of power concentrated in the executive leads to late budgets and informal negotiations behind closed doors, which in turn leads to efforts to reform the process.

To analyze changes in budget process, one has to look not only at the formal processes but also at the informal ones. Formal processes may be supplemented or supplanted by informal ones. For example, the formal process might include a fine division of responsibilities among legislative committees and between the executive

102

and legislative branches, but actual budget negotiations may be restricted to representatives from the chief executive and the leadership in each house of the legislature, bypassing legislative committees completely. Though the committees seem to be doing their jobs, they may be taking their cues from summit agreements in which they had no part. This informal negotiation process occurs at times at all levels of government. When and why does an informal, less visible process take over and when does it subside or yield to the more formal and visible one?

One answer is that more and tighter rules encourage evasions and informal adaptations. Divided government contributes to the need for informal and secret negotiations because the executive and legislative branches, controlled by opposite parties, use the formal process to thwart each other's priorities. Third, actual power may be highly one-sided, leaving one or more parties to the process with a limited scope of decision-making. The minority side sometimes holds the budget hostage to force behind-the-scenes negotiations rather than follow the formal process that disempowers them (see the minicase on New York on p. 105). Finally, if the formal process produces outcomes that are generally disliked or embarrassing, participants may switch to a less visible process from which it is easier to distance themselves, generating the "who, me?" defense.

When informal processes take hold, secrecy may increase (few people know how decisions are made; selected stakeholders may have disproportionate access) and the information content of the budget may deteriorate, as definitions erode, categories blur, and outcomes (such as the size of the deficit or the implications of borrowing) are obscured. Democratic participation, openness, and accountability may diminish.

Overview

One of the key elements of budget process that has changed over time is the relative balance of budget power between the executive and the legislature. Colonial history left a legacy of distrust of the executive branch, associated as it was with the British king and his appointees, so budgeting was initially located in the legislative branch. Over the years, power shifted more toward the executive to facilitate financial control and allow a more explicitly policy–oriented budget review process. The practice of departments' submitting budget requests directly to legislative committees, with limited executive review, gradually yielded to a process in which the chief executive is responsible for assembling, reviewing, and cutting back agency requests before handing them to the legislature. As part of this change, executive budget offices were created, grew in professional staff, and became more politically sensitive and policy oriented.

Sometimes the shift to more centralized executive budget making was the work of reformers through constitutional amendments; at other times, the legislature delegated budget authority to the executive. Though one might expect legislatures to hold tightly to budget control as an important source of institutional as well as personal and political power, they have not uniformly done so. Two factors stand out as reasons for legislative delegation of budget authority to the executive branch. If the legislature and the executive are of the same party and have similar policy goals, the legislature has been more willing to delegate budget power to the chief executive. Alternatively, if there was some sense of crisis and simultaneously a demonstration that the legislature was not able to organize itself to deal with the problem, the legislature was more likely to shift budget-making power to the executive branch.

When the budget power was constitutionally vested in the executive, it became difficult or even impossible to share that power formally with the legislative branch. If legislatures felt too disempowered, they resorted to more informal means to exert some control. When budget power was legislatively delegated to the executive, there was more possibility that the legislative branch could take back some budget power if the executive abused it or used it to thwart legislative will.

The extremely powerful governor in New York was the result of a constitutional provision urged by reformers in the early 1900s, a provision that was difficult to change. By contrast, legislative delegations of budget power to the executive have not always been successful or permanent. Sometimes delegated policy-making power has been used for purposes explicitly forbidden by the legislature or used to bypass legislative approval. Legislators have sometimes responded by trying to strengthen their own ability to perform the functions they had formerly delegated to the executive, increasing budget staff, improving their capacity to review budget proposals, and enhancing their capacity to evaluate executive branch performance.

When the legislature and the executive share somewhat equal powers, tumultuous budget battles can result if different parties control the two branches, leading to vetoes, late budgets, and sometimes failure to pass a budget at all—the so-called train wreck. The cost of creating order in such volatile situations may be more extended negotiations between the executive and the legislative leadership and more (judicious, one hopes) use of distributive politics—pork. Pork is generally considered bad and blamed on legislators, but it may be generated by executives trying to pass a negotiated budget in a two-party democracy where power is evenly divided. Executives may include the pork projects of particular legislators in their budget proposals (or in supplemental appropriations) in an effort to win legislative support for the whole package or for other, unrelated legislation. However, the cost and visibility of pork may undermine trust in government, generating new waves of budget process reform.

Minicase: New York State—Powerful Governor, Weak Legislature, Informal Budgeting

When the formal rules of budgeting do not seem fair to all the actors—when power is highly imbalanced—the formal rules may still frame the process, but informal negotiations may take over. This was the case in New York State where the state constitution grants the governor broad authority over the budget and gives the legislature little independent budget power.

The main power the legislature had was its ability to hold up the budget to force the governor to negotiate. So budgets were routinely late and were based on political trade-offs rather than technical estimates.[1] New York State's politics and budgeting were described as "three men in a room."[2]

In 2004, the court played a major role in determining the governor's budget powers. On the one hand, it ruled that the governor could include policy statements in the budget proposal; on the other, it interpreted a clause in the constitution to mean that the legislature could not amend a "budget extender," the governor's temporary budget if the legislature had not passed the governor's proposed budget by the beginning of the fiscal year. The legislature had to either accept this temporary measure as is or accept the onus of shutting down the government. Because the legislature had to pass budget "extenders" as is, governors had a strong temptation to put their policy proposals into such measures, including policies that the legislature might otherwise have rejected or amended. If the legislature tried to use delay tactics to force the governor to negotiate, governors would use an extender and pass their policy preferences without legislative approval. Because of the 2004 court interpretation, the legislature lost its one key power, the power of delay to force governors to negotiate. Budgets since then have been more timely.

With Governor Cuomo using this expanded budget authority extensively in 2015, the senate finance chair was working on a constitutional amendment to rebalance powers, despite a failed amendment effort in 2005. It is not clear how such an amendment will be worded or what its chance of success, but short of a constitutional amendment, the legislature has not only little budget power, it has little ability to resist the governor's policy proposals more generally.[3]

(Continued)

(Continued)

The New York case demonstrates that if the governor's budget power is constitutionally based, it can be difficult if not impossible for the legislative branch to stop further aggregation of power in the governor's hands.

---

1. Editorial, "A Hocus-Pocus Budget," *New York Times,* January 21, 2004.
2. Seymour Lachman and Albert Polner, *Three Men in a Room: The Inside Story of One of the Country's Most Secretive and Misruled Statehouses by a Former New York State Senator* (New York: The New Press, 2006).
3. Nick Reisman, "Senate To Consider Scaling Back Governor's Budget Power," Time Warner Cable News State of Politics, May 12, 2015, online at http://www .nystateofpolitics.com/2015/05/senate-to-consider-scaling-back-governors -budget-power/).

While most contestation over budget power is between the executive and the legislature, the governor's desire for policy dominance can result in fights with the courts, especially when the courts mandate some expenditure the governor would like to eliminate or reduce. Kansas Governor Sam Brownback's fight with his state's supreme court is a good example. (See minicase "The Governor Versus the Courts" below.)

Minicase: The Governor Versus the Courts

In Kansas in 2014, the supreme court ruled that the state's education funding was unconstitutional, ordering an immediate increase in funding to make the allocations more equitable. The legislature had been withholding the constitutionally mandated payments in recent years. The state was already facing a $700 million hole because it had cut the state's income tax; being ordered to pay more for schools was bound to be politically problematic, but the governor's response was startling. He proposed to reduce the power of the supreme court over the lower courts and enhance his ability to choose justices. A judge sued, questioning the constitutionality of the governor's proposals. Then the governor signed a bill to not provide any budget for the court if it ruled his proposals unconstitutional.[1] His aim was to create a court that would go along with his policy proposals. A former senator reported that "Gov. Sam Brownback argued in a private conversation with Republican legislators and members of the governor's inner circle the method of judicial selection in Kansas had to be transformed to place on the bench judges who vote the 'way we want them to' on cases."[2]

Meanwhile the legislature was working on possible constitutional amendments that would make the governor's proposals legal. In the interim, however, a lower court judge ruled that the law concerning the selection of chief judges was unconstitutional; that decision could result in defunding the entire state court system. The decision was put on hold while the attorney general appealed it.[3] Then four judges sued to challenge the law cutting off the court system's budget if they ruled against the governor's proposal.[4] At the request of the state's attorney general, a district court judge ruled that the defunding law could not be put into effect until the middle of March, 2016, giving all parties a chance to rethink their positions.[5]

In March, the senate narrowly approved a bill to allow impeachment of supreme court judges if they usurped the decision-making power of other branches of government. Before the end of March, the legislature, still under the threat that the court would close the schools if they failed, passed a revision of the school funding formula. The revision lowered payment to all the school districts and used the savings to hold harmless the school districts that would lose money. The state added to the plan only $2 million.[6] This leveling plan did not satisfy the supreme court. The legislature passed a new plan in June of 2016. The story is ongoing.

---

1. Mark Joseph Stern, "Kansas Gov. Sam Brownback Threatens to Defund Judiciary if It Rules Against Him," *Slate,* June 8, 2015, http://www.slate.com/blogs/the_slatest/2015/06/08/kansas_governor_sam_brownback_threatens_to_defund_judiciary_if_it_rules.html.
2. Tim Carpenter, "Ex-Senator Tim Owens: Ideology Drives Sam Brownback's Push for Judicial Reform," *cjonline,* February 9, 2015, http://cjonline.com/news/state/2015–02–09/ex-senator-tim-owens-ideology-drives-sam-brownbacks-push-judicial-reform.
3. Joe Palazzolo, "Kansas Court System Faces Potential Shutdown After Ruling," Lawblog, *The Wall Street Journal,* September 3, 2015, http://blogs.wsj.com/law/2015/09/03/in-kansas-ruling-puts-court-funding-in-jeopardy/.
4. Meryl D. Wilson, "Four Judges Sue to Overturn Law That Would De-fund Kansas Court System," *Lawrence Journal World,* September 5, 2015, http://www2.ljworld.com/news/2015/sep/05/four-judges-sue-overturn-law-would-de-fund-kansas-/.
5. Peter Hardin, "Court Orders No Kansas Judicial Shutdown, At Least for Now," Gavel Grab, September 23, 2015, http://gavelgrab.org/?p=99036.
6. Edward M. Eveld, "Kansas Lawmakers Approve School Equity Fix," The Kansas City Star, March 24, http://www.kansascity.com/news/politics-government/article68035677.html.

Contests over power between branches of the government have become common, but they can also occur within the executive branch between independently elected officers. Democratic attorney general Andy Beshear in Kentucky recently ruled Republican governor Matt Bevin's midyear cuts of higher education illegal, arguing that the cuts violate the state's constitution and the state's process for making midyear cuts. The governor does not have the power to make midyear cuts unless revenue falls below estimates built into the budget, a fiscal crisis that did not happen. He cannot remake the budget at will during the year according to his own priorities. The attorney general threatened to sue if the governor did not withdraw the proposal; the governor did not withdraw the proposal; the attorney general then sued the governor. In this case, the governor was not granted more budget power, he just tried to take it by executive order. The court will have to resolve the case.

Federal Budget Process Changes

The federal budget process has changed over time. These changes were precipitated by financial crisis, rising deficits, and perceived abuses of delegated powers. Budget rules have sometimes been too stringent, generating evasions or modifications; at times, the budget process has been ill matched to the problems it had to deal with, in which case it was ignored and deteriorated into *ad hoc* decision-making.

In 1921, the executive budget process was adopted; in 1974 the Congressional Budget Reform Act was passed, limiting some of the president's budgetary discretion and enhancing Congress's ability to check executive branch revenue projections and economic assumptions; in 1985 the Gramm-Rudman-Hollings Act was passed in an effort to curtail the deficit. After several iterations, that act was replaced by the Budget Enforcement Act (BEA) in 1990 in a further effort to help strengthen the norms of balance. Balance was achieved in 1998, after which the budget process gradually unraveled. Deficits returned after September 11, 2001 and the Bush tax cuts, and were exacerbated by economic downturns during the Bush years and then in the Obama administration. In 2011, the Budget Control Act was passed in an effort to cut spending and reduce the deficit.

In addition to these formal, structural changes, there have been many informal adaptations. After passage of the 1974 Congressional Budget Reform Act, the more equal budgetary power of Congress and the president during the 1980s and 1990s, compounded by government frequently divided between the parties, encouraged budget negotiations between Congress and the president. These summit agreements led to more centralization of control in the executive Office of Management and Budget and the congressional leadership to reach and carry out agreements.

Robert Reischauer, the former director of the Congressional Budget Office, once described the federal budget process as so complex that only a handful of people in Washington fully understood it.

The Creation of the Executive Budget at the National Level

At the national level, the 1921 Budget and Accounting Act created the executive budget and the Budget Bureau in the executive branch. This major change in budget processes illustrates both (1) the competition between branches of government for power over budgeting and (2) the role of environmental shocks and emergencies, which fostered increases in expenditures and debt, generating problems that were addressed through budget process reform.

A major stimulus for the 1921 reform was the increase in spending that occurred from 1899 to 1912, in part because of a more activist government. Federal spending during the last third of the nineteenth century was $200 million to $400 million a year. From 1899 to 1912 the level jumped to $500 million to $700 million a year.[1] The full proposal for reform in budgeting at the national level included not just presidential review of agency requests but also a line-item veto for the president and restrictions on the powers of the Congress to change amounts the president proposed. Presumably the president would control expenditures and reduce waste using these tools. President William Howard Taft supported the executive budget proposal, but Congress did not initially approve of the idea.

The pressure on Congress to give up some of its traditional power in the interest of saving money was reduced by budgetary surpluses in 1911 and 1912.[2] The Democrats in Congress preferred to strengthen Congress and let it do the job of controlling expenditures. World War I intervened, reducing the salience of the issue in the short run but raising expenditures and deficits to such a point that congressional opposition to the presidential budget proposal was reduced. Something needed to be done, and this reform promised lower taxes, lower spending, and elimination of deficits.

Congress reformed itself in 1920, before the shift to the presidential budget. The House of Representatives consolidated appropriations into a single committee in 1920. As a result of the congressional reorganization and centralization, some of the pressure for shifting budget power to the executive budget was reduced, and the eventual shift was not as extreme as the reformers originally envisioned. The president got the Bureau of the Budget, which was transferred to the Executive Office of the President in 1939, and responsibility for preparing and presenting the budget, but Congress did not give the president a line-item veto and retained for itself its powers to accept, reject, or alter the president's proposed budget.

Entitlements and Congressional Fragmentation, From the 1930s to the 1970s

During the Great Depression of the 1930s, in response to massive unemployment and resulting poverty, a new kind of program was initiated, which gave money to individuals who satisfied criteria the programs established. Called *entitlements,* these programs bypassed the appropriations committees and were scrutinized only by the authorizing committees of Congress. Considerable spending power was shifted to authorizing committees, which often favored additional spending, and control over spending was divided up among a greater number of committees, fragmenting the budget process and making coordination more problematic. In addition, World War II caused staggering spending increases during the 1940s. Congress responded with several unsuccessful efforts at reform.

From 1966 to 1973 several environmental changes took place that strained the budget process and gave additional impetus to congressional reform.[3] First were the costs of the Vietnam War. Rather than curtail domestic expenditures to help pay for the war and risk exacerbating domestic conflicts, the government ran bigger deficits. There was pressure to reduce spending and the size of the deficits.

At the same time, there were major policy splits between Congress and the president over the conduct of the war and over domestic spending. President Nixon impounded (withheld) billions of dollars of domestic spending that Congress had approved. Mistrusting the president and fearing the loss of policy control over spending, Congress increased its budgetary role and strengthened its capacity to examine and determine budget policies.

Congress Takes Back Some Budget Control, 1974

The two pressures—to reduce spending and control deficits and to take back some of the budget discretion that Congress had granted the president— combined to produce the 1974 Congressional Budget and Impoundment Control Act. The act moderately increased centralization and coordination, but equally important, it provided a professional staff of budgeters to help Congress check the analysis that underlies the president's budget proposal. It also revised the procedures that allowed the president to withhold funds that Congress had approved.

Congress centralized budgeting only to a limited extent. To the existing authorizing, taxing, and appropriations committees, the 1974 act added budget committees, whose responsibility was to come up with overall estimates of revenues and targets for spending in broad areas. Their plan was called "the budget resolution" and needed to be approved by both houses of Congress (but not the president). The other congressional committees were generally supposed to stay within the guidelines the budget resolution established. The new arrangement provided for some coordination between revenue and expenditure committees and some fiscal policy formation; at the same time, it did not greatly threaten the existing division of power.

Congress's reorganization of the budget process was also intended as a way to take back some budget initiative from the president, who, in the eyes of some, had abused the discretion he had been granted. The budget committees could accept presidential policies or, relying on the new Congressional Budget Office, could differ with the president on projections concerning the economy, the anticipated deficit, and the inflation rate. Congress could make its own fiscal policy. The new budget process also curtailed the president's ability to withhold spending that Congress had approved but that did not accord with presidential policy preferences. Congress was given the opportunity to object to proposed deferrals of spending and had to give assent to rescissions (permanent withdrawal of legislative appropriations) or they would not take effect.

Though Congress tried to enhance its own power to devise and implement fiscal policy, most of the distribution of power within Congress was left as it was to ensure that threatened appropriations, tax, and authorizing committee members did not quash the whole proposal for change. The compromises resulted in budget committees that had little real power or influence. Their ability to act as a brake on spending was limited.

Deficit Controls 1986, 1990

Despite the new congressional budget process established in 1974, deficits continued to rise, taking an upturn at the end of the Jimmy Carter administration and then growing even more rapidly throughout the Ronald Reagan administration. Slow growth of the economy and the effects of rapidly growing entitlement programs contributed to the mounting deficits, but tax reductions, military buildups, and overestimates of economic growth also contributed.

Because many of the causes of deficits were seen as difficult to control or politically off-limits, there was renewed focus on changing the budget process instead of tackling the deficit sources directly. Supporters of a strong executive proposed stronger presidential vetoes; proponents of smaller government argued for a constitutional amendment that would take discretion away from public officials of both branches by requiring a balanced budget and revenue limitations. Advocates of congressional power suggested further reforms of the legislative budget process. What finally passed was a peculiar compromise that did not change the balance of power much between the Congress and the executive branch but markedly limited the discretion of both branches if they could not meet guidelines on the reduction of the deficit.

The compromise legislation, named Gramm-Rudman-Hollings after its sponsors, called for setting deficit reduction targets each year, with the goal of eliminating the deficit in five years. Failure to achieve the annual target for deficit reduction triggered an automatic, across-the-board cut (with some exemptions for entitlements). In theory, the across-the-board cuts would be so obnoxious to all parties that they would choose to achieve the deficit reduction targets on time, so that the automatic feature of the cuts would not be invoked. What actually occurred, however, was that the rules were bent and most of the cuts were never made. Gramm-Rudman-Hollings was modified several times before it was finally replaced by the Budget Enforcement Act in 1990.

Gramm-Rudman-Hollings was not particularly successful. It may have had some marginal effect in reducing the rate of growth, but the deficits continued to grow. Both Congress and the president began "gaming" Gramm-Rudman requirements, to reduce the apparent size of the deficit just before the calculation would be made on whether to invoke Gramm-Rudman cuts (called *sequesters*) to get down to the mandated deficit levels. Gimmicks included overoptimistic estimates of growth in the economy, pushing back spending from one fiscal year to the previous one, and keeping new spending off-budget. Gramm-Rudman's one-year focus encouraged quick-hit, temporary revenue raisers that would do nothing to help balance the budget in future years.

Many legislators were reluctant to give up Gramm-Rudman because the symbolism was bad—it would look as if they were giving up on deficit reduction. Hence they decided to overhaul the legislation, trying to close the loopholes that had appeared and eliminate some of its worst features. In fall 1990, a new plan for deficit reduction was passed, with a number of features.[4] First, the Social Security surplus was taken out of the deficit calculations, so that the true size of the deficit problem would be clear. Second, the legislation included a "pay-as-you-go" (PAYGO) requirement, meaning that proposed increases in mandatory expenditures had to be balanced by compensating increases in revenues or decreases in spending for other entitlements, and proposed reductions in revenues had to be balanced by decreases in expenditures or an increase in some other revenue source. Third, the agreement set separate spending caps for defense, domestic, and foreign discretionary spending, in an effort to keep spending down.

The legislation addressed several problems that arose during Gramm-Rudman days. Congress had cut the defense budget but had used much of the savings on domestic spending increases; in the new process, each area of the budget had to come in at or under the ceiling; savings in one area could not be transferred to other areas. Those constraints made it easier to achieve savings to reduce the deficit.

Another problem of Gramm-Rudman had been that the target had to be reached only briefly; there were no sanctions if the deficit estimates increased later in the year. By contrast, the new Budget Enforcement Act added a feature called *look back,* a check on conformity with the new limits later in the year. If any of the three caps was breached (defense, domestic, or international), then automatic, across-the-board cuts would be invoked in the area that breached the limits. Sequestration or automatic cuts would also be invoked if pay-as-you-go provisions of the mandated portion of the budget were violated. If such breaches occurred late in the year, the legislation provided that the amount of the breach would be subtracted from the next year's ceiling.

An additional problem with Gramm-Rudman was its one-year time span, which encouraged temporary revenue increases that did not solve the problem for future years. The Budget Enforcement Act included a five-year resolution that discouraged that kind of action.

The new budget process was less rigid than the previous one because it provided exemptions for emergencies and built in flexibility related to changes in the economy. The rigid deficit targets were gone, but the mechanisms to help achieve balance were strengthened. The new process was easier to live with and hence more likely to be observed. The process was still laden with constraints, as Gramm-Rudman-Hollings was, and its separate spending ceilings for different areas of the budget explicitly determined which programs would have to compete with which other programs.[5]

Evaluations of the Budget Enforcement Act suggest that it worked better than Gramm-Rudman-Hollings. One scholar observed, "A complete reckoning of what has happened since the rules were devised in 1990 would show that Congress has achieved substantial deficit reduction by increasing revenue and cutting direct spending under existing law while also offsetting any deficit increases resulting from new legislation."[6]

Budgeting After 1998: Ad Hoc Decision-Making

By 1998, after years of effort, the national government achieved budgetary balance and was looking at surpluses over the next few years. But the budget process was geared for the elimination of deficits, not for allocation of surpluses. The level of discipline inherent in the Budget Enforcement Act was difficult, if not impossible, to maintain after balance was achieved. Legislators no longer adhered to the spending caps in the BEA and ignored rules requiring offsetting revenue decreases with increases elsewhere or with spending cuts. They ignored some provisions of the budget process and worked around others. Writing in 2002, budget scholar Allen Schick described the evasion of the spending caps:

> The arrival of a surplus a few years ago triggered a spending frenzy that vitiated the discretionary spending caps established by the 1990 Budget Enforcement Act and made a mockery of the BEA requirement that increased spending be offset by cuts in other spending or by revenue increases. In 2000 and 2001, discretionary spending soared more than $200 billion above the legal limits on annual appropriations. The caps expire at the end of 2002—which will at least enable politicians to be more honest about what they are doing. They no longer have to pretend that the census and other ongoing operations of government are national emergencies.[7]

When the BEA formally expired in 2002, it was not renewed. But the result was not more openness or integrity in the budget process. The process became less predictable, less open, and more *ad hoc*. Deficits swelled. The Budget Enforcement Act of 1990 had been layered on top of the 1974 Congressional Budget and Impoundment Control Act. With the expiration of the BEA in 2002, the budget process was still guided by the 1974 act. That process depended on Congress's ability to pass a budget resolution, balancing revenues and expenditures, either adopting the president's assumptions and totals or substituting Congress's. Once Congress agreed on the totals and roughly how they should be spent, it was supposed to divide up the totals among various committees and subcommittees according to the plan. The two-step process helped coordinate the work of the committees, maintain control of budget totals, and put Congress's policy imprint on the budget. After 2002, however, the provisions of the 1974 act were often ignored or bypassed.

As former Congressional Budget Office staffer Phil Joyce observed, there was insufficient consensus to come up with congressional targets and adhere to them. The lack of agreement meant that the budget process was operating without a notional budget constraint. As a result, Joyce claimed, "No one knows how much is enough—or too much—spending. And nobody knows—or everybody knows, but nobody agrees—when the deficit is too large or the surplus too small."[8] The congressional budget process could have retreated back to the 1921 executive budgeting process, but the executive budget proposal was not balanced either and so could not operate well as an informal budget constraint.

Perhaps not surprisingly in this environment, for fiscal years 1999, 2003, 2005, 2007, 2011, 2012, 2013, 2014, and 2015, Congress failed to pass a budget resolution, the central feature of the 1974 act.[9] It did pass a resolution for 2016. Even in the years when there was a resolution, it was usually late, and the process was not always predictable or open to scrutiny. For fiscal year 2004, Congress passed a budget resolution, but House and Senate appropriators decided not to give spending targets to the appropriations subcommittees, at least not in public. The targets would be fluid until the subcommittees had done their work and crafted their portions of the appropriations for 2004. The consequence of not making spending targets public was to obscure the impact of President George W. Bush's tax cuts, which ought logically to have translated into programmatic spending cuts. Had Congress implemented its budget resolution in the normal fashion, it might have roused considerable opposition to the president's policies by showing the cuts made necessary by the tax reductions. Such a result could have jeopardized the chances of passing budget legislation. By obscuring the appropriations subcommittee ceilings, legislative supporters of the Bush policies made the tax cuts look as if they had no consequences.

The result was damaging to the budget process. Appropriators indicated that they would allocate as they went along rather than set targets in advance, but other participants, including staffers, were not sure how that would work or if that would be the final process. Some observers wondered how a subcommittee could operate without a limit of some sort. They argued that the budget numbers didn't add up, which was a good reason not to allocate totals to the subcommittees, but that at the end of the legislative process, the Senate, according to its rules, had to conform to the budget resolution; that meant that appropriators would likely get caught at the end if they didn't work with some sort of limits built into the budget resolution.[10] It seemed likely, then, that spending targets of some sort would have to be in operation, even if they were informal and kept from public view or operated after budget appropriations had been crafted rather than before.

For 2005, Congress was not able to pass a budget resolution to guide the committees' work. The issue was disagreement on budget process, namely the lack of offsetting spending reductions to compensate for the Bush tax reductions. Moderate Republicans in the Senate refused to go along with a process that legitimated this budgetary imbalance, insisting on reinstating the PAYGO provisions of the Budget Enforcement Act. Enormous pressure was brought on these holdouts to concede and vote for the budget resolution, but they did not yield. Appropriations in the Senate proceeded without a budget blueprint. The result was that spending items with the highest visibility in an election year would be approved, while more routine but equally important priorities would be left on the cutting-room floor:

> Without the budget resolution and its cap on fiscal 2005 discretionary spending at $821.4 billion, Stevens' panel [Sen. Ted Stevens, R-Alaska] would be limited to $814 billion [the limit in the previous year's concurrent budget resolution] in total spending but with no budgetary points of order on the floor capping funds for each individual spending bill. That would lead to a situation where funds could be increased on the floor until reaching that $814 billion limit, meaning some spending bills could be left out of the process.
>
> Without a budget, Stevens said, they would "pray and connive to work something out," but election-year politics would necessitate amendments increasing spending on fiscal 2005 Defense and Homeland Security Appropriations bills on the floor and "there won't be any money left for anything else."
>
> "My problems are just enormous without a budget," Stevens said. "Just enormous."[11]

In the end, it was the House's cap of $821 billion, which mirrored the president's proposal, that framed the final agreement on appropriations. Appropriators had to come down to that total. The various subcommittees that prepare the appropriations bills agreed to an across-the-board cut in their recommendations to bring in the total near the president's proposal. "In the end, Congress kept the total defense and non-defense discretionary appropriations below the $822 billion spending limit set by President Bush by cuts to several programs originally scheduled for more funding and by a 0.8% across-the-board nondefense, non–homeland security programs reduction."[12]

The appropriations process did proceed without a detailed blueprint, but it did not proceed smoothly. Only four appropriations bills had passed by the beginning of fiscal year 2005, so Congress had to pass an omnibus appropriations bill to fund the remaining agencies. This legislation was put together hastily and was huge (three thousand pages), tempting legislators to stick in a variety of pet programs, projects, or policies in the certainty that other legislators would be denied sufficient time to read the legislation and oppose provisions of which they disapproved. Some such provisions were caught, but an unknown number survived in the "must-pass" legislation. Legislators described the result as chaotic.

Unable to come up with its own budget proposal, Congress relied on the president's proposal, but that was not a useful source of fiscal discipline because it was unbalanced. The executive budget was highly dependent on emergency supplemental appropriations, which did not require a revenue offset. In particular, the Defense Department was systematically underfunded during the budget process, with the idea that it would be funded separately, after the budget was approved, by a supplemental appropriation that would simply add to the deficit.

In the absence of formally agreed-upon budget resolutions, Congress has often had to resort to *deeming* resolutions, the choice of some figure for a ceiling and using that number in lieu of a formally approved budget resolution (see the mini-case "Deeming Resolutions and Ad Hoc Budgeting" on p. 118 for a description of how this informal adaptation works).

To complicate matters, the wars in Iraq and in Afghanistan were largely funded through supplemental appropriations, even though substantial parts of the need were known in advance, to the frustration of some members of Congress. Not having any idea of how much money would be required for defense during the year made it nearly impossible to budget for the remaining items or to judge how large a tax reduction would be possible; no one knew how much money would be left over after defense was accounted for.

For fiscal year 2007, the House and the Senate passed different budget resolutions, which they never aligned with each other. Only two of the appropriations bills passed, Defense and Homeland Security; the remaining portions of the budget were funded by a series of continuing resolutions for the entire rest of the year. For 2008 and 2009, Congress did better, passing the budget resolutions for both years.

Minicase: Deeming Resolutions and Ad Hoc Budgeting

When both Houses of Congress cannot agree on a budget resolution or during the interim prior to agreement on a late budget resolution, legislative committees need some notion of a ceiling within which to work. Each house is likely to deem or adopt a figure and treat it as if it were the ceiling in a resolution. There is no legal basis or technical definition of the word *deem* or any prescribed form or sets of information it must contain. Sometimes deeming resolutions have been simple one-house, single-issue resolutions or have been incorporated into rules for considering some piece of budget legislation; sometimes they have been provisions in laws on related matters. It has been an ad hoc process, invented to get around the lack of agreement on resolutions, changing with need each year.

What figure each house deems as its overall ceiling or committee allocation is highly variable. Sometimes the prior year's resolution is used. If one house has passed a new budget resolution, it may deem that resolution as if it were binding, even though the other house has not agreed to its totals. For 2013, the totals agreed to in the Budget Control Act of 2011 were deemed by the Senate and treated as if they were a budget resolution.

Deeming a constraint makes it enforceable in that house, but deeming resolutions may not contain all the information that a normal budget resolution would have, leaving some deliberations uncontrolled. Moreover, when the House and Senate have deemed different figures to guide their deliberations, there is likely to be more conflict and disagreement over appropriations legislation that must pass both Houses of Congress.

For 2011, the Senate did not pass a deeming resolution granting a given sum to the appropriations committee, although the budget committee had passed one; instead, needing to proceed with allocations, the appropriations committee set spending limits for subcommittees, known as subcommittee spending guidance. While undoubtedly useful, such informal procedures had no enforcement mechanism.

In short, some years, both Houses passed a budget resolution, as the Congressional Budget Act of 1974 required; some years the resolution was late and a deeming resolution was put into effect for the interim; some years there was only the deeming resolution; and in some years, there was no deeming resolution in at least one house but a still more informal procedure within the appropriations committee. The deeming resolutions were passed in different ways and had different content in each year, and the source of the notional limits also varied from year to year. Deeming thus illustrates the concept of ad hoc budgeting.

Source: Megan Suzanne Lynch, *The "Deeming Resolution": A Budget Enforcement Tool,* Congressional Research Service report for Congress, June 12, 2013, https:// www.fas.org/sgp/crs/misc/RL31443.pdf.

Since 1998 the budget process has fallen into disarray and become increasingly improvisational or ad hoc.[13] Budget scholar Allen Schick has argued that when the budget process produces outcomes that are disliked, such as big deficits, decision makers distance themselves from the process, procrastinate on accomplishing key tasks, and sometimes encounter policy stalemates. Despite intense conflicts, they still have to produce a budget, so they resort to inventing new ways of getting the budget passed each year. Large deficits contribute to this deterioration of process and evasion of the rules, but deficits are also the result of the lack of agreed-upon process. Without such a process to help manage deep conflicts, time and energy are consumed on policy disputes, leaving participants with no time or inclination to fix the process itself. The breakdown of budget processes is often accompanied by instability in policy and ad hoc scoring rules that make it nearly impossible to compare spending from year to year. (For illustrations of how ad hoc budgeting is reflected in unstable and confusing budget rules, see the minicase "Ad Hoc Scoring Rules" on p. 120.)

Schick contended that the cause of the breakdown of budget processes in the 1980s was a mismatch between a budget process geared for a rapidly growing economy and revenues and the reality of a slow-growing economy generating inadequate revenues. The budget process was unable to adjust in a timely manner. This structural imbalance led to deficits and from there to a deterioration of routines and the generation of ad hoc budget processes.

Since 1998 a somewhat different sequence has occurred, though some of the same elements have reappeared. The budget process was geared to reducing or eliminating deficits and was unable to adapt quickly to a period of budgetary balance, creating enormous pressure to ignore the difficult choices inherent in the established budget process. While the economy slowed a bit, the major revenue problem was due to policy choices to reduce taxes. Politicians had a specific agenda, in this case to reduce the tax burden on the wealthy, and were determined to carry it out regardless of the deficits and disruption of budget processes that resulted. Controversy about those policies led to stalemates and generated adaptations to get around the roadblocks, including omnibus appropriations bills that could not possibly have been read by those who voted for them. The desire to hide the negative consequences of those policies led to increased dependence on supplemental appropriations and favored the use of omnibus appropriations that would obscure cuts by burying them in three thousand pages of legislation. It also led to misleading and gimmicky accounting rules.

Minicase: Ad Hoc Scoring Rules

Ad hoc budgeting is often accompanied by instability of rules. Decision makers create new rules as they go along, not only rules for how to make budgetary decisions but also the rules for counting how much is being spent, estimating the size of the deficit, and figuring the size of revenue increases or decreases. Without stability in these rules, it is impossible to compare from year to year or from committee to committee or between the houses of the legislative branch. Once rules are up for grabs, the temptation is overwhelming to change them for short-term political gains, changing back again if additional political gains can be obtained that way. The result is chaotic, not only for the budgetary decision makers but also for the press and the public, who find it increasingly difficult to know the impact of current policymaking.

The George W. Bush administration allowed deficits to grow as a result of its policy of reducing taxes. Reducing the tax burden was a political priority, but the consequent growth of deficits was something of an embarrassment. The administration distanced itself from the results of its policies in a number of ways, one of which was to change the "scoring rules" that help measure the cost of legislation. On measuring the costs of tax cuts, the administration first argued that its cuts would be temporary, so that under the scoring rules, the Office of Management and Budget would only have to count a few years of the consequences, even though the financial impact increased after the end of that period. Then, a couple of years later, the administration argued that the tax cuts should be treated as permanent, so that their extension would not be scored as having any increased costs. The administration sought to dodge the implications of the tax cuts first in one way, and then it serpentined back to dodge the implications the other way.[1]

The administration's eagerness to change the rules to make the consequences of its policies disappear continued into President Bush's second term, when the administration proposed not counting the borrowing that would be required to set up private accounts for Social Security. Since those who pay into Social Security are in fact paying for the benefits of those who are currently receiving Social Security, setting up private investment accounts for young payers—diverting their contributions into their own private accounts—would require the government to borrow to pay benefits to current retirees—vastly expanding the deficit. Determined to adopt the privatization plan, the administration sought to make the borrowing disappear through new scoring rules.[2]

Ad hoc budgeting and rule making favor short-term partisan and political gains over long-term collective and institutional interests, and they erode the quality of information available to participants and the public. They also foster public cynicism that corrodes the trust necessary for democratic governance.

1. Robert Greenstein and Joel Friedman, "Budget Rule Change Would Make the Cost of Extending the Tax Cuts Disappear," Center for Budget and Policy Priorities, February 27, 2004, www.cbpp.org/2-27-04bud4.htm.
2. Jason Furman, William G. Gale, and Peter R. Orszag, "Should the Budget Rules Be Changed So That Large-Scale Borrowing to Fund Individual Accounts Is Left out of the Budget?" Center for Budget and Policy Priorities, December 13, 2004, www.cbpp.org/12-13-04socsec2.htm.

Recent Changes in Congressional Budget Process

The budget deficits of the Bush administration resulted from tax cuts, an economic decline in response to the attacks of September 11, 2001, and two wars. President Obama had his own deep recession to deal with, while continuing the wars in Iraq and Afghanistan. Deficits not only continued, they rose precipitously. One reaction was to try to change the budget process.

Congress's pay-as-you-go (PAYGO for short) provision in the Budget Enforcement Act of 1990 was in effect from 1990 to 2002. This provision was credited with helping to achieve balance in 1998. PAYGO was supposed to ensure that the federal government did not either cut taxes or increase entitlements without finding a way to offset the revenue losses or spending increases. The government was prohibited from making the deficit worse, although exceptions were to be made for emergencies. The PAYGO provision was to be enforced by a nearly across-the-board cut (sequestration) in a select group of mandatory (entitlement) programs if Congress failed to comply with the law. This threat was sufficiently strong that during the 1990s it was not necessary to invoke sequestration; compliance was high until the budget was in balance. The Senate maintained some kind of PAYGO rule (the exact nature of the rule varied) after the demise of the Budget

Enforcement Act; the House later adopted a PAYGO rule. In 2010, the rule was formalized into a law. During his campaign, President Obama had pledged to end the practice of using unfunded emergency supplemental appropriations to pay for the wars in Iraq and Afghanistan. Not only did the practice obscure the costs of the wars and give the Defense Department a blank check, but because the emergency supplementals were not offset by increased revenue or decreased spending, they added directly to the deficit. In 2010, the war supplemental dropped from about $100 billion to about $33 billion, and in 2011, the administration funded the wars through the regular appropriation process, without an emergency supplemental. (See Figure 4.1 for the proportion of emergency supplementals attributable to funding the wars.) Nevertheless, the debt continued its long rise, resulting from war spending, tax breaks, antirecession spending, and bailouts while the economy suffered a deep recession.

In 2011, Republicans forced a long-term deal to reduce spending as their condition for voting for a debt limit increase. Embodied in the Budget Control Act, the deal included caps for discretionary spending to last through 2021, with separate spending limits for security and nonsecurity spending for the first couple of years. In addition, the legislation set up a joint legislative committee to reduce the deficit by $1.2 to $1.5 trillion by 2021; if it failed to do so, then automatic cuts would occur, split evenly between defense and nondefense and including both discretionary and so-called direct spending (entitlements and debt). The committee failed to agree on savings, and hence the automatic cuts became law. Social Security and Medicaid were exempted, as were some other programs for low-income people. Medicare cuts were limited to no more than 2 percent.

The caps under the Budget Control Act were deemed, that is, taken in lieu of a congressional budget resolution that was the core of the 1974 congressional budget process. The Budget Control Act specified that the law was intended to be the congressional budget for 2012 and 2013. The 1974 act was thus superseded by the Budget Control Act. There was no congressional budget resolution until fiscal year 2016.

Several factors—the creation of a joint supercommittee that bypassed congressional committees and traditional rules of consideration of legislation, the establishment of ten-year spending caps and automatic across-the-board spending reductions, and the substitution of the Budget Control Act for the congressional budget resolutions required by the 1974 congressional budget act—all suggest ongoing budget process chaos on the one hand and a reduction in the role of Congress in the budget process over the next few years, in the name of deficit reduction. The cuts appear automatic, untouched by human hands, and thus avoid the blame that might normally accrue to legislators cutting programs.

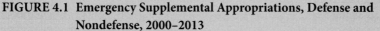

FIGURE 4.1 **Emergency Supplemental Appropriations, Defense and Nondefense, 2000–2013**

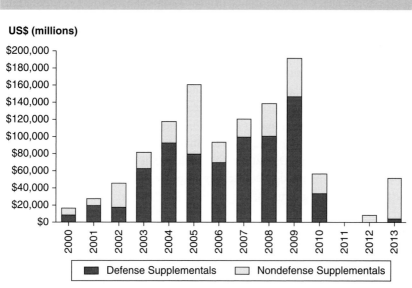

Source: Congressional Budget Office, Supplemental budget authority, http://www.cbo .gov/sites/default/files/cbofiles/ftpdocs/66xx/doc6630/suppapprops.pdf.

In January of 2013, the across-the-board cuts were scheduled to begin, and at the same time, the Bush tax cuts from 2001 and 2003 and the Obama tax reductions of 2010 were set to expire. If no action was taken, tax increases would affect nearly all taxpayers at the same time that broad spending cuts—including defense—were implemented, with potentially major effects on slowing down the economic recovery from the deep recession. The president and Congress negotiated painfully and slowly up until the last moment and a day beyond, before coming up with an agreement. The cuts were deferred for two months and the tax cuts were generally extended for the middle class, while the very wealthy would have to pay more taxes. This prolonged, intense, and closely watched conflict, with Democrats and Republicans generally lining up on opposite sides, took precedence over more normal budget processes.

Across-the-board cuts that would affect defense were unacceptable to many Republicans as well as to the administration and the Department of Defense. Because Obama had included spending for the wars in the budget, as opposed to in emergency supplemental appropriations, that spending too could have been subject to across-the-board cuts. To avoid this outcome and appear to continue to adhere to the Budget Control Act, Congress and the president agreed to an Alice in Wonderland approach to defense spending. The costs of the wars were taken "off budget" in an account called the Overseas Contingency Operations (OCO). Since this spending was considered off budget, none of the rules applying to on-budget spending applied. The spending did not have to be offset and it was not subject to across-the-board cuts. The president kept his word, the wars were not funded through emergency supplementals, they were estimated in advance, but other than being more transparent and occurring as part of the regular budget process, the Overseas Contingency Fund functioned in much the same way as the emergency supplementals had. Even when the wars were winding down, the OCO kept on expanding, for reasons explained in the minicase of the Overseas Contingency Operations fund below. The minicase underscores the conclusion that when budget constraints are perceived as too stringent, they give rise to evasions and gimmicks.

Minicase: Overseas Contingency Operations

The OCO was initially a small line item in the defense budget for emergency spending, but it became much bigger when the wars ceased to be funded by emergency supplemental appropriations. Though initially conceived of as a temporary fund, it has endured and will be difficult to eliminate. Because the fund is not bound by spending caps, Congress has shifted some of the regular base defense department spending that is capped into the uncapped OCO fund. Even as war spending winds down, these other expenditures remain. Were the fund to disappear, these costs would go back to the DoD budget and, unless DoD caps were raised to include the transferred amounts, would force cuts in other accounts to stay under the caps. Estimates for 2014 indicate some $30 billion of nonwar spending had been slipped into the OCO. A second reason that the fund is likely to endure is that the DoD is currently putting into the fund money for antiterrorism expenditures around the world and air strikes in Iraq and Syria. Those expenditures are not likely to go away any time soon. A third reason the fund will be difficult to eliminate is that it became a mythical source of money for nondefense spending, as elected officials tried to claim savings in the OCO as offsets for other desired spending.[1]

The way the accounting gimmick works is that the initial Congressional Budget Office projection of increasing OCO spending is treated as a baseline; any reduction from that baseline is considered a savings and hence can be used as an offset for new or expanded spending or to claim a reduction in the deficit. Since actual OCO spending did not approach that initial projection and the winding down of the wars means that war spending should come down further without programmatic cuts or caps, some have claimed the savings are fictional, the money wasn't requested and wasn't there to be cut. Nevertheless, those putative savings have been used to justify real spending increases elsewhere in the budget. Elected officials can thus publicly claim that their spending proposal does not increase the deficit.[2] Those in favor of smaller government want real program and spending cuts as offsets, not cuts from a projected baseline, and hence have opposed the use of the OCO in this fashion.

Senator Bernie Sanders, in arguing to use the OCO for some veterans' benefits, claimed the technique was legitimate or at least should not be opposed, because it already had been used by both Democrats and Republicans: "I have heard my friends on the other side of the aisle call this a budget gimmick. I disagree. Republicans and Democrats in the House and Senate have voted several times to count war-related savings as a reduction in the deficit. For example, virtually every Republican in the House of Representatives and Senate voted for the fiscal year 2012 budget resolution, introduced by Representative Paul Ryan, which counted $1 trillion in deficit reduction from 'phasing down overseas contingency operations'—not what I am saying, but what the Heritage Foundation points out. If the savings from winding down wars can be counted as deficit reduction, clearly we owe it to our Nation's veterans to use a very small percentage of this fund to make their lives a little bit better at home."[3]

1. National Taxpayers Union and Taxpayers for Common Sense, "Top 10 Reasons It's Time to Re-Think OCO," NTU Website, May 19. 2014, http://www.ntu.org/governmentbytes/detail/top-10-reasons-its-time-to-re-think-oco.
2. U.S Senate, Committee on the Budget, Republicans, "War Savings Offset Still a Gimmick," February 11, 2012, http://www.budget.senate.gov/republican/public/index.cfm/2012/2/war-savings-offset-still-a-gimmick.
3. Bernie Sanders, Senate Session on C-SPAN Website, February 26, 2014, http://www.c-span.org/video/?c4485656/sen-sanders-speaks-oco-funding.

Ad hoc budgeting continued for 2014 and 2015. In neither of those two years did the House and Senate both pass budget resolutions and agree on them. Recall that the budget resolutions are not law, they are passed and agreed to by both houses but not signed by the president. Instead of a normal budget resolution, for FY 2014, Congress passed and the president signed the Bipartisan Budget Act of 2013, which contained a section called "Establishing a Congressional Budget." It functioned like a budget resolution, with some major exceptions. The House and Senate each had passed separate budget resolutions, but instead of formally reconciling the two resolutions, the chairs of the budget committees of both houses together with a budget resolution conference committee negotiated an agreement that was embodied in the Bipartisan Budget Act. There was one major catch, however—there were no numbers in the agreement that would have been in a budget resolution. Instead a different mechanism was used, allowing the chairs of the budget committees to file a statement of budgetary levels. The statute, in other words, changed the budget procedure for 2014 and possibly for 2015, if no budget resolution were passed in that year. (In fact, there was no resolution in 2015.) The result was enforceable, it functioned like a deeming resolution but was temporary.[14]

The federal example makes it clear that the budget process changes—sometimes slowly—in response to the problem at hand. It can be difficult to back off publicly from rules that are harsh but aimed at popular outcomes, such as deficit reduction; that kind of pressure leads to efforts that seem to comply without actually doing so, whether the gaming of Gramm Rudman Hollings or the evasions the BEA spending caps once budget balance was achieved, or the imaginary savings of the Overseas Contingency Operations fund. When the formal rules do not work well, for whatever reasons, informal rules take over, which sometimes change from year to year.

Changes in Budget Process at the State Level

Budget process in the states has been somewhat less complicated than at the federal level, and while it has evolved over time, has been less ad hoc. Perhaps most important, the distribution of budgetary power between the executive and legislative branches has been somewhat different at the state level than at the federal level.

The same reform movement that brought executive budgeting to the federal government in the 1920s influenced the states first and went further there. In three states, New York, Maryland, and Illinois, the legislatures were disempowered, leaving them still struggling for a meaningful formal role. The remaining states balked at implementing the reforms in such an extreme way. In five states, Arizona, Colorado, New Mexico, Oklahoma, and Texas, the legislature develops the state budget independently of the governor.[15] Most states lie between the extremes of executive or legislative dominance: The governor may propose a budget, but the legislature may change the governor's budget or ignore it. Despite the exceptions, on average, governors have more authority over state budgets than the legislatures do.

History of State Budget Process

After an initial period of strong legislatures in the 1700s, state legislatures declined in public trust and responsibility. They tended not to be representative of voters, they were often too big, and were overly responsive to interest group and constituency demands. These flaws sometimes led to structural changes to limit their influence, including short sessions, constitutional constraints on what they could do, and early awards of line-item veto power to governors. (For an example of a state where the legislature was sharply curtailed constitutionally in the hope of controlling spending, see the minicase of Maryland, on p. 128.)

Governors' budget powers were gradually strengthened, but the executive branch, reflecting that same early distrust of state government, remained highly fragmented. Many key state officials were elected rather than appointed by governors, so these officials had their own power bases and were not under a governor's control. Governors and their lieutenant governors might be rivals rather than teammates, and the elected controller might be out to blame the governor for budget problems. Departments were often headed by commissions that appointed their own heads. Thus the governors' control was often limited. In many states, the competing elected officials were gradually eliminated in favor of appointees loyal to the governor, and the governor instituted accounting controls over the departments. The governors and their budget staff would examine the requests coming from the departments, formulate a budget proposal, and pass that proposal along to the legislature for response. Often the governors were granted a veto over legislative changes to their budget proposals. (For an illustration of the change from a legislatively dominated to a gubernatorially controlled budget process, see the minicase of South Carolina, on p. 130.)

Although the governors generally dominate the state budget process, the capacity of state legislatures to review the governor's budget and question the assumptions underlying it has improved. In the 1960s, as a result of the Supreme Court's one-man, one-vote decision, the redrawing of electoral districts, and the election of more representative legislatures, state legislatures began to reform and prepare themselves for a more active policy role. The budget was a key focus of that increased capacity. Many legislatures lengthened their sessions, changed from meeting every two years to every year, and added staff with expertise on fiscal and budgetary matters. These staff members do many of the same things for legislatures that the Congressional Budget Office does for Congress at the national level. They empower the legislature to question the assumptions in the executive budget and to formulate its own alternatives without jeopardizing budget balance.

In the standard model of executive budgeting, the governor's office gives budget instructions to the agencies, then collects proposals from the agencies, cuts them back, and forwards the whole budget proposal to the legislature for its consideration. In that model, the governor's policies form the framework for consideration of the budget. Most of the states now have some form of executive budget, but as long as the legislature continued to receive unedited budget requests directly from the agencies, the governor's budget power was diluted. The direction of change has been away from direct transmission from agencies to the legislature.

In 1983 the legislatures in forty-one states received budget proposals from the agencies before the governor's office had put the budget proposal together. By 1988 that number had risen to forty-three, but by 1997 only thirty-two states reported that the legislature received the proposals from executive agencies before the governor prepared the proposal. In 1983 three state legislatures received agency budgets only through the governor; by 1997 eight did.[16]

The National Association of State Budget Officers looked at the issue a little differently, asking whether the agency budget justifications were included in the governor's budget requests. If the agency budget justifications were included in the budget, the legislature would get the proposal from the agencies at the same time as the recommendations from the governor, and the two would be distinct. If they were not included, the legislature would see the governor's recommendations and might not see the agency requests at all. From 1997, when the question was first asked in the NASBO survey, until 2002, the numbers of states that included the agency's budget justification in the governor's budget proposal increased slightly, from thirty-nine to forty-two, but by 2008, the number of states in which the governor's proposal included the agency budget justifications had dropped to thirty-five or thirty-six (depending on how one defined agency budget justification) and stayed there through 2015. (Data is based on NASBO surveys, Budget Processes in the States, various years).

Minicase: Maryland's Legislative Budget Power

Maryland has gone the farthest in disempowering its legislature and empowering the governor with respect to the budget. Because of fear that the legislature would spend money irresponsibly, the legislature was permitted only to reduce, not increase, the governor's budget proposal. This restriction has been in place since 1916 and is embodied in the constitution, which makes it very difficult to change. Legislators tried unsuccessfully several times to put before the voters a constitutional amendment to let the legislature add to the governor's budget. Unable to add to the governor's budget proposal, the legislature devised other ways of exerting its influence. These techniques have not always been efficient or accountable and sometimes have triggered counter responses from the governor.

First, the legislature used its limited powers to cut out some items the governor wanted; the governor retaliated by adding those items back in a supplemental appropriation. In order to get legislative approval for that supplemental appropriation and to build support for other, unrelated policy initiatives, the governor added into the supplemental the pet projects that key legislators wished to include.[1] The negotiation of which items will be included in the supplemental is not open to the public.

Second, because the legislature cannot add to the governor's *current* budget proposal, legislators often pass expensive programs with budget implications for *future* years instead. In the 1970s, the legislature passed a law requiring the payments of one program to match the costs of a second program, a law signed by the governor, but without funding. A court ruled that the governor could not be forced under the constitution to fund such a law. The legislature responded with a constitutional amendment to require the governor to fund programs that were legally passed. This provision was approved by the public and amended the constitution, providing a limited channel for the legislature to address needs not given high priority by the governor. When the direct budgetary path was blocked, the legislature chose the path of substantive legislation with budgetary implications. With the mandated expenditure approach, program decisions are divorced from budgetary implications, so legislators can pass (and the governor can sign) more expensive programs than the state can afford.

Third, the legislature can add or expand programs if it can pass legislation establishing dedicated revenue specifically to pay for them. This ability leads to an excessive number of accounts and reduced flexibility. Revenue dedication means that revenue sources are tied to particular expenditures and can be spent for nothing else. When revenue is divided into many small pieces, each of which is necessarily connected to a particular program, there is insufficient flexibility in the budget to adapt to new situations.

The fourth adaptation is that the legislature has compensated for its relative powerlessness by micromanaging the agencies, a role that is inappropriate and inefficient.[2]

In 2015, the Republican governor clashed with the Democratic legislature over the budget. The legislature cannot increase the governor's proposals, but it can reprioritize, shifting money from one program to another. The legislature voted to reduce the governor's request for strengthening the pension

(Continued)

(Continued)

funding, to fund government workers' pay increase, and to increase spending on large school districts and on particular health programs. It did not reduce the state's structural deficit as much as the governor wished. The governor called these changes irresponsible and threatened to withhold the funds from the legislatively approved priorities.[3] The governor has the power to withhold up to 25 percent of an appropriation with the approval of the Board of Public Works (a three-member board consisting of the governor, the comptroller, and treasurer). The governor's powers over the budget, constitutionally based, remain utterly one-sided.

1. Roy T. Meyers and Thomas S. Pilkerton, "How Can Maryland's Budget Process Be Improved?" Maryland Institute for Policy Analysis and Research (MIPAR), University of Maryland, Baltimore County (UMBC), September 2003, http://user pages.umbc.edu/meyers/improveMD.pdf; also available at www.umbc .edu/mipar.
2. Roy Meyers's testimony to the House Appropriations Committee, Maryland General Assembly, March 9, 2004.
3. Jetta Johnson and Ovetta Wiggins, "Maryland General Assembly Passes Budget That Widens Split with Hogan," *The Washington Post,* April 14, 2015, http://www .washingtonpost.com/local/md-politics/maryland-lawmakers-governor-rush -to-complete-budget-before-midnight/2015/04/12/1dc466a6-e16c-11e4–81ea -0649268f729e_story.html.

Minicase: South Carolina's Legislatively Dominated Budget Process Begins to Budge

South Carolina is one of the few states that has a legislature-dominated budget process and still has a structure with many independently elected executive officials whom the governor does not control. Although the governor prepares a budget proposal and has a general veto and line-item veto power, he or she is still weak compared to the legislature. For one thing, the legislature has often overridden the governor's vetoes. Until recently, a joint legislative-executive budget and control board (created in 1950) controlled much of budgeting and financial management, instead of the executive alone, as occurs in other states. The governor only occasionally controlled a majority on the board and so could present a budget but could not necessarily influence what happened to it after that.

The governor's budget powers have been gradually growing. The governor received the authority to present a budget only in 1993. Gov. Mark Sanford ran for a second term on a platform of reorganizing state government, to reduce the number of elected officials in the executive branch and eliminate the state Budget and Control Board. He was not able to do so. With Republican majorities in both houses of the legislature and a Republican governor, Nikki Haley, giving high priority to these reforms, there has been more willingness in the legislature to give the governor more power over the budget and its implementation. In 2011, 2012, and 2013, several major legislative proposals were put forward to eliminate the joint executive and legislative Budget and Control Board and give many of its powers to the governor. Those bills did not pass.

However, in 2014, the legislature passed and the governor signed a restructuring bill that eliminated the Budget and Control Board and created a department of administration in the executive branch and transferred many of the functions of the old board to the new administration department. The Budget and Control Board ceased operating in June 2015.

South Carolina's budget process is changing, but not very quickly.

Sources: Luther F. Carter and Richard D. Young, "The Governor: Powers, Practices, Roles and the South Carolina Experience," South Carolina Governance Project, University of South Carolina, 2000, www.ipspr.sc.edu/ grs/SCCEP/Articles/ governor.htm; Fred Barnes, "Mark Sanford vs. the Good Old Boy Party; Can South Carolina's Government Be Brought Into the 21st Century?" *Weekly Standard,* August 6, 2007, www.weeklystandard.com/Content/Public/Articles/000/000/013/ 931dxyvm.asp?pg=2; Eric K. Ward, "House Axes Budget and Control Board in New Restructuring Plan," The Nerve Center, May 3, 2012, http://www.thenerve .org/house-axes-budget-and-control-board-in-new-restructuring-plan/; Eric K. Ward, "Politics Threatens to Derail Restructuring," The Nerve Center, April 25, 2012, http://www.thenerve.org/politics-threatens-to-derail-restructuring/; Seanna Adcox, "S.C. Senators Approve Restructuring Bill," *Post and Courier,* February 17, 2012, www.postandcourier.com/article/20120216/PC1603/302169998; Seanna Adcox, "House: Haley Shares in Blame for Bill's Demise," *The Charlotte Observer,* July 7, 2012, www.charlotteobserver.com/2012/07/07/3368412/house-haley-shares -in-blame-for.html. The South Carolina Department of Administration website, http://www.admin.sc.gov/search/node/note; GWDtoday.com "Gov. Nikki Haley Signs S.22—Government Restructuring Act Of 2014, 2/6/2014," http://gwdtoday .com/main.asp?SectionID=2&SubSectionID=235&ArticleID=28585.

In some states where there was a strong executive budget and a weak legislature, the legislature has gained power in budgeting in recent years; in those states where the legislature was strong and the governor weak, the governor's position has been strengthened. The state of Florida offers an example in which power over budgeting has gone back and forth between the legislature and executive, favoring the executive in recent years (see the minicase on Florida on p. 133).

Throughout the 1970s and 1980s, the general direction of changes in budget processes in the country was clear: Legislatures were becoming better organized, with more professional staff, and were taking a larger role in budgeting. That change led some to question whether governors overall were losing budgetary power. For the present, however, it seems that gubernatorial dominance of budgeting is safe. It is difficult to change constitutional provisions; it is even difficult to pass reform legislation if it threatens the governor's powers, because the governor has to sign the bill. The governors retain many important formal powers, such as very strong vetoes. Governors on average have not lost power with respect to the legislatures, but when government is divided—that is, when the legislature is controlled by one party and the executive branch by the other—legislators scrutinize the governor's budget proposal with an eye to policies with which they disagree. When the legislature and the governor are of the same party, they are likely to have a similar philosophy and similar policy goals, so legislators are more inclined to go along with the governor's proposals. One study argues that the governor gains more power from times of unity in government than he or she loses in times of divided government.[17] It is not so much that governors have lost power in recent years as that the legislatures have gained power. One way that legislatures can gain power without the governor's losing it is that each may care about a different area of the budget. Also, as the Florida case suggests, when the legislature cedes control to the executive over budget formulation, the legislature's role may change, increasing its power over budget implementation and program evaluation; if it gives up micromanagement of the executive through line-item budgetary controls, its scrutiny of agency plans and performance measures may increase.

One fundamental difference between the state and the national level is that at the state level the budget process—or parts of it—is often embodied in the constitution rather than in laws, making it especially difficult to change. Also in some states, power is so one sided that the weaker side has little leverage. These characteristics of state budget processes have resulted in the growth of many informal rules that allow change to occur. By themselves, the formal rules may not be good indicators of the actual distribution of power and may obscure the ongoing process of adaptation. The formal rules have to be viewed together with the set of informal rules they breed.

Minicase: The Executive and the Legislature in Florida's Budgeting

Changes in the balance of budgeting power between the legislature and the governor in Florida illustrate several themes. If governors and the legislature are of the same political party, the legislature is more likely to delegate budget power to the governor. When governors use that power to publicly threaten legislative district projects, legislators may protect those projects by making them less visible. Delegation of budget power to the governor may be accompanied by safeguards, so that the executive cannot ride roughshod over legislative prerogatives and policies.

Years ago, Florida's budget process was legislatively dominated. Governor Bob Graham, elected in 1978, expanded his role in budget preparation by implementing a program budget and creating an office of planning and budgeting in the executive office of the governor. Program budgets grant the agencies broader discretion over spending and give the governor more policy control. The legislature reacted negatively to the program budget format and the enhancement of executive budget-making power. In 1983 it began mandating the format and content of the budget in considerable detail and requiring the governor's staff and the legislative staff jointly to develop the budget instructions sent to the agencies. Most important, the new law directed the agencies to "submit their independent judgment of their needs to the legislature," so the governor could not change the agencies' requests before the legislature saw them. The legislature also strengthened its budgetary oversight role, extensively reviewing budget changes initiated by the executive during the year.[1] One observer summarized, "The balance of power in state budgeting in Florida is only slightly less legislatively controlled than in Texas, where a joint legislative council creates the budget."[2]

The governor's powers were strengthened vis-à-vis the legislature in recent years, because the governor and majorities of both houses of the legislature have been of the same party (Republican). As a result, the legislature generally has been willing to go along with the governor's priorities, including his demands for more budgetary power. Nevertheless, it retained some budgetary power for itself, redefining its role.[3]

When Gov. Jeb Bush was elected in 1998, he made it clear that he would not tolerate a system in which the legislature ignored the governor's budget proposals.[4] He insisted that all projects, including legislators' projects for their districts, go through an appropriate review process in the agencies. In 1999 Bush declared that in the budget for 2000, "all items, including member projects, must fall within the statewide budget policy priorities as set by the

(Continued)

(Continued)

agencies. And they must be within the established spending limits for the agencies and programs affected. Furthermore, member projects may only be funded with non-recurring dollars and those projects will be evaluated for their effectiveness in the next budget cycle."[5] If legislators added projects to the agencies' requests later in the legislative process, the governor vetoed them. Governor Bush vetoed many more projects in legislators' districts than had his predecessors, using the item veto against Republicans as well as Democrats.[6] He threatened to veto any appropriations that did not contain the projects or programs he supported.

Legislators protested the 550 vetoes of Bush's first year and then responded with various strategies to make the items they put in the budget less visible as a way to avoid the governor's veto pen.[7] In 1999 and 2000, Bush vetoed about $313 million in legislative projects; in 2001, the figure was $290 million. Then in 2002 the amount dropped to $107 million and in 2003 to a mere $33 million. It is not clear if legislators were hiding their projects better, were more selective in what they proposed so they passed gubernatorial muster, or the governor was backing away from using the veto against his allies in the legislature. Interestingly, however, in 2004 the governor returned to using the veto heavily, vetoing $349 million in legislative projects.[8]

In 2000 the Bush administration proposed a number of modifications to the budgeting system, which the legislature approved. Some of the changes were similar to those Graham sought earlier without success, such as a performance orientation embedded in a program budget. Along with the program budget, the legislature granted the executive branch more flexibility to move funds around. Most important, the legislature "removed the requirement that agencies submit preliminary Legislative Budget Requests, and thus limited opportunities for legislative intervention in framing departmental submissions."[9] With this provision, the governor could (finally) shape the agencies' budget requests.

At the same time that these reforms gave reality to executive budgeting in Florida, the legislature retained enough power to maintain its influence and some policy control. The new budget law increased the ability of agency heads to move money around from similar accounts, but only if in doing so they did not create any future obligations for spending or violate the intent and policy of the legislature. The new law required agencies to draw up plans and submit budgets that meshed with those plans, but it also required that the plans be submitted to the legislature for approval well in advance of the legislative session and that legislative budget requests be submitted to the governor and legislature at the same time. The new law required agencies to come up with and report on performance measures but also to present those measures to the legislature for approval.

The writers of the new law made sure that if key legislators felt that the governor was overstepping bounds, they could intervene to stop the offending spending. Furthermore, the reforms created the Legislative Budget Commission, consisting of fourteen members of both houses, including the chairs of the appropriations committees. The legislature gets recommendations from the individual departments and from the governor, and the House and Senate each prepare their own budgets. The Legislative Budget Commission is empowered to review agency spending plans and approve or disapprove of midyear changes to the approved budget. "In addition, the Chair and Vice Chair of the Commission, on behalf of the Legislature, may object to any agency action that exceeds the authority delegated to the executive or judicial branches, or is contrary to legislative policy and intent, regardless of whether that action is subject to legislative consultation or Commission approval."[10] Thus the legislature retained for itself the authority and capacity to make decisions, enforce its policy preferences, and question the governor's policy proposals should the need arise.[11]

Despite the much-enhanced budgeting powers of the governor and same-party domination of the executive and legislative branches, the legislature in Florida remains strong and somewhat independent of the governor. It maintains its own staff to make revenue projections based on monitoring the economy; it monitors budget implementation; it reviews programs; and it can and does reject some of the governor's policy proposals. Nevertheless, the governor still wields a powerful veto: In 2015 Governor Scott vetoed over $461 million from the legislative budget, including some top priorities of the leadership. Scott justified his vetoes by arguing that he cut projects that lacked statewide impact or that had not gone through the formal review process.[12]

---

1. Gloria Grizzle, "Florida: Miles to Go and Promises to Keep," in *Governors, Legislators, and Budgets,* ed. Edward Clynch and Thomas P. Lauth (Westport, CT: Greenwood Press, 1991), 98ff.
2. Karen Stanford, personal communication, March 18, 1999.
3. See Robert B. Bradley, "Florida: Ebb and Flow in Executive Legislative Relations," in *Budgeting in the States: Institutions, Processes, and Politics,* ed. Ed Clynch and Tom Lauth (Westport, CT: Praeger, 2006), chap. 8.
4. Richard S. Conley and Richard K. Scher, "'I Did It My Way': Governor Jeb Bush and the Line Item Veto in Florida (with Apologies to Frank Sinatra)" (paper prepared for The Citadel Symposium on Southern Politics, Charleston, SC, March 7–8, 2002).

(Continued)

(Continued)

5. Quoted in Fishkind and Associates, "Florida's New Budget Process," August 31, 1999 (Hank Fishkind, 90.7 FM,WMFE News), www.fishkind.com/radio/fnbspot.html.
6. Conley and Scher, "I Did It My Way."
7. Ibid.
8. Jackie Hallifax, "Bush Trims $349 Million out of State Budget," *Naples Daily News,* May 29, 2004.
9. R. B. Bradley, "Budgeting in Florida" (paper presented at the Association for Budgeting and Financial Management meetings, Chicago, October 7–9, 2004).
10. Legislative Budget Commission, statement of purpose, www.leg.state.fl.us/data/committees/joint/jlbc/LBCProcede.PDF.
11. Ibid.
12. Gary Fineout, "Florida Gov. Signs Budget, Vetoes Nearly $500 Million," *Tallahassee Democrat,* June 23, 2015, http://www.tallahassee.com/story/news/politics/2015/06/23/florida-gov-signs-budget-vetoes-nearly-500-million/29151631/.

Changes in Budget Process at the Local Level

Local governments are less partisan than states or the national government and have a completely different structure. Most important, local governments are subordinate to the states. In many key ways, they do not determine their own budget processes. There is continuing tension between the states and their local governments on the degree of local autonomy over the budget process. Occasional tension between the legislative and executive branches manifests itself mostly in adoption and abandonment of council-manager and strong-mayor forms of city government.

The states grant limited and often ambiguous autonomy to local governments through home rule laws or regulate the local governments directly through statutes, called *municipal budget laws.* Although cities do not have constitutions, the state may grant them a charter or allow them to adopt a charter that outlines what they may do and how they may do it. These charters typically include the form of government, including the powers of the mayor and council, and may embody detailed rules about the budget process. They can be changed in much the same way that constitutions can be changed, by a massive campaign and vote of the citizenry. Charter changes, while they do occur, are infrequent. Changes in the form of government also change the budget process, giving more budgetary power to the legislative body, to the mayor, or in some instances, to a commission.

State Control Over Local Budget Process

In the 1800s, states controlled the finances of cities through legislation. Sometimes these laws were specific to an individual city and sometimes they applied to a whole class of cities. Mayors would negotiate with the legislature for exemptions from tax limits, permission to borrow above a mandated limit, or consent to provide a particular service. Although there are still some remnants of the process of special legislation for each city, states gradually adopted a pattern of legislating for classes of cities or for all the cities and villages in the state.

In some states, laws specify nearly all aspects of the local budget process, including the forms on which budget requests are to be made, the accounts that may be used, the kind and size of contingency funds, and the ability to transfer revenue between funds. In other states, the laws are less restrictive and may only require submission of a balanced budget, a public hearing, and an independent audit at the end of the fiscal year. State governments specify which taxes or fees local governments may use and may limit the amount of revenue that local governments may collect or mandate the provision of particular services. The states may pass tax exemptions that apply to local governments, and they may or may not replace revenue that is lost in this way. When they limit taxation and simultaneously mandate service levels, states force their priorities onto local governments.

To the extent that states have mandated budget processes in the localities, several major questions arise. The first deals with persistence: Are the rules so rigid and long term that they prevent local governments from adapting to new situations? The second question deals with the neutrality of the rules—that is, whether the rules are aimed at improving financial management, or toward specific policy outcomes. The third deals with the extent to which states have encouraged or hindered democratic participation in the budget process or have overridden local priorities.

Persistence. Some states have provided a set of minimum standards for city budget processes, including which cities are allowed to adjust and modernize; in other states, budget rules have locked cities into clumsy processes designed for another time and another set of problems. In the latter cases, local governments need to continually finesse the state regulations or ask for exemptions or changes to a system that has become too complex, as one system of rules was laid over another.

Many states have included in their municipal budget laws a line-item approach to budget formats. At the time when it was coming into use in the early 1900s, line-item budgeting was a major reform and a considerable improvement over the way budgeting had been done. Before line-item budgeting, it was common to budget by naming particular expenses and how much they cost. A municipal budget might include an item for the police stables that read, "Horses and stables, $50,000." The reader would have no idea of the number of horses, the size of the barn, the number of employees, the quality or quantity of the feed, or the health of the horses. There was no way to tell if this was a successful operation at reasonable cost. When line-items were introduced, the purpose was to put each component of expense on a single budget line, so it would be visible and comparable to the price of such items available elsewhere. The costs for a stable might be broken out into thirty pounds of feed at $30, five stable workers, each paid $5 a week, and $10 for repairs to the roof. The idea was to make it known if the city was overpaying for supplies, personnel, or capital infrastructure.

The state budget laws typically required cities to include in the budget the expenditures by line item for the past year or two, the current year's expected expenses, and the projection for the next year. The goal was to make sure that the line items did not grow too quickly or without justification. In the early 1900s, just after the major expansion of municipal programs in the Progressive Era (roughly 1895–1910) and the inflation caused by the expense of World War I, keeping costs down was a major consideration. State requirements for local budget processes were designed to deal with those cost increases.

While line-item budgeting has some strengths, it also has some weaknesses. One of the major ones is that it obscures policy decisions by making line items rather than programs the focus of attention. In emphasizing spending controls, it deemphasizes management and planning. In those states where the state continues to require a line-item budget, local governments have to layer program budgets and performance budgets on top of the line-item format or issue separate documents with program and performance information.

The emphasis on cost controls became more extreme during the Great Depression of the 1930s. State rules for local budget making often broke revenues into small, earmarked portions, with tax caps for each function. The idea was that savings from one function should not be used to increase spending somewhere else, and revenue that came in over expectations could not be spent without formal rebudgeting and approval. The rigidity of this model led many cities to put expenditures where there was money, transferring costs into funds that had unspent totals, because it was illegal to transfer revenues out of those funds. In other words, the system was so inflexible that it was often gamed. Where such rules still apply, cities still game them in the same fashion.

Out-of-date rules concerning municipal budgeting have persisted nearly unchanged in many states. An example from Arizona suggests how long some of the state requirements last and the effort it takes to budget efficiently despite the regulations:

> Maricopa County in Arizona, the county in which Phoenix is located, ran into fiscal difficulties, and in getting out of them, became aware of how outdated the state laws were that controlled local budgeting and finance. . . . The state law was passed in 1912 when Arizona became a state. The county found it could not legally pay bills by wire, even though that would help the cash flow, because warrants had to be approved individually by the board. Once the expenditures were determined for the year, that total could not be exceeded, even if more revenues were available during the year. And totals for departments could not legally be shifted around at the end of the year without declaring an emergency. The accounting system was required to be cash based. However, exceptions were granted on an individual basis. The result was that staff had to fight the system continuously to do a good job of budgeting and financial management.[18]

In 1997, the law in Arizona was changed to allow local councils to make transfers between funds if the money was available and the purpose appropriate, without declaring an emergency. State laws regulating local budgeting do change, but slowly.

Lack of Neutrality. States have been periodically pressed by businesses and homeowners to lighten the burden of taxation. Some states responded to this pressure, especially during the Great Depression, by creating budget processes in cities that were biased toward reduction of property taxes and away from service delivery. Some states remained focused on the quality of financial management and avoidance of fiscal distress in their cities, but others, responding to antitax groups, structured local budget processes to keep taxes down and to keep the scope of government narrow. They created boards and commissions that could override local priorities and budget requests so as to keep expenditures down.

For example, Indiana's old budget process, established in the early 1920s, allowed any ten taxpayers to petition state tax commissioners on budgetary matters. The system favored taxpayers who wanted lower taxes, even when the majority of residents in a community were willing to have higher taxes and more projects and services.[19] During the Great Depression, when communities were in desperate need of more revenue to help the impoverished citizenry, the state relented and allowed some increases in taxation.

The flexibility and responsiveness of the Indiana system may have helped keep the basic structure intact for many years. Indiana's mandated budget process was exceptional in its bias toward lower taxes, but even the Indiana system gradually accommodated to the needs of local governments and the preferences of local voters, in addition to responding to the desires of organized antitax groups.

Democratic Controls. Nearly all the states require some level of direct citizen input into the local government budget process. Requirements include public hearings, which are often specified in great detail in terms of when they must occur, their scope, who must be present, and how long before budget adoption they must occur. Such rules have been in place for many years and demonstrate a desire to foster and preserve democratic responsiveness at the local level.

While the hearing requirement suggests a desire to make local governments responsive to residents, at least in part because of the states' vulnerability to interest groups, states have often mandated that local governments do certain things, such as increase police pensions or spending for public schools, overriding local preferences.[20] The states also sometimes tell the local governments that particular classes of taxpayers should get a particular tax break. When the states do not reimburse the local governments for costs they impose, the local governments are stuck: Either they have to cut back spending on some other service or project, or they have to increase revenue, often a difficult or even impossible task when the local governments are operating under state or local tax caps. Such unfunded mandates supplant priorities. Unfunded mandates alter the budget process by telling the local governments in effect: Do this first—subtract the cost from your available revenues, and then you can use the rest according to your own priorities. If used extensively, such mandates can erode local democracy by narrowing the decisions local governments and their citizens are allowed to make.

Local government officials and local taxpayers have been frustrated by unfunded state mandates. Opponents sometimes have succeeded in amending the constitution to curtail unfunded mandates. Other responses have been legislative rather than constitutional, limiting unfunded mandates or allowing local governments to avoid complying with mandates if the state does not provide funding for them. Legislators sometimes find ways to evade laws they have passed prohibiting unfunded mandates (see the minicase "Florida and Unfunded Mandates," on p. 142).

In Massachusetts, an unfunded mandates' provision was included in legislation sharply limiting property taxes. Under new, tight revenue constraints, local governments would be unable to absorb increases in spending mandated by the state, so a provision was included in a measure called "Proposition 2½" stating that if the state passed a mandate without fully funding it, then compliance with the mandate would be optional. To make the law workable, the state set up a local mandates office in the Office of the State Auditor, which would, on petition from a local jurisdiction affected by a mandate, investigate how much that mandate would cost. The local government could use the local mandates office's assessment as evidence in its petition to be exempted from the law. The office would try to figure out the aggregate costs and advise the legislature how to proceed and whether to fund the mandate for all jurisdictions. The law was passed in 1980, and since then, the local mandates office has several times declared that the legislature had indeed passed an unfunded mandate and recommended funding from the state. Despite the law and occasionally successful challenges to the legislature, local governments in Massachusetts are still burdened by unfunded mandates. First, the expensive mandates that preceded the 1980 law are not affected and remain in place. Second, the legislature has found a way of getting around the prohibition.

> For example, Lexington and Newton prevailed in an unfunded-mandate lawsuit against the state, successfully defeating a statutory amendment that expanded the local obligation to provide private school transportation. The state responded, however, by passing a second statute conditioning all state reimbursements for pre-1981 mandates on local acceptance of the challenged amendment. When the new statute was challenged by the same municipalities, the Supreme Judicial Court found that there was no violation of the prohibition. The court explained that there is . . . nothing to prevent the Legislature from forcing the acceptance of [the private school transportation amendment] upon reluctant cities and towns by providing benefits it has no obligation to provide.[21]

States sometimes promise and then fail to pay for mandates, especially when the states are experiencing fiscal stress. Even when a state does pay for its mandates, the results may still distort local decision-making. In Massachusetts, the professional development mandate passed by the state requires all schools to establish a training program for education-related employees within the public school system. The funding for the program comes from the local school budget; it can be supplemented by grants from the state, but those grants are conditioned on the locality's maintaining the level of public school spending of the prior year. Any municipality that reduces funding for public education from the previous fiscal year becomes ineligible for state funds for professional development.[22] The result is strong pressure to maintain school funding, even if some other pressing need presents itself.

Minicase: Florida and Unfunded Mandates

In 1990 Florida citizens approved a highly popular constitutional amendment to prevent the state government from mandating expenditures by or reducing revenues of the local governments. There were three exceptions: (1) if the legislature stated that the public interest required the legislation, (2) if the mandate were necessary to fulfill a law or a requirement of the federal government, or (3) if the cost were negligible. To enact a mandate that didn't fit into one of these exemptions would require a two-thirds vote of both houses of the legislature. Otherwise the local governments were free to ignore the mandate.

The legislature nevertheless continued to pass mandates, many of them unfunded. The legislature could grant a tax break to some particular group, and as long as the tax break was passed by two-thirds of each house, the resulting reduction in revenue at the local level was legal under the constitution. There were also a number of mandates whose individual financial impact was less than the minimum but which became expensive when added up. Nonrecurring losses, such as those due to tax holidays, were also legal under the constitutional ban on unfunded mandates. Anything to do with criminal justice was automatically exempted, so that legislation directing local police to arrest people for graffiti, for example, did not come under the limits of the law. Equally important, because the legislature did not stop trying to pass unfunded mandates, the cities and counties had to fight back after a law was passed that imposed large burdens on them.

The constitutional provision has been useful in that when the counties took the state to court over legislation shifting responsibility for juvenile justice to them, the court agreed that the shift was an unfunded mandate and illegal under the constitution. However, using the constitutional provision effectively has been an uphill battle for local officials. One official in a Florida county explained,

> Cost shifting and unfunded mandates mean that the state of Florida says that you will pay for a program. Whether it's something we like or don't like, they tell us we have to pay for it. Now we have a constitutional amendment that says that they can't do that without a two-thirds vote in the [Florida] Legislature. Sometimes, we've been successful because they didn't get the two-thirds vote, but they also have this loophole about health, safety and welfare. So, they put something in the legislation about health, safety or welfare—then they can do it without the two-thirds vote. . . .[1]

---

1. Douglas C. Lyons (interviewer), "Face to Face: A Conversation with Karen Marcus," *South Florida Sun-Sentinel,* October 29, 2004, www.sun-sentinel.com/news/opinion/sfl-facekarenmarcus,0,1790581.story?coll=sfla-opinion-utility. The *Sun Sentinel* keeps older articles in its archives, http://pqasb.pqarchiver.com/sun_sentinel/search.html.

In short, the states have had considerable influence on the budget process at the local level, but that influence has sometimes resulted in rigid, biased, and undemocratic outcomes. Overall, these negative consequences have abated in recent years, but unfunded mandates from the state are still a burdensome problem for local governments and are a bone of contention between the states and local governments, even when laws and constitutional amendments forbid them.

Forms of Government

Within the limits of state laws, cities have chosen different legal forms, which entail particular budget roles and processes. In the early days of municipal budgeting, after the Civil War, many cities adopted boards of estimate; in the early 1900s, there was a major move toward executive budgeting, concentrating power in the hands of the mayor. Later in the 1900s, a number of cities, particularly middle-sized ones, adopted the council-manager form of budgeting. Although many cities kept the form they chose for decades, some cities have shifted from one form to another, changing budget processes accordingly. Some hybrids have also occurred.

Municipal budgets originated as a spending control mechanism during the period of major spending growth after the Civil War. Early budgets were estimates of how much tax revenue would be required, based on detailed accounts of receipts and expenditures for preceding years. Officials submitted detailed requests. Typically, the head of the finance department, the controller, the auditor, or the mayor would receive and cut back these requests, or in smaller cities, the departments would forward their requests directly to the council or its budget committee. To control spending during the year, some cities adopted annual appropriations, setting maximum authorized expenditures for the year.

The 1870s and 1880s were years of sharp economic and governmental contraction for most cities. Budgeting focused on keeping government small and inactive. Beginning in 1873 in New York City, a form of budgeting appeared in which budget estimates from the departments went to a board of estimate, variously but generally consisting of the mayor, controller, president of the board of aldermen, and others. The frequent failure of independently elected officials to agree to the same projects slows down spending. Beyond that, the boards of estimate responded to public pressure to keep taxes down.

In the early days of the Board of Estimates in New York City, aldermen would add to the recommended budget. From 1873 to 1888 they added about $500,000 annually, but they were constantly overruled by the Board of Estimates. Over time, the aldermen added less and less.[23] By 1898, the charter granted the council some formal budget authority but only to decrease the estimates.[24]

From about 1895 to about 1920, the focus of budgeting shifted from keeping government small and nonintrusive to combining activism with efficiency and accountability. The result was a major push for a single executive responsible for the budget—the so-called strong mayor form of government. Executive budget reform reflected the Progressive Era themes: Government was a necessary counterbalance to business and a major provider of services but had to be controlled and responsive to the public. The single-executive reforms also reflected the idea of progress in an agreed upon direction rather than the random expenditures of a council and a pork-driven budget. At that time under this form of government, councils were sometimes radically disempowered.

The council-manager form began to gain popularity after World War I. In the council-manager form of government, the council was reduced in size and elected at large to reduce the influence of neighborhoods, ethnic groups, and political machines. This new council was given more budgeting authority, but it operated by hiring a professional manager who was responsible, either directly or through an appointee, for collecting and sifting the budget requests from the departments before forwarding them to the council for approval. This council-manager form was intended to be less political and more management oriented than the mayor-council form. Accountability was to be formally provided by the frequently exercised right of city councils to fire the manager if he (early managers were males, frequently engineers) did not do as they wished. But accountability was also provided by improved budget documents that demonstrated how well public money was being spent.

Major spurts in adoptions of the council-manager form occurred after the two world wars. From 1945 to 1959 the number of council-manager adoptions increased from 637 to almost 1,500.[25] One reason was that the infrastructures of the cities were in a state of neglect, and technical problems required competent staff and an activist approach. In the past few years, the number of council-manager cities has actually exceeded the number of strong mayor cities, but what has caught the eye of the news media has been some major cities' abandoning the council-manager form and adopting the strong mayor form instead.

Often in these abandonments of the council-manager form, a highly popular and well-known mayoral candidate pressed for charter changes that enhanced his or her own mayoral power. The shift often followed corruption scandals, long-term community decline, or severe financial problems with implications of incompetence or cover-up. In Richmond, Virginia, former governor Douglas Wilder campaigned in 2003 for a charter change to abandon the council-manager form and directly elect the mayor. Then he ran for the office, winning handily, after which in early 2005, the council gave him the line-item veto and enhanced appointment powers. In Oakland, California, Jerry Brown, another popular ex-governor, got an amendment to the charter onto the ballot before his landslide victory in the mayoralty race in 1998; the measure passed by a wide margin. San Diego had a successful abandonment election in 2004. There the mayor took on the manager's budget responsibilities, but the council received its own budget analyst and the ability to override the mayor's veto with only five votes. "The October firestorms exposed the severe underfunding of city fire services, the pension fund deficit has ballooned to $1.1 billion, and federal authorities are investigating errors and omissions in disclosure documents used to sell municipal bonds."[26] These issues weakened the city manager.

In each of these council-manager abandonments, successful elections to enhance the powers of the mayor followed years of unsuccessful efforts by mayors and their supporters. The time, circumstances, and candidates have to be right to secure a shift of budget responsibilities to the mayor.

Summary and Conclusions

At the federal and state levels, with clear distinctions between the executive and legislative branches, much of the change over time has to do with the shifting balance of budgetary power between branches of government. At the state level, more of the budget process is embedded in constitutions rather than laws, with the result that it is harder to change. Reformers can lock their policy preferences into processes that are binding for generations, a result that makes it difficult to adapt to changing circumstances and has major implications for democracy, since later generations are bound by the decisions and preferences of earlier ones. To get around rigid rules there may be more informal budgeting at the state level in processes that involve negotiations behind closed doors. At the local level, much of the ongoing tension is between the state government, which is legally responsible, and the local governments, which are legally dependent on the states, over the degree of autonomy the local governments have in budgeting. The tension is ongoing in part because the rigidity and durability of state laws make it difficult for local governments to adapt and to make decisions that match local preferences.

At all levels of government when a budget process becomes extreme in any way, there are pressures to move it back toward the middle. Thus in Indiana, state-mandated budget processes affecting the localities over time became more respectful of local priorities. Sometimes the pendulum seems to swing back and forth, as when strong mayor systems are replaced by council-manager forms of government, only to be replaced again by a strong mayor form. At the national level, if the president takes too much policy control away from Congress,

Congress responds by taking some power back for itself. Change is more likely when a budget process fails to accomplish that which is supposed to be its strength—Gramm-Rudman-Hollings failed to balance the budget; the council-manager form in San Diego failed to provide sound financial management.

Though change in the process will almost always be justified on the basis of its ability to solve some public problem, in reality it is difficult to distinguish between changes aimed at enhancing the power of individuals and factions and changes that are aimed at solving particular public policy problems. Citizens seem unable to distinguish between giving more power to popular elected officials and changing the structure for the long term. The politicians pushing for enhanced powers often seem to make charter amendments referendums on their own popularity.

The shifts in process through time can be visualized as pendulum swings between extremes, but the reality is that the pendulum sticks in places. Several factors cause that stickiness and slow the rebalancing of budgetary powers or revamping of budgeting processes. Among them are structural rigidities, constitutions, charters, and laws, on the one hand, and highly unbalanced powers, on the other. Those who are truly powerless in the budget process have trouble changing it, because those who would have to give up power choose not to; powerful governors reject the reform proposals of legislatures that would reduce their power. These sticky places hold up formal change and breed a variety of informal processes instead, some dysfunctional. Informal processes often change from year to year and typically are carried out behind closed doors.

Though the ideal might be some kind of equilibrium—a budget process that avoids the extremes and balances the voices of a variety of legitimate stakeholders—sometimes equilibrium is not achieved. Budgets may be held up, with chaotic results for program managers and those dependent on government spending. Fiscal discipline may dissolve, with spending routinely outrunning revenues, piling up debt for future generations and limiting the ability to address problems collectively. Much time can be wasted fighting over process each year instead of working out priorities. In short, budget processes can deteriorate into *ad hoc* negotiations behind closed doors, with key figures and consequences blocked from public view. These episodic failures of process highlight the importance of building consensus around relatively neutral rules that share budgetary power wisely, so there will be minimal pressure to work around the process or derail it.

Useful Websites

For a rich oral history of congressional budget process, see **G. William Hoagland's oral history interviews on the Senate Oral History Project website** (www.senate .gov/artandhistory/history/resources/pdf/OralHistory_HoaglandBill.pdf).

Hoagland was staff director of the Senate Budget Committee for many years. He gave his interviews in 2006 and 2007. Hoagland gave another oral history interview in 2011, which outlines in detail some of the **informal evolution of the congressional budget process** (http://digitalassets.lib.berkeley.edu/roho/ucb/text/hoagland_william.pdf). This oral history comes from a collection of interviews from a special project at the Bancroft Library at the University of California Berkeley, "Slaying the Dragon of Debt: Fiscal Politics and Policy from the 1970s to the Present," a project of the Walter Shorenstein Program in Politics, Policy and Values. There are many other interviews in this series besides Hoagland's.

The Government Printing Office offers both a convenient **history of the Senate Appropriations Committee through 2008** (www.gpo.gov/fdsys/pkg/CDOC-110sdoc14/pdf/CDOC-110sdoc14.pdf) as well as a **history of the Senate Budget Committee through 2006** (www.gpo.gov/fdsys/pkg/CDOC-110sdoc14/pdf/CDOC-110sdoc14.pdf).

For an idea of the mandates that federal and state governments impose on local governments, see **Virginia's Catalog of State and Federal Mandates on Local Governments** (http://www.dhcd.virginia.gov/index.php/commission-on-local-government/reports.html#Catalog-Mandates-Local-Gov), from the Commission on Local Government, Department of Housing and Community Development, of the Commonwealth of Virginia. The report is several hundred pages long, which gives an idea of the number of mandates. Some information is presented on each one, with an estimate of fiscal impact for new mandates. The report has been issued annually; as of July 2015, the reports were posted from 2009 to 2014, providing information about new mandates and deleted mandates over time.

The Council of State Governments (CSG) publishes an annual volume called the *Book of the States*. Table 4.4 lists the budget powers of governors across the states. A link to the 2014 and earlier editions can be found at **CSG Knowledge Center** (http://knowledgecenter.csg.org/kc/category/content-type/content-type/book-states). Because prior years of the volume contain similar tables, some historical tracking is possible, though CSG doesn't do a new survey every year.

The transcripts of the Maryland Board of Public Works meetings, at which the governor makes his request for midyear budget cuts, are online at http://bpw.maryland.gov/Pages/meetingDocuments_year.aspx.

For Florida, The Florida Channel posts videos of press conferences with key legislative budget leaders, such as the house and senate appropriations chairs, and also posts videos of conference committee proceedings as the house and senate try to reconcile their different versions of budget bills. Chairs of tax committees are also included in this archive. This raw data allows the viewer to feel as if he or she were present and suggests the scope of budget issues the legislature deals with (http://thefloridachannel.org/programs/state-budget-process/).

5 Expenditures

Strategies, Structures, and the Environment

The politics of expenditures is a politics of choice. Revenue is never sufficient to satisfy all possible claims on the budget, so governments have a formal and sometimes informal process for making budget requests, sorting through them, prioritizing them, trimming them back, and approving the resulting plan. If there is a tight ceiling on spending, those proposals low on the priority list may be cut deeply or eliminated completely. The stakes are high, the competition may be intense, and the associated politics is often lively.

Who gets what, who wins, and who loses, is not just a function of who can make the best case for public funds (strategy); it also depends on program structure and on changes in the environment that make some needs more urgent than others and sometimes overwhelm the budget. Winners and losers are also influenced by the political party in power and its agenda. The decision process, program structure, and even prior levels of debt may build in or lock in some priorities, so that they are not reconsidered at annual or biannual intervals but form a protected base, forcing more intense competition for the rest of the dollars not so protected. Some decisions are thus made for the long term, while others are shorter lived. The intergovernmental system, our federal government, with its cooperative and competitive elements, influences, if not determines, parts of the budget, through grants, loans, mandates, and cooperative programs run jointly by the national and state governments. The courts play their episodic role in expenditures, as they do in revenues and budget process.

Strategies

Though good strategy is not enough to determine the outcomes, program advocates try to devise the best case possible for agency or program funding. The following are strategies that are common and have often (though not always) proven effective over the years.

1. *Please the politicians.* Agency heads try to gain support by including in their budgets the policy preferences and/or pet projects of elected officials. Bureau chiefs or department heads often describe in their budget requests how their budget proposal will address the goals of the chief executive or legislators, such as increased food safety, fewer child deaths, or lower rates of errors in billing. At the local level, department heads often scrutinize council transcripts, looking for clues as to what the legislative body considers important, and slant their budget requests to include those preferences. In performance budgeting, where it exists, legislators, the executive branch, and sometimes members of the public set goals for the departments and programs that are then reflected in the budget requests.

Sometimes agency efforts to please legislators can result in choices that could not be justified on technical grounds of cost or efficiency. The federal government spends a great deal of money on contracts each year. These contracts are usually awards to U.S. companies, located in someone's congressional district. Awarding a contract or subcontract to a company in a particular legislator's district help gain that legislator's support for a program. Legislators sometimes reward campaign

---

Minicase: A $17,000 Drip Pan

From time to time, some outrageously overpriced commodity purchased by the Department of Defence (DoD) comes to light, such as an $800 toilet seat. The DoD is often blamed for poor financial controls and ineffective contracting, but the source of the problem may lie elsewhere. Consider the $17,000 drip pan for catching transmission fluid on Blackhawk helicopters. A competitive product from another company only cost $2,500. It turned out that the chair of the House Appropriation Committee, Kentucky representative Harold Rogers, wrote an earmark for the purchase into 2009 legislation. Not only was the company that provided the part located in Representative Roger's district, the president of the company was a frequent donor to Representative Roger's political reelection committee. Rogers delivered over $17 million in business to this company between 2000 and 2012. The DoD was not willing to offend the chair of the House Appropriations Committee by choosing a more cost-effective alternative.

Source: Eric Lichtblau, "Earmark Puts $17,000 Pans on Army Craft," *New York Times,* May 18, 2012, www.nytimes.com/2012/05/19/us/politics/behind-armys -17000-drip-pan-harold-rogerss-earmark.html?_r=1.

contributors with contracts through earmarks in appropriation legislation or other means (to see how this works, see the minicase "A $17,000 Drip Pan" below). Defying such earmarks risks loss of a legislator's support for a budget request.

2. *Build a geographic coalition.* When asking for program funds, administrators try to demonstrate that the program benefits everyone. If this is not possible, they might try to gain support by expanding small programs or locating physical facilities in multiple geographical locations, to win the support of multiple legislators in different states, building a coalition large enough to pass legislation.

One way to claim that a program benefits everyone is to describe what are called *positive spillovers,* that is, benefits that accrue to others not directly affected by a program. Backers of mass transit often argue that many others benefit from mass transit besides the riders. Drivers benefit from less crowded roads, for example, and reducing driving reduces dependence on imported oil, with benefits for the entire economy. Mass transit helps reduce pollution, a benefit to the entire service area.

Even with a vivid imagination, not all program advocates can claim much in the way of indirect benefits, but it may be possible to spread the direct benefits around a bit. One way of building a geographically based coalition is to spend money on defense contracts that are managed and built in a number of states and provide thousands of jobs. Main contractors often subcontract out parts of the work, gaining legislative support from more senators and representatives. The strength of such coalitions is sometimes such that even when the defense department backs off a project as ineffective and overly expensive, Congress keeps it going. The result is sometimes called a zombie program, one that cannot be killed, but isn't really alive and functioning either. One recent example is a high-tech blimp built for the army to detect cruise missiles; in 2015, the program was seventeen years old, had cost $2.7 billion, and did not work. The huge white blimps are vulnerable to storms and are sitting ducks in any kind of combat situation. Their computer programs have yet to function properly, and they routinely fail performance tests. Yet the blimps live (limp?) on. The blimp program sustains jobs in Maryland, California, Texas, Virginia, North Carolina, Massachusetts, Oregon, Alabama, New Mexico, and Utah.[1]

Because legislators have so much invested in physical facilities and workers based in their districts, closing a post office, military base, or government office in a legislator's district is dangerous. To minimize the anger of legislators in stricken districts, military base closings have been done by an independent commission appointed by the president and approved by the Senate. In the last round of closings in 2005, money accompanied the base closings to help repair economic damage to the communities in which they were located.

In part because of reduced staffing in the military, the Defense Department has extra space (estimated to be about 20 percent of DoD property), and to save money under the sequester (the across-the-board cuts mandated in 2011) the Department of Defense requested Congress to reconvene the Base Realignment and Closure Commission [BRAC], but lawmakers have not been friendly to the proposal. They fear the economic impact on their constituents and note how expensive prior rounds of closures have been.[2] One money-saving strategy for the DoD has thus been taken off the table for the near future.

3. *Build broader coalitions by adding constituencies.* Expanding programs so more people in more places benefit is not a possible strategy for all programs, but it is often possible to add a program that serves a different constituency or demonstrate a policy goal or achievement that appeals to a different set of legislators, thus expanding the potential coalition of support. One well known pairing occurs in the Agriculture Department, which services farmers and ranchers but also provides food programs for the poor and ensures food safety for the public, thus gaining support from legislators in both rural and urban areas. A second example occurs in transportation, which includes both highways and mass transit, serving both remote rural areas and large urban ones. These pairings have often been problematic and sometimes contradictory—food safety, for example, might require imposing costs or regulations on farmers who object to them. Supporters of highways and of mass transit have often been at each other's throats. Yet these odd bedfellows have generally benefited from their shared berth.

4. *Demonstrate effectiveness and efficiency.* Agencies that have been criticized for inefficiency or those that have had difficulty demonstrating their effectiveness sometimes engage respected sources to do performance evaluations and then use these evaluations in budget justifications to demonstrate that they are doing a good job. If agencies can demonstrate their effectiveness in achieving goals that Congress supports, they may be able to resist budget cuts.

Demonstrating performance became a little easier for some agencies with the passage of the Government Performance and Results Act (GPRA), which was updated in 2010. Critics have argued that Congress doesn't use the performance measures that it asks for, but more likely, it uses the information among other sources or at intervals. The executive branch too sometimes asks for and may use performance data. In 2012, as agencies prepared to submit reduced budgets under the Budget Control Act, the director of the executive Office of Management and Budget urged agencies to use evidence and evaluation in setting priorities for their budget requests.[3]

5. *Link programs to goals of (nearly) unlimited value.* Examples of programs with goals of unlimited or nearly unlimited value include national security, economic development, and job creation. Saving lives also fits into this category. Administrators who succeed at this strategy do not have to prove efficiency or even effectiveness.

Public employees trying to hang on to their pensions in states eager to reduce them argue that, collectively, retirees have a major impact on local economies, implying that cutting their pensions would pull the rug from under the state's economy. Firefighters asking for an additional ambulance note that every moment after a heart attack reduces the chance of survival, and further, that emergency medical technicians can revive people whose hearts have stopped. They thus link their budget request to a goal of unlimited value. (For an example of how this strategy has been used successfully, see the minicase on Homeland Security below; for an example of a failed attempt to use this kind of strategy, see the minicase on the Amtrak train wreck on p. 153.)

Minicase: Homeland Security—A Program Tied to a Goal of Unlimited Worth

If an agency can make the case that what it is trying to accomplish is so valuable that it is in fact priceless, it can write its own ticket, and it won't be judged or evaluated in terms of whether its programs actually achieve their goals or whether the spending is cost effective. One recent example is the Department of Homeland Security after the terrorist attack of September 11, 2001.[1]

As Richard Clarke, the chief counterterrorism advisor on the National Security Council, described, "As soon as we went to the Congress, they said, 'Just tell us what you need.' Blank check."[2] The budget allocation to the Homeland Security Department was also described as "a candy store without a price tag."[3]

The budget more than tripled from 2001 to 2013, and certainly would have been unsustainable if it had continued to grow at that rate. But the spending peaked in 2006 at $69 billion, then dropped, and with some variability, stabilized at about $45 billion a year. (See Figure 5.1 for a graphic illustration.)

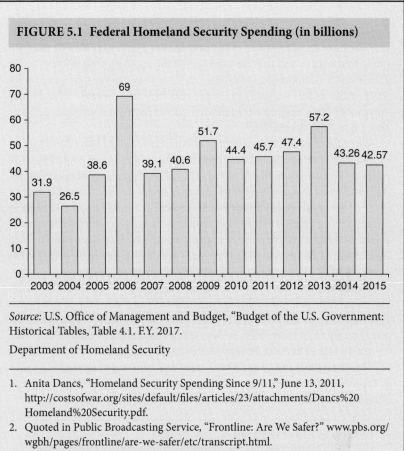

FIGURE 5.1 Federal Homeland Security Spending (in billions)

Source: U.S. Office of Management and Budget, "Budget of the U.S. Government: Historical Tables, Table 4.1. F.Y. 2017.

Department of Homeland Security

1. Anita Dancs, "Homeland Security Spending Since 9/11," June 13, 2011, http://costsofwar.org/sites/default/files/articles/23/attachments/Dancs%20 Homeland%20Security.pdf.
2. Quoted in Public Broadcasting Service, "Frontline: Are We Safer?" www.pbs.org/ wgbh/pages/frontline/are-we-safer/etc/transcript.html.
3. Anthony Cordesman, Center for Strategic and International Studies; ibid.

Minicase: Amtrak Train Wreck

Sometimes the claim that spending more money after a disaster will save lives does not work. If opponents of a specific spending proposal can delay action long enough so that memory of an accident subsides, they can often derail budget increases. In 2015, there was a massive Amtrak train wreck in Philadelphia, with loss of lives, on a stretch of track that lacked a functioning

(Continued)

(Continued)

safety feature (called positive train control) that would have slowed the train going into a curve and may have prevented the accident. One reaction to the accident was a democratic amendment to the transportation appropriation for $825 million for technology improvements for Amtrak. The House Appropriation Committee voted down the amendment and voted for a 20 percent cut to Amtrak's budget.

When the transportation appropriation bill came to the House floor, a group of Democrats moved to increase spending for positive train control to $750 million. The proposal was defeated, 182–241.[1] Opponents of spending for Amtrak argued that cuts were needed to stay under the 2011 caps and that the cause of the accident was not definitely known.[2] It would be some 18 months before the investigation of the cause of the crash would be completed and made public, by which time the sense of urgency would have long since passed. Some have argued that the loss of life from train accidents is negligible and that the money would be better spent on other safety advances, such as passenger underpasses that would prevent riders disembarking from trains from walking across the tracks. The political lobbying firm Capstone explained the reluctance to fund Amtrak in political terms: The main routes of Amtrak are in the Northeast, and there are many more riders in Democratic districts than in Republican ones. Hence the lack of Republican support for the Amtrak budget. [3]

The minicase is not about who is right and who is wrong on this issue, it is about the pressure to do something after an accident and the response of delaying, and hence possibly derailing, action to prevent a reoccurrence.

1. Keith Laing, "House Dems Seek to Boost Funding for Automated Trains," *The Hill,* May, 19, 2015, http://thehill.com/policy/transportation/242556-house -dems-seek-to-boost-funding-for-automated-trains).
2. Heather Caygle, "House Panel Votes to Cut Amtrak Budget Hours After Deadly Crash," *Politico,* May 13, 2015, http://www.politico.com/story/2015/05/amtrak -budget-house-panel-crash-117904.html.
3. *The Washington Report,* May 15, 2015, http://capstonenationalpartners.com/the -washington-report-may-15–2015/.

The strategy of using a disaster to motivate support for a spending proposal failed after a major bridge collapse in Minneapolis in 2007. Major highways in the United States are supported by federal grants, but the formula for distribution of the funds allocated 25 percent of the money to all states, regardless of need, leaving the states with more urgent needs with less money. The formula reflected the political requirement to extend the geographic benefits widely in order to get enough Congressional support to pass the legislation.

But in Minneapolis's case, there was another underlying cause both of the bridge collapse and the inability of the federal government to respond to the general problem of underfunding of bridge repairs. The money that states do receive need not be spent for bridge maintenance and repair. Many state legislators prefer to spend the federal money on new or expanded roads rather than bridge repairs, because developers who sometimes contribute to campaigns want the new projects. In the three years prior to the bridge collapse, legislators in Minnesota had diverted 50 percent of their bridge funding away from bridge repair and maintenance.[4]

After the bridge collapse with loss of life, Democratic representative James Oberstar advocated a dedicated source of funding for bridge maintenance, repair, and replacement for the national highway system. Oberstar's proposal passed the House by a wide margin in July of 2008, passed a Senate committee, and died right there. Later, in 2012, legislation (Pub. L. 112–141) eliminated the Highway Bridge Program, allowing further choices between new road projects and bridge repairs. That shift reflected the political choices being made at the state level throughout the country. In addition, the ban on earmarks that included transportation projects made it more difficult to get money for specific, geographically limited projects that had no way of gaining nationwide support.

6. *Make programs look cheap or free.* Opponents of spending proposals often argue that programs will cost too much or would require a tax increase, which is considered a political nonstarter. Program advocates have an easier time gaining approval for their requests if the costs are moderate or the program seems free. One budget strategy therefore is to make programs look inexpensive, by underestimating the costs or spreading them out over several years. Loan programs, because they appear free or nearly free, are easier to sell than grant programs, which clearly cost the government money. Those who wish to curtail a program or cut its budget often work to make invisible expenditures clearer or exaggerate the costs in a variety of ways, for example, by reporting many years of expenditure in a single budget rather than just one. The result of this strategy is to create a politics of cost estimation, where advocates' and opponents' estimates battle each other. In the midst of competing estimates, elected officials need a neutral analyst (See the minicase on the Congressional Budget Office on p. 156.)

One example of the kind of magical thinking that can result from supporting spending programs while seeming to avoid tax increases to pay for them occurred recently in Indiana. Gov. Mike Pence proposed a billion-dollar spending program on highways over four years, pledging that it would not result in any tax increases. The proposal would be funded by drawing down reserves that normally are set aside to moderate cuts during a recession and by borrowing. Pence did not discuss how the debt would be repaid or how the reserve fund would be rebuilt.

Sometimes a program can be made to look more or less expensive by a change in accounting and reporting rules. Education loans and loan guarantees provide one example. (See the minicase about higher education loans on p. 157.) In the example of college loans, the choice of structure of program delivery affected how expensive programs looked, what the actual costs of the program were, and how the benefits were divided among groups of claimants. The structure also influenced the vulnerability of the program to corruption.

Minicase: Congressional Budget Office and Scoring

In colloquial English, the term *scoring* means getting someone of interest into bed, but in budgeting it means estimating the cost of proposed legislation according to a set of rules. At the national level, the Congressional Budget Office (CBO) is responsible for doing this estimation and telling legislators what the cost impact of legislative proposals is likely to be and whether particular proposals meet the cost requirements under the existing rules. At the state level, the legislative budget office, assuming there is one, is usually responsible for what is called *fiscal noting*, attaching a note to a bill estimating the cost or revenue impact.

Given the importance of inflating or deflating costs as a budget strategy, scoring and fiscal noting take on considerable importance in budgeting. The legislative budget office can puncture a political claim, kill or support proposed new programs or program expansions, and enforce spending limits. To do this successfully, the legislative budget office must have a reputation as a neutral arbiter that does not bend the rules according to political party allegiances or policy preferences.

The Congressional Budget Office earned a reputation for being nonpartisan and, as a result, became a critical actor in some major policy decisions. During the Clinton administration, the president's proposal for health care reform was defeated, in large part because of a CBO judgment that costs that the government imposed on the private sector counted as governmental costs, even when they did not directly impact federal spending. The result made the program look too expensive. More recently, when the Obama administration pushed for health care reform, despite considerable skepticism on the part of the public and many budgeteers, the CBO estimated that the legislation would help balance the budget, as the president claimed. Had CBO ruled otherwise, it is doubtful that the controversial legislation would have passed.

In 2015, Congress mandated the CBO to use a scoring rule called *dynamic scoring*, which requires an estimate not only of the direct costs of legislative proposals but the long-term impacts on the economy. The methodology for making such estimates is very crude, and there is extensive political pressure to exaggerate positive effects on the economy. It remains to be seen if the CBO can maintain its reputation for impartial evaluation of the cost of legislation.

For more on the Congressional Budget Office and its role in health care legislation, see Philip Joyce, *The Congressional Budget Office: Honest Numbers, Power, and Policy Making* (Washington, DC: Georgetown University Press, 2011).

Structure

While strategy is important, it is far from the only factor in determining winners and losers. Program structure is also important. One major distinction between program structures is between *discretionary* and *mandatory* programs. Another important distinction has to do with the strength of walls around a program, that is, whether it has a dedicated source of revenue and how easy it is to transfer money out. The process of budgeting, the predictability and controllability of costs, and the degree of competition any program faces depend on program structure.

Two examples illustrate different impacts of structure on expenditures. The first is about the federal college loan program, where the structure influences how expensive the program looks; the second is about budgeting for immigration enforcement (see the minicase on p. 160), which suggests the impact of openness to the environment on the unpredictability of expenditures and describes the implications for budgeting when one agency controls the demand for services from a second agency.

**Minicase: Budgetary Implications of
Direct College Loans Versus Loan Guarantees**

The federal government has for years loaned money or guaranteed the loans of students paying their college or graduate school tuition. The idea was to provide loans to students who had no income and nothing to offer as collateral and hence would have to pay unaffordably high rates to banks. Direct loans from the government looked low cost, until credit reform in 1990 made

(Continued)

(Continued)

their real costs more transparent and made full costs visible in the year when the loans are issued. By putting the total costs over the life of the loans up front, loans appeared more expensive than loan guarantees run through private banks. In the loan guarantee program, banks lend money to students, while the federal government reduces the risk to lenders by committing itself to repay the loan if the student defaults. With zero risk, banks can afford to lend money to students at much lower interest rates than in normal unguaranteed loans. In fact, however, the complex program of loan guarantees run through private sector, profit-making banks was more expensive than the direct lending program. As a result, in 1993, a historic agreement to begin to restore the budget to balance included a provision to phase in a program of direct lending until the ratio of direct government loans to government guaranteed loans reached 60 percent.

In 1994, Republicans took control of both houses of Congress. The new Republican leadership in Congress slated the direct loan program for termination, preferring the program that worked through the private sector, allowing the banks to loan money risk free and make a profit from those loans. But many universities and colleges preferred the simpler direct loan program. The result was a compromise that forbade the Department of Education to encourage or mandate the direct loan program but allowed the private sector lenders to openly compete for the business. The consequence of the private sector's efforts to gain the loan business caused a shift back toward guaranteed loans but also resulted in a set of scandals revealed in 2007, involving kickbacks to universities to steer students to the private loan businesses. The kickbacks resulted in higher loan costs to students. The scandals fed pressure for publicly provided direct loans.

By 2008 and 2009, the economic environment had changed. The housing market sank in 2008, banks had little money to lend, and many opted out of the loan guarantee program. In the crisis, the federal government created a temporary program to buy the education loans of the private sector banks, creating a pool of funds that the banks could then relend. Ultimately, the reduced costs of direct loans compared to loan guarantees won out in tight government budgets and the loan guarantee program was terminated in 2010.

In this example, the portrayal of program costs as higher or lower influenced the outlays and choice of program structure between direct government loans and loan guarantee programs run by the private sector and backed by the government. Another factor was political contestation between ideologies and parties in 2004 (direct government programs on the left versus programs provided by the private sector on the right). Beginning in 2008, the economic environment, which reduced the amount of money that banks had to lend, and growing federal deficits created pressure to choose the more cost-effective program. Scandals among businesses competing for the loans, uncovered by news media, probably also played a part in taking the luster off the private sector provision of loans.

Sources: New America Foundation, "Federal Student Loan Programs History," http://febp.newamerica.net/background-analysis/federal-student-loan-programs -history; Associated Press, "College Loan Program 'Like Peeling an Onion,'" April 10, 2007, MSNBC, www.msnbc.msn.com/id/18040824/ns/business-personal_ finance/t/college-loan-scandal-peeling-onion/#.UAxX25HYF6E.

Discretionary Versus Mandatory Programs

A major distinction in structure of spending at all levels of government is the degree of discretion that officials have over spending. In so-called discretionary programs, officials can choose (control) the level of spending, increasing some and decreasing others, as long as they stay within overall revenue constraints. The level of competition is usually very high in discretionary programs—roads compete with mass transit, capital spending for construction may vie with operating budgets for salary and benefits, or programs for local police communications might compete with drug interception programs. Discretionary programs include direct service provision, such as police and fire at the local level, some grant programs, and many loan programs. Even spending for open-ended programs like immigration enforcement can be controlled, cut, or capped, although the result may be overloaded judges. By contrast, with mandatory programs, budgeters have less discretion. The spending may be automatic, based on need, demand, contract, or formula. Mandatory programs include debt repayment and entitlement programs like Medicare and Medicaid. They also include some state payments to local governments. Mandatory programs generally face lower levels of competition: They normally come first, while discretionary programs compete for the rest of the available pool of revenue.

Discretionary Programs: Direct Service, Grants, and Loans

The costs of some types of programs are more controllable during budget preparation than others. Budgeters work out how much a program is likely to cost during the budget year (or biennium) and allocate some or all of that amount to the program. Program administrators work to keep within those spending limits. If a school system gets a budget that is less than what it estimated it needed, it may have to reduce service levels by reducing the number of staff and increasing class sizes or eliminating courses, such as language or music classes, or it may delay necessary building maintenance. Direct service, some grant programs, and loans and loan guarantees fall in the category of more controllable—discretionary—programs.

Direct Service. At the national level, an example of direct service provision is the Department of Defense, which hires soldiers, buys planes and weapons, and fights wars. At the state level, highways, courts, and prisons are examples of direct service provision. At the local level, public schools, street cleaning and repairs, water and sewer service, and fire and police are direct service programs. Direct service programs do not just hand out money, they do something—put out fires, arrest criminals, fill potholes, or fly planes and drop bombs.

The cost of direct service programs can usually be estimated reasonably well in advance, but they are open to the environment. For example, budgeting for snow removal in the northern part of the country is difficult, because the timing and amounts of snowfall are unpredictable from year to year. Border protection costs depend on the number of people trying to get across illegally and the costs of detention centers depend on the number of people arrested. (See the minicase on immigration enforcement below.) Many services are demand based, such as fire calls or homeless shelters. To deal with such uncertainty, budgeters may have to estimate expenditures high, save money in a contingency fund, or build up fund balances from year to year to be in position to deal with an unusual demand situation—heavy snow or a bitterly cold winter or a war in the Middle East that creates an influx of refugees. Or they may have to stretch their existing resources in some way, requiring overtime, increasing workloads, or adopting new technology.

Minicase: An Open-Ended Discretionary Program—Immigration Enforcement

Budgeting for immigration enforcement, including border patrol, detention facilities, and judicial procedures, is complicated and unpredictable. Like a number of other programs, immigration enforcement is open ended and demand driven, based in part on the number of illegal immigrants trying to cross the border, a number which varies depending on economic conditions in the home country and in the United States. It also depends on policy, because the level and type of enforcement at any time influences the number of potential immigrants to be housed in detention facilities, the number of immigration hearings to be held, and the number of prosecutions for criminal activity. Two executive branch departments are involved, the Department of Homeland Security, which does the enforcement part, patrolling the borders and capturing border crossers, sometimes detaining them; and the Department of Justice, which is responsible for the administrative hearings and criminal trials. The decisions of the Department of Homeland Security affect the numbers of people that have to be processed by the Department of Justice, but there is often inadequate communication and coordination between the two, not only on policy but also on budget requests. As government staff try to adjust to fluctuating workload within a budget that cannot possibly keep up with changing demands, they sometimes work faster or adopt technical solutions, such as having judges hear cases remotely or putting four or five defendants into one trial.

Budgeting for immigration control is difficult, not only because of the unpredictability of the numbers of people who will be caught at any time but also because of the program structure, in the sense that there are three different agencies within Homeland Security that are active in pursuit of law breakers and two different departments involved, with separate budgets, separate budget priorities, and different appropriations subcommittees that make decisions without much reference to each other.

The result is uneven treatment. The courts sometimes get overloaded, resulting in long backlogs and judgments that are not well researched. While it is possible to deport someone summarily, without a trial, those who get a trial may have long waits because of the shortage of judges. The *Washington Post* reported in 2013 that immigrants waited an average of 550 days for a decision on their case. In California, the wait was 660 days. Many are held in detention for some time. The cost of each day for each person in detention in 2013 was estimated at $122.

The structure of the program, its open endedness and unpredictability, and the shared but uncoordinated responsibilities of two executive departments resulted in inadequate budgets and uneven justice—some would argue injustice.

Sources: Suzy Khimm, "Many Immigrants Facing Deportation Must Wait 550 Days for Their Day in Court," *Washington Post*, February 22, 2013, http://www .washingtonpost.com/news/wonkblog/wp/2013/02/22/many-immigrants-facing -deportation-must-wait-550-days-for-their-day-in-court/; Steven Redburn, Peter Reuter, and Malay Majmundar, *Budgeting for Immigration Enforcement: A Path to Better Performance* (Washington, DC: National Academies Press, 2011).

Grant Programs. An intergovernmental grant is a monetary award from a higher level of government to a lower level or from government to a nonprofit organization. Grant recipients may have more or less discretion about how the money can be spent. Grants may be highly specific about what may be done with the money, like giving a gift card that can only be redeemed to buy a pair of shoes, or they can be fairly broad, enabling the recipient to buy any of a variety of related goods. A broad (or block) grant might be for any public safety improvements, any of a variety of street improvements, or any of a range of social services.

The total amount of grants can be capped; capped grants are predictable in terms of costs. While many grants are discretionary and can be estimated in advance and reduced if needed by the donor government, some have more open-ended or automatic features, such as formulas, or have some mandatory features, such as California's constitutional requirement to make up for school revenues taken by local development districts.

The grants may come with strings, such as a requirement for matching contributions or requirements for maintaining previous levels of spending so the grant actually increases the amount of money spent on the target programs. Sometimes grants include mandates about tangentially related matters, such as requiring the states to have a legal drinking age of twenty-one; failure to comply with such requirements may result in reductions in grant amounts.

The purpose of intergovernmental grants is to encourage a given activity. Officials are likely to invest in activities where they get many grant dollars, even when those are not the top state or local priorities, because with grant funding, these activities look cheap or free to local residents who do not have to pay for them out of local taxation.

Grants are ways that the national government can get states to carry out federal policy mandates; they offer incentives to engage in certain activities or increase services levels. This tool is thus of critical importance in a federal system where the national government has limited authority to order states to carry out national policy. This system of grants has a weakness, in that the dollar amounts of grants may not match the costs of policy mandates, creating unfunded or underfunded mandates. State or local governments may be required to carry out particular policies but not be given enough money to do so.

Loans. Governments at all levels—federal, state, and local—may offer loans at below-market rates. Loan programs from the federal government help businesses recover from disasters, help states deal with high unemployment rates, or as described earlier, help students pay for college tuition. They help veterans buy homes. Compared to direct grants, these programs look very inexpensive, because the loans are normally repaid with sufficient interest to cover most if not all the defaults. Their relative inexpensiveness has advantaged this type of program. While the initial amounts to be lent are easily determined and controlled, if default rates should be higher than anticipated, the funds can run out of money.

Mandatory Programs

Mandatory programs are those that the government has to pay, has agreed to pay, and where the payment is automatic. They represent commitments made in the past, paid in the present. They include entitlements, debt repayment, loan guarantees, and pensions. Court orders can also be considered mandatory. One characteristic of mandatory programs is that budgeters do not *directly* control the amounts in any given budget year, whatever the costs turn out to be, they have to be paid. Future costs can be reduced or increased by changing the design of the program or reducing borrowing; but for the current budget year, the costs are what they are. This is when you pay for the goods and services you bought last year or ten years ago, and you do not have a second opportunity (usually) to undo those purchases or bargain over price. A second characteristic of mandatory programs is that the costs are often difficult to predict.

Entitlements. Entitlements are open ended. Total spending is not determined in advance. Every person or business or government entity that meets particular criteria is "entitled" to—that is, has a legitimate claim to—a predetermined level of benefits. The actual cost in any year is the result of the size of the benefit, which is usually known, and the number of applicants, which usually is not known in advance. Costs are controlled going forward by either reducing the size of benefits or tightening up the eligibility requirements, so that fewer individuals, businesses, or government units qualify for benefits. Entitlement costs are sometimes called uncontrollable, which is misleading, because they are not uncontrollable but require a different kind of legislation, a redesign of program characteristics rather than a direct spending limit.

Even with program redesigns, however, entitlements remain open to the environment, because actual costs in any given budget cycle depend on the number who actually apply for benefits. Entitlements are therefore less deterministic than discretionary programs, and absent the political will to reduce benefits or curtail eligibility, program costs may grow out of hand.

It is not just that entitlements are less predictable than discretionary programs; they reduce the flexibility in the budget, because their claim on the budget takes priority over the discretionary programs that are structurally easier to cut on short notice. What makes entitlement spending particularly problematic for budgeters is that the revenues that pay for them tend to decrease just as more people become eligible for them, during a recession. Entitlements may consequently result in deficits or cuts in discretionary programs.

Debt Repayment. Governments incur debt for a variety of reasons, and that debt must be paid back in a timely fashion, with interest. Debt repayment often comes first in a budget. At the state and local levels, it may be possible to borrow when interest rates are low and use the proceeds to pay off more expensive loans, thus reducing the debt burden. Debt can sometimes be spread out over more years, substituting a new, longer-term note for an older, shorter-term one, thus reducing the annual payments, if not the total amount borrowed or the interest rate. With these exceptions, debt is rigid; debt locks in future payments, which means that it locks in past priorities. If you borrow to pay for a project, then the next administration is stuck paying for your project, even if it would have preferred to spend the money on something else.

Repudiating public debt is rare. It is not possible for the national government to declare bankruptcy, and generally speaking, it is not possible for states either because, to be eligible for bankruptcy, states would need to be able to prove that they absolutely could not raise taxes to pay the bills. Some states allow their local governments to declare bankruptcy. Local governments, controlled by the states, might actually be in a position in which they cannot raise taxes. One of the key issues in a state's decision about whether to allow a local government to declare bankruptcy under federal law is which of the local government's creditors will not be paid. Under a bankruptcy proceeding, all creditors are likely to take a hit, including banks or bondholders. When the state steps in and takes over local finances, there is more discretion about canceling and renegotiating labor contracts, cutting pensions, selling assets, or cutting services more deeply. A state receiver, taking over a local government's finances, can decide that employees' wages will be cut but bond holders will get all that they are owed or vice versa.

Pensions and Other Post-Employment Benefits. Pensions and other post-employment benefits, such as health insurance, are a form of delayed payment for services already received. Employees get some of their wages when they work and the rest after they retire. Because governments have already received the benefit from the work of the employees, the governments they worked for are obligated to pay the rest later. These payments become controversial when state and local governments fail to put aside enough money in current budgets to pay for future benefits. In defined benefit pension plans, the costs to government depend on how old people are when they retire, how long they have worked at what salary levels, how long retirees live and continue to collect their pension, and on the rate of inflation. A market crash may reduce the value of the money that the government has invested to pay the pensions, requiring additional contributions. Whatever the costs, the governments are obligated (mandated) to pay them, but as demonstrated in Chapter 2, raising taxes is difficult or impossible. Raising them to pay for public pensions would be highly unpopular.

Not everyone agrees that delayed compensation is a mandate, and many elected officials would like to just reduce what they owe, abandoning health insurance for retirees, requiring larger employee contributions to pensions and health insurance, and reducing cost-of-living adjustments for those already retired. Less drastically, many governments are redesigning pension systems to make them more affordable going forward. One popular proposal is to eliminate defined benefit plans, the cost of which varies with the return on investment, pushing up costs when recessions pull revenues down. Recommendations include substituting defined contribution plans, in which government employers contribute a fixed sum each year, regardless of what the stock market does, how long people live after retirement, or what the rate of inflation is. From the employees' perspective, this is a greatly reduced benefit that leaves them with considerable financial insecurity. With mandatory expenditures, the costs may rise beyond expectation or affordability, tempting some to want to change mandatory programs to discretionary ones that can be more easily predicted, controlled, and cut back.

Constitutional and Court Requirements. If the constitution or a court directive requires a given payment, that directive is a mandate, and it thus must be paid. Courts have ruled that some jails or prisons are overcrowded, resulting in inhumane conditions. The constitution bans cruel and unusual punishment, and so the governments responsible for overcrowded jails or prisons have to pay for new or expanded facilities or divert some prisoners to other facilities or to house arrest or change the laws so that not so many people are incarcerated. Government can be mandated to spend money on something, regardless of whether the budget has sufficient revenue to cover the costs. Constitutions are supposed to trump every other card, other than bona fide emergencies, creating a nonnegotiable mandate (see the minicase on California and redevelopment agencies below, for an example).

**Minicase: California and Mandatory
Spending on Redevelopment Agencies**

In California, there was no discretion in the state's responsibility to replace funds lost to the school districts when redevelopment agencies took (legally) some of the schools' revenue.[1]

(Continued)

(Continued)

Citizens in California had passed Proposition 98 in 1988, a constitutional amendment requiring the state and local governments together to maintain a minimum level of education funding, determined by formula. So when local redevelopment agencies began to rely heavily on a form of financing, called tax increment financing (TIF), allowing cities to use revenue for their economic development projects that would otherwise have gone to the school districts, the school districts lost the use of those funds and the state was required to make good on the losses. While the legislature can suspend these payments to the schools by a two-thirds vote for a single year, the result is higher payments in following years to catch up. This state spending is automatic and unavoidable, because it is constitutionally mandated.

Proposition 13 in California had limited property tax assessments, curtailing local revenues. One adaptation was for local governments to expand the tax base through TIF funding. The dollars involved were huge and getting larger year by year. In the Great Recession, California was hard hit, and its finances were in a mess; the state simply could not afford to keep paying the school districts to replace the money they lost to TIF, but neither could it violate the constitution. The governor argued that the money would be better spent directly on the schools instead of redevelopment activities, so he proposed elimination of the redevelopment agencies.

The state offered the local governments the option of keeping the development agencies if they voluntarily made the school districts whole; in other words, if the cities instead of the state replaced the school's losses from the TIF. The court ruled this latter option illegal, so the economic development agencies were terminated.

1. Mac Taylor, "The 2012–13 Budget: Unwinding Redevelopment," California Legislative Analyst's Office, February 17, 2012.

In recent years, some governors have been treating court mandates as something they can resist in various ways. Thus in Illinois, when the government was without a budget, because the Republican governor and Democratic legislature were at loggerheads, the governor insisted that regular state employees continue to work and get paid but blocked payment to many nonprofits serving needy populations. When an agency serving the developmentally disabled sued, a federal court mandated the state to pay up, but the governor failed to do so, claiming lack of funds. Washington state ignored court requirements for school funding for three years before the court imposed huge fines. The state of Kansas also has been wrestling with the courts for several years over required education equalization payments, which were cut back during the Great Recession and not restored afterward. Moreover, the courts found the overall spending on education in Kansas insufficient. This sharp uptick in conflict can result in huge fines or school shutdowns as well as drawn out and expensive court fights.

Walled Programs, Earmarked Revenue

Some programs are broken out of the general budget, have earmarked revenue or raise their own nontax-based funds, do not compete for funds with other programs, and may spend their money only for designated purposes. These include special districts, government sponsored enterprises, and trust funds.

Government-Sponsored Enterprises. The federal government has set up a handful of government-sponsored enterprises (GSEs). These are quasi-public, quasi-private organizations. On the private side of the ledger, these GSEs are businesses that bring in their own revenues. GSEs are privately owned, some by investors, others by their borrowers. GSEs do not have the power to tax, and their staff members are not government employees. However, on the public side of the ledger, they pay no federal or state income taxes and they have implicit—but not explicit—government backing. They are created by an act of Congress and their scope of responsibilities is limited by government charter. They can borrow and loan money and issue loan guarantees. The purpose of the federal GSEs is to make credit markets work more smoothly. This odd structure has been problematic. (For the dramatic history of two large federal GSEs, see the minicase "Fannie and Freddie" below.)

Minicase: Fannie and Freddie

The national government includes two huge government-sponsored enterprises (GSEs): The Federal National Mortgage Association (FNMA), nicknamed Fannie Mae, and Freddie Mac, the Federal Home Loan Mortgage Corporation (FHLMC). The goal of these two GSEs is to make more mortgage money available to lend. They buy mortgages from commercial lenders. The commercial lenders who sell their mortgages to Fannie and Freddie get their money back immediately rather than over the life of the mortgage, and thus can relend it immediately. Over the years, these GSEs have made money, requiring no taxpayer support, but they had implicit federal government and taxpayer backing, which enabled them to borrow at below-market rates and improve their profitability.

(Continued)

(Continued)

In the 1970s and 1980s, Fannie and Freddie began to issue mortgage-backed securities; that is, they bought mortgages, insured them, pooled them, and sold shares of the pool. They also held some of the mortgages in their own portfolio.

As commercial lenders accepted more and more high-risk borrowers before the bubble in property prices burst and as variable mortgage rates became more popular, Fannie and Freddie came to hold a riskier portfolio. When the real estate market collapsed and the foreclosure rate skyrocketed, the value of the portfolio declined. The GSEs had to make good on their guarantees to buyers of mortgage-backed securities. Investors lost confidence: Shares of Fannie and Freddie tumbled more than 90 percent in one year. Fears of undercapitalization led investors to worry that the GSEs might declare bankruptcy.

In September 2008, the government took over both Fannie and Freddie. For now, a federal regulator makes their business decisions. The executive Office of Management and Budget continued to treat the GSEs as outside the budget, estimating the cost of the bailouts at $130 billion, while the Congressional Budget Office treated them after 2008 as if they were on-budget governmental entities, boosting the cost estimate to $317 billion.

Fannie and Freddie returned to profitability by 2012. Considered by some elected officials as a "cash cow" or source of revenue, it seems unlikely that efforts to privatize Fannie and Freddie will succeed, despite a major lobbying effort. Both are likely to remain under government conservatorship for the time being, though reform efforts may reduce the risk of a repeated meltdown.

Programs like the GSEs that look free may be far from free in fact. The implicit government backing of the GSEs, along with the impact on the housing market and economy of failure of these two giants, made it desirable for the federal government to bail out these two quasi–private sector organizations, at great public cost.

Source: Matt Cover, "The True Cost of Fannie, Freddie Bailouts: $317 billion, CBO says," CSNnews.com, June 6, 2011, http://cnsnews.com/news/article/true-cost-fannie-freddie-bailouts-317-billion-cbo-says. See also Congressional Budget Office testimony, *The Budgetary Cost of Fannie Mae and Freddie Mac and Options for the Future Federal Role in the Secondary Mortgage Market,* before the Committee on the Budget U.S. House of Representatives, June 2, 2011, www.cbo.gov/sites/default/files/cbofiles/ftpdocs/122xx/doc12213/06-02-gses_testimony.pdf.

Additional source: Inspector General, Federal Housing Financing Agency, "The Continued Profitability of Fannie Mae and Freddie Mac Is Not Assured" (white paper report, 2015), https://origin.www.fhfaoig.gov/Content/Files/WPR-2015-001.pdf.

Publicly Owned Enterprises. Privately owned, government-sponsored enterprises are characteristic of the federal government, while state and local governments sometimes spawn enterprises that are fully government owned. Common examples at the local level are golf courses, electricity production, water works, airports, and sewage treatment plants. Public transit is also often run as a public enterprise. At the state level, tollways and lotteries often operate as publicly owned businesses. These enterprises provide some or all of their own revenue from fees for service. Their revenues are generally restricted to paying for their own operations, though they are sometimes required to subsidize other governmental functions and sometimes they are subsidized by general taxation. Because they are mostly if not completely walled off from other programs, the level of competition between them and other public programs is generally low.

Programs that bring in their own revenue in the form of fees or charges for service may seem free or cheap and so escape the scrutiny that other programs confront. Their budgets may be relatively secure in the sense that they are unlikely to lose their revenue to other programs. However, to the extent that their charges are market based and their services discretionary, program managers may have to worry about how high they can set fees without losing customers. This situation would apply to public buses, golf courses, and water parks, for example. But when the charges are for services that people must have—for instance, water or sewer services—determining the appropriate rates may be a political process and service quality may be a public controversy. Some local governments buy and resell electricity, using the profits to spend on other services to hold down unpopular property tax rates.

Trust Funds. Government trust funds allow very little discretion. They tie a given revenue source or tax amount to a specific spending program. The earmarked revenue can be spent on nothing other than what the trust fund specifies is legitimate and approved.

Budget analysts are quick to argue that there are no *real* trust funds in government, because elected officials can change the revenue stream or the spending constraints. What we have in government is a structure like a trust fund but not as inviolate. (See for example the minicase on New Jersey's fund diversion on p. 170.) This structure is called a trust fund, for lack of a better word. Examples of these government trust funds at the national level include Medicare and highways. The former is paid for through a payroll tax and premiums paid for by retirees; the latter is funded through gas taxes. Unemployment insurance is a joint program between the national government and the states; the revenue mostly comes from a tax on employers, though in some states employees also contribute, and fund balances draw interest. This money is held in trust funds until it is spent to support unemployed workers. Many states have transportation trust funds. At the state and local level, pensions are held in trust funds.

**Minicase: New Jersey's Fund Diversion From
the Unemployment Insurance Fund**

Public sector trust funds are less than inviolable because elected officials can change them, sometimes underfunding them or diverting their earmarked revenue to other purposes. To pay for unemployment insurance, New Jersey taxes not only employers but also employees. The state reportedly diverted $4.6 billion between 1993 and 2006 from the employee share to balance the budget and to pay for hospital charity care. Businesses feared that the diversions would lower the amount of money in the trust fund to such a point that a recession would break the bank—forcing increased taxes on businesses to pay for the unemployed.[1] The fund did in fact run out of money during the recession in 2009 and was forced to borrow $1.75 billion from the federal government. The state missed its debt repayment in 2011 and 2012, with the result that the state owed interest on its borrowing; when this happens, an automatic increase in the rate businesses pay for unemployment insurance kicks in.[2]

This particular diversion will not reoccur, because in 2010, voters in the state overwhelmingly approved a constitutional amendment prohibiting the diversion of funds from the unemployment program for other purposes. With this source of funds blocked, Governor Christie has been aggressive in diverting other funds, particularly for environmental cleanups and clean energy, in order to balance the budget without tax increases.[3]

---

1. New Jersey Policy Research Organization Foundation, *NJ Unemployment Insurance Trust Fund Diverted Revenues, Low Balance Threaten Fund's Health,* 2006, www.njprofoundation.org/pdf/ffd0906.pdf.
2. Stacy Jones, "Threat of Unemployment Tax Hikes Have Employers Seeing Red," NJ.com, January 20, 2013, http://www.nj.com/business/index.ssf/2013/01/unemployment_tax_fund_has_empl.html.
3. Mark J. Magyar, "Raids on Dedicated Funds Climb under Christie," NJSpotlight, July 8, 2013, http://www.njspotlight.com/stories/13/07/08/raids-on-dedicated-funds-climb-under-christie/.

Trust funds guarantee or lock in program priorities and funding, but they can get into financial trouble if something happens to the dedicated stream of revenue or if the expenditures exceed the amounts built up in the trust fund. As the New Jersey minicase demonstrates, fund diversions, sometimes questionable and hotly contested, can drain revenues. Three of the major federal trust funds have run into financial difficulty in recent years, all for different reasons: the federal

Highway Trust Fund, Medicare, and the Unemployment Trust Fund. Pension funds at the state level are also struggling, with many of them cutting back benefits and changing eligibility requirements.

The Highway Trust Fund ran into difficulty for several reasons. Intentional underspending in the Highway Trust Fund created fund balances that appeared to offset deficits elsewhere in the budget—even though those totals in the trust fund could not be spent on other programs. In frustration, program supporters passed legislation requiring the estimated revenues in the trust fund to actually be spent, with the result that the large fund balances disappeared. A second reason for the Highway Trust Fund's difficulty is that its source of funding is the federal excise tax on gasoline, which is levied on a per gallon rather than a per dollar basis. Greater fuel efficiency resulting in fewer gallons sold and less discretionary driving because of the Great Recession held revenue down, so that revenue no longer matched the normal requirements of road construction and repair. To add to this problem, some of the trust fund revenue has been diverted, as legitimate purposes for spending have been expanded to include bike paths, covered bridge restoration, and other projects outside road construction and repair. Highway advocates actively resent sharing their fund with mass transit as well.

Medicare is an entitlement that is maintained as a quasi trust fund, with its own dedicated revenue source. In more recent years, it has had a revenue problem, because most of its revenue is from the currently employed and the long and deep recession threw many people out of work. Of those who found jobs, many took positions paying less than the ones they left. But other factors have been even more important, because as an entitlement, Medicare serves all those who are eligible after they reach age sixty-five, and more people are living past this age. As an entitlement program, it is open to the environment in the sense of having to pay health care providers' bills, which are going up faster than the economy in general. The Medicare trust fund is thus becoming depleted, putting pressure on politicians to either increase revenue or decrease benefits or eligibility or somehow bend down the cost curve for health care. With so many people depending on the program, politicians are understandably reluctant to tackle this issue.

The Unemployment Trust Fund ran into trouble for different reasons, also related to its structure. The unemployment insurance program is a joint program between the federal government and the states and so represents a form of cooperative federalism. Like Medicare, it is both an entitlement program and a trust fund. All those who meet particular criteria, such as losing their jobs through no fault of their own and actively looking for work, are eligible for payments of some proportion of their prior wages. As an entitlement program, it is open to the environment so that changes in the economy that affect the number of unemployed automatically affect the costs of this program. Employers pay taxes to both the state and the federal government, and proceeds are held in trust funds, which in theory can be spent on no other purpose than unemployment compensation.

The national government pays for the administrative costs of the program, lends money to the states when their trust fund balances are too low to deal with the cost of claims, and funds extensions of eligibility for benefits during especially long recessions. The states determine the formula for benefits and their duration as well as the rate of taxation on businesses.

Because the states control both taxes (revenues) and expenditures, they have the basic tools to manage balance in their trust funds. Nevertheless, because the costs for this program go up during recessions when unemployment is high, balance is problematic for the states, because it is difficult (perhaps impossible) to raise taxes on businesses during a recession in order to pay higher unemployment costs. To handle this problem, states normally build up their unemployment trust funds when unemployment is lower, and then draw the funds down during recessions.

When state unemployment payments empty the entire state trust fund, states can borrow from the federal government portion of the trust fund. They have several years to begin paying back; if they fail to do so, they have to pay interest on the debt, and the taxes businesses pay automatically jump to a higher rate.

During the recession that began at the end of 2007, many states borrowed from the federal Unemployment Trust Fund. Initially, Congress waived the interest on this debt, but the waiver expired, leaving states with not only an urgent need to repay their loans but also with a bill for the interest. Failure to pay on time would result in large increases in taxation on their businesses, and interest payments were not supposed to be drawn from a states' unemployment trust fund, which is earmarked solely for payments to the unemployed.

The states' choices could include benefit reductions, some kind of temporary tax surcharge, or borrowing on the market. Businesses faced with increasing payroll tax burdens have pressured the states to reduce program benefits. At least six states opted to shorten the time that unemployed workers can receive maximum benefits to less than twenty-six weeks. Eight states made it more difficult to qualify for benefits.[5] Some states, such as Arkansas, Rhode Island, and Indiana, reduced the amounts that could be paid to claimants.[6]

For states with good credit ratings to pay the government back, it was cheaper to borrow than it would have been to force businesses to pay the penalties for late payment, as the federal government interest rate is 4 percent. Some states either borrowed or were planning to borrow money, charging their businesses the lower cost of these loans rather than the higher federal interest.

While businesses advocated cuts in benefits for the unemployed, advocates for the poor have noted that the trust funds that ran out of money were often inadequately funded during years of low unemployment. Wages generally rise with inflation, so that the payouts for insurance also rise with inflation (they pay roughly half the lost wages), but the taxes employers paid were calculated on a fixed estimate of wages rather than one that was growing with inflation. The necessary result over time has been structural imbalance and deficits. Program advocates, supported by a Government Accountability Office study,[7] argue for indexing the base in order to assure that their trust funds are built up sufficiently during the good years. Of the sixteen states that had a policy of raising the base on which the tax was calculated by pegging it to inflation, more than two-thirds maintained solvent funds and averted the need to borrow with its associated costs.[8]

In the case of the unemployment insurance trust funds, time was a key element in the narrative; failure to tax sufficiently during the boom years resulted in deficits during the bust years. As a result, pressure to raise taxes on businesses occurred during the Great Recession, when businesses and the state economy could least afford the increase. The business community pressured elected officials instead to cut services to the unemployed. Program opponents attacked the character of the long-term unemployed while advocates for the program pointed out that cutting the benefits reduces aggregate demand during a recession—people cannot afford to buy the goods businesses sell, making recessions deeper and longer than they otherwise would be. Program supporters have linked unemployment benefits to a highly valued goal for the collectivity, but this strategy has not been overwhelmingly successful. Only two states have adopted legislation that would more adequately fund their unemployment trust funds, while many more have reduced benefits to workers.

Special-Purpose Governments. States have limited the amounts some local governments may borrow. These constraints have often been expressed as a percentage of the total assessed value of property in the governmental entity. To get around these limits, some governmental functions broke off from general government, establishing a single-purpose government covering the same territory. The debt limits apply to each of the overlapping governmental units, greatly adding to the borrowing power of local governments. Ten special-purpose governments could borrow ten times what a single government could borrow. Special-purpose governments like these typically spend more on the function they provide than general-purpose governments do. For example, a park district that is independent is likely to spend more than a park department that is part of a city and has to fight with the fire and police departments for funding. In a general government, other functions compete for expenditures; in special-purpose governments there is no competition. The disadvantages are that if there are many special-purpose governments, as in Illinois and California, the level of overlapping debt can be very high, and it is impossible to prioritize and make tradeoffs between programs.

The Environment

Success in winning the budget battle depends not just on strategy and structure but also on the environment, broadly defined. The examples given earlier in the chapter highlight the importance of the economic environment, including the level of revenues and unemployment. The rise and fall of housing prices and the practices of commercial mortgage lenders helped bring down Fannie and Freddie. Changing demographics are also important, such as the implications of an aging population for medical insurance programs like Medicare.

The environment affects expenditures in other ways as well: The level of illegal immigration impacts border control costs. Wars affect defense spending, the weather affects snow removal costs, and efforts to recover from emergencies like major hurricanes or earthquakes may increase spending for years. A war in the Middle East may increase gasoline prices, pushing up the costs for public works and police, which rely heavily on vehicles. Medical price inflation affects government spending for Medicare and Medicaid. When governments are required to limit their total spending to the growth in the economy or are mandated to maintain a level of spending on education that is proportional to growth of the economy in the state, the environment directly impacts the budget.

Many programs are demand driven. The costs of the fire department depend to some extent on the number and severity of fires; the costs of worker's compensation programs depend on the number and severity of job-related accidents and illnesses; the costs of a women's shelter depend on the number of battered women who show up needing assistance; the costs of a homeless shelter depend to some extent on the severity of the winters as well as the availability of single-room occupancy rental units. When a particular spring delivers temperatures that go up and down across the freezing mark, producing large numbers of frost heaves in the roads, the costs of road repairs soars. The spending is not optional; the local governments are responsible for fixing the roads. The automatic nature of these responses to the problems confronted by the collectivity reprioritizes expenditures.

The list of environmental influences would not be complete without considering politics and political realignments, that is, shifts not only in the majority party but in the policies backed by each party. A strategy of privatization and increase in contracting is likely to have more success when Republicans are in power, while a strategy of publicly provided programs, such as student loan programs, is more likely to be successful when Democrats dominate the political setting. This element of the environment was much in evidence in the student loan minicase.

Strategy, Structure, and Environment Combined: The Medicare Example

In any given program, strategy, structure, and environment combine to influence spending levels. The following illustration is meant to show how the themes developed in this chapter have worked out in one program, Medicare. Note that strategies have been employed by supporters and opponents inside and outside of government. The environment in this case includes the impacts of recession and unemployment, inflation of medical costs, and demographic changes. Structurally, Medicare is an entitlement operated as quasi trust fund, supported by a combination of payroll taxes and insurance premiums and bolstered by general revenue. The fact that Medicare is an entitlement program has made it especially vulnerable to the aging of the population, and its dependence on payroll taxes for revenues has increased its vulnerability to recession.

The federal Medicare program is a political football, loved by some who want to use it as a blueprint for universal health care coverage and hated by others who see it as a symbol of big government and the first step on the slippery slope to socialism. Considered the electrified third rail of politics, because of its popularity with the public—touch it and your political career is over—its financial problems have proved difficult to address. Both supporters and opponents are eager to show and possibly exaggerate its financial problems, the former in order to stimulate a solution, the latter in order to cut it back.

Some facts are clear, despite the political and partisan controversy. Medicare is expensive, and the costs rose over time and were projected to keep on rising. In 2014, Medicare spending was about 16 percent of the federal budget. Medicare's annual report for 2014 describes Medicare spending in 2013 as 3.4 percent of gross domestic product, projected to rise to 5.5 percent in 2040 and to 6.3 percent in 2080. These projections are highly uncertain. Basing their judgments in part on such rough projections and in part on history prior to 2010, many academics and politicians have described Medicare spending as *unsustainable.* They argue that something must be done soon to cut spending, but this simple narrative obscures more than it clarifies.

In reality, the actual rate of growth in Medicare spending has been coming down, not going up, in the last few years. Some of the older projections proved too high. For example, CBO projected the costs of the new drug program portion of Medicare when the program was passed in 2003, but that prediction proved too high, in part because actual enrollment in the program was smaller than expected and in part because of competition between plan sponsors. There has also been a major shift to more use of generic drugs instead of more expensive name brands. Actual expenditures in 2013 were about half what was projected in 2003.[9] Further the Congressional Budget Office estimates for total Medicare spending have come down almost every year after 2006. Both the projections and the reality actually dropped after the passage and implementation of the Affordable Care Act. "The difference between the current estimate for Medicare's 2019 budget and the estimate for the 2019 budget four years ago is about $95 billion."[10] The practice of medicine seems to be changing, which suggests that the recent trends are likely to continue.

Calling the growth of Medicare unsustainable is a political tactic, a bit of rhetoric intended to convince decision makers and the public that spending needs to be cut, without detailed policy analysis that would produce a more efficient and effective program. The word *unsustainability* helps frame the issue for political debate and narrows the solution options to those preferred by some.

One clue that unsustainability is a political, action-forcing term is that is it used to describe only some program increases, not others. Those who want to bring down the size of the deficit and reduce the level of debt describe deficits and debt levels as unsustainable. Unsustainable is the term used to describe anti-recession spending by those who oppose it. On the left, it is used to oppose buildups in military spending; those on the right who support military spending do not describe the military budget as unsustainable. "Unsustainable" has seldom, if ever, been used to describe spending on domestic security, which grew rapidly after the events of September 11 in 2001, despite the helter-skelter way the money was spent. In other words, *unsustainable* is not a word used to describe all rapidly growing programs; it is used to describe spending increases one opposes.

How Good Are the Numbers?

How good are the numbers is the first question to ask in getting behind the rhetoric. How badly off is the Medicare trust fund, really, and how reliant is it on general taxation, adding to the deficit or squeezing out other higher priority spending?

Seldom mentioned in the public discussion is that the Medicare trust fund has been more or less in balance, with income equaling or exceeding expenditures in most years. The Great Recession has been an exception. According to Medicare's annual report in 2014, the hospital insurance portion of the fund (Part A) is projected to run a surplus from 2015 to 2022. For Part B, the medical portion of the Medicare funds, and part D, the pharmaceutical portion of the funds, the 2014 annual report predicted surpluses in some years through 2023 and deficits in others, but overall the report predicted that there would be higher fund balances in 2023 than in 2015. These figures assume positive impacts of the Affordable Care Act in the short run and assume that after the end of that period an increasingly old population will increase medical costs to the funds.

The current projection for the hospital insurance portion of Medicare is that it will run out of money by 2030, but this prediction is highly sensitive to factors that change from year to year. First, because revenue for the hospitalization portion of Medicare is based on an earmarked payroll tax (FICA), a recession in which many people are unemployed or take lower paying jobs depresses revenue; economic recovery improves the revenue picture. Trust fund administrators can only guess at the rate and level of economic recovery after a long and deep recession. Second, based on a comparison of CBO's August 2010 and April 2014 baselines, Medicare spending in 2014 will be about $1,000 lower per person than was expected in 2010.[11]

The Medicare annual reports assume the cost increases will be unsustainable and simultaneously assume that they will be sustained, which is illogical: If Medicare costs are unsustainable, they will be curtailed in some manner. This process is already well under way, with movements within the medical industry to reduce unnecessary testing and surgical procedures, reduce hospital readmissions, and require evidence of the effectiveness of drugs and other medical interventions. Medicare began and expanded a process of competitive bidding, which will also help keep expenditures down.

Moreover, the projections of unsustainability depend heavily on demographic projections. These studies assume that as the baby boomer generation (the large cohort of babies born in the years immediately following World War II) ages, they will need more medical care and, with increased life spans, will need that expensive care for longer periods of time. But since these projections go out until 2080, one needs to consider that after the baby boom is a baby bust, a smaller cohort, fewer children born and less demand on the health care system. Also, improvements in life expectancy may be accompanied by better health and improved quality of life rather than more illness and prolonged expensive care. Predictions of Medicare spending skyrocketing as a proportion of gross domestic product assume a slow growing economy and more rapidly increasing medical costs, but we really don't know about either one, let alone both. The degree of change from year to year in the projections suggests the degree of uncertainty of the long-term projections. The size of the problem is not as clear and concrete as the rhetoric suggests.

How Much Should We Be Spending on Health?

As budgeters and policy analysts, the second question one ought to ask is whether the nation is in fact spending too much on health care. Sometimes spending increases rapidly as priorities change in response to current problems, such as a change in demography (an aging population), a war (or two wars), or threat to health or life. Increased spending is not itself an indication of budget failure or a mandate to cut back that particular cost increase. It might just be evidence of the adaptability of budgets.

The political message has been to cut back Medicare, because it is growing, rather than to examine budget priorities and trade-offs more generally. This framing is to some extent a function of spending through a trust fund, which isolates a program from the rest of the budget, setting it up so it should raise its own revenue and should balance over time. But since much Medicare funding also comes from general taxation and this trend is likely to continue (despite a law passed in 2003 that requires the president to propose solutions if the proportion of Medicare funding from general taxation goes above 45 percent), the question becomes what priority health care spending should have in comparison to other programs and what the optimum level of spending should be on health care. Are we spending the right amount, too much or too little, or are we spending too much money on the wrong things? Are we getting too little health for the amount of money we are spending because of the way the program is structured, the incentives, and the administrative costs?

One approach to answering the question of how much is the right amount is to compare U.S. spending on health care to health care spending in other developed countries. Although these studies do not focus solely on Medicare, the results are suggestive. Studies of total health care spending in developed countries, including public and private spending, show the United States as an outlier. Not only do we spend way more than other developed countries when compared to the average health spending of Organization for Economic Cooperation and Development (OECD) countries, but the United States spends substantially more than predicted by income alone. Generally, spending on health care and income are closely correlated, but not in the United States—we spend a higher proportion of our wealth on health care than other countries do.

What also stands out from these cross-national studies is that the United States is far more dependent on privately provided health care than any other OECD country. Our public spending on health care is comparable to many other OECD countries, but our private spending is much higher. If this additional spending were getting us much better health outcomes, one could argue that it just reflects our values as a nation. On two aggregate measures of outcomes, longevity (average age at death) and infant mortality, we do worse than average. We do somewhat better than average on cancer treatment and in-hospital surgery but less well on prevention and treatment of chronic health problems, such as asthma.

There is only a weak relationship between the amount of money spent and health outcomes. So for us, the issue is not so much how much we spend, but on what we spend it that matters. What we spend it on is a function of how programs are structured. The high use of private sector health care provision and the complicated insurance and payment systems we use raise the cost of administration, without providing any improvement in health care; we spend more on outpatient care, including same-day surgeries, than other countries, an increase that resulted in part from efforts to control Medicare payments to hospitals by relating payments to diagnosis. Hospitals then relocated less expensive surgeries to separate facilities engaging in same-day surgery.

When compared to countries that also have a combination of public and private systems, Switzerland, Germany, Japan, France, and Canada, we spend more per capita on program administration and somewhat more on hospitalization but much more on outpatient care, doctor visits, both generalists and specialists, dentists, and same-day surgery. One would imagine that the same-day surgery would cut the costs of hospitalization and nursing home care, but those costs are still considerably above the average.

The costs for hospital services are generally higher in the United States than in other countries, as are the costs for medicines, accounting for some of the differences from other countries; in addition, the United States has more diagnostic equipment, which is used more frequently, and perhaps as a result, we perform more discretionary surgery, some of which is probably unnecessary.[12]

This brief comparison with other countries suggests that we are spending much more than other countries on health care and only getting a moderate amount of improvement as a result (see Figure 5.2 for a comparison of U.S. health care costs and our average life spans compared to that of other developed nations). We may be over testing, and doctors may be practicing defensive medicine to prevent lawsuits, which suggests the need for reforming the system of lawsuits against doctors for malpractice. The United States has the highest obesity rates among the OECD countries reporting. Factors such as diet and exercise may have

FIGURE 5.2   Relationship Between U.S. Health Care Spending and Life Expectancy in OECD Countries

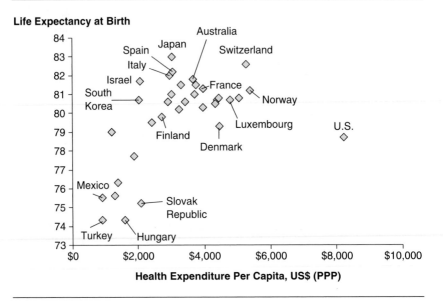

Source: OECD Health Data 2012, October 2012. http://www.oecd.org/els/healthpoliciesanddata/oecdhealthdata2012-frequentlyrequesteddata.htm.

Note: Data are for 2010 or the most recent available year. Data for Belgium excludes investments. Data for the Netherlands is current expenditure.

PPP = purchasing power parity.

more influence on longevity and health than spending on emergency room care, implying that building bike paths and making bicycling safer may result in better health outcomes than more spending on traditional health care. Improving accessibility to primary care for chronic illnesses may also reduce expensive hospitalizations.

From the perspective of budgeting, the walls around Medicare, intended to protect its revenue from being taken by other programs, have worked against solutions that involve more spending in other programs. The problem has been framed as Medicare spending, which must be reduced or cut back, without due consideration for what spending elsewhere would increase prevention and create better health outcomes less expensively. Stricter enforcement of clean water and clean air acts may reduce the incidence of cancer, asthma, and chronic obstructive pulmonary disease (COPD) and help improve longevity. More testing of medicines once in use may reduce medicine-induced illnesses, a major cause of hospital admissions in the United States. And greater coverage by public insurance—Medicare and Medicaid—is likely to result in reduced costs for administration. Spending more in the right places is likely to reduce costs and improve health outcomes.

The problems of Medicare are not inevitable results of an aging population. They can be solved, but only if one gets past the rhetorical framing that takes most solutions off the table. The problems are not likely to be solved by simple cuts in payment to providers, which just seems to produce more spending in other areas and overprovision of testing and surgery. Rather, good budgeting would start with a goal, the quality of outcomes to be achieved, such as a reduction in child mortality of a given amount. With a goal in place, it would then call for designing a program that will be effective in gaining that outcome in a cost-effective manner. Locating the source of increased costs and the reasons and incentives for those higher costs and working out new solutions may be necessary to bring spending into line. In order to control costs and assure cost effectiveness of entitlement programs, budgeting is going to have to marry policy analysis. (Budgeters marrying policy analysts may not do the trick, but it might help.)

Summary and Conclusions

Actual spending on programs depends on strategy, structure, and environment. The level of competition for spending, the level of flexibility and discretion, and the point of control all vary with the structure. The trend at the national and state level and, to some extent at the local level, has been to decrease flexibility, to put spending on automatic pilot, but such programs are vulnerable to the environment and may run into financial trouble. Budgeting successfully for these programs requires a different set of skills, with much more policy analysis, because the point of control is in the program design, not the annual spending numbers. For the strongly walled programs, whether set up as privately owned corporations, self-funding public enterprises, or special districts, solutions may lie outside their narrow program funding decisions.

More spending in one area may lower costs in another area. Making buses, fire houses, and school buildings "greener" may lower operating costs; increasing pollution controls may lower health costs; increasing spending for education and training may lower costs for unemployment insurance, welfare, courts, and prisons. The recent revision to the Government Performance and Results Act emphasizes the need to consider crosscutting goals and performance, measuring the contribution of all those programs that work toward the same goal. If well implemented, those crosscutting evaluations may help budgeters think outside the walls of walled programs.

Useful Websites

Many states have begun transparency programs that include websites with detailed financial information. For a listing of state transparency sites and what they include and do well, see **Following the Money 2012: How the 50 States Rate in Providing Online Access to Government Spending Data**, published by the CALPIRG Education Fund (www.calpirg.org/sites/pirg/files/reports/Following%20the%20Money%20vCA%20web.pdf). Among the most highly rated are **Texas's Transparency website** (www.texastransparency.org) as well as **Kentucky's Transparency Portal** (http://opendoor.ky.gov/Pages/default.aspx).

The federal transparency site is at USA spending.gov (https://www.usaspending.gov/Pages/Default.aspx). It has downloadable data for analysis. The data include grants, loans, and contracts. The site has a keyword search. You can search multiple years from 2008 to 2015. Possible topics include the degree to which contracts were competitive and the geographic location of the contracts. In addition to the raw data describing contracts in any given year, there is a convenient summary. For example, in 2015 there were 135,842 contracts that were not competed with a dollar value of $67.6 billion. The user can track such figures year by year. The site also has some handy interactive graphics and a list of the largest contractors and the amount of their contracts. Raw data is also available for earlier years but is not displayed in the same fashion as the more recent years.

Some cities have transparency sites as well, such as the **City of Chicago, Illinois** (www.cityofchicago.org/city/en/progs/transparency.html) and **Albuquerque, New Mexico** (www.cabq.gov/abq-view/).

For the federal level, the **president's budget proposals** are online (www.whitehouse.gov/omb). Agency presentations to congressional appropriations subcommittees, which contain their budget strategies, often can be found on the agencies' websites but may also be found at the **Government Printing Office** (www.gpo.gov). The **digital versions of Senate appropriations hearings** (www.gpo.gov/fdsys/browse/committee.action?chamber=senate&committee=appropriations&minus=test&treeid=treemenu4&openuls=0&ycord=0) and **House appropriations hearings** (www.gpo.gov/fdsys/browse/committee.action?chamber=house&committee=appropriations&collection=CHRG&plus=CHRG) are available from 1998 on (older hearings are available in hard copy at depository libraries).

Also available are webcasts (some audio only) and **selected testimony transcripts of recent Senate hearings** (www.appropriations.senate.gov/hearings-landing.cfm); also for recent events, the **House maintains an archive of hearings and committee markups** (http://appropriations.house.gov/calendararchive/), some in video, some in audio only, and selected transcripts of testimony. The House's archive is searchable by appropriation subcommittee, such as Agriculture, Defense, or Housing and Transportation.

C-SPAN, the public affairs network, covers many hearings live on the web (www.c-span.org). The schedule of hearings that they cover is listed on their website.

Tracking appropriation bills as they pass Congress is relatively easy on the **Library of Congress** website (www.congress.gov). The site has a separate section on appropriation bills each year, including continuing resolutions.

For a description of Proposition 98 in California that dedicates a portion of state money for education, see the **Proposition 98 Primer**, from the California Legislative Analyst's Office (www.lao.ca.gov/2005/prop_98_primer/prop_98_primer_020805.htm).

For information on implementation of **GPRA's crosscutting goals**, see the federal website (http://goals.performance.gov/goals_2013).

For information on the **joint federal state unemployment insurance** and the timing and outstanding amounts of state borrowing from the federal government trust fund, see the National Conference of State Legislatures (NCSL) website (www.ncsl.org/issues-research/labor/state-unemployment-trust-fund-loans.aspx). As of June 2015, five states still had outstanding loans from borrowing that began in 2008 or 2009.

Estimates for **cost savings for the initial year of Medicare competitive bidding** for equipment and projections for savings over time can be found in an electronic publication via the Centers for Medicare and Medicaid Services site (www.cms.gov/Medicare/Medicare-Fee-for-Service-Payment/DMEPOSCompetitiveBid/Downloads/Competitive-Bidding-Update-One-Year-Implementation.pdf) with **other initiatives for costs savings in Medicare and Medicaid** available from the home page (www.cms.gov).

6 The Politics of Balancing the Budget

Balancing the budget by cuts and layoffs is absolutely the worst thing to do. Cuts and layoffs only compound the problem, create renewed deficits. And if the next budget is balanced with further cuts and layoffs, the Miami-Dade County would be on its way to becoming a banana republic!

—Farid Khavari, "Facts About Balancing the Budget," *Gold Coast Chronicle,* May 27, 2012

The debt and the deficit is just getting out of control, and the administration is still pumping through billions upon trillions of new spending. That does not grow the economy.

—Rep. Paul Ryan, Fox News Sunday, February 1, 2010

The most important constraint on budgeting is the requirement for balance: Revenues must equal or exceed expenditures over a given period of time. Balancing is a key part of budgetary decision-making, but it is not always successful. Rebalancing the budget normally requires revenue increases and spending decreases. The possibility of increasing taxes evokes ideological and class differences about whom to tax and how heavily; similarly, decisions about which expenditures to cut and by how much incur intense debate that divides the young from the old, Democrats from Republicans, and the poor from the rich. The issues are so contentious that they are often not resolved. A 2011 congressional committee (nicknamed the supercommittee) set up to devise a plan to rebalance the federal budget failed dramatically, even though the alternative was widely unacceptable automatic across-the-board spending cuts.

Especially at the national level, and to a lesser extent, at the state level, governments sometimes incur deficits to moderate negative trends in the economy, maintain spending for unemployment benefits and welfare during a recession, or deal with emergencies, such as those caused by earthquakes or hurricanes. When deficits are caused by emergencies or by declines in the economy, the borrowing required to cover them is temporary and is not particularly harmful. Budgets have to be flexible and responsive to the environment, and some borrowing may be necessary to that end. Governments at all levels may experience deficits for a less worthy reason: The decision makers are unwilling to make difficult choices. Elected officials may choose to reduce taxes or keep them low, to gain popularity, without cutting spending proportionately. Sometimes deficits occur because revenues are growing more slowly than expenditures and decision makers are unwilling to risk loss of voter support by increasing taxes or fees or cutting services. In recent years, some elected officials have been so bent on reducing taxes that they create deficits. When elected officials do not make the necessary tough decisions, they often propose new budget processes and more rigid budgetary constraints instead, with the idea that these decision rules will save them from themselves or from their colleagues, insulate them from popular demands, and obscure their responsibility for painful outcomes.

Although the decisions that have to be made to reduce or eliminate deficits may be politically unpopular, the solution of ignoring hard decisions and running deficits is not popular either. Both the public and the financial community oppose deficits. After the federal budget was balanced in the late 1990s, public concern with deficits naturally fell off, but it reawakened with the resurgence of massive deficits in the George W. Bush administration. As the economy sank in the Great Recession, the Obama administration added bank and business rescues and financial aid to the states, further ballooning the deficits. Worry about the deficit, however, fell behind concern with fixing the economy and creating jobs. Public officials found themselves in a bind. Fixing the economy, say those on the right, requires reducing taxation, especially on businesses and the wealthy, potentially adding to the deficit; fixing the economy, say those on the left, requires more public spending, potentially worsening the deficit.

Because none of the choices seem good, when governments run chronic deficits, those responsible for them often deny them or minimize their size and importance. The definition of balance may be loose, applying only to some portions of the budget or only to the proposed and not the approved budget. Or deficits may be obscured by delaying expenditures or selling assets for one-time revenue. Budgets may look balanced but not really be balanced. For example, at the national level, the deficit is usually presented including the Social Security surplus, which is misleading, because Social Security is off-budget and its surplus cannot be used to defray the deficit. The quality of the budget numbers suffers under these circumstances. Between bad numbers and fuzzy definitions of what constitutes a deficit, it can be extremely difficult to figure out the real size of a deficit.

By the time those in charge of the budget decide to act, the deficit may be very large and proportionately difficult to cut back. Whose programs should be cut back and by how much? Where can cuts legally be made? How can resistance from interest groups be minimized? Whose taxes should be raised and by how much? Can expenditures be shifted to other levels of government, or can grants to state or local governments be reduced to cut the size of the deficit? Can states take revenue from local governments to balance their own budgets? How can the appropriate actions be taken while maintaining accountability and acceptability to the public? How can politicians make such unpopular choices and still maintain their support base? The politics of budget balance revolves around how and why budgets become unbalanced as well as how to rebalance them and who gets hurt in the process. In exploring this decision stream, it may help to return first to the characteristics of public budgeting outlined in Chapter 1 as they apply to budget balance:

- Public budgets are constrained by the requirement for balance. Governments do have a "bottom line." The bottom line in businesses is profit; in government, it is balance.
- The politics of balance involves multiple actors with conflicting policy goals.
- Budgets are open to the environment. Automatic spending, including entitlements, is especially vulnerable to changes in the economy, and some program structures may be simultaneously affected by a drop in revenues and an increase in demand. Recessions trigger deficits unless sufficient savings have been put aside in contingency accounts and the recession is either mild or short-lived.
- Deficit politics has to resolve the separation of taxpayer and budget decision maker, by negotiating publicly acceptable solutions. This is so difficult to do that decision makers may minimize the size or importance of deficits or obscure responsibility for politically difficult decisions. Acceptability may trump accountability.

Balance as a Constraint

A broad definition of budget balance is that revenues equal or exceed expenditures for some stated period of time. Governments in the United States try to balance their budgets, and most of the time, most of them succeed. This is true even in the absence of clear legislative or constitutional requirements for budgetary balance. This frequently positive outcome occurs because balance is a norm that budgeters accept; it is intrinsic to budgeting. A budget would not have much meaning if there were no balance constraint. Moreover, those who evaluate the creditworthiness of governments, and hence control the cost of public sector borrowing (higher risk = higher cost for borrowing), downgrade governments that cannot balance their budgets, warning potential investors that there is a risk they will not be repaid on time or at the agreed upon rate. Markets thus enforce the discipline of balance.

Having said that budgets generally balance, however, doesn't tell you as much as you might think, because in practice balance is variously defined (see the minicase "Is the Wisconsin Budget Balanced?" on p. 188 for an example). At the state and local level, budgets may be technically balanced by using revenue or fund balances left from a prior year, even if in the current budget year expenditures exceed revenues. Similarly, budgets are normally considered in balance at state and local levels when contingency funds, so called rainy-day funds, are drawn down. Internal borrowing, from pension funds or from funds with their own earmarked revenues, may also be used to balance the budget. At the national level, fund balances in trust funds may be applied against deficits in other funds in the calculation of aggregate deficits, even when those funds are earmarked and cannot be spent to cover deficits elsewhere. At the national level, deficits are calculated based on actual revenues compared with actual outlays, which makes delaying outlays particularly tempting. Some states delay paying vendors in years when budget deficits threaten. In some states, it is possible to balance the budget with borrowed money. However it is defined, the balance constraint is real, and many states during the Great Recession had to cut spending midyear in order to come up with balance by year end.

Most of the time, balance is determined one year at a time, but sometimes balance occurs over several years. Trust funds in particular are structured to balance over time. If all outstanding obligations were to be deducted from this year's revenue, a budget might not be balanced, but if those same obligations were matched against several years' anticipated revenues, that same budget might be balanced. The federal Highway Trust Fund illustrates this somewhat looser definition of balance over time (see the minicase on p. 189).

Minicase: Is the Wisconsin Budget Balanced?

In January 2012, Gov. Scott Walker in Wisconsin claimed the state's budget was balanced, while the secretary of the Department of Administration claimed the budget was not balanced. This was not a disagreement between members of opposite political parties: Both men are Republicans on the same team. Walker could argue the budget was balanced, because he relied on cash accounting, which depends only on the cash on hand at a given time. The amount of cash is influenced by borrowing, by delayed spending for goods and services already purchased, and one-time revenues that do nothing to cure structural imbalances between revenue and expenditures. (A structural deficit means that revenues are not growing as fast as expenditures, over time.) By contrast, Mike Huebsch, the Department of Administration secretary, was using generally accepted accounting principles (GAAP) used by all other Wisconsin governments. In this approach, bills and revenue are assigned to the period in which they were incurred, regardless of when the money goes out the door. The governor claimed a $68 million surplus, while the Annual Financial Report in December listed a deficit of $3 billion.

Governor Walker wanted to take credit for a balanced budget or at least avoid blame for deficits during a bitter recall election, but Huebsch wanted to reduce the number of people eligible for medical assistance coverage under the new federal Affordable Health Care Act, which he could do if the state could demonstrate that it was running in the red. Defining balance turns out to be a political choice rather than a technical or legal one. The easiest way to obscure a deficit is to choose an accounting system that allows maximum flexibility for when expenditures are counted.

Source: Editorial, "Our View: State Has Yet to Balance its Budget," *LaCross Tribune,* January 25, 2012.

Another way that the constraint of balance can be loosened or tightened is to change the point at which the budget must be balanced: when the executive proposes it, when the legislature passes it, when the governor signs it, or at the end of the year. According to a 2010 study, forty-four states required the governor to propose a balanced budget, forty-one required the legislature to pass a balanced budget, but only thirty-eight required the state to finish the year with a balanced budget, prohibiting any deficit to be carried over into the following fiscal year. These numbers were based on the perceptions of finance officers, how they see the process, rather than on the text of the law or constitution.[1] Practice depends in some cases on informal understandings or interpretations and sometimes on court cases. Prohibitions on borrowing to balance the budget are sometimes interpreted to be a balanced budget requirement, but strictly speaking they are not, because they don't address delayed payments for goods and services already received, sale of assets to balance the budget, or carrying a deficit forward from one year to the next.

Minicase: Balance in the Federal Highway Trust Fund

The national level Highway Trust Fund is an account based on gas taxes primarily for building and repairing the nation's highways. When projects are finished, the states bill the federal government for reimbursement from the Highway Trust Fund. Revenues have to be greater than obligations, not just greater than outlays, because the states are running up bills that they have not yet submitted for reimbursement. By next year, there should be more money in the fund to pay off the bills that are being incurred now but that will not be presented until next year or the year after. So how can anyone tell if the trust fund is really balanced at any time? How can Congress or the president ensure that the states do not spend more money than the fund can expect to receive? And if there is a surplus, how does anyone know how much it is?

When money is committed by the states, it shows up in the trust fund as obligated but not yet spent. So the total in the fund remains high, although much of the money is already committed and cannot be spent on anything else. The result of not subtracting this committed money from the trust fund total is to make the balance in the fund look greater than it really is. This can help to make the federal budget as a whole look balanced, if the "surplus" in the Highway Trust Fund is counted as part of the consolidated balance of the federal government. But the result is misleading.

Attributing future expenses to the present year's budget is equally misleading, as matching several years' expenditures against a single year's revenue would normally result in deficits for that fund. To avoid this problem, Congress, through the Byrd Amendment to the Federal-Aid Highway Act of 1956, restricted the growth of future commitments to a level not to exceed the current year's unexpended balance plus projected income for the following two fiscal years.[1]

The result does provide some protection against overspending, but it does not yield an exact figure for budgetary balance or an exact estimate of the surplus. To calculate a surplus in this situation, one has to subtract the actual obligations from the present unobligated revenues plus estimated

(Continued)

(Continued)

unobligated future revenues. The number is spongy, in part because until bills are actually presented for projects approved or under way, the exact cost is not known, and in part because the calculation depends on estimates of revenues for the present and the next two years.

1. John W. Fischer, *Transportation Trust Funds: Budgetary Treatment* (Congressional Research Service, Washington, DC: April 6, 1998), 98–63, http:// digital.library.unt.edu/ark:/67531/metacrs816/m1/1/high_res_d/98 -63e_1998Apr06.pdf.

The constraint against borrowing to balance the budget does not guarantee a balanced budget or good financial management. For example, Louisiana in 1988 got around the prohibition. State officials confronted a deficit that had been rolled over from year to year. They had been covering that deficit through internal borrowing and delayed payments to vendors. It would have been better management and more accountable to borrow long term to pay off the short-term obligations and spread out the deficit repayment over a period of years, but the state was forbidden to borrow to balance the budget. So the state created a special district to issue the debt. The special district had the same boundaries as the state. It levied a 1 percent sales tax to pay off the bonds.[2]

Though states sometimes evade the rules they operate under, because they feel the constraints are too tight or result in poor management, the general direction has been toward more restrictive rules mandating balance. In 2004, for example, California voters passed a referendum requiring the legislature to pass a balanced budget, mandating that the state resolve midyear shortfalls before the end of the year and prohibiting the state from borrowing to cover end-of-year shortfalls.

Washington state strengthened its requirements in 2012, though the balance requirements before the change were not particularly weak. If a cash deficit occurred during the year, the governor was required to implement across-the-board cuts. In 2012, the state added a kind of "look forward" requirement, so that the legislature had to assure balance not just for the current biennium but also for the next one, four years at a time. There were complicated exceptions to the rule, including the results of collective bargaining; the rule was legislatively based, not constitutionally based, and so could be changed in the future; further, it was not to take effect for several years. The definition of future balance was based on generous projections of revenue. Even considering these softening features, however, a legislative requirement to pass a budget that would be in balance for the next four years added a new and potentially powerful constraint to budgeting in Washington state.[3]

Indiana, which is forbidden to borrow to balance the budget, is in the process of adding a constitutional amendment to require a balanced budget, which is considered by some to be a stronger and more inclusive constraint. The governor called for such an amendment in his state of the union speech, even though the state budget has routinely been balanced. The legislature passed the proposal in 2015, but before it can be placed before the public, it must also pass the next independently elected legislature.

Tightening the balance rules may be one way to try to restore balance and/or maintain it in the future, but it can also be a way of keeping down expenditures and controlling the size and intrusiveness of government. The additional constraints can vary from a moderate change in the budget process that makes the linkage between revenue and expenditure decisions tighter and more authoritative, to a change in statute making the requirements for balance more inclusive and more difficult to get around, to a change in the constitution narrowly specifying the conditions under which deficits may be run or forbidding deficits or borrowing to pay them off. At the national level, deficit hawks have repeatedly put forth proposals for a balanced budget amendment to the constitution.

There is no evidence that more severe constraints work better than milder ones or even informal ones. On the contrary, there is some suggestion that more severe constraints encourage unintended consequences, such as asset sales—which are often a bad deal for the public—and delayed payments to vendors. The more draconian the requirements, the more likely they are to generate responses that meet the letter rather than the spirit of the rules.[4] Illinois, for example, has a constitutional requirement for a balanced budget, but has routinely evaded the spirit of the requirement through interfund sweeps, through pushing off bills into future years, and by diverting money owed to the pension funds. In some years, the state has borrowed money to pay into the pension system.

Multiple Actors, Ideologies, and Deficits

Who gets involved in the politics of balance, and how do those actors come down on the variety of policy issues involved in budget balancing?

The public plays an indirect role by putting pressure on elected officials to balance the budget. Citizens argue that their personal budgets have to balance, and hence governmental budgets should also balance. At the same time, citizens often want something for nothing, demanding lower taxes without cuts in their services or benefits. When elected officials comply with the demand for lower taxes and more services, they create deficits; when the elected officials try to reduce or eliminate deficits, the need to give the impression of not raising taxes or cutting services leads to evasion, distortion, and erosion of transparency.

Interest groups and agency heads may contribute to deficits by making it difficult to raise specific taxes or cut particular programs. When cuts are being proposed, interest groups and agency heads may work to protect programs that benefit them. However, neither individual interest groups nor bureau chiefs typically have distinct policies toward deficits (as opposed to policies toward maintaining the programs that benefit them). The appropriate size of government and level of taxation are issues that affect the rich and the poor differently, and thus class-based coalitions often take sides in debates on budgetary balance. An alliance of labor unions may oppose a consortium of business groups.

Elected officials in both the executive and legislative branches, responding to party platforms, constituency demands, and the ebb and flow of intergovernmental revenue, are key actors in this decision stream. Courts also play a role in budget balance, by judging the legality of efforts to balance the budget and by adjudicating bankruptcies.

These actors take sides on the appropriate size of government; the role of the budget in the economy; the appropriate role of each level of government; and the outcomes—that is, whose taxes will be increased and/or whose programs will be cut, by how much, and with what effect.

The Appropriate Size of Government

Budgets can be balanced by allowing revenues to increase; by freezing revenues at current levels and cutting expenditures to match; or by reducing revenues and cutting expenditures deeply to create balance at a new, lower level of spending. Allowing revenues to increase to reduce deficits is a fiscally conservative but socially more liberal position, without major implications for current program spending. Liberals hope to increase taxes on the rich to pay for programs for the poor. Achieving budget balance by deeply cutting programs is a more politically conservative position. Some conservatives press for cuts in taxes as a way to force cuts in expenditures, using the requirement of balance as a vehicle to reduce the scope of government. They hope to reduce the tax burden on the rich and simultaneously reduce services to the poor and dismantle regulations that hamper businesses and reduce profitability.

The Role of the Budget in the Economy

Should the budget be a tool of control over the economy to dampen economic swings, to control inflation and unemployment levels? Political liberals have accepted the need for deficits during recessions because of the need to increase unemployment benefits and maintain welfare spending at the same time that government receipts decline as a result of falling incomes. Liberals are more comfortable with using government spending as a way to jump-start a stalled economy. Some conservatives oppose deficit spending as a technique to help stimulate the economy when it is weak. They prefer that the budget not be responsive to economic cycles at all and argue that expenditures should be cut back when revenues fall during recessions. Other political conservatives will tolerate deficits during recessions if the deficit is caused by tax reductions to businesses and the wealthy. They argue that this policy will increase the supply of capital and thus stimulate the economy and create jobs. Not only conservatives and liberals line up on this issue but also interest groups that represent business and labor.

The Role of Each Level of Government

Where should the burden of providing services and benefits be placed? If balancing the budget becomes a valued goal at the federal level, there may be a strong temptation to balance it at the expense of other levels of government, cutting back grants and passing on program responsibilities. The states may do the same with local governments. Cities and towns may try to give service responsibility back to the state government or to townships, counties, special districts, or the private sector. Each level of government has an interest in passing on expenditures to other levels and preventing expenditures from being passed to itself.

The Choice of Outcomes

Which functions should continue to be performed? Whose benefits and programs should be maintained or cut? The politics of balance may lightly veil a bitter politics of outcomes, with protection or termination of particular programs or benefits as the goal. Interest groups, service recipients, and agency heads may take sides on this issue to protect their programs.

These four issues summarize what many of the actors in this portion of the budgetary decision-making process are trying to achieve. Liberals are trying to maintain the scope of government, while conservatives are trying to shrink it. Working people and their representatives want the budget to be used to keep the level of employment high, while businesspeople and their representatives prefer that the budget be used to keep taxes low. Each level of government wants to balance its budget, possibly by shifting the costs of programs and the burden of taxation elsewhere. Interest groups, legislators, beneficiaries of programs, and agency heads try to protect their programs from cuts that are proposed to balance the budget.

The Environment, Unpredictability, and Deficits

Deficits occur in part because budgets are open to the environment. Deficits can occur no matter how hard public officials work to balance the budget. The courts may declare that patients cannot be committed to a mental hospital without treatment or that overcrowding of prisons is cruel and unusual punishment, so governments have to increase treatment in mental hospitals and build more prisons and hire more guards. Hurricanes, floods, blizzards, or exceptionally cold or hot weather can increase spending. Riots; explosions; killings by terrorists, ideologues, or police; and political demonstrations can all require extra staff hours, more equipment—such as cameras—improved training, or better public relations. War, with its overriding urgency, can increase expenditures without reference to current revenues.

Unexpected losses of revenue can result from courts' declaring some tax unconstitutional, which may require the restoration of the revenue to the taxpayers. The passage of tax limits can freeze or reduce revenues for state and local governments. Borrowing may become more expensive just when a government is planning to issue a bond. The costs of medical insurance or gasoline can surge unexpectedly or relentlessly. A sudden downturn in the economy can shrink revenues below expectations. At the local level, a business may close unexpectedly or move to another state, causing a decline in property tax revenue and leaving people without jobs and income, reducing sales tax revenues. Cycles of boom and bust in residential property can increase and then decrease revenues from property taxes.

The intergovernmental revenue system introduces considerable uncertainty for state and local governments. With competitive grants, the potential recipients do not know whether they will receive the money. Sometimes intergovernmental aid is set up as an entitlement, so that all cities that have an unemployment rate over a given threshold are eligible for particular kinds of aid. Those paying for the program cannot estimate its cost; those who might receive the aid do not have any way of knowing in advance whether they will be eligible. When state governments give aid to local governments in the form of entitlements, the problem is exaggerated because the state governments have to balance their own budgets. To meet unexpected increases in costs, they have to set aside contingency funds, which may be inadequate to the purpose. At times states incur obligations to their local governments that they do not have the money to fund. Local governments that included revenues from the state in their budgets have to guess how much they will receive of what they were entitled to.

A related problem with intergovernmental revenues is that when the donor-level government is in financial trouble, it may hold back the money it is supposed to give to the recipient for weeks or months, earning interest on the holdback to help with its own financial problems. Or the donor can delay payments into the next year, forcing those who planned to use the money to borrow in anticipation of receiving it later.

Some expenditures depend on the demand; the supply of the service is not determined by how much money is budgeted. The problem of demand-driven costs is particularly acute at the federal level, because so much of federal spending is now composed of open-ended entitlements. That means that if there is an increase in the number of people eligible for a given program, the money must be found to pay them, regardless of what is happening on the revenue side. Entitlements decouple revenue and expenditure decisions and hence make budgets more vulnerable to deficits.

Long and severe recessions contribute most directly to budgetary imbalance, because they simultaneously increase expenditures for unemployment relief and welfare and reduce revenues because so many people are out of work or earning less. It is politically very difficult to raise taxes when many people are unemployed and perhaps equally difficult to reduce the benefits of people who are desperate for them because they have lost their jobs. Moreover, reducing public spending to balance the budget may worsen the recession, because people have even less money to spend to keep the economy going.

The environment may also contribute to deficits when the economy of a whole region is gradually declining and with it the amount of taxable wealth. The costs of delivering programs and projects does not decrease proportionally to the tax base, because service costs may be related to lane miles of road or linear feet of water pipe, neither of which shrink with population or with loss of businesses, and because remaining population may be poorer and more in need of public services than those who leave. The result may be a long-term disequilibrium between the cost of government and the availability of revenues. Either governments must continue to raise tax rates, taking a greater and greater share of people's income, against which the public will eventually rebel, or they must continue to cut back programs and projects, potentially exaggerating the decline. In the face of such continuing negative choices, officials may run deficits.

In short, many deficits stem from changes in the environment. These changes may require more flexibility than the budget can deliver. Forbidding deficits—which is one response to them—seems futile in the face of the openness of the budget to the environment. The budget can be made less open to the environment and it can be made more flexible so that it can adapt without deficits. But the most common response seems to be to run the deficits and then worry about how to eliminate them in a timely and fair manner.

Increasing Stress Between Payer and Decider

The difficulties created by the separation of payer and decider may become acute when governments run deficits. The public wants balance, but it simultaneously wants to maintain services and programs that it likes, and it does not want to increase its tax burden. Decision makers are faced with a series of politically unacceptable choices. Citizens may argue for taxing someone else and cutting someone else's programs, but for the decision maker there may not be many legal options that satisfy those conditions.

The unpopularity of deficits, when combined with the unpleasant options available to reduce them, creates a tendency to hide or minimize deficits. The budget may lose much of its ability to provide public accountability. Balance may be redefined, the system of accounting may be changed to a cash basis to hide deficits, long-term capital borrowing may be used to cover operating deficits, expenditures may be pushed off into the next year, or funds may be borrowed between accounts inappropriately and possibly without record (with or without an intent to repay). Revenues may be overestimated or expenditures underestimated to make the budget, as passed, look more balanced than it is. The longer this hiding goes on, the more convoluted and uninformative the budget becomes.

How, then, can a deficit situation ever be fixed? A number of pressures work to reveal the extent of the problem and restore balance. For example, if there has been a lot of internal borrowing, agency heads and program beneficiaries whose funds are being borrowed may become desperate enough to complain. Second, internal borrowing may become so tangled that auditors can no longer certify the honesty and integrity of the financial records, a warning sign of trouble that may bring the situation to public attention. Third, newly elected politicians have an incentive to reveal deficits and attribute them to their predecessors. Fourth, if the amounts involved grow large enough, they necessitate public borrowing, which means turning to the financial markets for funds. Banks and other investors require evidence of sound financial practice and require higher interest rates to compensate for higher perceived risks. If the situation is sufficiently serious, the market may close completely. The more desperate a government is to borrow, the more it needs to restore its fiscal integrity to be able to do so. After a deficit is acknowledged, the difficult task of restoring balance remains. When many programs are entitlements that benefit nearly everyone and other programs have intense interest group support, it is difficult to know where and how to cut expenses while maintaining acceptability to the public.

State governments, with their requirements for annual balance, have so little time to deal with emerging deficits that borrowing to balance the present budget and paying back over a period of years may seem to be the only viable solution. That can mean borrowing internally by not funding pensions fully—in essence borrowing against the future, with the idea that the situation will improve later and funds can be restored. In that case, the problems being created are not likely to come home to roost while current elected officials are in office. States may borrow against anticipated revenue sources, such as tobacco settlement money they are due in the future but need now. Sale of assets, such as highways or privatization and issuance of long-term leases, may provide temporary infusions of cash. (See the minicase of Chicago's parking meter lease below for an example of what can go wrong in such deals and also the minicase of Iowa's privatization of Medicaid on p. 198.)

These one-time revenues cannot address a long-term structural imbalance between revenues and expenditures, but they tend to dampen the sense of urgency, lower the estimates of deficits in the short term, and hence reduce the embarrassment of running deficits and the need to make politically unpopular cuts in services or programs. In extreme cases, states have borrowed long term to cover an accumulation of short-term operating deficits. That makes the cuts more manageable and the levels of service disruption less noticeable.

Minicase: Chicago's Parking Meters

Sale or lease of assets brings in one-time revenues, but sometimes these deals go awry. The case of Chicago's parking meters is a good illustration of what not to do and how not to do it. In 2008, Mayor Daley leased thirty-six thousand parking meters to a private consortium for $1.2 billion for seventy-five years, giving up that revenue stream. The city's inspector general argued it was worth much more than the city got. As soon as the consortium had control of the meters, it jerked up parking costs, as much as fourfold, to the highest in the nation. Under the terms of the lease, the city owed the

(Continued)

(Continued)

consortium money each year for any meters the city took out of commission for any purpose, such as road repair. According to the mayor, a later revision made the contract a little less bad for the city, though his claim was disputed. The city's inspector general reported that the city had not done its homework on the finances of the parking meter deal to fill a budget deficit in 2009 and had not sufficiently examined alternatives.

Minicase: Iowa's Privatization of Medicaid

Not all privatization deals are fiscally unfortunate, but estimating savings can be tricky. Advocates of privatization can be tempted to exaggerate the potential savings, and companies can be tempted to lowball to get the contract and later increase the costs. Opponents assume that reductions in cost mean reduction in the quality of services provided.

When the Iowa governor privatized the management of its Medicaid program, turning the program completely into managed care, the state department of human services estimated a savings of $51 million in the first six months, an estimate that legislators used when passing the budget. When legislators asked for the documentation to support the estimate, the department could not offer any. The most benign interpretation is that having come up with the estimate, they then discarded any documentation; a less kind interpretation is that the figure came from unidentified experts offering a wide range of possible outcomes. Since the governor was pushing the privatization proposal, staff may have chosen from that range a figure that would justify the governor's decision.

The uncertainty reportedly was not conveyed to the legislators. The savings predicted may not materialize. Privatization may look like a good way to balance the budget, but it can present major managerial and ethical problems. The first sign of trouble occurred when an administrative law judge recently recommended that one of the four contracts with private sector providers be thrown out, "noting that the company failed to disclose details of its 'integrity agreement' with the federal government after the 2014 convictions of three former executives involving the misuse of Medicaid money. In addition, WellCare had paid $138 million to resolve claims that it overbilled Medicare and Medicaid, and the firm had also hired two former Iowa legislators, who improperly communicated with the Branstad administration during the bidding process."[1] (See Figure 6.4 on p. 213.)

1. Dana Milbank, "Iowa's Radical Privatization of Medicaid Is Already Struggling," *Washington Post,* December 11, 2015, https://www.washingtonpost.com/opinions/iowas-radical-privatization-of-medicaid-is-already-failing/2015/12/11/58b21362-a01b-11e5-bce4-708fe33e3288_story.html.

Other sources: Jason Clayworth, "Iowa Can't Show the Math of Medicaid Savings Estimate," *The Demoines Register,* October 15, 2015, http://www.desmoinesregister.com/story/news/investigations/2015/10/14/iowa-cant-show-math-medicaid-savings-estimate/73922744/; Josh Levitt, "Branstad's Medicaid Privatization Plan is Officially a Disaster," Iowa Democratic Party press release, October 15, 2015, http://iowademocrats.org/branstads-medicaid-privatization-plan-is-officially-a-disaster/.

When cuts are necessary, one response is to make them where they are least noticeable to prevent citizen complaints. Such cuts break the visible link between taxes paid and services produced; it appears as if cuts can be made without reducing services. The model of invisible cuts encourages elected officials to keep on cutting, as there never seems to be any harm or public outcry.

Another approach is to cut across the board, to give the impression of fairness. To the extent that this strategy is employed, it prevents cutting more deeply the programs that have more waste or those whose services can be more easily dispensed with or provided by the market. It may work if the cuts are temporary but be inefficient if the problem is long term and structural. It can also be a difficult strategy to implement, as interest groups that perceive their programs are about to be cut will fight to protect them, regardless of what is happening to other programs.

A third approach is to cut the programs that have the weakest interest group support, including programs that have no powerful interest group support, such as personnel or foreign aid. A related strategy is to cut the programs of political opponents—either the ones that serve opponents' constituents or the ones into which opponents have in the past hired most of their political supporters.

Some programs are mandated by a higher level of government or may be required to be performed at a given level by the constitution or a charter provision or by the courts. In such cases, spending is cut back not where the priorities are lowest, but wherever it is legal to cut. At the state and local levels, public works programs may be most severely cut, because they have projects that are not yet committed, delaying them will save some money in the short run, and such cuts are usually permissible under law.

The four characteristics of public budgeting—constraints, variety of actors and goals, openness to the environment, and the separation of payer and decider—provide some common themes for the politics of deficits at different levels of government. Nevertheless, there are some important differences among the federal, state, and local levels that influence how each level deals with deficits when they occur.

One difference is that state and local governments are generally required to balance their budgets, if not in the current year or biennium, then in the following one. The federal government is not so constrained. When changes in the environment push up the costs of entitlement programs at the federal level, the increased costs show up as increased deficits; at the state level, the costs have to come out of a contingency fund or reduced spending for other budgeted expenses. Because state and local governments generally have to balance their budgets every year or at least in a short period of time, there may be more pressure to delay payments, push up revenue collection, or shift more program costs to local governments. States and localities sometimes build up budgetary surpluses to guard against deficits. Another product of the state and local requirement for balance is that efforts to hide deficits may be more intense.

A second difference between the levels of government is that the role of deficit spending in regulating the economy is most salient at the federal level. State governments are only marginally involved in efforts to control the economy, and local governments are generally too minor a part of the economy to control it no matter how they spend their money. State and local prohibitions on running deficits make it impossible for them to spend more during a recession, even if such spending could stimulate economic growth. A third difference has to do with overall size. At the federal level, the tremendous size of budget deficits and their chronic nature create a noisy and stubborn problem with potentially major impact on the national economy. Deficits are rarer and more tractable at state and local levels, in part because the requirements for annual or biennial balance make it more difficult (though not impossible) for large deficits to accumulate from year to year.

The Politics of Deficits: The Federal Level

Deficits were a fact of life at the federal level for many years, but they became particularly large in the late 1980s and early 1990s (see Figures 6.1 and 6.2). They were brought under control by 1998, only to grow again, to record levels, after 2001. In recent years the deficit has been coming down again. As of August 2015, the Congressional Budget Office estimated the federal deficit for fiscal year 2015 at $426 billion, compared to $1.3 trillion in 2011.

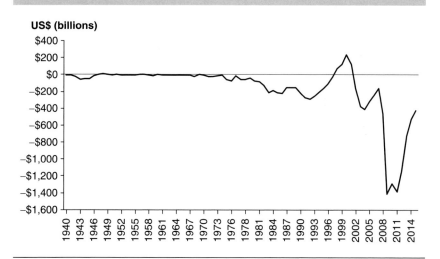

FIGURE 6.1 Federal Surplus or Deficit in Current Dollars, 1940–2015

Source: OMB, *Historical Tables*, FY 2017, Table 1–3

Note: *CBO Estimate. The CBO estimate is used for 2015 because it is updated during the year.

From the beginning of the republic to the 1930s, deficits were associated primarily with wars, and debts were paid off after the wars were over. During the Great Depression of the 1930s, politicians responded to falling revenues and the urgent need for aid for the poor by allowing deficit spending. The Depression forged a new role for the federal government to help minimize swings in the economy and the attendant social and economic distress. After the Great Depression, an economic theory, Keynesianism, emerged that argued that deficits for this purpose were not necessarily harmful and that spending during recession actually helped stimulate the economy. Deficits incurred to offset recessions and stimulate the economy are supposed to be temporary, but since the middle of the 1970s, deficits have occurred nearly continuously.

Since the 1970s, politicians who promised to eliminate deficits have often failed to do so, creating the impression that deficits were out of control. Whatever acceptance there was of moderate-sized and occasional deficits began to evaporate when the deficits became huge. In 1974 the federal government had a deficit of $6.1 billion, which was four-tenths of 1 percent of the gross national product (GNP). By 1992 the deficit had reached $290 billion—$340 billion not counting the Social Security surplus.[5]

FIGURE 6.2 Federal Surplus or Deficit as a Percentage of GDP, 1940–2015

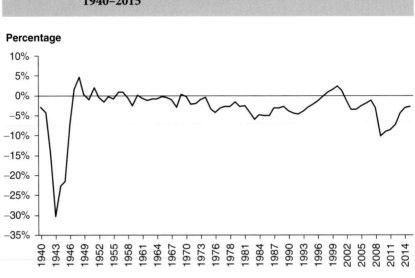

Source: OMB, *Historical Tables*, FY 2017, Table 1–2.

Note: The Congressional Budget Office estimates are somewhat lower than OMB's for deficits in dollars and also somewhat lower for estimates of the deficit as a proportion of GDP.

The Clinton administration focused on eliminating the deficit, and by 1998, the budget was more or less in balance. All that changed very quickly in the Bush presidency, for a combination of reasons. The September 11, 2001, attack on the World Trade Center and the Pentagon resulted in sharply higher costs for antiterrorist activities. The intelligence budget was $26.7 billion in 1998; it took a leap upward in 2001.[6] By 2007, the total was $63.5 billion and reached $78.6 billion by 2011.[7] Government documents leaked by Edward Snowden indicate that intelligence spending in 2013 for defense and nondefense agencies was approximately $75 billion. For 2016, the budget request was for $71.8 billion. These numbers have come down only slightly in the past few years. The costs for intelligence gathering are dwarfed by the costs of wars undertaken at least partly in response to the terrorist attacks. Depending on how inclusive the researchers have been in defining what is included in the cost of the wars, estimates vary from the Defense Department's $1.2 trillion over ten years from 2001 to 2011 to Neta Crawford's estimate of $4.4 trillion through 2014.[8] The larger estimate is for a longer period and includes obligations as well as actual outlays, including the costs of treating the injuries of veterans. Throughout the Bush administration the wars were funded by emergency supplemental appropriations, which did not require offsetting revenues or spending cuts, so war costs added directly to the deficits. In the Obama administration, the costs of the wars have been tucked into the Overseas Contingency fund, which is "off budget," does not follow any of the rules for on-budget items, and hence is not offset by revenue. As a result, war spending still adds directly to the deficit.

In addition to war and antiterrorism activities, a recession began mid-2001. Making the revenue problem more serious, the Bush administration granted two major tax reductions in 2001 and 2003. By the end of 2007, a second recession had begun; the Bush administration responded by reducing taxes again, which cost an estimated $170 billion, beginning to bail out the auto industry with loans, and working to rescue the banks. The program, called the Troubled Asset Relief Program (TARP), was signed by President Bush in October 2008.

The Obama administration took office in the midst of this recession. This one, unlike 2001, was long and deep, with widespread unemployment. His administration was marked by the continuation and expansion of the two wars, continuation of the Bush tax cuts, and the bailout of General Motors, Chrysler, and the banks. The recession, triggered by the bursting of the real estate bubble, left many banks and financial institutions in severe financial trouble; loan activity was frozen, which made the economic downturn more severe. President Obama was not happy about continuing the TARP program, but found it necessary:

> ... if there's one thing that has unified Democrats and Republicans, and everybody in between, it's that we all hated the bank bailout. I hated it. You hated it. It was about as popular as a root canal.

> But when I ran for President, I promised I wouldn't just do what was popular—I would do what was necessary. And if we had allowed the meltdown of the financial system, unemployment might be double what it is today. More businesses would certainly have closed. More homes would have surely been lost.

> So I supported the last administration's efforts to create the financial rescue program. And when we took that program over, we made it more transparent and more accountable. And as a result, the markets are now stabilized, and we've recovered most of the money we spent on the banks.[9]

The Congressional Budget Office estimated as of 2015, the costs of TARP to the public would be only about $28 billion of the $440 billion program spending, the rest of the spending had been recovered.[10]

The Republicans demanded an extension of the Bush tax cuts of 2001 and 2003, which benefited primarily the wealthy, as the price of support for Obama's request for an extension of the federal unemployment payments. To this, Obama added a cut in payroll taxes to working people as a stimulus to the economy and antirecession aid to the states, to prevent massive layoffs of teachers, police, and firefighters. The federal government also helped the states pay for Medicaid during the deepest parts of the recession. The financial assistance to the states included some funds for so-called shovel-ready projects to employ construction workers quickly.

There is no way around these numbers. In 2000, receipts from both on-budget and off-budget accounts represented 20.6 percent of GDP, while expenditures were 18.2 percent. By 2011, receipts had dropped to 15.4 percent of GDP, while expenditures had increased to 24.1 percent. The resulting deficits were not merely big; they were enormous. (See Figure 6.3 for a sense of the impact of reducing revenues and increasing expenditures.) After 2011, with spending curbs and across-the-board cuts, the winding down of the wars, and recovery of much of the TARP bailout funds, along with recovery from the recession, the deficit has roughly halved from its peak.

FIGURE 6.3   Total Federal Spending and Receipts, as a Percentage of GDP, 1930–2016

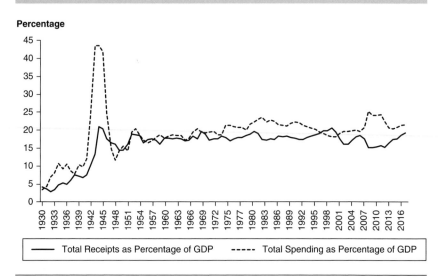

Source: Office of Management and Budget, "Budget of the U.S. Government," Fiscal Year 2016, Historical Tables, Table 1.2. https://www.whitehouse.gov/omb/budget/Historicals.

Note: Data for 2015 and 2016 are estimates.

The trends from 2001 to 2011 reflect political stalemates in which neither party could completely enforce its will on the other. While the Republicans fought for tax breaks for business and the wealthy, the Democrats fought for middle- and working-class tax relief; while the Democrats sought extension of benefits for the unemployed and jobs for public sector employees at the local level, Republicans sought to cut spending and opposed any kind of tax increase. Even though the bank and automobile bailouts were begun in a Republican administration, the expansion of government into the economy angered some on the right. To them, government ownership of shares of business looked like socialism; to the left it looked like a rescue of the economy but only for the upper classes, while the poor were being kicked out of their homes when they could not pay their mortgages. The only political agreement that seemed possible was support for further tax reductions and increased spending for the financial sector.

Republicans used the size of the deficit as a wedge to argue for cuts in spending. They refused to support an increase in the debt limit, which would have allowed the government to pay its bills, until an agreement was reached to cut back spending. Their proposals excluded tax increases, forced cuts in programs for the poor, and ended further effort to bail out the economy. They successfully insisted on the level of cuts and forged an agreement to establish a supercommittee to designate which programs' budgets would be reduced and by how much. The committee, composed of both Democrats and Republicans, failed to reach agreement, leaving the cuts to be made across the board, including defense.

Not long after the agreement was reached, Republicans backed off from it, demanding deeper cuts in other programs and exemptions from cuts to Department of Defense spending. The original agreement involved cuts of $1.2 trillion over ten years, but with the failure of the supercommittee to agree on tax increases or spending cuts, the fallback position was invoked, across-the-board cuts of more than $1 trillion, including defense, but exempting the neediest. Confronted with half a trillion dollars in cuts to defense, Democrats wanted to soften the cuts with some tax increases; Republicans refused to consider them. Instead, House Republicans proposed to reduce defense cuts by cutting food stamps, Medicaid, and other social programs. "The Congressional Budget Office estimated that the bill would push 1.8 million people off food stamps and could cost 280,000 children their school lunch subsidies and 300,000 children their health insurance coverage through the federal and state Children's Health Insurance Program. Elimination of the social services block grant to state and local governments would hit child abuse prevention programs, Meals on Wheels and child care."[11] This proposal seemed less aimed at reducing the deficit than shifting cuts from defense to social services.

Some Republicans wanted a guarantee that a balanced budget amendment to the Constitution would pass Congress before they would support an increase in the debt ceiling. They did not get that guarantee, but the balanced budget amendment did reach the floor of both the Senate and the House of Representatives. The House failed to get the necessary two-thirds majority to pass a constitutional amendment in November of 2011. Both a Democratic and Republican version of the balanced budget amendment failed in the Senate in December of 2011. While these proposals failed, they illustrate the renewed effort to come up with a budget process that would tie the hands of Congress, which would somehow force balance and discipline or would force the cuts in spending that some preferred. Sen. Orin Hatch from Utah, who sponsored the Republican version, argued, "Congress will not kick its overspending addiction alone, but only if required to do so by the Constitution itself."[12] The wording of one of the proposals was suggestive, in that it required a supermajority vote to raise taxes or allow spending to exceed 18 percent of GDP. Spending hadn't been that low as a percentage of the economy since 1966.[13] The balanced budget amendment thus may have been more about achieving a smaller government and keeping taxes low than about balancing the budget.

As discussed earlier, the solution to the controversy over whether the across-the-board cuts would include the Defense Department was shifting war costs into the Overseas Contingency Operations account, which was "off budget" and hence did not come under the requirement for across-the-board cuts. Some of the regular Defense Department expenditures were also shifted into the fund making the DoD base budget look smaller.

The Politics of Deficits: States

When they are facing deficits, the states, like the federal government, have to decide whether and how much to raise revenues or cut expenditures, with similar implications for the scope of government. Just as at the federal level, there are problems of defining what constitutes a deficit and of measuring the size and importance of deficits. Just as the federal government has to decide how much of a financial burden it can shift to the states or the private sector, states have to decide how much expense to absorb from or pass on to local governments and how much service burden they can unload on them. But the requirement of annual (or biennial) balance in the states creates some differences from the national government.

States are especially stressed by recessions that increase the cost of entitlements while simultaneously decreasing revenues. If only the states could put off rebalancing until the recession was over and the economy had recovered, they might avoid deep cuts, but state laws do not permit deficits to run for several years. It takes time and political risk to raise revenues; the short time line for states to achieve annual or biennial balance means they have to make deep cuts, sometimes even multiple times in a single year, to balance their budgets. In an effort to minimize the need for such gap closings, the states have often relied on more-or-less legal, if not always fiscally conservative, methods to tide themselves over until the economy improves. When confronted with high deficits, many states do some cutting but also some temporizing. They frequently use budget gimmicks of various sorts to prevent deeper cuts in programs and staffing, hoping that if they put the tough decisions off into the future, the economy will recover and balance will be easier to achieve later. Many states borrow; they draw down whatever reserves they may have in rainy-day funds; they delay or suspend payments to local governments and to vendors. Some states move paydays, delay tax refunds, speed up fee collections, or sell buildings and lease them back. Several states have engaged in a kind of arbitrage, borrowing money in the government market where interest is relatively low, giving the proceeds to the pension funds that invest in the private sector at higher rates of return. The pension funds are expected to pay back the loans and make some money in the process, lowering the amount the state has to contribute to the pensions.

States wrestling with balanced budget requirements sometimes use budget gimmicks to not only react to deficits but to obscure or minimize them. If the deficit is small or defined away, they will not have to raise taxes or cut services, both of which are politically unpopular. For example, Rep. David Obey, D-Wis., reported a number of years ago, "I come from a state with a balanced budget requirement. In the six years that I served in the legislature, Wisconsin's indebtedness doubled, because they engaged in all kinds of phony-baloney devices, off-budget accounting, dummy building corporations, all the rest, that simply defined out of the budget all kinds of spending that was really governmental."[14]

Another gimmick to make a budget look balanced is to accelerate tax collections, which produces a one-time windfall for the state. For example, if a state changes from a quarterly to a monthly collection schedule, it can collect fifteen months' revenues in twelve months. On a quarterly basis, it could collect taxes the first of the year for the preceding three months; the second payment would be at month three for the preceding three months; the third payment would be at month six for the preceding three months; and the final payment for the year would be at month nine for the preceding three months. But if the state goes to monthly collections at that point, it can collect the taxes for months ten, eleven, and twelve, for which it would normally have to wait until the next fiscal year.[15]

A similar gimmick is to put off some expenditures into the next fiscal year. That increases the next year's expenditures, but by then the recession may have ended so that increased revenues will cover the extra expenditures. A way to push expenditures into the following year is to change the basis of accounting from modified accrual to cash. Under cash accounting, expenditures that are incurred this year but not paid until next year are officially counted as next year's expenditures. Under accrual accounting, they would be counted as part of this year's expenditures.

In Illinois, the governor changed the accounting system from modified accrual to cash in 1978, making the budget look more balanced that year.[16] In addition, the cash budget changed the definition of a deficit. A cash budget measures deficits by looking at the available cash balance at the end of the year rather than matching revenues and expenditures during the year. The available cash balance is eminently suited for manipulation: Any cash on hand goes into the available balance, even if it is a loan. The available balance is also affected by speedups in revenue collections, delays in paying vendors, and manipulating the timing of drawdowns of federal funds. "When an administration commits itself to a specific end of year available balance, it can manipulate the revenue processing system to bring about an available balance consistent with its prediction."[17] Perhaps most important, the cash balance is always positive and hence makes it look as if the state is running a surplus, even when it is running a deficit.

Budget gimmicks reduce the amount of spending cuts or the size of tax increases that might otherwise be necessary, helping elected officials avoid hard political choices that make enemies. These techniques are not necessarily bad; it makes sense to avoid deep cuts and expensive restructuring to eliminate a deficit that will disappear on its own as the economy recovers. They can be harmful if they go on too long and allow huge buildups of unpaid obligations; moreover, they obscure the true financial picture, reducing accountability.

One of the more constructive responses that many states have adopted is to create and expand rainy-day funds, to be used when the economy falters and revenues decline below expectations. In the ideal case, money is put into these funds during years when revenues are growing and drawn down during recessions when revenue falls. Funds that are depleted during recessions have to be replenished over the next few years. Such funds, if they are big enough, can help prevent the need for midyear cuts. Some states are more successful than others at building and using rainy-day funds. The funds are often too small to function as intended or have to be repaid before the economy and revenues recover.

When midyear cuts are necessary, it is often the governor who has to make the cuts; in some states governors can do this on their own initiative, in others, proposed cuts must be approved by the legislators. While legislators have not been eager to do the rebalancing themselves, they have not always been eager to give the governor unlimited power to change the priorities in the budget mid-year. Fifteen states give the governor unlimited authority to cut the budget during the year.[18] It is more common for legislators to give the governor limited authority to cut back the budget, either across the board—that is, without changing legislative priorities—or up to a given percentage without legislative approval.[19] Governors are thus expected to help balance the budget during the year and are often granted considerable discretion in doing so. But if more action is required that might seriously change legislative spending priorities, the governor generally has to come back to the legislature for approval.

Although there are sometimes controversies over whose programs will be cut, the states do not have enormous flexibility in what will be cut back. When budget cuts are necessary, the discretionary portion of state budgets is cut first, such as highways, education, police, prisons, courts, and shared revenue or grants to the local governments. Other spending may be mandated by law.

Even within the so-called discretionary budget, there may be limited discretion. For example, Proposition 4 in 1979 in California limited appropriations growth to the percentage increase in the cost of living and the percentage increase in the state or local government's population. In reaction, citizens passed Proposition 98 in 1988, which requires a minimum of 40 percent of California's general fund to be spent on education. Similarly, Colorado's TABOR amendment caused serious budget cuts year after year, including in K–12 education funding. In response, citizens passed a referendum ensuring funding for those schools. The result was that higher education was nearly the only expenditure left that could be cut. State universities' budgets were sharply reduced. It is partly this lack of options that makes it so tempting for states to pass along costs to the local governments or take local revenues to pay state bills.

Passing the Buck to Local Governments

Because local governments are subordinate to the states and have to take orders from state governments, the states can decide to pass the burden of paying for programs and projects onto their local governments. That is, the state can command the local governments to perform a particular service at a higher level or in a different manner than before, without giving the local governments the money to pay for the new requirements. The states can also claim local revenues. A third possibility is for the states to balance their budgets by cutting financial aid to local governments, even if that aid was a replacement for revenues the state took away from them.

Each of these three strategies has the possibility of aggravating the financial condition of the local governments. Because the states are ultimately responsible for the fiscal health of the local governments, they have an interest in not squeezing them too hard, but at the same time, the states have to balance their budgets each year or biennium and have few choices about what to cut. Therefore, state officials may adopt any or all three of these strategies, if they have no rainy-day fund, if they have an inadequate one, or if they decide not to use the one they have. Some states give in to the temptation to balance their budget on the backs of the local governments.

State Unfunded Mandates. States may help balance their budgets by passing along expenditures to the local governments that the state would normally pay for. These burdens can make it more difficult for local governments to balance their budgets. In 1996, the citizens of Oregon passed a constitutional amendment prohibiting the state from imposing unfunded mandates on the local governments. What made this measure urgent was that the local governments were confronting rigid statewide limits on their ability to raise taxes. The provision required public reaffirmation of the amendment in four years: It was enthusiastically renewed.

In 1996 twenty-eight states had some type of mandate restraint program established by constitutional provision, statute, or both. Of the twenty-eight states, seventeen provided for the reimbursement of all mandates; nine provided reimbursement of selected mandates. The extent of reimbursement could be full, partial, or a combination. By 2007, thirty-five states had either a constitutional or statutory provision to require reimbursement of some sort for state mandates.[20]

States have generally found it difficult to abide by limitations on their ability to pass costs along to their local jurisdictions, but such laws or constitutional provisions do seem to help local governments fight back, despite the disproportionate power of the state compared to the localities. For example, in Washington state, the local governments won a number of lawsuits brought against the state to recover costs the state had mandated.[21] However, laws barring unfunded mandates overestimate local government's ability to resist state imposition of costs, since the statutory provisions may be overlooked in practice. Even a constitutional amendment may be circumvented. When a state is in financial trouble, it often finds a way to avoid paying for mandates.

In California, a constitutional amendment required the state to fund mandates on the local governments, but when the state didn't have the money, it merely postponed the payments. In 2004, Proposition 1-A required the state to either pay for mandates or suspend or terminate them, but money owed from before 2004 could be paid out over time. The response of the state has been to annually suspend the mandates, making compliance optional for the year, and making state payment unnecessary. Since the mandated activities are in some cases required by the federal government, are still in the statute books, may be reinvoked in any future budget, and may be built into curricula and processes already, schools and local governments cannot easily suspend many of these activities. As a result, they simply lose the reimbursements for the activities that they were formerly mandated to perform. As of the 2012 budget, the state still owed over $1 billion in backlogged mandate compensation, no provision for any payment on the backlog was included in the budget, and over fifty mandates had been suspended, many for over a decade.[22]

Once a mandate has been suspended, the state is not only freed from the obligation to compensate the local governments for compliance, it is also freed from paying for the costs of the mandate before the suspension. Hence the state department of finance annually scrutinizes the list of mandates and suspends as many as possible. In addition to the suspension of mandates and reimbursements, the state manages to avoid the requirement for reimbursement entirely for mandates for which the local governments can raise fees, such as in solid waste and recycling.[23]

State Tax Grabs. States can also help balance their budgets at the expense of the local governments by taking over local government tax revenue. The state may take over a local source of revenue or require the local governments to remit money to the state. When California ran into fiscal difficulties, it took more than $40 billion from local government revenues over twelve years. Initially the state took property taxes that were going to the local governments and gave them instead to the schools and community colleges, thereby reducing its own expenditures on education. Then after September 11th, 2001, when the state's financial position worsened, the state reneged on replacing revenues lost through a reduction in the car tax. The state then delayed payments on mandated expenditures, leaving the local governments to find whatever money they could to fulfill the state requirements. Collectively, these losses aggravated financial problems at the local level, in some cases causing or at least contributing to staffing reductions in police and fire departments.

The local governments in response proposed a constitutional amendment to restrict the state's revenue grabs. Eventually a compromise was worked out in which the state promised to stop taking the local governments' revenues but retained some leeway in case of severe fiscal exigency. The amendment "prohibits the Legislature from taking car taxes, local property tax money and sales-tax money from local governments unless the governor first declares a fiscal emergency and two-thirds of legislators agree. Even then, the money must be paid back in full within three years."[24] In addition, the measure requires the state to pay back the costs of mandates for which it had not paid the local governments for several years, and it allows the local governments to decide not to comply with future unfunded mandates if they cannot afford to pay for them or disagree on their importance. The amendment protecting local government revenues had wide bipartisan support and passed easily in November 2004.

Despite the 2004 amendment, in 2009, the state legislature took about $5 billion from local government funds. In response, in 2010, an alliance of local government groups put an initiative on the ballot to prevent the state from taking local government revenues for public safety and transportation. The measure passed 60.7 percent to 39.3 percent. These included gas taxes as well as locally imposed hotel taxes, parcel, utility, and sales taxes, earmarked for public safety and transportation.[25]

Cutting State Aid to Local Governments. The temptation to cut reimbursements and shared revenue can be overwhelming when a state runs into fiscal difficulty or if the state's policy makers want to reduce taxes or keep them low and need to find a place to cut to balance the budget.

Many states cut their local aid during the Great Recession; some failed to fully restore that funding after the recession, even when there were budget surpluses and even when cities, such as Detroit, were in severe fiscal stress. For example, after accounting for inflation, thirty states were still funding locally provided public education in 2014 through 2015 at levels lower than before the recession hit.[26]

In Wisconsin, between the 2005 through 2007 budget and the proposed 2013 through 2015 budget, state spending on direct aid payments to counties and municipalities dropped by 17 percent in inflation-adjusted dollars.[27] In 2015, years after the end of the last recession, state aid was still lower than it had been in 2002.

Ohio reduced its local government funding by $1.5 billion between 2010 and 2015. The estate tax, which funded local governments, was eliminated; the state eliminated local taxes and failed to replace them with promised state revenues; property tax relief was curtailed; and the local government fund was cut back.[28] Between 2003 and 2011, Minnesota's aid to local governments dropped 24 percent in nominal terms—inflation correction indicates about a 50 percent reduction.[29] (See Figure 6.4 on p. 213.)

FIGURE 6.4 Minnesota's History of Funding Local Governments, in Constant Dollars per Capita, 1972–2014

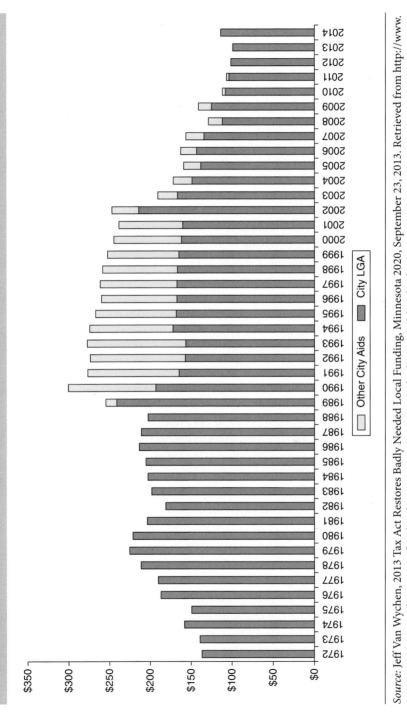

Source: Jeff Van Wychen, 2013 Tax Act Restores Badly Needed Local Funding, Minnesota 2020, September 23, 2013. Retrieved from http://www.mn2020.0rg/issues-that-matter/fiscal-policy/2013-tax-act-restores-badly-needed-lga-funding.

Note: Figure 6.4 shows what happened to state aid to local governments in Minnesota from 1972 to 2014.

A report on Minnesota critiqued the administration of its state aid program, saying,

> Most of the state's financial woes since 2002 have not been resolved by increasing state taxes or by cutting state government expenditures, but by shifting the problem on to local governments through cuts in state aid. From 2002 to 2008 per pupil state aid to Minnesota school districts has declined by 13.4 percent, while per capita state aid to Minnesota cities and counties has declined by 36.7 percent and 31.3 percent respectively after adjusting for inflation in government purchases.[30]

This reduction in state aid to local governments in Minnesota occurred while the state was shifting significant service mandates to the local governments. Governor Dayton, a Democrat who took office in 2011, has partly restored the local government funding, but as of 2015, funding was still noticeably below the level in 2002.[31] In 2015, Republicans in the legislature were working to reduce funding to particular cities.

For Michigan, from 2002 to 2013, state revenue sharing dollars dropped from over 900 million annually to around 250 million. The Michigan Municipal League estimated the cumulative total revenue losses at over $6 billion. The revenue sharing losses were usually accompanied by reduction or elimination of local revenue sources, for which the state was supposed to compensate the local governments but had failed to do so.[32] Detroit, which filed for bankruptcy, lost over $732 million between 2002 and 2013 from the state reductions.[33]

New York State has had a program of state aid to local governments intended to reduce local property taxes called AIM (Aid and Incentives for Municipalities). Funding for local governments in the AIM program outside New York City grew from $578.6 million in 2004 to $1078.2 million in 2010. Funding dropped to $714.7 million by 2012 and stayed there through 2015.[34]

Maryland increased its aid to local governments from 2002 to 2008, which was a period between recessions. From 2008 to 2014, it decreased aid, with local health departments and cities and counties the biggest losers. See Table 6.1 on p. 215 for the details.

In Maryland, the steep drops during the great recession have not been completely reversed since the recession ended. Aid to counties and municipalities dropped from a high of $904.6 million in 2008 to a low of $380.6 million in 2011. There was some increase after that, but funding is still well below the levels of a decade earlier. Aid to counties and municipalities dropped 5 percent in 2008, 18.6 percent in 2009, and a whopping 46 percent in 2010. The year 2011 saw a further drop of 4.2 percent. Aid increased 38.4 percent from 2010 to 2015, but that increase has not been enough to compensate for earlier losses: From 2008 to

TABLE 6.1   **Average Annual Increase/Decrease in State Aid to Local Governments: 2002–2008 Versus 2008–2014, Maryland**

	2002–2008	*2008–2014*
Public Schools	10.3%	2.1%
Libraries	5.9%	−0.7%
Community Colleges	4.8%	1.7%
Local Health Departments	2.6%	−8.2%
Counties/Municipalities	4.1%	−8.7%
Retirement Payments	9.5%	7.2%
Total State Aid	8.8%	1.3%

Source: Overview of State Aid to Local Governments Fiscal 2015 Allowance, Department of Legislative Services Office of Policy Analysis, Annapolis, MD, January 2014, p. 4, http://dls.state.md.us/data/polanasubare/polanasubare_ intmatnpubadm/polanasubare_intmatnpubadm_staaidrep/Overview-of-State -Aid-to-Local-Governments.pdf

2015, the annual average change in state aid for counties and municipalities has been a negative 6.9 percent.[35]

Pressure Cooker

In the recession beginning in late 2007 and during its aftermath while the state economies were still weak, state aid to local governments, including to public schools, was often deeply cut; the resulting stress on the local governments was offset by federal aid for two years, but by the end of 2011, that assistance had ended. On the local level, financial problems typically develop more slowly than at the state level, because local governments are less dependent than the states on income taxes (which drop quickly during a recession) and more dependent on property taxes, which tend to be more stable. But the recession that began in December 2007 was caused by the bursting of a housing bubble, which means that real estate prices fell, reducing local government revenue from property taxes. With sales taxes also depressed by the recession, local governments experienced sharper revenue declines than normal in a recession.

Sometimes reductions in aid came simultaneously with a shift of responsibilities to the local governments. For example, North Carolina diverted portions of the education lottery—earmarked for local schools—to the state's general fund. The legislature cut out funding for new school buses in 2013, forcing costs onto local governments; afterward, the state increased the number of miles a school bus could drive before it had to be replaced by the state from 200,000 to 250,000. The state has to replace fewer buses, but with more, older buses on the road, repair costs inevitably increase. The state pays a given amount for maintenance, but if a school district runs over that ceiling for maintenance costs, it has to pick up the excess.

California, mandated by the courts to reduce prison overcrowding, devolved responsibility for low level offenders to the county jails in 2011, providing funding for the newly decentralized function. Local governments were naturally anxious that the state continue to provide the resources for this new responsibility, especially in light of the state history of revenue grabs. AB 109 provided a permanent source of funding—a vehicle license fee and a portion of the sales tax. In 2012, Proposition 30 was passed by the voters, to make constitutional the dedicated sources of revenue the 2011 legislation provided. Nevertheless, it is not clear that the dedicated revenue sources—1.0625 percent of the sales tax and $12 of the $25 vehicle license fee—will be sufficient to cover program costs. If recession reduces state sales tax revenues, money for the program may become inadequate.

Some states, in an effort to help their local governments weather the financial storm, have granted local governments new or expanded taxing powers. For example, in Massachusetts, in the 2010 budget, the legislature allowed the local governments to raise a tax of .75 percent on restaurant meals. But in other states, no new taxes were permitted, and increases in existing taxes were prohibited or curtailed, making the problems more rather than less severe.

When the local governments were simultaneously confronted with reduced property tax revenues, reductions in state aid, and the end of federal assistance, they had few options. They could cut staffing and services, raise taxes, or get the state to ease up on unfunded mandates, allowing the local governments more flexibility in how to carry out their responsibilities less expensively. Raising taxes was politically difficult and sometimes legally impossible, and getting more money from the state seemed like a nonstarter. Being responsible for the health and safety of their respective residents, there was only so far they could cut staffing and programs and still carry out their responsibilities. As a consequence, across the country, the local governments argued for more flexibility, to become more efficient at delivering services.

A number of states are reviewing and some have revised state mandates on local governments. For example, Texas passed a comprehensive mandate relief measure that allows school districts to furlough teachers, reduces contract termination notification and minimum salary requirements, and expands the Texas Education Agency's authority to grant waivers for the 22:1 student-teacher classroom ratio.[36]

Ohio also passed an education mandate relief bill, with a somewhat different slant:

> The legislation . . . lifts the unfunded mandate requiring schools to offer all-day kindergarten and places the authority to charge tuition for all-day kindergarten back in the hands of most districts. Other provisions include the elimination of the requirement that school districts set aside a specified amount per pupil into a textbook and materials fund, and ending a policy requiring school districts to establish family and civic engagement teams.[37]

In New York State, an extensive effort was made to review mandates and include recommendations from local officials. Legislation passed in 2011 was estimated to save about $125 million a year, but many of the serious recommendations from the special commission, called the redesign team, were not adopted by the legislature. The proposals that passed included reduction in paperwork requirements and permission for local governments to piggyback on federally approved vendor lists and contracts. Local governments were permitted to use their own labor on small contracts, and statutory salary requirements for police chiefs were eliminated. Some of the micromanagement by the state was eased, requirements for reporting reduced in frequency, and small school districts were permitted to share a superintendent. While these adjustments are clearly in the right direction for local governments, they are not earthshaking. Among rejected proposals were a constitutional amendment to prevent the passage of additional unfunded mandates and a provision that would have allowed local governments to ask for a waiver from mandates.[38] In 2012 Governor Cuomo's mandate relief council turned down fifty-one out of sixty-five requests for relief; the following year the council received only four requests and acted on only one of them. Created in 2011 to hear local government grievances, by the end of 2014, it closed up shop.

When states are unable or unwilling to prevent or alleviate the fiscal stress of their local governments, they find themselves responsible for their local governments' financial problems. Some states have laws allowing them to impose a kind of receivership on local governments, in which the state government chooses a financial manager who may exert extraordinary decision-making power over the local government's finances. In Michigan, a new law was passed in 2012, called the Local Financial Stability and Choice Act. By 2015, six struggling cities were in state receivership; in addition, Detroit had had a state appointed financial manager, who endorsed bankruptcy for the city. In Pennsylvania, the state took control over the finances of twenty-seven cities, including the cities of Harrisburg,

Scranton, and Reading. A separate oversight board was created to deal with Philadelphia's financial problems.[39]

Some states permit their local governments to declare bankruptcy under federal law. Under Chapter 9 of the federal bankruptcy law, local governments can gain some protection from their creditors while they reorganize and work to improve their finances. Twelve states grant local governments unlimited authority to declare bankruptcy; fifteen states impose conditions on declaring bankruptcy or offer municipal bankruptcy to some jurisdictions. In these states, the local government in fiscal trouble may have to get permission from the state to declare bankruptcy under federal law—permission which may not be granted. Twenty-two states have no law enabling local governments to use the federal bankruptcy provisions, while one state (Georgia) has a prohibition.[40]

Under federal bankruptcy law:

> To establish insolvency, a judge must determine that the municipality cannot use its reserves, reduce expenditures, raise taxes, borrow, or postpone debt payments to pay its obligations to creditors. In a Chapter 9 case, a bankruptcy court is prohibited from interfering with the municipality's property, revenues, or political or governmental powers. Consequently, the court may not require the municipality to sell property, raise taxes, or remove officials from office. However, a municipality's unreasonable failure to exercise its taxing powers could violate its duty to act in good faith— disqualifying the municipality from bankruptcy protection.[41]

With the consent of two-thirds of the creditors, when a local government declares bankruptcy, a court may impose a plan that will have the impact of changing prior agreements and contracts. Creditors may get some proportion of what is owed to them, retirees may have their pensions or health care coverage reduced, or wages and benefits for current employees may be cut.

When a state takes over the finances of a local government through the appointment of an emergency financial manager rather than allowing bankruptcy, the local elected officials may lose autonomy. A city may be forced to sell property to pay bills, to raise fees, or to meet some obligations while retreating on others. Given the differences between what an emergency financial manager can do and what a bankruptcy judge can do, the decision between state control and bankruptcy is likely to be controversial.

States had been limited in how much fiscal stress they could impose on local governments to ease their own financial burdens, because they are ultimately responsible for the fiscal condition of the local governments in their boundaries. But recently an escape hatch seems to have opened—bankruptcy. Municipal bankruptcies historically have been rare in the United States, but there has been an increase in the last few years. The list includes Vallejo, Stockton, and San Bernardino in California; Jefferson County, Alabama; and Detroit, Michigan.

Detroit's bankruptcy in 2013 has been the largest to date. The case of Detroit involved some poor decisions by the city, cuts in state aid, a takeover by the state, and finally adjudication by a federal bankruptcy judge. (See the minicase "Detroit Bankruptcy" below.)

Minicase: Detroit Bankruptcy

The underlying cause of Detroit's financial problems was a long-term erosion of its tax base, especially the failure of the auto industry in which both General Motors and Chrysler eventually declared bankruptcy. With the erosion of its industrial base came a loss of jobs and population. Then a deep recession worsened the city's revenues. Michigan's policy of cutting back on aid to local governments made the revenue problem worse. The end of federal antirecession assistance also played into the financial difficulties of the city. Inadequate revenue forced layoffs that reduced contributions to the pension funds at the same time that the recession reduced the value of existing pension holdings, increasing the amount of money the city owed to the pensions.

A city in financial trouble sometimes adopts complicated, risky, and possibly illegal strategies. Banks, investment houses, and financial advisers eager to make some money sell such schemes to anxious city officials. When these strategies go sour, the city is left with unsupportable levels of debt. Such problematic arrangements featured in Detroit's story.

In 2005, Detroit workers successfully sued to force the city to contribute what it owed to their pension fund. With no money to pay for the court settlement, the mayor wanted to borrow money to put into the pensions. However, the city had already reached its state-mandated debt limit, making ordinary borrowing impossible.

Financial advisers and bankers helped the city work out a plan to get around this limit. The city created two service corporations—spinoff organizations from the city with independent borrowing power—whose sole function was to borrow money on the city's behalf. To encourage and protect potential investors, the city agreed to a variable interest rate on much of the borrowed sum. If interest rates rose, the city would have to pay a higher rate of interest on much of the $1.4 billion it was borrowing. Encouraged by the banks and financial advisers, the city then swapped the variable rate loans for

(Continued)

(Continued)

fixed rate loans at 6 percent, as a guarantee against a rising rate. But then, instead of rising, the interest rates fell, leaving the city with an expensive fixed rate of interest instead of the less expensive variable one. The banks with whom the city was dealing required a very high penalty fee to cancel the contract. In 2009, when the city's credit rating was downgraded, violating the terms of the swap agreement, the city restructured the agreement to reduce the risk to the banks of the city's default, depositing its revenue from casinos directly into an escrow fund from which the banks could draw money if the city defaulted. Later, when the city defaulted on its payments, the banks took the city's casino revenues.

In March 2013, Governor Snyder appointed Kevyn Orr from the law firm Jones Day to be the city's emergency financial manager. Jones Day represented both the city and the state in the bankruptcy proceedings. Orr had broad authority to change the city's budget, renegotiate or void union contracts, sell city assets, privatize services, and deal with creditors on the city's behalf. Under Michigan law, a city can declare bankruptcy only if that course is recommended by the state-appointed emergency financial manager.

Orr rejected the possibility of getting out of some of the city's obligations on the ground that those obligations had been illegal. He argued that the chance of success in court was only 50–50, and the city didn't have time for a lengthy court proceeding. As an expert in bankruptcy law, he undoubtedly knew that interest swaps and other derivatives get favorable treatment in federal bankruptcy proceedings.

Orr began negotiations with the city's creditors. Offering only pennies on the dollar to obligations that he determined were not secured, not surprisingly, he was unable to get all the parties to agree voluntarily to his proposals. Failing to get such agreement, he petitioned for bankruptcy for the city. He wanted to change the pension system to a defined contribution rather than a defined benefit plan, which puts much more risk on the employee instead of the employer, he advocated deep cuts in employee health care, he proposed deep pension cuts as a way of forcing labor concessions and recommended only modest reductions in the amounts owed to the banks holding the interest swaps. While he was managing the city's finances, he skipped the city's contributions to the pension funds, while maintaining payments on outstanding bonds and the interest rate swaps and continuing to pay "certain important" vendors.[1] Orr had exaggerated both the extent of the pension's underfunding—as a result of borrowing, the pension was reasonably well funded—and had also exaggerated the relative importance of the pension and health insurance obligations compared to other obligations of the city.

The bankruptcy judge ruled that Detroit was eligible for bankruptcy and that pensions could be reduced despite the state constitutional prohibition on reducing pensions. However, he rejected Orr's proposal for how much the banks should be given to terminate the interest rate swaps and consequently how much of the city's casino revenue could be recovered and used to reduce future borrowing and help restore city services. Orr's first proposal to the bankruptcy court was to pay 80 percent of what was owed to the banks holding the interest rate swaps; when that was rejected, he proposed 60 percent. When the judge rejected this proposal as well, Orr and the banks agreed to a 30 percent settlement. The final deal approved by the bankruptcy judge also cut the pensions considerably less than Orr's original proposal.

The governor generally kept a low profile while this was going on, but with his backing, the state did eventually contribute some money to prevent creditors from forcing the sale of art in the city's museum and to reduce the impact of cuts on retiree pensions. Despite this late-stage support, the *Washington Post* argued that Governor Snyder had "pushed Detroit into bankruptcy."[2] *The New York Times* similarly noted that "Gov. Rick Snyder of Michigan on Friday defended his decision to force Detroit into bankruptcy as a necessary step to halt its decades-long decline and resolve its spiraling debt crisis."[3]

The Jones Day lawyers who represented both the state and Detroit in bankruptcy proceedings believed that bankruptcy was the only way to solve Detroit's problems and that the emergency financial manager could not possibly come to voluntary agreements with all the creditors and thus avoid bankruptcy. They expressed that opinion in emails before one of their own, Kevyn Orr, was appointed as the emergency financial manager. They felt that the purpose of the emergency financial manager was to check off the boxes and make it look as if all possible alternatives had been exhausted, thus making Detroit eligible for bankruptcy.[4] It thus appears that the governor, the law firm representing the city and the state, and the emergency financial manager all felt that Detroit had to declare bankruptcy. One likely reason was so that the pensions could be cut, bypassing constitutional guarantees for pensions.

It is possible that there was no realistic alternative for Detroit besides bankruptcy, even if every possible alternative had been tried and failed, but forcing the city into bankruptcy seemed predetermined, other rescue options were not seriously discussed. Some states prefer to avoid bankruptcy for their cities, because they can exert more control over the outcomes with an emergency manager and because bankruptcy in one jurisdiction has a contamination effect of hurting others in the state, but if there is a constitutional

(Continued)

(Continued)

protection preventing reductions in pensions, bankruptcy may seem like a good way to get around the constitution and reduce pensions. At the same time, federal bankruptcy law protects payments for various derivatives, such as interest rate swaps. If the goal was to cut worker and retiree pensions and protect the banks, bankruptcy was a reasonable tactic. The bankruptcy judge just didn't go along to the extent that the state's appointed financial manager proposed. There is always that risk with a bankruptcy proceeding.

1. The quotation marks are in the original Reuters article. "Property Taxes, Skipped Pension Payments Boost Detroit's Cashflow," Oct 16, 2013, *Reuters,* http://www .reuters.com/article/2013/10/16/usa-detroit-quarterly-idUSL1N0I62I620131016.
2. Michael Fletcher, "Gov. Rick Snyder Could Be the Country's Most Unusual Republican. Can he save Detroit?" *Washington Post,* June 13, 2014, http://www .washingtonpost.com/business/economy/gov-rick-snyder-could-be-the -countrys-most-unusual-republican-can-he-save-detroit/2014/06/13/ccea36e8 -e7b6-11e3-afc6-a1dd9407abcf_story.html.
3. Bill Vlasic, "Michigan Judge Rules Against Bankruptcy Push," *New York Times,* July 19, 2013, http://www.nytimes.com/2013/07/20/us/breadth-of-bankruptcy -fight-detroit-faces-becoming-clear.html).
4. Alan Pyke, "Banking on Bankruptcy: Emails Suggest Negotiations With Detroit Retirees Were Designed To Fail," July 23, 2013, Thinkprogress.com, http:// thinkprogress.org/economy/2013/07/23/2342511/banking-on-bankruptcy -emails-suggest-negotiations-with-detroit-retirees-were-designed-to-fail/).

A key element in the Detroit fiscal meltdown was the complex financial arrangements the city made with the banks to pay for the pension underfunding. Complex financial dealings that looked too good to be true were also part of Jefferson County, Alabama's bankruptcy case. (See the minicase on Jefferson county on p. 223 for details what happened in Jefferson County.) The state's role was critical in both Alabama and Michigan. Not only did both states have to decide whether the state was willing to bail out its ailing local governments, providing new revenue sources or substituting its own credit rating for that of the failing local government, enabling it to borrow, but both states had to decide whether to allow or prevent their local governments from declaring bankruptcy. Also, in both Jefferson County and Detroit, the courts played an important role. In Detroit, a court ruled that the city had to pay what it owed into its pensions, and later the bankruptcy judge ruled that worker pensions could be cut despite a constitutional guarantee; in Jefferson County, a court ruled that the county had to fix a leaking sewer system, and a judge ruled that new revenue sources were illegal. While theoretically the outcomes might be the same regardless of whether a court-appointed official or a state-appointed one took over the local government's finances, bankruptcy normally means negotiating with all the major creditors, so that they all take some losses, while a state-appointed official might control the local government, cut spending, or reduce labor contracts, in order to make sure that the banks and bondholders are paid in full. The result may be higher taxes and lower service levels for poorer residents and better outcomes for the richer investors. In the legislature, those who represent richer districts may resent demands to bail out poorer ones and resist any deals that require such payments. In a bankruptcy proceeding, state-elected officials lose control over the choice of outcomes.

As one might imagine, bond insurers, the ones who have to make the bondholders whole if a jurisdiction declares bankruptcy, have argued against bankruptcy proceedings. One bond insurer, the only one active in 2012, suggested it might not insure bonds in a state that does not have a procedure for examining and possibly preventing local governments from declaring bankruptcy and abandoning their debts, leaving the insurer with the bill.[42]

Minicase: Why Did Jefferson County, Alabama, Declare Bankruptcy?

In December of 1996, responding to a lawsuit arguing that its leaking sewer system was violating the federal Clean Water Act, the county issued debt to repair the sewer system. The project cost more than initially projected, and the financing was more expensive than it should have been, causing a huge run-up in fees that homeowners paid for sewerage. In 2002 and 2003, J. P. Morgan refinanced the bonds, converting what had been primarily fixed-rate bonds into variable-rate issues and linking the sale with interest rate swaps. The deal was supposed to save the county money, because interest rates on the bonds would be based on auctions that would occur at short intervals. Any increase in interest rates due to the auctions was supposed to be offset by the interest rate swaps, an investment by the county with the bank that was supposed to return more money if interest rates rose.

The deal was corrupt from the start. The bank had paid out millions in bribes to county officials and their friends, some unrelated to the deal, to get the business, and then charged the county much higher fees, which were not revealed, to cover the extra costs. But the really serious trouble started in 2008, when the auction market froze. In accordance with common practice, Jefferson

(Continued)

(Continued)

County had sold the sewer bonds with insurance to protect the buyers, but the bond insurers, as a result of the housing crisis, lost their top ratings. Many institutional investors were permitted to invest only in bonds insured by top-rated companies, forcing them to dump the bonds insured by the companies with lowered ratings. With so few buying, many of the bond auctions failed.[1] Investors dumped Jefferson County's sewer bonds on banks that had agreed to serve as buyers of last resort, triggering contractual requirements for the county to pay off its debt in four years rather than the expected thirty or forty years.[2]

With no auction prices to fix the interest rates, the county was forced to pay a default interest rate, which was much higher than the auction rates had been. When municipal auction rate notes are issued, they typically include a default rate of interest, which in this case was capped at 12 percent.[3] The investment linked to the bonds—the interest rate swaps that depended on interest rates at the time—did not generate more revenue for the county as they were supposed to, because interest rates fell sharply. During the recession, banks were not lending and hence not paying high interest rates to attract capital for them to lend out. The county had to pay very high interest rates on its bonds and got very low returns on its linked investments, all the while paying high transaction fees. In September of 2008, Jefferson County defaulted; it failed to make a payment of principle of $46 million on the bonds.

Default on the bonds made it impossible for the county to refinance to take advantage of lower interest rates; no one would lend money to a county that could not pay back its debt in a timely fashion. To make matters worse, in 2009, a new tax was declared illegal by the court. The state tried again with a different tax, which was declared illegal in 2011. Each of these events threw the county into a desperate situation with regard to revenue.

The county tried to negotiate with its creditors and worked out a deal that would reduce its obligations to the banks but required state cooperation to replenish the revenue of the county and to create an independent sewer authority to issue bonds on the county's behalf, with a state-backed guarantee. The state refused to go along, forcing the county into bankruptcy.

1. William Selway, "Jefferson County's Path From Scandal to U.S. Bankruptcy Filing: Timeline," *Bloomberg,* November 9, 2011, www.bloomberg.com/news/2011-11-09/jefferson-county-s-path-from-scandal-to-u-s-bankruptcy-filing-timeline.html.
2. Goodwin Proctor, "Jefferson County, Alabama, Files Historic Municipal Bankruptcy," November 18, 2011, www.goodwinprocter.com/Publications/Newsletter-Articles/Goodwin-Alerts/2011/Jefferson-County-Alabama-Files-Historic-Municipal-Bankruptcy.aspx.
3. Gretchen Morgenson, "As Good as Cash, Until It's Not," *New York Times,* March 9, 2008.

The Politics of Balance in Cities

While large bankruptcies draw the eye, they remain relatively rare. Most cities try to maintain year-end balances to tide them over when recession hits, but they are often unable to predict downturns in the economy and must reduce expenditures during the year to balance the budget.

At the local level, as at the state level, considerable effort may be spent to hide or minimize deficits, especially ones that are not the result of immediate environmental calamities. Cities use many of the same tactics that states do, including borrowing between funds (sometimes invisibly and without intent to repay), changing the basis of accounting so that some expenditures are counted in the next year's budget, delaying paying bills, and borrowing from pension funds by not making the required employer contribution. Cities may also hide deficits by borrowing outside the city for operating expenditures, pretending they are borrowing for capital expenditures. They sometimes shift expenditures from a fund that is poorer into another that is richer.

Depending on the definition of deficit used, cities can sometimes make the budget look balanced by drawing down reserves, which may be technically legal but obscures the fact that the city is running an operating deficit. Or the budget can be balanced with revenues from the sale of property, from grants, or from other one-time income. Overestimating revenues also makes the budget look more balanced than it is.

When deficits occur unintentionally during the year, the normal response is to gather unspent money and defer spending it until the crisis is over or until the council has had a chance to act on priorities. The result may be heavier cuts in some areas than in others; the intent is not to choose program areas but to find money that is as yet unspent. Capital projects are often delayed if the money is not yet spent or irrevocably committed.

When a deficit is imminent in the following year's budget or when a deficit is carried over from one year to the next, the manager or mayor makes recommendations for how the deficit gap is to be closed, and the council must approve or reject the recommendations. In this situation, program priorities must be decided, revenue increase and expenditure decrease weighed, and the scope of services reevaluated. Formally, the council often has the legal power to make the decisions, but in reality, the distribution of power between the mayor, manager, or administrator, on the one hand, and the council on the other, is highly variable.

The issue of scope of services is unlikely to arise in response to a midyear revenue decline, but it can arise as local governments wrestle with what appears to be an impending imbalance in the next year's operating budget. For example, in the 1970s, when cities were dealing with fiscal stress, if they were responsible for a range of functions, they often tried to shift some of them to other levels of government. Services such as courts, city universities, and museums were shifted to other levels of government or to the private sector. Some cities gave their planning functions to the county. In some states, cities were able to shift some or all of their share of welfare to the state as well as some of the cost of policing.[43] A number of counties have given responsibility for the courts to the state.

The minicase "The Politics of Deficits—An Urban Example" illustrates how budgets can become structurally unbalanced; that is, revenue grows more slowly than expenditures over time. The case also illustrates how difficult it can be to cut spending when every program seems to have a political protector or be exempt from cuts. In this minicase a change in structure was required, with a strengthened linkage between revenues and expenditures and sufficient central authority to cut back spending proposals. The case occurred in the 1970s when the option of increasing federal aid was still open; had it occurred more recently, it would probably have a different ending.

Minicase: The Politics of Deficits—An Urban Example

The city of Southside (a fictional name given to protect the anonymity of those involved) ran deficits that were hidden in the budget from 1972 to 1976.[1] During the later part of this period, there was no recession to blame. The initial causes of the deficit included hiring at the same time a young and inexperienced city manager and an inexperienced budget officer. But the city's problems went well beyond hiring a few inexperienced people. It was suffering from long-term erosion of its economic base, as heavy industry in the region declined, leaving behind many unemployed and a reduced demand for housing. The result was frozen or slow-growing revenues from both sales and property taxes. Department heads and elected officials seemed unwilling or unable to cut back expenditures proportionately. Elected officials at one point actually reduced property tax rates despite increasing costs. The young city manager did not have enough power to force department heads to cut expenditures, so he tried to reduce labor costs instead, incensing the city's employee unions and actually increasing labor costs.

The young manager initially hid the deficits and then tried to publicize them as a way to force the council to make the requisite cuts. He used his budget message to warn council members about emerging deficits, but council members later argued that they did not understand that the budget had to balance fund by fund. They said they were looking at the bottom line, which showed a cash balance. Cash balances are nearly always positive at the end of the year and are misleading indicators of the existence of a deficit.

The deficits were hidden in part by inappropriate, secret internal borrowing, especially from the cash flow of the water fund. The director of the water department worried that he could no longer do his job properly. He pleaded his case emotionally at a budget hearing. Auditors refused to certify the condition of the water fund because its records were not complete—the first public acknowledgment of serious financial trouble.

The second key event in forcing the deficits into public view occurred as the council and manager struggled to deal with the long-term decline of the city's economic base. They helped promote a new regional shopping center on the edge of the city. To carry out their end of the bargain required annexations, property acquisitions, and capital outlays for water, roads, traffic signals, and a new police substation. The city had to borrow by issuing a bond. The bond issue meant that Moody's, one of the major bond evaluators, would have to examine and vouch for the city's creditworthiness, or potential bond buyers would not risk their money. The evaluation of the city's creditworthiness was a disaster; the staff had to struggle to retain any rating at all. The problem was now public. The city had to take action to avoid complete humiliation and maintain the marketability of its bonds.

The manager tried to cut back spending by the departments but was hampered by the independence of the department heads. The police and fire chiefs were hired and fired by a police and fire board appointed by the mayor. Thus they were not directly responsible to the city manager and felt free to ignore his budget advice. The fire department was spending more than its budgeted allocation; police department expenditures had grown rapidly in response to urban riots a number of years earlier, and the manager was unable to cut them back. He requested cuts by other department heads, and they also refused. The manager was further stymied when he tried unsuccessfully to cut council members' pet capital projects. In frustration, the manager tried to cut some of the union contracts and restructure the unions so they would be easier to deal with, but ended up with some expensive, arbitrated settlements that further unbalanced his budget. The manager was then fired and replaced with a more senior manager.

The new manager froze departmental budgets and increased revenue by increasing federal aid, an option still open in the late 1970s. Perhaps more important, he changed the budget process. The manager had control over the street department head, who was responsible to him, and fired him. The manager forbade department heads to communicate directly to the council unless they went through him, to prevent end runs in which department heads got protection for expenditures from the council before they appeared in the budget request. The new manager insisted on the right to hire the

(Continued)

(Continued)

police and fire chiefs and was successful, so that they reported to him. The fire department was broken out of the general fund and set up with its own earmarked taxes, reducing the drain on other funds. The new manager had more authority to enforce balance.

The case of Southside indicates that cities sometimes do run deficits, but because such deficits are illegal, their size may be obscured. When that happens, the deficit can grow to a substantial portion of all spending and make remedies politically difficult. Because decision makers believed that the public would not tolerate an increase in the property tax, the option of reducing spending was explored, but the young manager failed to make significant cuts. When the city finally resolved to handle its deficit problems, it chose budget process reform as a solution, giving the manager more power to balance the budget. The deficits seemed to result as much from failure of structure as from economic circumstances, so a reform of structure was a logical response.

1. Irene Rubin, *Running in the Red: The Political Dynamics of Urban Fiscal Stress* (Albany: State University of New York Press, 1982).

Summary and Conclusions

Budget balancing is more than a technical activity that readjusts spending and revenue decisions. It is linked to issues about the scope of government, because balance depends on decisions to raise taxes and maintain scope or cut spending and reduce services or shift them to other locations. Balance is also linked to spending priorities: When expenditures are cut back, some programs will be protected and others cut back disproportionately, or all programs will be cut across the board. Balance is linked to federalism, because one level of government may seek to balance its budget at the expense of others. The relationship between states and their local governments is complicated by the fact that the states are responsible for the financial condition of their local governments; states can only shift so much of the burden to local governments before they are confronted with the need to solve the financial problems of the local governments. Some states have gotten out of this box by allowing their local governments to declare bankruptcy under federal bankruptcy law. Finally, the politics of balance is linked to the politics of process, as governments shift budget-making power in attempts to increase discipline, control expenditures, and systematically and authoritatively link revenues and expenditures.

Many of the issues involved in budget balance bring out ideological differences between Democrats and Republicans, liberals and conservatives, and business and labor. The politics of balance is closely linked to the politics of budget implementation. A budget can become unbalanced during the year because of environmental changes or because gimmicks used to make the budget look balanced cause problems during the budget year. Budgeters may overestimate revenues and underestimate expenditures, so that the budget as submitted looks balanced, but it will become unbalanced during the year. At the state and local levels, the budget may have to be changed during the year to rebalance it. Requirements for balance also encourage interfund transfers during the year, to make the budget look more balanced than it is. The importance of changes that occur during the budget year is discussed in the next chapter.

Useful Websites

Governing Data (www.governing.com/data) and its companion *Governing by the Numbers* (www.governing.com/blogs/by-the-numbers) provide useful and often graphical explanations of quantitative data in the news, such as employment numbers, the locations of municipal bankruptcies, and public sector layoffs.

The Brookings Institution (www.brookings.edu) often posts studies of interest to budgeters. One in particular provides some in-depth backup for this chapter: *Structurally Imbalanced: Cyclical and Structural Deficits in California and the Intermountain West,* by Matthew Murray with Sue Clark-Johnson, Mark Muro, and Jennifer Ve (www.brookings.edu/~/media/research/files/papers/2011/1/05%20 state%20budgets/0105_state_budgets.pdf).

Three resources concerning rainy-day funds are particularly helpful: a brief primer on state rainy-day funds (www.taxpolicycenter.org/briefing-book/state -local/fiscal/rainy-day.cfm), one with more detail on how rainy-day funds are structured (www.itep.org/pdf/pb25rdf.pdf), and recent experience and suggestions for reforms of rainy-day funds (www.cbpp.org/cms/index.cfm?fa= view&id=3387).

There have been a number of commissions and policy recommendations for how to rebalance the federal budget. The president's National Commission on Fiscal Responsibility and Reform issued a report in 2010, called *The Moment of Truth* (www.fiscalcommission.gov/sites/fiscalcommission.gov/files/documents/ TheMomentofTruth12_1_2010.pdf). The report has been referred to as the Simpson-Bowles report after its cochairs, Erskine Bowles and Sen. Alan Simpson. Minutes and videos of the commission's meetings were posted online (www.fiscal commission.gov/meetings).

A second set of recommendations was worked out by the Bipartisan Policy Center, released at about the same time as the Simpson-Bowles report. This report, titled *Restoring America's Future: Reviving the Economy, Cutting Spending and Debt, Creating a Simple, Progrowth Tax System,* was cochaired by Dr. Alice Rivlin and Sen. Pete Dominici, R-NMex., http://bipartisanpolicy.org/library/restoring-americas-future/.

There is an excellent description of the role of the federal bankruptcy law, Title 9, that governs municipal bankruptcies, "Chapter 9—Bankruptcy Basics," from the U.S. courts website, http://www.uscourts.gov/services-forms/bankruptcy/bankruptcy-basics/chapter-9-bankruptcy-basics.

restricts the ability of the governor to reduce or add to line items during the year and prohibits the governor from proposing a budget based on revenues that have not yet passed the legislature. This unusual reduction of gubernatorial power occurred despite objection from bond rating agencies. It happened in part because there was a Democratic governor and Republican legislature and in part because the governor appeared to use these midyear cuts not just to rebalance the budget but also to remake the budget according to his own priorities, without risking a legislative veto override.

The conflict began when Governor Nixon cut $170 million from the legislatively approved budget by reducing or eliminating forty-five programs; of that sum, $50 million was supposed to go for disaster relief. Opponents charged him with using the storm relief as a ruse to refashion the budget more to his liking. A later study claimed that only $7.8 million was actually spent on disaster relief. He was sued for exceeding his authority. When the lawsuit was thrown out of court, opponents proceeded to curtail his authority by public referendum. The measure passed 56.8 to 43.2.

Source: Allison Hiltz, "Missouri Voters To Decide Governor's Role in The Budget Process," NCSL, October 24, 2014, http://www.ncsl.org/blog/2014/10/24/missouri -voters-to-decide-governors-role-in-the-budget-process.aspx.

How is this tension between adaptability and accountability resolved? First, budgets are generally implemented as passed. The requirement to do so is taken seriously, so that consideration of important policy issues that arise during the year is often delayed until the next full, open budget process. Second, the legislative bodies carefully monitor budget implementation to ensure that important policy decisions are not slipped in among the routine adaptations.

Policy-related budget decisions may be allowed during the year under particular conditions. When new presidents are elected, they may be given fairly broad discretion to reshape the existing budget to fit their policies. Or Congress may design and implement new programs for relief of farmers in the middle of a drought or to help the unemployed during a deep recession. These decisions are made in the normal way, by the usual committees; what is unusual about them is that they feed into the budget in the middle of the year and they may be made in haste. In these cases, the changes have high visibility and widespread public acceptance. They do not threaten accountability.

Despite the care with which budgets are normally implemented, deviations from the budget that are not routine and minor sometimes occur. These may be of two kinds: The first is a violation of fiscal control, resulting in overspending or waste, fraud, or abuse. The second is a violation of policy control, in which someone in the executive branch makes policy changes in the budget without going through the whole formal, public business of lawmaking. If the consequences are serious enough, irritating enough, or embarrassing enough, the chief executive or the legislature may increase control over budget implementation to prevent a recurrence. The legislature may increase its control over the executive; the chief executive may increase control over the agencies. The result may be an increase in the number and severity of constraints over budget implementation.

Tools for Changing the Budget

Budgets can only be changed in specific ways after the budget year has begun. These include supplemental appropriations and rescissions; deferrals and other holdbacks; transfers *between* accounts or funds; and reprogramming, shifting money between programs or projects *within* accounts or funds. (State and local governments use funds as the point of control, the national government uses accounts, but they function similarly.)

A *supplemental appropriation* is a budget law that adds money to some existing function or new purpose during the year. The money can come from fund balances, unexpected revenue increases, or contingency accounts, or it can come from rescissions—that is, withdrawals of previously granted legal authorization to spend money. In some cases, however, there may be a supplemental appropriation without extra funds to pay for it. In such cases, supplemental appropriations are paid for by borrowing and contribute to deficits.

A *deferral,* a term used at the federal level, occurs when the executive delays spending money that has been appropriated for a specific project or program. At the state or local level, a chief executive may ask for a *holdback,* usually a fixed and small percentage of the approved budget of all or nearly all agencies, that agencies are prohibited from spending. Alternatively—or in addition—capital projects may be frozen or personnel lines left unfilled. Holdbacks can be insurance against fluctuating revenues or unexpected expenditures, or they can be used to create a pool of funds to spend for special, politically favored projects.

Interfund transfers take money from one appropriation account or fund for a designated purpose and spend it in a different fund or appropriation account, presumably for a related purpose. Such transfers normally go back to the legislative body for approval; they represent a sort of budget amendment and reprioritization. *Reprogrammings,* by contrast, are transfers that occur within funds or accounts, often within the same administrative unit. They may shift money from one line in the budget to another, from one project to another, or from one category of spending, such as capital improvements, to another, such as supplies or contractual services. Rules typically govern the allowable amounts of such shifts and sometimes govern where the money can come from. At the federal level, some reprogrammings require advance notice to congressional committees, while others only require after-the-fact reporting. Without those reports, Congress could lose control of budget implementation and have little idea how the money legislators approved had actually been spent.

Supplemental Appropriations, Rescissions, and Deferrals

Supplemental appropriations and rescissions are most common at the national level as tools for reshaping the budget midyear. Both are laws, passed in the normal manner. They may be initiated by the president or by Congress, and if initiated by the president they may be raised, lowered, or denied by Congress. Supplemental appropriations were used extensively in the 1970s and most of the 1980s. Figure 7.1 shows the amounts of supplemental appropriations compared to the size of deficits and the size of the total budget through 2010. In 2011, there was no proper budget, just a series of continuing resolutions, funding agencies for the whole year. There were no supplemental appropriations. Supplementals contributed directly to the deficits, because many of them were treated as emergency spending, the budget rules did not require any additional revenue or spending reductions to offset the additional expenditures.

After budgetary balance was achieved in 1998, the pressure to limit emergency supplementals was reduced, and they began to grow again. Items that were not clearly emergencies or unpredictable crept into the emergency supplementals, where they did not have to be offset by new revenues or budget cuts elsewhere. Perhaps the most glaring example was the funding of the 2000 census with emergency supplemental funding, which is to say, by deficit spending. Elected officials could not argue that the census was not anticipated well in advance or represented an emergency.

After 2002, when the Budget Enforcement Act lapsed and the response to September 11, 2001, began to cause increases in spending for antiterrorist activities and war, spending through supplementals soared, as did the deficit. The wars in Afghanistan and in Iraq were funded through emergency supplementals until 2008, even though many of the expenses could have been anticipated in the regular budget. The effect was to swell the deficit.

Why fund wars with supplemental appropriations? By leaving a huge chunk of spending out of the regular budget and funding it later during the year, the president made the deficit look smaller when he submitted his annual budget proposal. If the real size of the deficit were widely advertised, there might have been more pressure to curtail it and hence to limit the tax reductions that were

FIGURE 7.1 Supplemental Spending as a Percentage of the Deficit and Budget Authority, 2000–2010

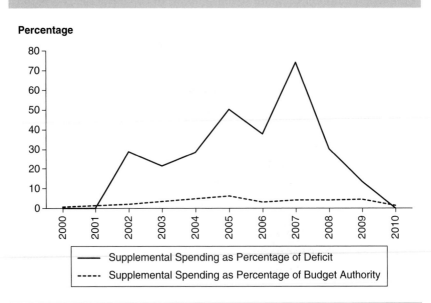

Source: For the supplemental appropriations, Congressional Budget Office, "Supplemental Appropriations 2000–2010," http://www.cbo.gov/sites/default/files/cbofiles/ftpdocs/66xx/doc6630/suppapprops.pdf; budget authority and deficit data are from the Office of Management and Budget, "Budget of the U.S. Government," Historical Tables, 2012, Tables 1–1 and 5–2. The figure for the deficit includes both on-budget and off-budget; the on-budget figure alone would be considerably higher.

the cornerstone of the George W. Bush administration. Second, emergency supplementals for war are nearly impossible to vote against; they receive very little congressional scrutiny and provide maximum flexibility to the Department of Defense in spending the funds. The DoD preferred supplemental appropriations, because they gave more discretion in spending than regular appropriations. Third, when the administration borrows to pay for a war, present voters do not have to pay for it, and hence they are less likely to oppose the policy that launched the war. The costs of the war are obscured.

The Obama administration vowed to end the funding of the wars through emergency supplemental appropriations, because much of the need for war spending could be estimated in advance. In fact, he did reduce the level of supplementals. During his administration, war costs were anticipated in the budget, but much of that spending was taken "off budget" in the Overseas Contingency Operations (OCO) fund. Because the OCO was "off budget," its outlays did not have to be offset with additional revenues or spending cuts and hence added to the deficit just as the supplementals had. There were no supplemental appropriations in 2011 or 2012. For 2013, supplemental appropriations cost $50.5 billion, mostly for relief for hurricane Sandy destruction, with almost no defense spending; for 2014, the levels were down again to a modest $225 million.[1]

While *emergency* supplementals do not have to be offset, sometimes they are, and *nonemergency* supplementals have routinely been offset. Rescinding or legally withdrawing permission to spend money for some program is a common way of funding (offsetting) a supplemental appropriation. Sometimes, however, rescissions occur independently of supplemental appropriations; they must be passed by both houses of Congress and signed by the president just like other legislation.

At the national level, rescissions were used extensively by presidents until 2000, but the George W. Bush and the Obama administrations have not used them much. Congress continued to use rescissions, cutting over $80 billion during the eight years of the Bush administration and another $40 billion during the first four Obama years. This recent history brings into question the idea that only the president has the will to cut the budget and therefore that more power must be shifted to the executive branch.

While paying for particular supplementary spending through selective rescissions has become less common, rescissions that cut many programs by a single percentage have become more common. "The total amount of budget authority reduced pursuant to the FY2013 across-the-board rescissions was in excess of $2.3 billion." This kind of rescission is a way of enforcing agreements on budget totals.[2]

Rescissions are common at the state level. Because states are forbidden to run deficits, when revenues drop unexpectedly during the year, the state may have to rescind spending authority granted to its agencies in the annual budget. In anticipation of such rescissions, agencies sometimes hold back some of their budget rather than spend at the normal rate, to have some money on hand to cut if a rescission occurs. New hires may be delayed until it is clear that a rescission will not take place or will not be large enough to prevent new hires. Capital projects may be delayed, with the idea that money set aside for them need not be spent this fiscal year and can be applied for again in later years. It is difficult or impossible to cut in a rational manner to cope with rescissions that occur during the year; what is cut is what has not yet been committed. If rescissions become common, agencies are likely to organize their expenditures so there will be resources to cut midyear. They may change the ratio of permanent to temporary employees, for example, so that there will be enough temporary staff to cut, if necessary, on short notice. The later in the year a rescission occurs, the harder it is to implement. An 11 percent rescission that occurs in the last half of the fiscal year effectively cuts 22 percent of the remaining revenues for the year. In some states, the legislature grants the governor power to cut the budget midyear up to a given percentage without coming back for legislative approval. These are called midyear cuts rather than rescissions, because rescissions by definition have to be approved by the legislature and signed by the governor.

Deferrals are not based on formal legislation passed by the legislature and signed by the executive. The executive decides to delay (defer) some expenditure, presumably for technical reasons, such as a project not being ready to begin. In the past, however, presidents have found it tempting to use deferrals in somewhat the same way as governors use line-item vetoes—to take out of the budget legislative add-ons to executive budget proposals. All a president had to do was delay indefinitely any expenditure of which he disapproved. Such policy-based delays violated the constitutionally required balance of powers, as the presidents ignored Congressional decisions with which they disagreed. In response, Congress included in the 1974 Congressional Budget Reform Act a requirement that the president propose deferrals to Congress; if Congress did not disapprove, the spending could be deferred. This procedure was declared unconstitutional in 1983 in the *INS v. Chadha* case, because under the 1974 Congressional Budget Reform Act, one house rather than both houses could veto a presidential proposal. From then on, so-called legislative vetoes were considered illegal.

Congress responded to the elimination of its veto power over deferrals by putting its rejections of them into supplemental appropriations and passing them as they would other laws. In 1986 when Ronald Reagan deferred some $10 billion that he did not want spent, "Congress's response was to insert a provision in that year's supplemental appropriation bill nullifying most of the policy deferrals."[3] If the president wanted the supplemental appropriation, he had to sign the bill including the rejections of his deferrals.

Congress questioned the president's legal ability to defer funds for policy purposes. In 1987 the U.S. Court of Appeals for the District of Columbia agreed with Congress, barring any kind of policy-based deferral.[4]

"Deferrals" is a term applied to the federal budget. At the state and local level, the related mechanism is called a "holdback." Most holdbacks at the state level are not policy related. They are a tool used to rebalance the budget during the year, if revenues are inadequate to fund the budget that was passed and signed into law. Because governors usually have line-item vetoes and sometimes have amendatory vetoes, normally it is not necessary for them to withhold spending on projects that the legislature might add to their budget requests; they can just line out or veto those parts of the budget bill.

Though the intent is to give the governor power to reduce spending during the year to rebalance the budget if revenues fail to meet projections, the governor's holdback authority can be used to simply not spend the money that the legislature has added or added back to the governor's budget proposal. The aggressive use of this tool has generated many lawsuits by those whose budgets have been cut in this fashion.

For example, in 2010 Governor Paterson in New York withheld hundreds of millions of dollars in school and local government funding, prompting a lawsuit against him by the teachers' union, the school boards, and others. The legislature had rejected the governor's budget cutting plan, which included cuts to the schools. The governor signed the budget approved by the legislature then proceeded to withhold the spending. The lawsuit charged the governor with violating the constitutional separation of powers and the constitutional mandate to fund education.[5] The funds were paid after the lawsuit was filed, but the lawsuit continued. Then for a second time during the year, the governor delayed payments to the schools, saying he would pay them two months later if cash was available at that time; later he argued that cash was insufficient to make the payment by the stipulated time. This second delay prompted a second lawsuit.

Two earlier cases in Connecticut by cities and school districts established that when revenues were insufficient to pay the budgeted amounts, the governor's power to withhold funds that had been legally appropriated and signed by the governor did not extend to aid to cities and school districts. The governor's powers to withhold budgeted funds applied only to the budgets of state agencies.[6]

Minicase: Using Holdback to Change Legislative Priorities—Maryland

Governor Hogan in 2015 held back $68 million that the legislature granted to pay for an education equalization formula. He wanted to spend the money on the pension fund instead, since the legislative budget took money due to the pension fund to spend on other programs. Hogan also planned to use the $68 million to fund a one-time increase in public employees' wages and to restore cuts he had made to Medicaid and mental health programs. Overruling the legislature's decision, the governor roused much opposition from affected local government officials. Despite opposition, he did not back down, so the legislature passed a bill that required the governor to fund the education program in the future. The governor said he would allow the bill

(Continued)

(Continued)

to become law without his signature, as he did not have the votes to prevent an override if he vetoed the measure.

Source: Len Lazarick, "Hogan Rejects Pressure for School Aid, But Surrenders in the Long Term," *The Maryland Reporter*, May 14, 2015, http://marylandreporter .com/2015/05/14/hogan-rejects-pressure-for-school-aid-but-surrenders-in-the -long-term/.

Reprogramming

Reprogramming is taking some or all of the money that has been budgeted to one program or project and transferring it to another in the same account or fund during the fiscal year. Reprogramming may make good managerial sense if the money cannot be appropriately spent as budgeted and other urgent needs for the money occur during the year.

Reprogramming can help an agency adapt to unexpected contingencies without requiring a supplemental appropriation. Some agencies intentionally underspend to create a pool of funds that can be spent elsewhere. However, extensive reprogramming can alter the approved budget and change the legislative priorities reflected in the appropriations. To monitor changes taking place and prevent changes that threaten legislative policies, the legislative body may set guidelines for reprogramming, limiting the total amount that can be shifted, reducing the size of the units within which flexible choices can be exercised (say, from accounts to subaccounts), requiring advance notice and explanation of reprogramming, or requiring extensive quarterly reporting after the reprogramming has taken place. Another approach is to prohibit large year-end carryover budgets or other possible sources of reprogramming funds.

Reprogramming does take place at the state and local levels and sometimes becomes controversial, but it has been a more visible issue at the national level. Congress has tried to maintain agencies' ability to adapt to changing situations, while preventing them from using reprogramming to thwart its will. It does this by issuing guidelines to control rather than prevent reprogramming. Guidelines often include wording such as, "Reprogramming may be used for unforeseen events but only if delay until the next budget cycle would result in excessive costs or damage." Prohibitions include any projects for which Congress has already denied funding and reprogramming into areas where Congress has just cut the budget. These guidelines may appear in committee report language (without the force of law) or appropriation legislation (with the force of law). Committees often ask the agencies to report in advance reprogrammings above a given dollar amount, which gives the committee members a chance to object if the reprogramming has policy implications or is otherwise questionable.

Overall, Congress's experience in controlling reprogramming has been successful. The number of requests for reprogramming has been moderate, and there have been few abuses. Nevertheless, in recent years, reprogramming has become controversial. Efforts to balance the budget and reduce spending, especially in the discretionary portion of the budget, have resulted in renewed interest in reprogramming. War and the antiterrorism campaign have also seemed to require more budgetary flexibility. Presidents claimed broad discretion to move money around within accounts, but Congress fought back, worried that legislative priorities might be tampered with if reprogramming authority was broadened.

Conflict over reprogramming may be a function of the relationship between an agency and a congressional committee but can also indicate policy disputes between the president and Congress. At the federal level, appropriations legislation awards each agency a total amount of money, broken into separate accounts for different purposes. These accounts are generally very large, with many different things inside. Those totals for each account are fixed in law and may not be exceeded; transfers between accounts are carefully controlled and monitored. But inside these broad appropriation accounts, the administration theoretically has discretion to spend the money according to need. At the federal level, appropriations are not passed with detailed subaccounts or even more detailed line items that force the executive to spend money as Congress directs. By writing the legislation for broad accounts with firm controls only on the totals, Congress grants the administration considerable discretion to adjust the budget within accounts according to need, but members worry about how that discretion will be used and whether items or policies of particular concern to legislators will be ignored or overturned.

The congressional appropriations committees are divided into twelve subcommittees, each of which deals with a particular set of departments and agencies. Each executive branch agency presents to its appropriations subcommittee in Congress a budget justification, outlining how it intends to spend the money it requests from Congress. These justifications are the subject of appropriations hearings. At these hearings, members discuss the proposals and express their intentions about how the money should or should not be spent. They further spell out their concerns and give directions in committee reports that accompany the appropriations legislation. These reports do not have the force of law, but agency administrators generally comply with what they know their congressional budgeters want them to do.

Congressional committees expect agencies to spend their budgets in accordance with the information presented in these budget justifications, sometimes down to details of organizational structure and number of authorized positions. They expect agencies not to make major changes during the year without at least notifying the relevant committees.

In order to balance legitimate executive branch needs for discretion with congressional need for control, Congress has established reprogramming guidelines. These guidelines tell agencies the circumstances under which changes are and are not permissible, when agency officials must inform congressional committees of changes, and what kind of changes must be reported. Some subcommittees require agencies to get advance permission to make substantial changes in the budget.

Congressional committees provide flexibility to the executive branch, with the condition that if members disagree with how that discretion has been or is going to be used, they can invite a discussion, negotiate, suggest alternatives, or "veto" or otherwise prevent the action. Congress's ability to influence executive branch choices about how the money will be spent encourages members to grant broader discretion to the administration.

Generally speaking, presidents have wanted more discretion over how to spend the budget during the year, and Congress has tried to balance the need for executive discretion with the need for congressional policy control. But President Herbert Hoover was an exception, able to see the importance of legislative control of policy in the budget (see the minicase below for details).

Minicase: Herbert Hoover and Legislative Vetoes

While some presidents have chafed at legislative interference in what they consider their rightful authority to make changes within an appropriation account, the idea of legislative control (vetoes) over executive discretion was put forward initially by Herbert Hoover (president from 1929 to 1933).[1] Hoover had asked for unilateral authority to reorganize the executive branch, and he suggested that Congress retain an ability to veto his decisions if they disapproved. Hoover believed presidents had usurped too much legislative power and needed to work out ways to restore to Congress its role in budgeting. He wrote, "I felt deeply that the independence of the legislative arm must be respected and strengthened."[2]

---

1. Louis Fisher, "The Legislative Veto: Invalidated, It Survives," *Law and Contemporary Problems* 56, no. 4, Symposium Elected Branch Influences in Constitutional Decisionmaking (Autumn, 1993), pp. 273–292.
2. Herbert Hoover, *The Memoirs of Herbert Hoover: The Cabinet and the Presidency 1920–1933* (New York: MacMillan, 1952), www.ecommcode.com/hoover/ebooks/pdf/FULL/B1V2_Full.pdf.

Congress's specification of reprogramming rules, including legislative vetoes of executive actions, provided flexibility to the executive and therefore was tolerated for decades, until the Supreme Court declared congressional vetoes unconstitutional in 1983, in *INS v. Chadha*. The Chadha decision was aimed at congressional vetoes of presidential deferrals, that is, presidential decisions to withhold funds that Congress had granted. The court's judgment that legislative vetoes of deferrals were unconstitutional was often considered to include all legislative vetoes, including those addressed at executive reprogramming. Despite Chadha, however, reprogramming controls, including legislative vetoes, have survived to the present. Chadha may have strengthened the president's hand in demanding more discretion, but Congress has by no means given up the battle to control for what purposes that discretion may be used.

It is not clear that the Chadha case ought to apply to reprogramming constraints. The Government Accountability Office (GAO) judged that unofficial processes of control, such as through committee communications and reports accompanying legislation, were not prohibited by Chadha. Moreover, the GAO offered its institutional opinion that Chadha only applied where Congress had made a clear delegation of authority to the executive branch, in which case it could not later withdraw that delegation without further formal legislation, but if there was no grant of discretion or if the grant were ambiguous, then Chadha did not apply.[7] According to this interpretation, when Congress passes a law that forbids increasing an account or decreasing an account by more than 10 percent or prohibits reprogramming to fund a project that Congress had denied, requiring an agency to seek congressional permission for an exception, Congress is not violating Chadha, because it did not grant discretion in the first place. The legality of reprogramming guidelines has never been tested in the courts.

Legal niceties aside, there is the practical reality: If the administration insists too strongly on its freedom to use money in an appropriated account in any way it sees fit or uses its discretion to thwart congressional will, Congress can respond by reducing or cutting an appropriation completely or reducing the amount of discretion it grants to the executive branch. Despite the complaints of some presidents, the system of reprogramming rules, both formal and informal, persists. It serves both sides: The executive gets some discretion, and Congress gets some control over how that discretion is used.

Most congressional committees or subcommittees get around the Chadha prohibition on legislative vetoes by including congressional vetoes only in reports, which do not have the impact of law, or only requiring notice of reprogramming. However, some have continued to insist that departments or agencies obtain committee or subcommittee approval before carrying out a major change of purpose or executive defiance of congressional intent.

This process of Congress granting the executive discretion but monitoring and controlling its use became highly contentious during the George W. Bush administration. As President Bush signed legislation into law, he made statements about what parts of the laws he was signing he considered unconstitutional and was not going to implement. In these signing statements, citing Chadha, he claimed that discretion, once granted, could not be constrained in any way; within a given budget account, the administration could use money as it saw fit.

Bush argued against the requirement for advanced notice to Congress of intent to reprogram, saying that he would inform Congress after the fact and then only as a courtesy, not because he was legally bound to do so. His administration attacked in particular the requirement sometimes written into law or included in committee reports that substantial changes required appropriations committee approval before they could take place. He argued in the signing statements that if a reprogramming had to go back to a committee for approval, it was akin to a one house or one committee rejection of a presidential deferral of spending banned under Chadha and therefore was unconstitutional.

President Bush claimed that his role as commander in chief allowed him freedom to start new programs without notifying Congress if warranted by national security. Congress, in contrast, generally prohibited reprogramming for the purpose of creating new programs without congressional approval.

Obama, in an early signing statement in his administration, repeated some of Bush's arguments with regard to reprogramming. He particularly opposed the advanced permission requirements but was more willing to provide Congress advance notice of reprogramming. The repetition of the same language in a signing statement in late 2011 demonstrated that this was an intentional statement of policy rather than an unthinking carryover from the Bush era.[8]

Congress has not backed down in the face of these executive branch claims.[9] To deal with Chadha's prohibition on legislative vetoes, appropriations subcommittees that require advance permission for changes within accounts grant little discretion to the administration initially; they therefore are not curtailing an existing grant of discretion without benefit of law. The following language from the Transportation and Housing and Urban Development (THUD) subcommittee in 2003 illustrates how little discretion may be granted:

> As in previous years, the Committee reiterates that the Department must limit the reprogramming of funds between the program, projects, and activities within each account to not more than $500,000 without prior written approval of the Committees on Appropriations. Unless otherwise identified in the bill or report, the most detailed allocation of funds presented in the budget justifications is approved, with any deviation from such approved allocation subject to the normal reprogramming requirements.[10]

The House Appropriations report for THUD for 2015 maintained the advanced approval requirement, stating that such approval must be received from both the House and Senate appropriations committees but granted more discretion, raising the total for triggering a reprogramming to $5 million or 10 percent of an existing program, project, or activity. [11] The list of things the agency could not do without advance permission includes creating or terminating a program, increasing funds or personnel for any program previously denied by Congress, redirecting money that had been specified in a report for a given purpose, increasing or decreasing a program or activity by more than 10 percent, or reorganizing offices in a different manner than specified in the budget justification.

The Department of Interior, Environment and Related Agencies appropriations included reprogramming guidelines that would be triggered for changes over $1 million, a low trigger allowing little discretion. The language for prior approval was a little gentler but reached the same goal. The agencies covered by the appropriation could proceed with their reprogrammings after submission of their request to the appropriate committees, if committee members did not object. Any significant departures from the budget justification, including any change in the organizational structure, required a reprogramming process.[12] The congressional committee also monitored closely any effort to create a pool of funds that might later be used for changes in the budget that Congress had already approved.

The 2015 House report for Defense appropriations included detailed instructions for reprogramming by type of expenditure, including requirements for obtaining advanced permission from the committee. The trigger for requiring a formal reprogramming for personnel was $10 million, but significantly, the committee report forbade below the threshold reprogrammings to be used to increase or decrease any items Congress had shown a particular interest in. In other words, DoD was not allowed to use a large number of small reprogrammings, too small individually to report on, to bypass congressional intent on specific items.[13]

As these examples suggest, how much discretion the executive branch has to change the budget once it has been passed remains a subject of contestation. Agencies can get caught between the executive and legislative policies. When an executive branch agency violates reprogramming guidelines, adhering to the president's and OMB's interpretation of the law rather than Congress's, members of Congress notice and chastise the agency officials and sometimes punish them.

For example, HUD had been pleading for more flexibility but got the following reaction from legislators on its appropriation subcommittee in 2010:

> The Committee reiterates that no changes may be made to any program, project, or activity if it is construed to have policy implications, without prior approval of the Committees on Appropriations. The Committee is dismayed that on many occasions the Department has taken action on new initiatives without seeking, or before receiving, formal approval, as required in Section 405 of the appropriations act. For example, the Committee was displeased to learn of the establishment of the Disaster Relief Enhancement Fund (DREF), a diversion of funds to a new initiative without an approved reprogramming request. Examples such as this diminish the Department's credibility, especially in light of the Department's recent requests for increased flexibility.[14]

Congress has been serious about enforcement of reprogramming rules. One method of enforcement has been to require agencies to submit reports within sixty days after budget appropriations are passed, establishing the baselines from which the reprogramming triggers are calculated. If the trigger for a formal reprogramming request is a change of more than 10 percent in a program or activity within an account, Congress wants to know 10 percent of what dollar amount and which programs or activities are affected. Equally important, Congress expects agencies to highlight in these reports items of congressional interest. By requiring that agencies include such items in reports, Congress assures that agency administrators notice and acknowledge these particular items.

If agencies fail to follow reprogramming guidelines, committees threaten to reduce or eliminate the discretion they have provided. The following excerpt is from the report accompanying the 2013 appropriation for Commerce, Justice, Science and Related Agencies.

> The Committee is concerned that, in some instances, the departments or agencies funded within this appropriations act are not adhering to the Committee's reprogramming guidelines that are clearly set forth in this report and in section 505 of the accompanying bill. The Committee expects that each department and agency funded in the bill will follow these notification policies precisely and will not reallocate resources or reorganize activities prior to submitting the required notifications to the Committee.

> The reprogramming process is based on comity between the Appropriations Committee and the executive branch. The Commerce, Justice, Science, and [R]elated [A]gencies appropriations bill provides specific program guidance throughout this report and tables accompanying the bill. The process is intended to provide flexibility to meet changing circumstances and emergency requirements of agencies, if there is agreement between the executive branch and the Congress that such a change is warranted. Reprogramming procedures provide a means to agree on adjustments, if necessary, during a fiscal year, and to ensure that the Committee is kept apprised of instances where nonappropriated resources are used to meet program requirements, such as fee collections and unobligated balances that were not considered in the development of the appropriations legislation.

> In the absence of comity and respect for the prerogatives of the Appropriations Committees and Congress in general, the Committee will have no choice but to include specific program limitations and details legislatively. Under these circumstances, programs, projects, and activities become absolutes and the executive branch shall lose the ability to propose changes in the use of appropriated funds through the reprogramming process between programs, projects, and activities without seeking some form of legislative action.[15]

Subcommittee chairman Frank Wolf, R-Vir., was clearly irritated by a reprogramming violation: "Last year, you disregarded the Committee's direction and proceeded with an unprecedented $165 million dollar reprogramming to support the purchase of the Thomson prison in Illinois, something that was actively sought as an earmark request by Senator Durbin, but was not included in the President's budget nor in any appropriations act. In fact, Congress had denied a similar reprogramming in FY11, and subsequently rescinded the funds that had been identified by the Department as a potential source for the Thomson purchase."[16] Reprogramming money for a project that had already been rejected by Congress was clearly in violation of reprogramming guidelines. The chairman concluded that the result would be the loss of administrative flexibility.

Because most reprogramming is routine, it is not highly visible. By contrast, failure to follow reprogramming guidelines, for whatever reason, is likely to create a public conflict. In one recent case, an administrator for the National Weather Service was discovered to have engaged in unauthorized reprogramming for at least several years, possibly longer. The revelation led to his resignation under pressure (see the minicase on the National Weather Service, p. 249).

Contingency Funds

Contingency funds are sums of money budgeted for unknown and unpredictable purposes. There are some contingency funds—or discretionary funds—at the federal level, but contingency funds are more important at the state and local levels. At the national level, contingencies are generally funded by supplementals, which, if not offset with additional cuts or revenue increases, increase the size of the deficit; at state and local levels, it is illegal to run deficits, so a variety of special funds are set aside for different contingencies. At the local level, departmental budget justifications are normally included in the budget, so a detailed plan of how money is to be spent is part of the budget legislation. Most city agencies thus do not have much flexibility regarding how budgeted money will be spent. To create discretion during the year, administrators have to build it into the budget by establishing pools of uncommitted revenue to be allocated during the year.

Cities and states can use their year-end fund balances—money left over from the prior fiscal year—as a kind of emergency kitty, and they can create separate accounts specifically to handle contingencies. The more money there is in contingency funds, the less is needed in the year-end balance and vice versa. A city or state may intentionally not spend all the money that was budgeted so as to create a pool of money that can be rebudgeted if necessary. Pools of flexible funds can be created by overcutting in response to pessimistic revenue estimates. For example, in a study of Cincinnati during a period of fiscal stress, the city cut back expenditures in line with a worst-case revenue scenario, creating moderate amounts of slack in the retrenchment budget. The council used the slack to add police and fire personnel after the 1976 cuts. In 1980, the manager elicited supplemental requests from departments to use revenues that had exceeded the pessimistic predictions in the budget. The manager then selected those requests that dealt with deferred maintenance, the problem that he saw as the highest priority.[17] How such "savings" are used and who will control them are policy-laden issues.

Minicase: The National Weather Service Reprogramming

In the spring of 2012, a story broke that the National Weather Service (NWS) had been reprogramming out of a technology modernization account into salaries for at least two years—2010 and 2011—without notifying Congress. Agency officials had been wrestling with a structural imbalance for years and apparently ran out of solutions. Taking money from the modernization accounts may have seemed like the only possible option.

One source of the underfunding has been the salary increases for federal employees. Each year, the president proposes and Congress passes or changes a figure for salary increases for federal employees, but Congress typically does not appropriate enough money to pay for the raises. The expectation is that most agencies will be able to fund at least some of their salary increases from vacant personnel lines and savings from turnover when highly paid senior staff retire or leave an agency and younger less expensive ones replace them. The executive Office of Management and Budget assigns each agency an inflation increase to its budget, which may be more or less than the cost of the salary increase. For the National Weather Service, the OMB inflation increases were often considerably less than the cost of the salary increases.

To pay for the mandated salary increases, the NWS had to reduce the number of staff. However, Congress was unwilling to let the agency reduce its field staff, especially its hurricane warning center, which left only administrative staff at headquarters that could be cut. After several years of this process, any flex in the system was used up. An agency administrator began to move money from technology modernization to salaries, to maintain the size of the field staff. The trouble was that he didn't notify Congress of this reprogramming in accordance with the guidelines governing the agency.

The formal answer to why the agency didn't report to Congress as required was that staff had been inadequately trained on the reprogramming guidelines, but it is possible that they believed that they were not bound by the guidelines.

Once the reprogramming was discovered and made public, it could no longer continue without congressional notice. The agency needed to put forward a formal reprogramming notice to a congressional committee angry at the misuse of funds and violation of procedures. The Department of Commerce reprogramming guidelines require only notification, not advanced permission, but both the agency and congressional committees acted as if congressional permission were required. If Congress blocked or delayed the reprogramming, the NWS employees would be forced to take time off without pay (furloughs) to make up the difference during hurricane season.

(Continued)

(Continued)

Some members of the authorizing committee for the weather service were so upset by the implications of the unauthorized reprogramming that they asked the appropriations committee to hold up the agency's budget until a clearer story could be told and proposals to address the underlying problems, including the underfunding as well as the compliance issues, could be worked out. In the end, the appropriations subcommittees approved the weather service's request for reprogramming.

The National Weather Service story hints at the complexity of reprogramming controversies. In this case, the administration systematically underfunded the NWS, which was of intense interest to members of Congress. The result was a reprogramming, which went unreported either because of executive branch policy or because of lack of knowledge of the reprogramming procedures. As the story became public, the extent and duration of the underfunding became clearer. Equally intriguing, the *advance notice* clause in the reprogramming guidelines was treated as if it meant *advanced permission* was required—this may be one way that Congress gets around Chadha limitations.

The use of funds built up through conscious overestimation of expenditures or underestimation of revenues also occurs in cities not experiencing cutbacks. The following excerpt from an interview with a city manager indicates that he believes that some cities use their balances to make minor but policy-related changes during the year:

Q.   What about year-end balances, how are they used?

A.   They are strictly an accounting device. We don't play any games at all with the statements. I could, because most people don't read accounting statements. Some managers do use it. They purposely underestimate revenues and overestimate expenditures, so that will happen. The council may ask the manager to find money to fund a project during the year. The manager then can do it. The council thinks it's magic.

The project, for which the council asks midyear support, may be one for which the need developed during the year, or it may be a pet project, with political payoff that could not be funded as part of the regular budget but could be funded midyear without much scrutiny or comparison to other projects.

While the need for contingency funds at the local level is substantial, year-end balances combined with contingency funds seldom exceed 8 percent to 10 percent of the budget in midsized or larger cities. Such balances can be proportionately much larger for smaller cities, villages, or counties, which have limited discretion and small budgets. One of the major purposes of such contingency or emergency funds is to provide money for labor agreements. Contingency funds may be drawn down to fund a particular capital project or to tide the city over in a recession to prevent having to cut the budget during the year. In some cities, at some times, a portion of the contingency funds may be spent for special council projects, with explicit council approval. The budget may thus change somewhat during the year, with negative impact on public accountability, but the amounts involved are normally quite small, maybe 2 percent of the total budget.

Interfund Transfers

Interfund transfers are shifts of money between appropriation accounts or funds. At the federal level, because the amounts of the individual appropriation accounts can be very large, most of the need for transfers can be accommodated within accounts, with minor reprogramming and without fanfare. In cities, however, individual funds (the local analog to federal appropriation accounts) are sometimes narrow, covering only one function and having only a limited number of dollars. Some of these funds may be spent for related functions, so interfund transfers may be planned and budgeted in advance. Formal transfers occurring during the year are treated as budget amendments and must be approved by the council. Hence they are not secret and do not bypass the regular budget process.

There should be little reason for unanticipated transfers, and normally there are few of them. Sometimes, however, there is some informal borrowing, especially from cash-rich to cash-poor funds. If the borrowing is not approved by the council or becomes a long-term loan or if a loan is not fully repaid, the implications are policy laden rather than technical. For example, if a general fund borrows from a water fund and does not repay the loan, the water fund may develop deficits.[18] The fund showing the deficit will have to cut services or increase user fees or taxes to eliminate it. The result may be raising water fees to pay for police services, a result that is not only inequitable but secret. If the deficits are not eliminated, borrowing costs for the water fund may go up, forcing the city to pay unnecessarily high interest charges on future water projects. This practice is probably not common, but it does sometimes occur, and when it does, there are policy implications.

Summary and Conclusions

For the purposes of accountability to the public and managerial predictability, most of the budget is implemented as passed. Nevertheless, some flexibility has to be built into budget implementation, because budgets are open to the environment. Rivers flood, countries invade each other, hurricanes knock down trees and houses. The economy waxes and wanes, reducing or increasing revenues beyond expectations and reducing or increasing the number of those eligible for entitlements. If more people commit crimes and are caught and sentenced to prison, there has to be some way to pay for their imprisonment, even if the numbers were not correctly predicted when the budget was put together. Budgets also adapt to the priorities of newly elected officials, who must initially work within the framework of budgets put together by their predecessors.

Budgets adapt through a variety of techniques, including supplemental appropriations, rescissions, deferrals, reprogramming, contingency funds, and interfund transfers. Some techniques are more common at one level of government than another. The federal government can run deficits, so it can borrow to respond to an emergency. State and local governments generally cannot run legal deficits and so have to build up reserve and contingency funds to draw down in emergencies, and they often hold back on spending during the year in case revenues do not materialize. Contingency funds and deferrals of this sort are common at state and local levels, but supplemental appropriations are relatively rare. Interfund transfers are fairly common at the local level; reprogramming within accounts is more important at the national level because accounts are so large that moving money around inside them usually provides sufficient flexibility.

Most of the changes in the budget during implementation are the result of technical changes and adaptation to the environment, but the flexibility that is absolutely necessary to budgeting also allows for some changes because of policy considerations. If Congress adds to the president's budget, the president may try to rescind or defer that unwanted spending; to bypass the president's opposition, Congress may package the spending the president disapproves of with supplemental requests that the president urgently needs. Especially where the executive and legislature are from different political parties, executives have been known to alter the legislatively approved budget during budget implementation to spend on priorities they prefer. Governors can often veto spending they don't like or want, but if there is a veto proof majority in the legislature, their vetoes can be overridden, so reshaping the budget during the budget year may be a preferred option.

In general, the amount of money spent on policy-related changes during the year is quite limited, and in some cases, as with policy-related deferrals at the national level, it has been reduced to near zero, but the amounts can rise and fall. When policy-based midyear changes become noticeable, conflict may push issues of budget implementation to center stage.

Useful Websites

When signing legislation, the president may object to portions of legislation, with the argument that these portions of the law are unconstitutional and he (or she) has no intention of carrying them out. Some of these signing statements have concerned budget implementation, demonstrating the battle between Congress and the president over budget implementation. To read the **presidents' signing statements**, see the American Presidency Project (www.presidency.ucsb.edu/ signingstatements.php?year=2011&Submit=DISPLAY#axzz2CDlcsNQX), and for an **interpretation of signing statements**, see the Congressional Research Service report, *Presidential Signing Statements: Constitutional and Institutional Implications*, 2012, by Todd Garvey (www.fas.org/sgp/crs/natsec/RL33667.pdf).

A good summary of the **history of use of rescissions** initiated by the president and or by Congress was done by the Government Accountability Office: *Updated Rescission Statistics, Fiscal Years 1974–2011* (www.gao.gov/assets/600/592874. pdf). The Congressional Budget Office publishes periodic reports on supplemental appropriations.

An intriguing thesis from the Naval Postgraduate School is available (www .dtic.mil/dtic/tr/fulltext/u2/a473540.pdf) in which Chad Roum examines **Department of Defense reprogramming requests and congressional responses** from 2000 to 2006 in *The Nature of DoD Reprogramming*, 2007; Roum's thesis is also available at http://calhoun.nps.edu/bitstream/handle/10945/3406/07Jun_ Roum.pdf?sequence=1&isAllowed=y.

Agencies and departments that reprogram typically leave a paper trail. The District of Columbia posts its quarterly list of approved reprogrammings, including the small ones that did not meet the level required for a formal reprogramming request. To see what they look like and what they were for, see http://cfo .dc.gov/page/reprogramming-reports. Data are quarterly from 2012. An example of a DoD reprogramming request for unclassified spending is posted at http:// comptroller.defense.gov/Portals/45/Documents/execution/reprogramming/ fy2013/prior1415s/13–14_PA_Replacement_Sources_for_FY_13_09_PA_ Implemented.pdf.

8 Controlling Waste, Fraud, and Abuse

> I was told if you do this (job) right, you'll eventually have people trying to shut you down.
>
> —Inspector General Stephen Street, Louisiana

> . . . getting investigated by the state auditor's office is like a visit from your accountant. An inspector general investigation is more like the Texas Rangers walking in.
>
> —Rep. Dan Gattis, Texas

The dynamic of budget control tends to follow a pattern over time: (1) an initial grant of broad discretion to the executive or to specific executive agencies; (2) a perception of abuse; (3) closer oversight, more reporting responsibilities, and possibly additional constraints written into committee reports and statutes; and (4) agency reaction to reduced flexibility. If politicians become overburdened with politically irrelevant decisions about budget execution or if the original problem seems to have been resolved, there may be (5) a gradual lessening of the intensity of oversight.

The central part of this process involves the perceived abuse of discretion and the reaction to that perception. Years ago, Sen. Edmund Muskie, D-Maine, described his impulse to increase control over implementation when an agency defies congressional or committee intent. When he learned that the Environmental Protection Agency (EPA) had misused its budgetary discretion, Muskie told agency officials that they had been granted "legitimate administrative discretion to spend the money, not defeat the purposes. Then to have you twist it as you have, is a temptation to this Senator to really handcuff you the next time."[1] "Handcuffing" involves writing into legislation detailed constraints that reduce the agency's discretion over budget implementation.

Portions of this cycle of discretion, abuse, and control were illustrated earlier when the National Weather Service abused its discretion by failing to follow congressional reprogramming guidelines during budget implementation and when Governor Nixon of Missouri cut legislatively approved spending during the year and reallocated at least some of it according to his own priorities. The weather service got its budget in the end, though it was held up, but the agency administrator lost his job; Governor Nixon permanently (that is constitutionally) lost some of his executive budget discretion.

Sometimes, the issue that evokes a cycle of control is not divergence from the budget as passed but a failure of implementation of a different sort, such as corruption, inefficiency, or ineffectiveness. Collectively, these problems are called *waste, fraud, and abuse.* A variety of overseers are tasked with finding and addressing these problems.[2] Of these, the inspectors general are among the most important. Inspectors general are more or less independent program and financial auditors who work with a team within or across specific departments or agencies. They examine financial reports, look for instances of fraud, waste, and abuse, and make recommendations to attack the structural sources of these problems. Inspectors general are widespread at the national level, common at the state level, and occur in some cities and counties.

Overall, inspectors general at all levels of government have been effective, saving millions, in some cases billions, of dollars of public money and helping to restore public trust after revelations of corruption. For example, the Office of the Inspector General of the Department of Transportation recently played a role in bringing a criminal wire fraud charge against Toyota for deceiving both the public and the National Highway Traffic Safety Administration when the company falsely claimed it had fixed a safety issue on its vehicles. The agreement required Toyota to pay a $1.2 billion penalty.[3] In fiscal year 2014, the federal IG (inspector general) community as a whole "identified potential savings of over $46.5 billion as well as program efficiencies and enhancements."[4]

At the state level, there is no estimate of savings or impact across states, but a few illustrations make the point of the effectiveness of some IG offices. These reports of accomplishments are not necessarily typical of other IG offices and may exaggerate the dollar gains, since IG offices often report identified *possible* recoveries or dollar savings rather than actual ones. Nevertheless, the reported accomplishments are impressive.

In Massachusetts, the 2013 annual report of the inspector general's office noted the following achievements: "The Office's work led to state and federal indictments, legislative initiatives, and reforms and policy changes at the state and local levels. The Office's efforts also resulted in settlements and the imposition of fines totaling $4 million. In addition, the Office identified $42.5 million in potential cost savings per year for the Commonwealth. The Office's direct appropriation in the 2013 fiscal year was $2.3 million. This means that for every dollar that the Legislature appropriated to the Office, the Office identified or helped recoup twenty dollars in savings and recoveries for the Commonwealth and other public entities."[5]

In Louisiana, the inspector general reported "for every dollar appropriated to OIG from the state general fund in Fiscal Year 2013–2014, $9.93 in fraud, corruption and waste was identified. Included among these numbers was a theft of over $1 million from the Department of Health and Hospitals that resulted in a ten-year prison term, over $1.8 million in tax credit fraud that resulted in a 70 month federal prison term, and over $15 million in identified waste following Hurricane Isaac. Not included among these numbers was an additional $4,578,286 in fraudulent tax credit payments that OIG was able to prevent from going out."[6]

In cities, inspectors general with substantial power and independence have also racked up impressive scores. In Washington, D.C., for example, the IG office reported for 2014 having identified $42 million in potential savings and claimed responsibility for $2.2 million in fines, penalties, restitutions, recoveries, and civil monetary actions and more than $3.7 million in civil recoveries. The office also boasted of participating in multiagency effort that shut the doors of home health agencies believed to have defrauded the district of over $100 million.[7]

Such successes do not come easily. Investigating waste, corruption, and fraud perpetrated by and against government agencies is a sensitive process with many potential pitfalls.

The Politics of Finding Waste, Fraud, and Abuse

When waste or corruption becomes widespread or severe, public anger may result in the creation of an office of the inspector general. The inspectors general (IGs) are the heroes come to restore financial integrity and public trust, but the more successful they are, the more they threaten customary ways of doing business. Inspectors general may make programs, administrators, and administrations look bad. They can be downright dangerous if they find evidence of fraud or corruption. To prevent prosecution or bad publicity, IGs may be starved, throttled, or forced to focus on minor issues. They may not get the access or cooperation they need to get their work done. As a result, IG work may give the appearance of reform without its substance. IGs have sometimes been compared to junkyard dogs—snarling, barking, threatening to bite, but on a relatively short leash.[8]

The IGs can be effective in their complex role only if they are independent of direct political control, but their independence may make it difficult for them to function cooperatively to bring about managerial changes within their agencies. Criticism of past administrations may be welcome, but describing the current administration as poorly managed or corrupt is likely to create tumult and may appear partisan.

The right balance between total independence and total subservience can be hard to find. What happens if IGs are too close to their department heads or the executive who appointed them and as a result, pull their punches? What if the IGs abuse their power and intimidate staff? What if IGs silence whistle blowers or come to conclusions condemning agency practices without sufficient evidence? On what grounds and with what evidence should IGs be removed and by whom? To be truly independent, removal by politicians should be difficult, which means that the IGs should police themselves. Is that a reasonable expectation, and how effective is this process? In order to function, IGs must be above reproach, but that is a tall order.

Inspectors general have been compared to junkyard dogs; they may have a threatening bark, but are often held on a short leash.

Federal Inspectors General: "Straddling a Barbed Wire Fence"

The federal IG offices illustrate the discretion-abuse-control cycle. A series of scandals and abuses led to the passage of the federal Inspector General Act.[9] The first inspector general was appointed in the Department of Agriculture in 1961, in response to the Billie Sol Estes scandal: "Estes had been revealed to have parlayed fraudulent warehouse receipts, mortgages, and financial statements into a fortune from the Department of Agriculture, despite the fact that his activities were suspected by three different audit units within the Department."[10] Widespread reports of cheating in Medicare and student loans as well as overbilling and overtesting of Medicaid patients prompted Congress to create an IG for the Department of Health, Education, and Welfare in 1976. The 1978 Inspector General Act installed IGs in twelve federal departments and agencies, specifying that the inspectors general would be appointed by the president and would report to both agency heads and Congress. The inspector general system gradually spread to other departments and agencies; in the smaller agencies, inspectors general were not appointed by the president.

The matters that inspectors general are supposed to examine and their ability to force compliance with requests for information have increased over time, but the budget and the staffing levels of IG offices have sometimes decreased or have not increased proportionally to the size of their responsibilities, reducing what the IG offices can accomplish. Moreover, in recent years, a number of IG offices have been occupied by temporary rather than permanent heads, weakening those offices for a period of time.

Staffing Out of Balance With Work Load. In 1993, there were sixty federal offices of the inspector general, employing fifteen thousand;[11] by 2003, there were only fifty-seven offices, employing eleven thousand.[12] At present, there are seventy-two federal inspector general offices: Thirty-two are presidentially nominated and Senate approved; one the president alone appoints, and thirty-nine are appointed by the agencies they scrutinize. Combined, these offices employ an estimated fourteen thousand personnel. With a vastly expanded mission, more mandated reports, and many more offices, there were fewer employees in federal IG offices in 2014 than there were in 1993.

The reduction of the IG workforce reflected some reorganization and elimination of agencies as well as the downsizing of the federal bureaucracy. One needs fewer overseers in a smaller bureaucracy, and reportedly, many IGs felt they needed to take cuts proportional to those of their agencies. However, all of the reductions may not have been voluntary. If a department or agency head is displeased with the expressed point of view of its inspector general, the administrator may cut the budget and staffing of the office. Also, the National Performance Review, during the Clinton-Gore administration, took aim at offices whose role was detailed oversight, arguing that these overseers intimidated frontline managers, making them risk averse and preventing them from innovating. As a result, IG offices were among those targeted for particularly deep personnel reductions.

The IG offices were cut at about twice the rate of the federal civilian workforce in the years between 1993 and 2003. The federal civilian workforce was reduced by about 13 percent,[13] whereas the IG staff shrank about 26 percent. It was widely rumored in the IG world that the disproportionate reductions represented a kind of revenge for unfriendly or critical studies and bad publicity.[14]

The reduction in staffing occurred simultaneously with an expansion of the role of the IGs. The Chief Financial Officers Act required federal agencies to prepare financial reports and have them audited, and the IGs were called on to examine those new financial reports. In addition, IGs have taken on more responsibility for criminal investigations and computer security. As the agencies that the IGs worked for cut back staffing, they often increased their contracting out, sometimes without retaining sufficient staff in-house to supervise the contracts. That created more work for IGs. The budget cuts and staffing reductions therefore understate the degree to which the IGs were being pressed.

For example, in the Department of Defense, the budget doubled, from $300 billion to $600 billion, while staffing in the IG office remained nearly unchanged. According to one report, "In fiscal 1997, there was one IG auditor for every $642 million in DoD contracts. By 2007, the ratio had declined to one auditor for every $2.03 billion in contracts."[15]

From fiscal years 2001 through 2006, the State Department's budget increased from $13.7 billion to about $24 billion, an increase of 55 percent when adjusted for inflation, in order to manage an expanding role in the global war on terrorism. During this same period, the State Department's IG's budget increased from $29 million to $31 million, which, when adjusted for inflation, was a decrease of about 6 percent. In addition, of the 318 authorized staff in the State Department's IG's fiscal year 2006 budget, the actual onboard staff averaged 182 or about 57 percent of the authorized level and about 20 percent less than in fiscal year 2001.[16]

In recent years, staffing recovered somewhat from its low point of eleven thousand in 2003. From 2005 to 2011, budgets for the sixteen cabinet level inspector general offices increased by 45 percent on average, and staffing for those offices increased 17 percent.[17] However, sequestration—the across-the-board cuts passed in 2011 to take effect in 2013—seems to have halted the recovery. From 2013 to 2015, 32 percent of IGs responding to a survey reported a decline of 5 percent to 10 percent in staffing, while 13 percent reported a decline of more than 10 percent.[18] The survey did not identify individuals who responded or in which offices they worked, but a few examples from major departments illustrate the continuing problem of increased scope of work with stable or shrinking staffing levels. The OIG office in the Department of Agriculture showed a decrease in staffing from 2012 to 2015 of 3.5 percent. The Office of the Inspector General in Health and Human Services dropped from a peak of 1800 in 2012 to 1660 in 2013 to 1557 in 2014, a decrease of 13.5 percent. The latter decrease occurred during the implementation of the Affordable Care Act. The Department of Justice IG office reported relatively constant numbers over this period. The Department of Labor reported a decline of 7.5 percent from 2013 to 2015 in staffing paid from appropriations.

Growing Independence. The trend toward greater scope for investigations and more independence for federal inspectors general is clear. For example, as IGs got deeper into fraud cases, they began to press for broader authority to engage in criminal investigations. Years earlier there had been considerable opposition to IGs engaging in criminal investigations—supporters of the business community and representatives of those being investigated wanted to curtail the power of the IGs to investigate their activities. The FBI and the Department of Justice were concerned about losing control of their investigations. Part of that concern may have been based on protection of turf, but it may also have been related to the attorney general's desire to be able to put a stop to particular investigations. Opposition to the IGs as criminal investigators gradually diminished, as they demonstrated that they could save a lot of money by investigating cases of fraud against the government.

A procedure emerged in which each investigator in an Office of the Inspector General had to ask the permission of the Justice Department (the U.S. Marshal Service) to engage in a criminal investigation, and the permission applied only to that case. The case-by-case approach was so clumsy that it was gradually replaced by an annual blanket grant of criminal investigation powers to particular IG offices, enforced by a memorandum of understanding that included requirements for training. The permission could be revoked for cause, such as abuse of power. IGs feared administrative delays in granting such blanket approvals, which could threaten or terminate ongoing investigations, so they asked for a statutory grant of power to do criminal investigations under the general oversight of the Department of Justice. Rather than assuming that they could not engage in such investigations unless the Justice Department gave approval, the IGs wished to assume they could do so unless the Justice Department said otherwise.

The FBI and the Justice Department initially opposed granting this authority to the IGs. By 2000, however, the Department of Justice had relinquished its objections, saying that the marshal service was swamped with work as a result of the deputations and a legislative deputation would eliminate that extra work.[19] After 2001, the criminal justice agencies were so absorbed in antiterrorist activities that overseeing each inspector general office's criminal investigations may have seemed a much lower priority. By 2002, the proposal had passed as part of the legislation creating the Department of Homeland Security. (The presidentially appointed IGs received statutory authority, but the agency-appointed IGs still operated on a permission basis.)

The result was only a marginal improvement. As the price for his support, the attorney general required a provision in the legislation allowing him to cancel any investigation without revoking the permission of an entire office.[20] Otherwise, to stop a particular investigation that might have security implications, that contradicted an existing law enforcement case, or that was politically threatening, the attorney general would have had to shut down a whole office's investigations, with possible negative publicity. What he asked for and got was more surgical precision in the level of his control. The IGs got more independence but did not gain much in the way of freedom from control by the administration in these criminal cases. The permission of a whole office could still be revoked for systemic reasons, such as failure to train staff adequately for dangerous situations or in the use of firearms or for abuse of power.

Early in the George W. Bush administration, several highly questionable firings and appointments of politically connected IGs stirred the fears of the IG community concerning the degree of their independence. In one incident, a highly accomplished and respected IG in NASA was forced to resign, and the president immediately appointed a replacement who had spent a year on the White House staff. The fired IG had been critical of the deep budget cuts in the agency and the extent and manner of contracting out.[21] Whether or not the forced resignation was because of the IG's strong and critical positions, other IGs felt pressured and threatened.

The inspectors general began to press for the rest of their legislative agenda, which included a legislative basis for the Council of Inspectors General, along with some funding for it, and fixed terms of office rather than service at the pleasure of the president. They also worked for clarification of the grounds for firing a sitting inspector general. With fixed terms, IGs could only be fired for stated cause.

The Office of Management and Budget (OMB)—as the executive office that works most closely with the IGs to see that they are implementing administration policies and not their own preferences—opposed fixed terms. In a hearing, the OMB representative argued that the IGs did not need any more independence.

Congress passed an IG independence reform bill in 2008. Reacting to the proposal before it was passed, President Bush threatened to veto the bill if it included a fixed term for the IGs and the provision that IGs could be dismissed only for good cause, because such terms would reduce his ability to fire them. He also objected to a provision that would allow the IGs to submit their budget proposals directly to Congress, bypassing the normal executive review and approval process. Further, Bush objected to giving the council of IGs a basis in law, though it is unclear why he objected to that provision. The final bill was altered to address most of the president's objections but did contain some provisions strengthening IG independence:

- The legislation provides that each IG shall be appointed without regard to political affiliation and solely on the basis of integrity and demonstrated ability in accounting, auditing, financial analysis, law, management analysis, public administration, or investigations.
- It requires that the president or agency heads inform both houses of Congress of the reasons for removing or transferring an inspector general at least thirty days prior to the removal or transfer. Before the law was passed, the president was required to communicate the reasons to Congress but not before an IG's removal or transfer.
- It provides salary increases for IGs, to pay them as senior-level executive employees, but with a prohibition on bonuses or cash awards. The reason was to make the IGs less dependent on the approval of the heads of their departments.
- The law gives the IG council a legislative basis, combines the two existing councils into one, and provides for a chair to be elected by the IGs, although there is still to be an "executive chair" from OMB. A funding stream is identified to support the new council. The council will send the president a slate of candidates for vacancies, though he is not required to choose his nominee from this list.
- The IGs' subpoena power is specifically expanded to include access to electronic and tangible items, and it is made clear that all IGs may recover funds defrauded from their agencies under the Program Fraud Civil Remedies Act. Similarly, all IGs would now have clear law enforcement authority.
- It allows IGs to obtain their own legal counsel. The bill allows them to seek counsel from other IG offices, have their own counsel reporting directly to them, or obtain counsel from the Council of the Inspectors General.

- It establishes separate budget lines in the requests of the IGs, agency heads, and the president for the operations, training, and support of the IGs, so that Congress can clearly track the resources a president intends to provide them.
- It requires agencies to have a direct link on their Internet home pages to the office of their inspector general, so that IG reports and materials are easily accessible and so that the public can directly report instances of waste, fraud, and abuse.[22]

Instead of vetoing the measure, as he had threatened, President Bush signed it but made it clear in his signing statement that he would not be bound by it. The president objected to IGs having access to legal counsel separate from the department's legal counsel, although most of the major IGs already had this source of independence. He also objected to the provision that the president include in his budget proposal the original IG budget request, in addition to his own recommendation, and in cases where the recommendation was to cut the services of the IG's office, to include the IG's discussion of the president's request. The president rejected this directive, claiming it violated his right under the Constitution to make recommendations to Congress.

For the IGs who are not presidentially appointed, their independence was improved by the Dodd Frank act in 2010. The act defined the agency head to whom they reported as the whole board or commission, in agencies that had such boards or commissions, and required a two-thirds majority to fire them rather than a single individual. The majority of them felt that this change made them more independent.[23]

Generally, the IG reform act was implemented as intended. While the president did not always break out the IG offices in his budget proposal as required by the reforms,[24] the budgets for the IGs are much clearer than they had been before 2008. The administration has allowed the IGs to outline their requests for comparison with OMB recommendations, and when an IG office felt that the budget proposal was too low, the IG was able to complain publicly about the request. In several major cases, the increased transparency made it clear that overall agency spending was increasing, while IG office expenditures were being cut: In the president's request for 2011, Department of Defense spending was increased by 3.4 percent, while the IG office was cut by 2 percent; even more strikingly, the Department of Energy budget was proposed for a 7 percent increase, while its IG office was slated for a cut of 17 percent.[25]

While the level of independence of IGs has decidedly improved, some problems remain. Although presidents can no longer fire an IG without notifying Congress in advance and stating their reasons, it is still possible for agencies to sideline an IG by putting him or her on involuntary paid leave. A Senate report noted the example of the IG in the National Archives and Records Administration who was put on paid leave in 2012 for two years while charges against him were investigated.[26]

A major challenge to the 2008 reforms occurred in 2009, when the Obama administration fired a sitting IG for what appeared to be personal and political reasons. The administration had asked for the resignation of the IG of AmeriCorps, a domestic volunteer corps somewhat similar to the Peace Corps. By asking for a resignation rather than firing the IG, the administration tried to circumvent the 2008 reform requirement to give Congress an explanation for a firing thirty days in advance. However, the IG would not quit, ultimately suing to get his job back. (He lost the suit.) The administration then put the IG on involuntary leave, while delivering a list of reasons for firing to the Congress. The administration thus complied with the letter, if not the intent, of the 2008 reforms. (For further details, see the minicase "President Obama Fires an IG" below.)

In 2014, a number of the IGs complained to Congress that some agencies were refusing to hand over documents, either delaying investigations or making them impossible. Sometimes the agencies involved claimed other laws, including national security requirements, took precedence over IG access, but IGs responded that the refusal to comply with document requests sometimes had nothing to do with sensitive material. The FBI rejected the IGs' request for an organizational chart, claiming the request had to go through the FBI's general counsel's office.[27]

In August of 2015, the IG council pleaded with Congress to make IGs' independence clearer after "The DOJ's Office of Legal Counsel ruled that the department's IG can only obtain sensitive information such as wiretaps and grand-jury testimony if given permission by other Justice officials overseeing the cases in question. While permission may be granted upon request, some information will be barred from access by IGs altogether."[28] Bills have been introduced in Congress to clarify the IGs' access to such documents, but as of 2015, these bills had not proceeded beyond the committee level.

Minicase: President Obama Fires an IG

Gerald Walpin, the IG of AmeriCorps, had been selected by President George W. Bush and carried over into the Obama administration. Walpin had never worked in investigations or auditing and had no prior experience in an IG office. He was not familiar with the norms of IG offices, such as refraining from speaking to the press about an ongoing investigation, nor was he familiar with how a government office operates; for example, at one point he confessed to complete lack of experience or knowledge of procedures for investigating charges of discrimination in employment. Columnists and bloggers suggested that he was an active Republican, donating to Republican candidates and supporting their campaigns, though he had never worked in the White House or on a congressional staff. But even if he had been scrupulously nonpartisan and highly experienced, he would have had a difficult time finding himself in a Democratic administration as the inspector general of a pet program of the president and the president's wife. Virtually anything the IG criticized would be considered political and antagonistic to the administration.

Republicans had long stalked AmeriCorps, attacking it for association with a number of their issues, such as a volunteer who escorted women safely inside an abortion center and a small number of volunteers who helped collect money for ACORN, a community organizing group that earned Republican anger for registering poor voters (who would likely vote for Democratic candidates). Having a Bush appointee as IG in AmeriCorps gave Republicans an opportunity to find violations that could bring down the entire program.

Whether or not Walpin intentionally played into the Republican agenda, from the administration's point of view, Walpin's reports were potentially lethal. His most controversial findings dealt with abuse of funds by a former basketball star, Kevin Johnson, who ran a charity that received AmeriCorps funding. Johnson was a well-known Obama supporter. Not satisfied with a claim for repayment from the charity Johnson ran, Walpin pushed to assure that Johnson would be prohibited from receiving any future federal grants. When Johnson ran for and won the mayoralty of Sacramento, this prohibition threatened to prevent the city from receiving antirecession funds from the administration. The acting U.S. attorney took over and negotiated a settlement that did not take the whole population of the city of Sacramento hostage. Walpin complained loudly about this arrangement as insufficiently punitive on the one hand and leaving the government open to further abuse on the other.

When AmeriCorps board members approached the administration asking for Walpin to be relieved of his duties, the administration responded quickly, asking for Walpin's resignation. When Walpin refused to resign, the administration put Walpin on administrative leave and responded to congressional complaints about lack of advance notice by describing in detail its list of complaints against Walpin. The administration did not initially but did eventually comply with the requirement for advance notice to Congress.

(Continued)

(Continued)

Whether or not the administration was justified in asking for Walpin's resignation—cases have been made on both sides—the AmeriCorps IG office remained without a permanent head from 2009 until 2012, and its budget was drastically reduced. While these actions certainly suggest the administration was trying to protect a program (Americorps) that had been seriously attacked—the House voted to eliminate AmeriCorps funding completely— one can't help wondering about the effectiveness of an IG who seemed out to destroy an agency rather than make it work better. Why would the board cooperate with him or implement his recommendations? Where is the line between legitimate investigation and creating a threatening environment? What should an administration do about an IG appointed by a president of the opposite party, known for choosing candidates for political loyalty rather than experience, an IG who seemed to have an agenda to publicly embarrass an administration by helping to bring down a program that symbolized the president's goals and values?

The acting U.S. attorney who arranged the negotiated settlement with Johnson referred Walpin's case to the IG council for possible disciplinary action, for failure to abide by accepted rules of evidence and for publicizing his cases before they were complete. The integrity committee of the IG council did not discipline Walpin, but their standards for initiating an investigation were high—that is, investigations would occur when the case involved gross mismanagement, gross waste of funds, abuse of authority, or misconduct so serious that it would undermine the integrity or independence expected of an IG or senior IG staff (from the procedure manual, 2009). The charges laid against Walpin were not that serious. The integrity committee argued that Walpin had sufficiently and satisfactorily addressed the matter and further inquiry or investigation was not warranted. Self-policing in this case did not produce a solution or publicly clarify the norms and rules of investigations.

Sources: Andrew Walzer, "Media Trumpet Walpin Claims Without Noting Acting U.S. Attorney's Allegations," Media Matters for America, June 18, 2009, http:// mediamatters.org/research/2009/06/18/media-trumpet-walpin-claims -without-noting-acti/151309; a series of articles by Byron York in the *Washington Examiner* detail the case from an pro-Walpin perspective, beginning with "What Is Behind Obama's Sudden Attempt to Fire the AmeriCorps Inspector General?" June 10, 2009, http://washingtonexaminer.com/article/135590; Evan Harris, "More Details Emerge In President Obama's Firing of Inspector General," June 13, 2009, ABC News, http://abcnews.go.com/blogs/politics/2009/06/

more-details-emerge-in-president-obamas-firing-of-inspector-general/; Ed
O'Keefe, "Documents Detail Case for Walpin's Dismissal," *Washington Post*,
July 1, 2009; Committee on Oversight and Government Reform, U.S. House of
Representatives, "Politicization of Inspectors General," October 21, 2004, http://
oversight-archive.waxman.house.gov/story.asp?ID=726; Huma Khan, "President
Obama Fires Controversial Inspector General," ABC News, June 12, 2009;
"Letter to Senator Grassley From the Board of the Corporation for National and
Community Service," *Washington Post*, June 17, 2009, www.washingtonpost
.com/wp-srv/politics/documents/board_letter_to_grassley.pdf; Senate Finance
Committee, Sen. Charles E. Grassley, Ranking Member and House Committee
on Oversight and Government Reform, Rep. Darrell Issa, Ranking Member, "The
Firing of the Inspector General for The Corporation for National and Community
Service," Joint Staff Report, 111th Congress, November 20, 2009, http://oversight
.house.gov/wp-content/uploads/2012/02/20091120JointStaffReport1
.pdf; Justin Elliott, "GOP Inquiry Fails to Show Obama's Firing Of AmeriCorps
IG Was Politicized," November 20, 2009, TPMMuckraker, http://tpmmuckraker
.talkingpointsmemo.com/2009/11/issa_grassley_inquiry_hits_white_house_on_
walpin.php; Molly Ivins, "Attacks on AmeriCorps Are Mean-Spirited, Stupid,"
Seattle Times, October 30, 1995, http://community.seattletimes
.nwsource.com/archive/?date=19951030&slug=2149598; Lee Speigel, "White
House Plays Hardball; Says Fired IG Walpin Was 'Confused, Disoriented'
Engaged in 'Inappropriate Conduct,'" June 16, 2009, ABC News, http://abcnews
.go.com/blogs/politics/2009/06/white-house-plays-hardball-says-fired-ig-walpin
-was-confused -disoriented-engaged-in-inappropriate-co/; Josh Gerstein, "W.H.
v. Grassley on Walpin Clearing," November 10, 2009, Politico, http://www
.politico.com/blogs/joshgerstein/1109/WH_v_Grassley_on_Walpin_clearing
.html; "Gerald Walpin, Response of IG Gerald Walpin and the OIG To the
Complaint," ABC News, http://a.abcnews.go.com/images/Politics/PCIE_
Response_Report_FINAL_5_20_09.pdf; Ed O'Keefe, "Records Indicate Tension
Between Agency's Fired IG and Officials," *Washington Post*, July 1, 2009.

In the Walpin case, the inspector general council judged that the charges
against Walpin did not meet their standard of seriousness. But what about a case
in which there really were serious charges? How did the case come to light, who
investigated, and what did the IG council do? If the IGs are to be independent of
politics, they must be able to self police. The minicase (see p. 268) of the IG from
the Department of Commerce suggests the IG council is not very effective at
policing its own, not only because it lacks the staff to investigate and often takes
the IGs' words as truth, but also because IGs control their subordinates' careers
and can threaten them if the subordinates report bad behavior. Reports of serious
misbehavior may never reach the IG council.

Minicase: Who Guards the Guards? Not the Guards Themselves

Todd Zinser was the Commerce Department inspector general, appointed in 2007; he resigned under congressional pressure in June 2015. Zinser became a focus of congressional investigation because his office had failed to bring to congressional attention the National Weather Service's evasion of the reprogramming rules, about which his office had received a hot-line tip. In an odd move, Zinser had allowed the National Weather Service to investigate itself. He denied knowing about his office's preliminary investigation, but the congressional committee chair was not convinced that was possible.

A complaint had been filed with the IG council charging Zinser with promoting and protecting a woman with whom he had undue intimacy. Zinser denied the charge, and the council accepted his denial. Zinser's closest aides and appointees and possibly Zinser himself forced staff to sign choke orders, forbidding them to bring complaints against him to the IG council. Thus, the more serious charges, from Congress' point of view, of beginning an investigation without warning Congress about the issue and then handing the investigation over to the agency being investigated were never reported to the IG council. It was a congressional committee that did the investigation, and it was members of Congress who wanted the IG to step down.

Sources: Josh Hicks, "Lawmaker Seeks Ouster of Commerce Department Inspector General," *Washington Post*, March 30, 2015, http://www.washingtonpost.com/blogs/federal-eye/wp/2015/03/30/lawmaker-seeks-ouster-of-commerce-department-inspector-general/; Sarah Westwood, "Commerce Inspector General Resigns Amid Growing Scandal," *The Washington Examiner*, June 4, 2015, http://www.washingtonexaminer.com/commerce-inspector-general-resigns-amid-growing-scandal/article/2565597.

It is easy to be too close to the administration, too protective of it, and hence to be hesitant to issue hard hitting reports, but it is also easy to be too far from the administration, too sympathetic to the opposite party from the administration, too eager to find fault and be bent on destruction or embarrassment rather than problem solving. Agency heads, fearing bad criticism and bad publicity, sometimes fail to cooperate with IGs. Presidents, less able than ever to fire sitting IGs, even those appointed by their predecessors, cannot count on loyalty from IGs, which may contribute to alternative measures of control, such as cutting IG budgets and staffing and failure to appoint permanent IGs.

Failure to Appoint Permanent Inspectors General. In recent years, many federal IG offices have had only acting heads, sometimes for years. An IG office with an acting head has less clout and visibility than one with a presidentially appointed, congressionally approved inspector general. As of October of 2015, there were nine acting inspectors general among the thirty-three presidentially appointed offices. Of those nine offices, the president had nominated permanent nominees for four.

The Office of the Inspector General in the Department of Interior had an acting head for over six and half years. Under pressure to name a candidate, in June of 2015 President Obama finally nominated the acting IG for the permanent position. As of December 2015, it looked as if the Senate would not confirm his choice. The Agency for International Development has been without a permanent IG for over four years. The Department of Veterans' Affairs IG Office had an acting head for over a year and a half, before he was asked to step down amidst charges from whistleblowers that he had done little to uncover fraud and abuse. He was followed by another acting appointment for another four months, before the president nominated a permanent inspector general. The CIA head position was vacant for more than half a year without a presidential nominee for the position.[29] The Department of State operated with an acting IG from January 2008 to June 2013.

Sen. Ron Johnson, chairman of the Senate Homeland Security and Government Affairs Committee, pointed out at a hearing that temporary IG appointees "are not truly independent" and because of their interim status "do not drive office policy, and they are at greater risk of compromising their work to appease the agency or the president." Johnson was particularly concerned about the lack of a nomination for the Veterans' Administration, arguing that the acting IG, Richard Griffin, "has shown alarming signs that he lacks independence from the agency, including his failure to release more than 140 reports to the public and to Congress, his fighting to keep documents from Congress, and reports that he has lost the trust of whistleblowers at the agency."[30]

The increased independence of IGs, including the difficulty a president has in firing a sitting IG—even one who may have been appointed by a predecessor of the opposite party—may be contributing to the president's slowness in nominating permanent IGs. Since acting IGs are often interested in being appointed to the post of permanent head of their office, they may pull their punches in an effort to please their department heads and become overly protective of the agencies they are supposed to investigate. They may thus be more controllable than presidentially nominated and congressionally approved Inspectors general. (For an example of an acting IG who got too close to department political staffers, see the minicase of Homeland Security, on p. 270.)

Minicase: Acting IG for
Homeland Security–Too Close to the Department

The acting IG for Homeland Security, Charles K. Edwards, stepped down, after a congressional investigation of charges of nepotism, misuse of office, and an overly close relationship with the administration.[1]

He was charged with delaying investigations and altering reports to protect the administration. The investigation began because Edwards reportedly withheld information and soft-pedaled the incident in which the president's security detail dallied with prostitutes in Colombia. According to a report by a congressional oversight committee, he shared drinks and dinners "with department leaders and gave them inside information about the timing and findings of investigations." He was charged with accepting guidance from the political advisers of the department head on the wording and timing of three reports. Reportedly, he asked the secretary's advisers how he should respond to questions at a hearing. Committee officials concluded that because he was actively seeking the permanent appointment, he was not engaging in real oversight.[2]

Edwards stepped down in December 2013, just before he was to testify on these issues. This forced resignation was prompted by a congressional investigation, not by the IG council. Congressional committees, especially when dominated by the opposite party from the administration, may be eager to read hard-hitting critical reports from inspectors general; if acting IGs are too tame, too hungry for the permanent job to offer incisive and serious analysis, then committee members have an interest in replacing that IG with a more aggressive permanent appointee. The IG council, on the other hand, has an interest in protecting the inspector general community; it has a high bar for evidence against a sitting IG, permanent or temporary.

Edwards, in defending himself against charges of nepotism and abuse of office, argued the IG council had reviewed and dismissed similar allegations against him. However, it is not clear that the IG council took the charges seriously. "Only after the Senate started investigating Edwards in June did the council set up an investigation of Edwards by the Transportation Department's inspector general. . . . Until that time, complaints against Edwards were either dismissed or languished at the council." Moreover, the "Council for Inspectors General on Integrity and Efficiency usually only meets four times a year and lacks the tools to investigate and hold inspectors general accountable for abuses."[3]

---

1. U.S. Senate Subcommittee on Financial and Contracting Oversight, Committee on Homeland Security and Governmental Affairs, "Investigation Into Allegations of Misconduct by the Former Acting and Deputy Inspector General of the Department of Homeland Security," Staff Report, 2014, 04–24.

2. Carol Leonnig, "Probe: DHS Watchdog Cozy With Officials, Altered Reports as He Sought Top Job," *Washington Post*, April 24, 2014, http://www.washingtonpost .com/politics/probe-dhs-watchdog-cozy-with-officials-altered-reports-as-he-sought-top-job/2014/04/23/b46a9366-c6ef-11e3-9f37-7ce307c56815_story.html.
3. Susan Crabtree, "Internal Government Watchdog System Broken, Experts Say," *The Washington Examiner*, May 16, 2014, http://www.washingtonexaminer.com/ internal-government-watchdog-system-broken-experts-say/article/2548508.

The inspectors general need to be independent to carry out investigations, but even when there is a permanent appointed head, their independence can be compromised by political appointment, by budget subordination of the IG offices to the department heads, and by their responsibility to both Congress and the department secretaries. The IGs continually struggle to gain and maintain sufficient budget, staffing, and independence to do their work.

If inspectors general become caught between departments and Congress, they can be rendered useless. The GAO evaluated the first IG, in the Department of Agriculture, negatively. There was "limited use of the office as a management tool, partly because of concern over external disclosure of inspection findings through routine distribution of reports to congressional committees and others."[31] Reported one observer of the inspector general system, "In my opinion, the IG's independence will not be any better defined than it has been and will always be a subject of dispute. IGs are 'straddling a barbed wire fence.'"[32]

State and Local Inspectors General

Thirty-three states have at least one inspector general in a major agency or department (see Table 8.1). Some of the offices are created by statute and hence are permanent; some by executive order, which can be revoked or continued by the next executive; and some only by fiat of an agency or department head. In some states, only one or a few agencies have IGs, but eleven of the states have an inspector general system that is statewide or nearly statewide in coverage. These tend to be in states known for a culture of corruption, such as Illinois, Louisiana, New York, and Massachusetts.

Some IGs have broad powers, including subpoena and criminal investigation powers, and others have much more limited scope and power. Equally important, the offices vary considerably in how independent the IGs are from department heads or the governor. To some extent these variables interact; for example, some states grant IGs broad powers but keep them leashed by making the IGs responsible

TABLE 8.1 State Inspectors General

State	Date Created	E/S/A	Department(s)	Appointed by/Reports to	Independence
Arizona	1991	S	Corrections	Works independently of the director.	Unknown
	2004	E	Transportation	Reports to the director of transportation department.	Low
	2009	S	Medicaid; health care cost containment system	Reports directly to the director of Arizona health care cost containment system.	Has full subpoena powers, can impose fines, refer criminal cases for prosecution
			Department of Economic Security	NA	
			Children and Family services	NA	
Arkansas	2013	S	Medicaid	Appointed by the governor with advice and consent of the senate; reports directly to the governor; serves at the pleasure of the governor.	Low
California	1994	S	Youth and Adult Corrections staffed as of 1998	Governor appoints, Senate confirms.	Moderate; no fixed term
	2005	S	Dept. of Corrections and Rehabilitation	Governor appoints, Senate confirms; six-year term, can be removed only for cause.	High

State	Date Created	E/S/A	Department(s)	Appointed by/Reports to	Independence
	2011	S	Dept of Corrections and Rehabilitation	2011, office budget reduced 45 percent; most staff transferred to state auditor; scope of authority drastically reduced; studies to be requested by governor, chair of senate rules committee, or assembly speaker.	Low
	NA	A	Highway Patrol	Reports directly to commissioner of California Highway Patrol.	Low
Colorado	1995	S	Corrections	Department of Corrections head appoints and removes.	Low
Florida	1994	S	Governmentwide	An IG in each department reports to agency head who hires, fires; there is a chief IG.	Moderate; agency head cannot prevent or prohibit the IG from "initiating, carrying out, or completing any audit or investigation"
Georgia	2003	E	Governmentwide	Governor hires, fires, reports to governor.	
	2007	A	Human Services		
	Before 2008	NA	Dept. of Community Health, includes Medicaid	Appointed by and Reports to commissioner of Community Health.	Low

(Continued)

TABLE 8.1 (Continued)

State	Date Created	E/S/A	Department(s)	Appointed by/Reports to	Independence
Illinois	2003	E	Governor's agencies IG	Appointed by the governor; reports to the governor.	Low
	2008	S	Statute, includes all executive officers	Executive IG, governor appoints, Senate confirms; removal only for cause; five-year term.	Statute prohibits political basis of appointment; removal only for cause; relatively high independence
	1993	S	Children and Family Services	Reports to department director, the governor, annually to the legislature; has separate budget; appointed by governor, Senate confirms; four-year term.	Moderately high
	1994	S	Health Care/ Medicaid	Appointed by and reports to governor, via the executive IG, Senate confirms; four-year term; budget under the department.	Moderate
	2007	S	Human Services	Governor appoints; reports to both governor and department head; four-year term; independent budget line.	Moderate
	1993	S	Attorney General IG	Attorney general appoints, Senate confirms by three-fifths vote; reports to the attorney general; may also report to the Ethics Commission; five-year term; removal for cause w/o hearing; independent budget.	Moderately high

State	Date Created	E/S/A	Department(s)	Appointed by/Reports to	Independence
	1993	S	Secretary of State IG	Secretary of state appoints, Senate confirms by three-fifths vote; five-year term; removal for cause w/o hearing; independent budget.	Moderately high
	1993	S	Office of Comptroller	Controller appoints, Senate confirms by three-fifths vote; five-year term; removal for cause w/o hearing; independent budget.	Moderately high
	1993	S	State Treasurer	Treasurer appoints, Senate confirms by three-fifths vote; five-year term; removal for cause w/o hearing; independent budget.	Moderately high
	1993	S	Legislative IG	Legislature appoints, staff chosen by leadership, not IG; legislature controls budget; cannot initiate investigation unless approved by Legislative Ethics Committee.	Five-year terms; but employment of staff subject to approval of at least three of four legislative leaders; overall, low
Indiana	2005	S	Executive agencies	Governor appoints; term coincides with governor, removed only for misfeasance or malfeasance.	High
Kansas	2007	S	Department of Health and Environment	Selected by and reports directly to director of Health Department; budget and administration controlled by department; Senate confirms; can be removed only for cause.	Moderate

(Continued)

TABLE 8.1 (Continued)

State	Date Created	E/S/A	Department(s)	Appointed by/Reports to	Independence
			Medicaid	Senate confirms. The state privatized Medicaid, department proposed making position unclassified (at the pleasure of the governor, i.e., less independent). Position generally vacant, Senate proposes eliminating.	Lower than low
	1998	A	Juvenile Justice	Designated by and Reports to the JJA commissioner.	
	1989	NA	Transportation	Reports to director of Fiscal and Asset management, who reports to secretary of transportation.	
Kentucky	1977	S	Health, includes Medicaid	Secretary hires and fires.	Low
	1999	S	Environmental	Governor appoints/fires.	Low
	2002	E	Transportation	Governor appoints/fires.	Low
Louisiana *	1988, 2008	E/S	Governmentwide	Reports to governor, who can no longer choose whether to make reports public, under a reform in 2008.	Initially low; improved in 2008

State	Date Created	E/S/A	Department(s)	Appointed by/Reports to	Independence
Maryland	1990	A	Human Resources, includes chairing team with responsibility for Medicaid integrity	Reports to secretary.	Low
	1994	A	Public Safety	Reports to secretary.	Low
Massachusetts	1998	A	Mental Health	Reports to secretary.	Low
	1981	S	Governmentwide	Governor, AG, state auditor choose; two of them can remove; five-year term.	High
Michigan	1972	S	Family Independence Agency	Agency director appoints.	Low
	2010	E	Medicaid-Health services	Governor appoints, independent of department; has own budget; IG classified civil servant; reports to Health Services director and governor.	Moderately high
Minnesota	2011	A	Human Services, includes Medicaid	Reports to department commissioner or deputy commissioner.	NA
Missouri	2004	A	Corrections	Investigative arm of the department; reports to the director.	Low

(Continued)

277

TABLE 8.1 (Continued)

State	Date Created	E/S/A	Department(s)	Appointed by/Reports to	Independence
Nebraska	2012	S	Child welfare Corrections	Ombudsman, chair of legislative HHS commission, and chair of Leg. Executive board appoints; five-year term, renewable; part of legislative branch.	High
	2015	S		Subdivision of the Office of Public Counsel.	Relatively high; subject to control of the public counsel, but has term of five years, removal requires assent from chair of executive board of legislative council and chair of judiciary committee of legislature
				Appointed by Public Counsel with approval by chairperson of the executive board of the legislative council and chairperson of the judiciary committee of the legislature. Reports to the director of Corrections and to Board of State Prison Commissioners.	
Nevada	NA	NA	Corrections	Reports to the head of Corrections and to Board of State Prison Commissioners.	Permanent employee, can be fired for cause
New Jersey	2005– Terminated in 2010; functions merged with Comptroller	S	Statewide		Moderately high
	1988		Transportation	Reports to the department commissioner.	

State	Date Created	E/S/A	Department(s)	Appointed by/Reports to	Independence
New Mexico	1989	A	Human Services, includes Medicaid	Department secretary appoints.	Low
	2012	NA	Corrections	Reports to deputy director for administration of corrections department.	
New York	Before 1996	A	Correctional Services	Reports to the commissioner.	NA
	1996**	E	Governmentwide, agencies under the governor	Governor hires, fires; reports to governor's secretary; salary established by governor but with a floor; term ends with term of governor who appointed.	Low/moderate
	1992	S	Welfare	Governor hires with advice and consent of senate.	Low
	1996	S	Workers Compensation	Governor hires.	Low
	2006	S	Medicaid	Governor appoints, with approval of Senate; governor fires at will.	Low
	2008	E	Comptroller	Comptroller appoints, may be removed for cause; serves until end of term of comptroller.	Low

(Continued)

TABLE 8.1 (Continued)

State	Date Created	E/S/A	Department(s)	Appointed by/Reports to	Independence
North Carolina	2008	S***	Transportation	Appointed by and reports to the secretary.	Training and experience requirements for internal auditors were made less explicit, possibly weaker, in amendments of 2013; efforts to mislead an auditor or block investigation were made a second-class misdemeanor. Low
Ohio	1990	S	Gubernatorial agencies	Governor appoints, with advice of Senate.	Moderate; same term as governor
Oklahoma	1979	A	Human Services, includes Medicaid	Department head appoints.	Low
Oregon	1990	A	Corrections	Reports to director and deputy director.	NA
Pennsylvania	1987	E	Gubernatorial agencies; and in 1994 part of the department overseeing welfare fraud	Governor appoints, fires, reports to governor.	Low

State	Date Created	E/S/A	Department(s)	Appointed by/Reports to	Independence
South Carolina	NA	A	Corrections	Department head.	Unknown
	2011	E, then S	Cabinet offices; after July 1, 2012, all state agencies	Governor appoints, with Senate advice and consent; reports to governor and agency head of agency being investigated.	Initially low; now moderate; legislation in 2012 sets it up as separate agency outside the governor's office, only six investigators; specified reasons for removal by governor; a four-year term; has subpoena powers; agencies required to cooperate
Tennessee	2004	A	TennCare, includes Medicaid	Governor appoints; reports to state finance commissioner.	Moderate, does not report to the Tenncare administrator; has subpoena powers
	NA		Department of Human Services	Reports to the commissioner.	NA
Texas	1999	S	Criminal Justice	Governor appoints, reports to board of criminal justice.	Moderate Has subpoena powers
	2003	S	Human Services: TANF, Medicaid, SNAP	Governor appoints; governor claims IG reports to governor; department claims IG reports to commissioner; IG does not control budget.	Very low

(Continued)

TABLE 8.1 (Continued)

State	Date Created	E/S/A	Department(s)	Appointed by/Reports to	Independence
	2007	S	Youth Commission	Hired by and reports to board of trustees of youth commission.	Moderate; in 2011, independence slightly enhanced
	1984?	S	Public Safety	Appointed by, serves at the discretion of, and reports to the Public Safety Commission.	moderate, improved in 2011
Utah	2011	S	Medicaid	Governor appoints with advice and consent of Senate; two-year term; governor may dismiss for cause.	Moderate
Virginia	1984	S	Corrections	Reports to Department of Corrections, secondarily to secretary of Public Safety and Board of Corrections.	Moderate
	1999	S	Mental Health	Reports to governor, legislature confirms.	Moderate; term not concurrent with governor
	2000	A	Transportation	Reports to transportation commissioner, board, secretary, and the governor.	NA
	2012	S	Statewide IG	Governor appoints, legislature confirms; five-year term; renewable; part of legislative branch.	Moderate

282

State	Date Created	E/S/A	Department(s)	Appointed by/Reports to	Independence
W. Virginia	1979	A	Human Services, includes Medicaid	Department head hires; direct reporting to department head.	Low
Wisconsin	2011	A	Health Services, includes Medicaid	Civil service job, not political appointee; separate budget line.	Moderately high

Notes: The original table several editions ago was prepared with the research assistance of Brian Frederick. Updating has been done by the author. Data are for the most recent incarnation; if office was created by a governor but later recreated by statute, the date and statutory status are given here. Level of information available is uneven from office to office. Degree of independence is a subjective, composite variable, using available data, including, where known, term of office (term is more independent than lack of term; term not coterminous with governor's is more independent than if coterminous); firing for cause only is more independent than firing at will; statutory authority implies more independence than establishment by executive order, but establishment by executive order suggests more independence than administrative creation; departmentwide, but reports to the governor gives some independence; governor controls report release is less independent than if office of inspector general controls release, especially to the public. Having its own budget line and minimums is more independent than reliance on the department or program being evaluated controlling the IG budget. Not all information was available for each IG office; more information might change the evaluation of the degree of independence.

*Louisiana's IG was created by executive order, which has been continued from one administration to the next but acquired a legislative basis in 2008.

** New York has had an inspector general for the executive branch (agencies whose heads are appointed by the governor) since 1986, but Governor Pataki revoked the prior executive order by Governor Cuomo and issued his own in 1996 with broadened powers.

*** North Carolina's transportation inspector general was not actually established by statute but was part of the implementation of a law requiring internal audits in larger executive departments, passed in 2007.

E = Executive order (of governor); must be renewed by each governor or office ceases.

S = Statutory; permanent unless rescinded by law.

A = Administrative order (of department head); exists at the pleasure of the department head.

NA = Information is not available.

only to the department head. Massachusetts is an exception in that the IG has broad powers and is not controlled by either the governor or the department heads. One result has been a series of efforts by governors to eliminate the IG office and control the investigative function (see the minicase "The Massachusetts Inspector General Versus the Governor" on p. 287).

A number of states have given inspectors general responsibility for investigating Medicaid abuses. Recently created IG offices in Michigan, Minnesota, Utah, and Wisconsin have all been aimed at Medicaid abuses. Medicaid, a jointly funded federal and state program to provide health care for the poor, is one of the major state-level expenditures, and as such, there is great interest in assuring that there is as little fraud in the program as possible. However, because it is a joint federal and state program, the federal government also has an interest in assuring that the state administered programs are as free of fraud as possible, as well as in assuring the quality of care. The inspector general for the federal department of Health and Human Services has responsibility for overseeing and reporting on the results of state-level Medicaid fraud control units, created and governed by federal law. There are forty-nine state-level fraud control units, plus one in the District of Columbia. Most of them are located in the attorney generals' offices, not in inspector general offices, which raises the question of who does what and why there are two such structures. The location of the fraud control units in attorney generals' offices suggests a focus on criminal prosecution as well as financial recoveries. By law, the federally created fraud control units focus on medical providers, not on recipients of Medicaid assistance.

In Texas, which has both a Medicaid fraud control unit in the attorney general's office and an inspector general in the health department focusing on Medicaid fraud, the attorney general's office described the division of responsibility in the following fashion:

> The Texas Medicaid Fraud Control Unit was created in 1979 as a division of the Office of the Attorney General. The Unit has three principal responsibilities:
>
> - investigating criminal fraud by Medicaid providers;
> - investigating physical abuse and criminal neglect of patients in health care facilities licensed by the Medicaid program, including nursing homes and Texas Department of Aging and Disability Services homes;
> - assisting local and federal authorities with prosecution.
>
> The Unit does not look into fraud committed by Medicaid recipients. The Texas Health and Human Services Commission Office of Inspector General is responsible for those investigations.[33]

New York State, like Texas, has both a Medicaid fraud control unit in the attorney general's office and an inspector general in the health department, both of whom focus on Medicaid fraud. The IG focuses more on civil cases and recoveries, referring criminal cases to the attorney general. The IG also has responsibility for fraud prevention and for coordination of fraud control efforts between state offices that service Medicaid patients. The IG office makes recommendations for procedures to help prevent fraud and oversees implementation of its recommendations. The IG can investigate both service providers and service recipients. As in Texas, the federally designated Medicaid fraud control unit focuses on investigation and prosecution of health care providers for improper or fraudulent Medicaid billing schemes, kickbacks, and substandard medicines and equipment.

State reliance on inspectors general who focus on either recipient false claims or provider fraud outside the government bring in more money and are generally less threatening to elected officials than those who focus on program failures, inefficiency, and corruption among elected and appointed officials. The relatively low threat level from Medicaid IGs for sitting elected officials combined with public concern with fraud in public welfare programs may explain the readiness of states to adopt this particular inspector general. However, because they can actually recover money found in fraud, the level of intensity of oversight can become a problem, as illustrated in the New York State minicase on the Medicaid IG below.

Minicase: New York State and Medicaid

New York State created an IG to oversee its Medicaid program when the *New York Times* in 2005 revealed the extent to which the program was riddled with overpayments and fraud. Since Medicaid is a joint federal-state program, the federal government lent $1.6 billion to New York to overhaul program implementation, with the condition that the money be paid back by 2011. The new IG for Medicaid was zealous in uncovering waste and fraud, demanding repayment of money spent in error so the state could pay back its loan to the federal government.

The industry rebelled at what its members considered nitpicking audits and claimed the IG treated paperwork errors as fraud. Instead of allowing health providers to file amended bills, the IG demanded repayments. Legislators who were beholden to Medicaid service providers for contributions took up their cause, urging the IG to back off. Under pressure, Governor Cuomo fired the inspector general.

The legislature then passed a bill curtailing the IG's authority, which the governor vetoed. At the same time, the governor urged the next IG to work

(Continued)

(Continued)

out procedures in a more amicable fashion with providers. A number of cases the first IG had begun to investigate were dropped. Legislators threatened to bring back the legislation to curtail IG powers if the new negotiated arrangement turned out to be unsatisfactory. The level of recoveries fell sharply after the federal deadline for repayment had been met.

The first theme of this case is the role of the press in revealing the level of waste and fraud in the system in a compelling and embarrassing fashion. Without the initial revelations, there would not have been an IG for Medicaid.

Second, shared responsibility between levels of government is the key to understanding what happened. The federal government picked up half New York's Medicaid bill in most years, so the federal government had an interest in reducing the amount of waste and fraud in New York's Medicaid program. By lending the state money to fix its system and requiring repayment within five years, the federal government put pressure on New York to recover enough money from providers to pay back the money it borrowed. The IG could not just identify problems; the providers had to pay back the money they had incorrectly collected. Under the conditions of the loan, the state changed quickly from extremely lax to very stringent oversight and enforcement. When the federal debt was paid off, policy became more conciliatory.

The third theme is that the Medicaid providers were not powerless. They were major employers in the state and major contributors to political campaigns. When they complained about enforcement and the money they were being required to pay back, legislators listened.

Source: Based on Nina Bernstein, "Under Pressure, New York Moves to Soften Tough Medicaid Audits," *New York Times,* March 18, 2012.

IGs who focus on service providers outside government sometimes have to deal with blowback from those they oversee. For IGs who focus on government employees, blowback comes from agencies, from the legislature and/or the governor. If IGs are not politically controllable, their offices may be terminated. New Jersey offers an illustration of a governor terminating an IG office, while the minicase of Massachusetts has a different ending. (See the minicase of Massachusetts, on p. 287.)

In New Jersey, an inspector general office was created in 2000 to examine contractors for school construction projects and bar those who had records of corruption or shoddy work from bidding. With many corruption cases falling outside the scope of the existing IG, acting governor Richard Codey created a statewide IG position by executive order in 2004. The legislature gave the office a statutory basis in 2005 and increased its independence. The IG was given a fixed term of office and could be removed by the governor only for cause after being heard. The IG had a dual reporting structure, to the governor and also the president of the senate and speaker of the house. Reports were to be made public. This independence must have been considered a threat, because after the first five-year term, the IG office was merged into the comptroller's office in 2010. Former inspectors general now work for the comptroller, but the title "inspector general" has disappeared. The comptroller is a gubernatorial appointee for a term of six years, renewable. (Prior to 2007, the comptroller was directly elected.) The comptroller, Matt Boxer, was a former employee of Gov. Chris Christie when Christie was U.S. attorney for New Jersey. Appointed by Democratic governor Jon Corzine, Boxer's budget, authority, and staff were greatly expanded under Christie when Christie became governor. Christie merged both the state IG's office and the Medicaid IG into the comptroller's office. Although the comptroller continues to act in an independent fashion, Governor Christie seems more comfortable with this structure and with an old friend and colleague in control of the investigation function.[34]

Minicase: The Massachusetts Inspector General Versus the Governor

Massachusetts was the first state to establish a statewide inspector general system. The office was created by statute as a result of a perceived culture of corruption in public construction, especially in the building of the University of Massachusetts campus in Boston. The inspector general was granted a broad mandate and considerable independence, with a five-year term that could be renewed one time. Its reports were to be public, and the office was granted subpoena powers in the original legislation. But four years later the legislation was amended, so that requests for subpoenas have to go through a board known as the inspector general council that included the state's attorney general, auditor, comptroller, and public safety secretary. Approval requires assent from at least six of the eight members. This process has proved unworkable. The IG asked for independent subpoena powers in December of 2012, a request that met with considerable opposition.

The Massachusetts inspector general is not appointed solely by the governor but by a majority among the governor, attorney general, and the state auditor. Because the IG does not report solely to the governor, has a fixed term, and can only be fired by the same majority that hired him or her, the IG exercises considerable independence from the governor. The IG has broad investigative powers, which can be politically threatening. While the governor cannot control the IG directly, he or she may propose to cut the IG's

(Continued)

(Continued)

budget or eliminate the office entirely. Those recommendations have to be approved by the legislature before they can take effect.

In 2003. Gov. Mitt Romney proposed to eliminate the office and shift some of its functions to the state comptroller, who reports to the governor. He proposed to eliminate the IG's subpoena powers and the requirement that state officials cooperate with the IG's investigations. Under his plan, reports could be kept confidential. Romney continued his campaign to eliminate the IG office from year to year, despite lack of legislative support. The prior governor, Paul Cellucci, had also tried to eliminate the inspector general's office. Most states that have IGs do not grant them as much independent power as Massachusetts does. As a result, there is less conflict with the governor, and whatever conflicts there are, are more easily kept under wraps.

Sources: Frank Phillips, "The Governor Looks to Cut the IG's Office," *Boston Globe*, February 28, 2003; Scott S. Greenberger, "Legislators, Romney Budget Aide Spar Over Inspector General Office," *Boston Globe*, January 30, 2004; Office of the Inspector General, Massachusetts, Annual Report for 2005, August 2006; Sean P. Murphy, "Vetting Urged on Inspector General Power Bid," *Boston Globe*, December 3, 2012; Pamela H. Wilmot, Executive Director for Common Cause, Testimony to the Massachusetts House and Senate Ways and Means Committee, March 28, 2003, partly reprinted in *South Coast Today*, www.southcoasttoday.com/apps/pbcs.dll/article?AID=/20030401/OPINION/304019918&cid=sitesearch.

When a governor creates an inspector general office, he or she normally wants to limit the powers of the IG, to create the appearance of integrity without fear of public embarrassment or worse; when the legislature creates an inspector general office, it is often for the purpose of ferreting out corruption and embarrassing the administration, which may be of the opposite party. Under those circumstances, the legislature may want a strong, independent inspector general. But when there is an inspector general for the legislature, to find corruption in the legislature or recommend ethics rules, the legislature may not be so keen on empowering the office. Illinois, which has had an IG for the state legislature, made the position part time and gave the office no additional staff, not even a secretary. As a result, many issues which might have been worth exploring escaped his view. In the ten years after the creation of the position, the inspector general handled 163 complaints, an average of a bit over sixteen a year. The law allows for limited investigation, weak punishments (fines), and almost no public disclosure. "To launch a probe, Homer needs approval from the Legislative Ethics Commission, which is made up of eight legislators, half from each chamber, half from each political party." He can only investigate ethics act violations, not issues such as bribery, extortion, and personal use of campaign funds.[35]

Inspectors General in Cities and Counties

A number of cities and counties have adopted the inspector general model in recent years, usually as a result of corruption and lack of public trust. These include New Orleans; Chicago; Philadelphia (created by executive order); New York; Houston; Baltimore; Albuquerque; Washington, D.C.; and Palm Beach County. Jacksonville, Florida, added an IG office in 2014. Montgomery County, Maryland; Miami-Dade County, Florida; and Cook County, Illinois, also have inspectors general. Palm Beach County has jurisdiction not only over the county but also over the municipalities inside the county.

The level of independence and powers of these offices vary greatly. IGs may dream of being ferocious junkyard dogs, but they may not be given sufficient authority to do the job, or they may be leashed or tamed by the chief counsel's or mayor's office. (See the minicase on Baltimore below.) Which cases IGs may investigate may be sharply curtailed or their reports may not be made public. They may end up investigating whether an alderperson sent out one inappropriate e-mail on a city computer or whether one employee misused a credit card rather than more far-reaching and systematic issues of waste, fraud, and abuse.

Minicase: Baltimore's Departing IG

Sometimes Inspectors general leave on their own volition to take a different job. Their departure is often a commentary on the lack of cooperation, resources, or independence to do the job. When Baltimore's IG, David McClintock, left Baltimore before his term was up, the departure provoked questions about why. His answer was he was taking a job in Jefferson Parish, Louisiana, because that office had more independence. The Baltimore office was created in 2005 by mayoral order. The mayor could dismiss the inspector general at any time for any reason, and the annual budget was dependent on the decisions of the board of estimates and city council each year. The office therefore had no protection from political influence or interference. Further, the IG reports to the city solicitor, an appointee of the mayor who serves at the pleasure of the mayor. Jefferson Parish had solved all those problems. The office was included in the city charter and was given a dedicated revenue source.

Source: Mark Ruetter, "Inside City Hall: Sharpening the teeth of Baltimore's Watchdog," *The Baltimore Brew*, February 5, 2013, https://www.baltimorebrew .com/2013/02/05/inside-city-hall-sharpening-the-teeth-of-baltimores-watchdog/.

In cities with a history of corruption, there is a tendency to create powerful and independent inspectors general, who inspire fear rather than cooperation and may have a difficult time getting the access they need to do their work. Chicago is a case in point. The Chicago IG was granted broad powers to initiate investigations at his or her own discretion and the right to issue subpoenas. The IG can be removed only for cause and has an opportunity to appeal to the council in case of attempted dismissal. The IG has a four-year term that is not coterminous with the mayor's or council's. The ordinance establishing the IG office mandates agency compliance with IG subpoenas and makes it a crime to resist the subpoena or block an investigation.

Joseph Ferguson, the City of Chicago's inspector general, had a fight on his hands right from the start. His predecessor had sued the administration after the law department refused to hand over documents related to an investigation of a no-bid contract awarded to a former city worker. Ferguson became the plaintiff in the ongoing case, and the law department continued to resist turning over unedited documents, claiming the inspector general was not granted the power to hire his own attorney and sue the city and that the documents were protected by client-attorney privilege.

The circuit court sided with the city legal department, but the appellate court reversed the decision, judging in favor of the inspector general. The issue ultimately came before the Illinois Supreme Court. The court decided that the inspector general had a right to issue a subpoena and to enforce it but did not have the power to hire his own attorney to take the city attorney to court. That power was granted only to the city attorney, in this case the object of the subpoena. The result therefore appeared absurd, as the city attorney would have had to sue himself in court. The court concluded that because the inspector general reports to the mayor, he should have brought his argument to the mayor and asked for resolution in that way.

Because the implication of the court's decision is that the city's attorney's office has the right to issue or block each of the IG's subpoenas and that the inspector general has no way to enforce the subpoenas if the city attorney does not go along other than to ask the mayor for help, the other elements of IG independence do not count for much.[36] The story has a more or less happy ending, as the mayor and the inspector general eventually came to an understanding and began to work together.

New Orleans, like Chicago, has had a history of corruption. New Orleans created a very powerful, independent inspector general to clean up the mess and keep it clean. The ethics board chose the inspector general for a four-year term, and the IG could be fired only for cause by a two-thirds majority of that same board.[37] A two-thirds vote of the entire city council is necessary to eliminate the office, which is operationally independent of the mayor's office, the ethics board, and the council. The establishing ordinance gave the inspector general subpoena power.[38] While Chicago tried to leash its IG by arguing that his office reported to the city attorney's and hence was indirectly controlled by the mayor, in New Orleans, that route was impossible; the IG was clearly independent of the mayor. Instead, the strategy was foot dragging. The office was set up in slow motion, with new obstacles at every step.

With the mayor's support, the council had put a proposal to establish an inspector general on the ballot in 1995. The public approved the charter provision, which is analogous to a constitutional provision at the state or national level and provides a strong legal basis for the IG office. But while the public may have wanted an IG, public officials were less eager to implement the public's mandate. The implementing legislation wasn't passed until 2006, and the office didn't get started until the following year. Even then, the funding source was in doubt, making it impossible to hire staff. A second charter amendment in 2008 created a stream of revenue for the office so that it would not be dependent on mayoral or council approval in order to pay the staff.

The first IG, Robert Cerasoli, left after seventeen months, reportedly for health reasons, but most likely he was feeling the strain of setting up his office with uncertain funding and difficulty gaining access to documents. In New Orleans, he said, "information technology is in a terrible state. Getting access to information people regularly access in other places is a major problem. Public documents aren't being made public, if they exist at all. And I don't think the city government truly understands what the inspector general is supposed to do—and might provide more resistance as it becomes more clear."[39]

The problem of access continued under Cerasoli's successor, who had a confrontation with the police chief over the denial of access to files. The result was the signing of a protocol on sharing documents and an improved computerized database. The IG has a broad mandate and an ambitious set of planned investigations; he has issued reports to the public at regular intervals and has identified major opportunities for savings. The mayor has promised cooperation. The problems seem to be gradually working themselves out.

Houston had a different approach to controlling the inspector general. The city set up a toothless IG with limited scope of inquiry in 2004, by executive order, a weaker basis than either ordinance (Chicago) or charter (New Orleans). The inspector general's office was initially located in the police department, to investigate employee wrongdoing. The city attorney was tasked with protecting IG office documents and determining what would be released. The office was shifted to the attorney's office, under the mayor's office, in 2010. The IG could be fired at any time, another sign of lack of independence.

A new IG was hired in 2010, after the shift from the police department to the attorney's office. When asked by a reporter, the IG indicated he didn't think that it would be appropriate to release the results of investigations, just an overall report of goals and accomplishments.[40]

The IG resigned after fourteen months on the job. He argued that he was not resigning under protest but advised that the office needed to be independent, not under the mayor via the city attorney, and should have subpoena powers. The office was tasked only to look into matters of violations of city rules and procedures.[41] As one journalist opined, "Inspectors general in other cities root out fraud, conflicts of interest; Houston's IG only has power to investigate complaints of vulgar language or unlawful tamale sales."[42] The office did not issue any reports over the year prior to the IG's resignation.

Houston leashed its IG by locating it in the attorney's office, making the IG office dependent on the city attorney for budget, allowing the IG to be fired at will, and granting no criminal investigative power. This was not an IG that elected officials needed to be afraid of. Palm Beach County had a different set of problems—and solutions. The county had been dealing with charges of corruption over several years. From 2007 to 2009, four county and city commissioners were convicted of federal corruption charges, and in 2009 another longtime county board member was charged. She had directed bond sales to companies her husband worked for and apparently accepted bribes from developers receiving city contracts.

In the face of this corruption, a grand jury in 2009 recommended the creation of an ethics commission and an IG office. The board of county commissioners complied, creating the IG office by ordinance (the equivalent of a statute at the state level). The first IG took office in June 2010. In November of 2010, the public overwhelmingly approved a charter amendment that gave charter authority (equivalent to a constitutional requirement at the state level) to the IG office and extended the scope of the IG office to include cities within the county.

The IG office that was set up in Palm Beach County is relatively powerful and independent. The IG serves a four-year term, and future IGs will be selected by the IG committee, which is composed of the ethics committee, the state attorney, and the public defender. The IG was granted subpoena powers. However, problems began to arise when the scope of the office was extended to include the cities in the county, some of whom were reluctant to go along with the plan. Several protested the arrangements for paying for the IG's services, while some attempted to redefine waste, fraud, and abuse, watering down the definitions so fewer cases would qualify for investigation. In setting up procedures to deal with the IG investigations, some city officials established rules for employees to follow, if contacted by the IG office, that were likely to prevent an investigation. These procedures treated any inquiry from an IG like a criminal investigation, requiring an attorney to be present and requiring the meeting to be set up by an employee's superior. If a subordinate was reporting on questionable behavior by a superior, this procedure would have a chilling effect.[43] In the interim, before the situation could be legally resolved, the county picked up $400,000 in costs that the cities would not pay.

By 2015, fourteen cities petitioned for a rehearing after a judge rejected all their arguments about why they should not pay a share of IG costs. The judge was not sympathetic, telling them that they should have followed the will of their citizens in the referendum. The ongoing resistance of these cities to the inspector general had reportedly crippled the office, leaving it with only half of the necessary budget and fewer staff.[44] When their request for a rehearing was denied, thirteen of the localities appealed the decision. It is not clear whether the strength of their opposition stemmed more from the money they would have to pay or from their reluctance for their activities to be scrutinized by the inspector general.

In sum, a number of cities and counties have established their own IGs in recent years. Either a major scandal or a culture of corruption has triggered the creation of the office, but mayors and department heads are no more likely to welcome unfettered investigations than are executive officials at the state or federal level. What do public officials do when they are confronted with a strong IG whom they fear they will not be able to control? The examples suggest a variety of techniques, from limiting the scope of investigations, to denying the office subpoena powers, to controlling the budget of the office or denying access to unedited documents. In New Orleans, the response was to delay implementation as long as possible. The cities in Palm Beach County came up with a novel approach—redefine waste, fraud, and abuse—raising the level of seriousness that would warrant or allow an investigation.

For students of budgeting, it is important to watch not only the development and expansion of IG systems but also their actual structure and degree of independence. The trend at the local level, as at the state and national level, has been to gradually increase the independence, power, and scope of responsibility of IG offices. But this outcome has not come easily; it has been fought out year after year, and sometimes the inspector general has quit in frustration or been so hogtied he or she ends up investigating minor personnel squabbles and fails to issue reports on investigations. It is also important to keep in mind that fully leashed IGs who report to a department head, the mayor, or manager may have the best chance of having their recommendations for reducing waste actually implemented, though they may avoid investigating malfeasance of supervisory staff who can fire them or prevent them from initiating an investigation.

Campaigns to Reduce Waste, Fraud, and Abuse

The tension between appointed officials' policy control over investigations and the IG's independence is endemic to the system and adds a political dimension to budget implementation. A second source of politics in budget implementation is political campaigns to reduce waste, fraud, and abuse. During his first term, President Reagan launched a national campaign to reduce waste, fraud, and abuse in the federal government as had his immediate predecessors. Not only did his campaign make headlines, but examples of fraud and waste kept hitting the newspapers, making the issue particularly salient. Military purchases of $2,000 toilet seats, $600 hammers, and $7,600 coffeepots became public; military procurement became the subject of congressional hearings. During Reagan's second term, military procurement became a widely publicized scandal.

Reducing waste, fraud, and abuse seems like an ideal political campaign issue, because it fits the public conception that there is waste in government, promises to clean it up, and offers to reduce tax burdens by cutting fat and leaving services alone. On closer examination, however, such campaigns are fraught with difficulties both political and technical.

Campaigns against waste, fraud, and abuse often make the naïve assumptions that there is fat in the public budget and that the fat is easily recognizable and surgically removable. In fact, the amount of fat is not easily determined, and it is almost always attached to something of value. For example, trying to get able-bodied people off the handicapped rolls requires tightening eligibility requirements. Inevitably, some people who are both eligible and needy will also be taken off the rolls. There is a very real trade-off between denying aid to people who need it and preventing the undeserving from getting it.

Second, waste, fraud, and abuse recur, no matter how much is reported eliminated, because a small number of mistakes are inevitable in any large and complex operation.[45] Thus, a campaign to eliminate waste, fraud, and abuse can be embarrassing because the more you "save" the more you demonstrate how much more waste, fraud, and abuse exist. "No matter which administration is blamed, constant harping on fraud and abuse goes beyond its necessity as a deterrent to the point of further weakening an already dangerously tottering image of the governmental process."[46]

Moreover, much of the source of waste is systemic, which means that really getting to the base of the problem may mean revealing structural problems that require new processes and major reorganizations. To eliminate wasteful purchasing in the military would require a drastic overhaul of the way the military is funded and managed. Such a change is a long-term proposition, not something that can be accomplished by a brief political campaign with highly publicized results and then silence.

Campaigns against waste, fraud, and abuse are useful political tools to bring down an opponent or discredit a predecessor, but they can boomerang and be used against one's own administration. Such campaigns are inherently political, regardless of their technical components.

Summary and Conclusions

Legislative bodies tend to become angry when they think their will has been thwarted. They do not tend to get as excited about poor financial management, but auditors and inspectors general do get upset about poor financial management, especially when it leads to major losses of money. Auditors and inspectors general do not have line authority to make improvements; they have to persuade the management of their agencies to accept their recommendations. They have to develop a working relationship with the managers they are observing, while maintaining their independence and reporting to the executive and sometimes the legislature and the public as well.

Improving financial management is not a neutral and technical topic, even when it is handled quietly, but when mismanagement involves millions or billions of dollars and makes government look bad, those who report it become unwelcome presences. Efforts to control the auditors or put a particular spin on their findings have sometimes marred the independence of the inspectors general.

Can inspectors general be granted too much power and independence? To the extent that IGs generate fear and resistance, they are likely to get less agency cooperation, experience less successful investigations, and recover less money. Their advice on improved systems of control is less likely to be implemented. The job of the inspectors general is difficult, requiring a set of skills that may include criminal investigations, financial auditing, public relations, and political negotiations. They need to know when to push forward and when to fall back. Overemphasis on dollar recoveries, as in New York State, may make IGs nitpicky and bring about counter pressures to weaken the office. The choice of IGs for political loyalty, tempting because of the political harm that they can do, may also undermine the system as a whole. Despite the tensions, the job of the IGs is critical, not only in assuring that public money is spent efficiently and effectively but also in maintaining public support for government.

What happens when Inspectors General go awry? If they go overboard in protecting an agency or in attacking it? What happens if IGs themselves commit some rules violations? Can they effectively police themselves? This chapter suggests that the IG council at the federal level is less than effective as a watchdog of watchdogs, with more of an interest in protecting the status of the IG system as a whole than punishing or admonishing individual IGs. To be effective, they would have to devote more time and resources to looking into questionable behavior brought to their attention, but misbehavior may not be brought to their attention since those (few) IGs who misbehave have the power to prevent their subordinates from bringing cases to the council. The role of checking and restraining IGs thus falls to the president and the Congress, who make major waves when they try to bring down a sitting IG. The disciplining of IGs is not a visible issue at the state and local level, in part because they are often tightly leashed. The attacks reported in the press have been more on the office of the inspector general—its budget, it scope of investigation, and its powers—than on individual inspectors general.

Useful Websites

For the federal level, the **Council of the Inspectors General on Integrity and Efficiency,** created in 2008, maintains a website that posts its **annual reports to the president** and includes measures of potential savings and various other measures of accomplishment (for 2011, www.ignet.gov/randp/FY2011-Annual -Progress-Report-to-the-President.pdf). It also relates the number of federal IG offices and the approximate level of staffing in any given year.

The Congressional Research Service did a useful summary of legislative issues on the inspectors general. Wendy Ginsberg and Michael Greene, "Federal Inspectors General: History, Characteristics, and Recent Congressional Actions," CRS, December 8, 2014, https://www.fas.org/sgp/crs/misc/R43814.pdf.

Many inspectors general's offices at all levels of government have their own websites. Some post their reports as well as the scope and reporting structure of the office. In the case of the **Chicago inspector general**, the extensive legal case over the IG's powers is documented on the website (http://chicagoinspectorgen eral.org/major-initiatives/ferguson-v-patton/).

The **Association of Inspectors General** (http://inspectorsgeneral.org/), which includes state and local inspectors general, includes model legislation for the establishment of an IG office and sometimes issues of concern to the IG community.

POGO, the Project on Government Oversight, has a handy website called **"Where Are All the Watchdogs?"** (www.pogo.org/tools-and-data/ig-watchdogs/ go-igi-20120208-where-are-all-the-watchdogs-inspector-general-vacancies1 .html) that tracks inspector general vacancies at the national level.

9 Budgetary Decision-Making and Politics

Budgetary decision-making includes five distinct but linked clusters: revenues, process, expenditures, balance, and implementation. Describing each decision stream separately tends to emphasize their independence. This chapter is about how they fit together into one decision-making process. Looking at the decision strands together also illuminates their differences and common themes.

A simple model of budgetary decision-making would assure that the definition of balance, the budget process, and the revenue estimates would be in place in that order before the beginning of decision-making about expenditures and that the spending decisions would begin with targets for spending that keep within revenue estimates. Evaluations of how much was actually spent for what should precede the formation of the following year's budget. However, real budgeting is less linear but more flexible and adaptive.

Real-Time Budgeting

Budgeting is characterized by five streams of decision-making that depend on one another for key pieces of information. The streams do not follow each other in a logical sequence. They occur at different intervals and last for different lengths of time. To make the key decisions in any one stream, actors may have to look backward, to the last time the decision was made in another stream, or forward, to anticipated decisions, or even sideways, to decisions being made at the same time. Much of this information is tentative; it can and does change as the budget moves toward implementation. Budgets continually readjust, in real time, to account for information coming from the environment and from each decision stream.

Budgetary decision-making takes the shape it does because of the characteristics of public budgeting described in Chapter 1. First and foremost, budgets are open to the environment—to the economy, to the weather, to a variety of emergencies, to mandates from courts and other levels of government, and to changes in public preferences and political leadership. Openness to the environment means that estimates of revenues and expenditures may have to be revised several times during the budget process as better information becomes available. Budgeters cannot make one estimate at the beginning of the budget process and stick to it. Openness to the environment means that budgetary decisions that were generally agreed to may need to be remade.

A second characteristic of public budgets is that a variety of actors with different goals compete for limited resources. Budgets have to be able to deal with competition between these actors. When they disagree, they may hold up whatever decisions they are in the process of making. Budgeting has to accommodate this kind of conflict and the resulting delays, because unlike many other political decisions, budgets have real deadlines. The later they are, the less useful they are, so the problem of late decisions has to be handled in some way.

The budget process is segmentable: Each part and even each group of actors can proceed without the whole being known. For example, when policy disagreements prevent Congress from passing a budget resolution that sets revenue and expenditure limits, each house separately deems a set of guidelines to work within and worries about getting agreement between their respective plans later. This informal adaptation allows decision-making to continue.

The different strands of decision-making can proceed as if they were independent, referring to one another, bargaining when necessary to reach accommodation. If one decision-making strand gets stuck—as, for example, when a tax increase is being considered but has not yet been decided on—other decision streams can proceed if budgeters make assumptions about what will occur and adjust their own work when the final outcome is known in the revenue stream.

The decision clusters need information from one another to complete their work. The revenue cluster cannot proceed without some knowledge of spending requirements and balance constraints. Decisions about how to reduce a deficit are dependent on revenue and spending estimates. Spending estimates depend on revenue estimates and balance constraints. Implementation depends on decisions throughout the process to that point, especially on the degree of underestimates of revenues or overestimates of expenditures and the balance constraints. Revenues, expenditures, balance, and implementation all depend on the process stream to organize them and allocate power to them. Information coming from other decision streams may appear as a constraint, but one that is flexible rather than rigid. Thus, a figure for estimated revenues already fed into the expenditure stream may change if the prediction of the economy changes. Or it may change if a decision is made in the expenditure stream that requires more revenue.

Constraints from other decision streams are flexible, not only because the environment changes but also because actors in one stream can sometimes force a change in another stream. Actors who want to spend more money may be able to force a change in the tax structure or in revenue estimates; they may even be able to force a change in the definition of balance. Actors who want to reduce revenues may act to cut expenditures and define balance to suit their purposes.

Real-time decision-making allows the streams to be disrupted or interrupted and repeated. Budgeters have to have contingency plans to deal with missing information or late decisions. They may push up the urgency of decisions that are causing roadblocks by linking them to other urgent matters. The overlap of decision clusters allows solutions in one stream to resolve roadblocks in another stream. A solution in the revenue stream may unlock a problem in the expenditure stream; a change in process may solve problems of linkage between the streams.

A Comparison of the Decision-Making Streams

The focus of this book is to make clearer the nature of politics in public budgeting. What budgetary politics looks like depends on where you look. Narrowly conceived interest groups compete with one another for tax breaks or spending increases; broad coalitions of interest groups that approach class interests compete for control of the scope of government services. In some of the decision strands, interest groups have little role. Some areas of the budget are policy laden, whereas others appear policy neutral and technical. To get anything like a realistic view of politics in the budget requires a look at each strand of budgetary decision-making.

Revenue politics is characterized by both a policy orientation and active interest group participation. The policy issues include who will be taxed and what the level of taxation will be. Narrowly defined interest groups try to deflect taxes from their constituents; broader coalitions of interest groups become involved in efforts to determine the distribution of taxation among income groups and the overall level of taxation. The fairness of taxes is one of the major considerations in this strand of decision-making.

The politics of process revolves around several policy issues, plus bargaining among the actors. One cluster of policy issues includes how much of a policy focus the budget should have, how clearly policy issues should be articulated, and concomitantly, how much conflict should be expressed and resolved during budgetary decision-making. A second policy issue is how citizen and interest group preferences should be expressed. How much access should individuals, interest groups, agency heads, and the press have to budgetary decision-making, and how much secrecy should there be? The result of these policy choices influences not only the level of accountability in the budget process but also the level and nature of public expenditures and the amount of conflict that occurs in the budget process. A third set of issues is what biases the process should build in, for example, toward lower taxes or lower spending or more accountability and transparency. The politics of process also revolves around the bargaining between budget actors for more power over budgetary choices. The bargaining over the distribution of power and negotiations over key policy issues are often intertwined.

The expenditure stream is characterized by active interest group involvement as well as extensive bargaining and competition. The competition among interest groups generally prevents one interest group from controlling budgetary decisions. At times, an emphasis on policy trumps the interplay of interest groups. The choices of which programs to fund and at what level may be carefully analyzed and considered against some ideal of the public good. Legislators can resist even powerful interest groups when they choose; to do so, they use the budget process to insulate themselves from possible backlash.

The politics of budget balance evokes three key issues: (1) the role of the budget in managing the economy, (2) the scope of government programs, and (3) which level of government will balance its budget at the expense of which other level of government. What programs will be terminated, whose programs will be cut back, and what will be the balance between revenue increases and spending decreases? The outcome of each of these policy decisions is far reaching. As a result, coalitions of interest groups representing wide segments of society take different positions on the politics of balance; liberals and conservatives, Democrats and Republicans, take opposing stances.

The politics of implementation is marked by tensions. On the one hand, the goal of budget implementation is to maintain accountability by implementing the budget almost exactly as passed and on the other, to allow necessary changes to adapt to changing circumstances. Moreover, some actors press to reshape the budget during the budget year to accomplish some policy goal that was not agreed to or not sufficiently funded during budget deliberations. Generally, the technical accountability model is triumphant, but at the cost of considerable effort in monitoring potentially policy-laden budget changes. Implementation politics can pit executive discretion against legislative prerogatives, invoking constitutional battles between branches of government, requiring court adjudication. This is one area where the courts play a major role.

In short, no one view of politics in the budget stands alone. There is bargaining among actors in budget decision-making, but it is framed by policy concerns expressed through the budget process. Interest groups are active in budgetary decision-making, but they are controlled or can be controlled both by competition among themselves and by the budget process, which gives or denies them access to decision-making. There is a contest between more technical and more policy-oriented approaches to budgeting, but in most areas, there is some kind of balance between them. There are policy issues in the budget, but they may be played up or toned down by the budget process and format. And there are constitutional constraints that frame intergovernmental relations and the division of powers between the branches, constraints that sometimes are enforced by state or national supreme courts.

Common Themes

Though each strand of budgetary decision-making generates its own political pattern, some themes run throughout the chapters. One is the tension between openness and secrecy; a second is the increase in intense partisanship and ideology, with resultant rigid stands and budgeting by extortion; and a third is a pattern of action and reaction, deterioration and reform, reform and deterioration. Fourth, in most of the decision strands, federalism is apparent in the interaction between levels of government.

Openness Versus Secrecy

One theme that cuts across the decision clusters is the tension between keeping decision-making open and reporting accurate and meaningful information, on the one hand, and on the other hand, limiting public participation and either not reporting information or showering the public with loads of disaggregated data that are difficult to interpret.

In taxation, taxes can be more visible, such as income taxes, paid in a lump sum once a year, or less visible, paid in small increments, such as sales taxes, or less visible still, as in value-added taxes that appear to be levied on businesses and are included in the final sales price. Tax expenditures are even less visible, though sometimes listed and estimated, they do not appear as revenue in the budget. Budget processes can be more or less open to the public and interest groups. As for expenditures, spending on contracts may be lumped together so that no individual contract or contractor is visible. Expenditures can be obscured through complex rules and through less visible spending tools, such as guaranteed loans and insurance. The so-called black budget blocks information on defense and security spending. In budget balance, deficits can be obscured through a variety of accounting techniques, including the use of cash accounting and interfund transfers. Spending can appear to be offset by reducing totals in other programs that were predicted to spend more than they actually are spending—fictitious savings. In after-the-fact budget accountability, acting Inspectors general can be tempted to pull their punches or even rewrite damaging sections of reports. The question of how open budgeting should be is not simple. Open processes, with lots of public participation, not only take longer but are sometimes contentious. They may raise expectations to unrealistic levels, causing disappointment and frustration all around. Public and interest group demands may make it difficult or impossible to reduce spending or eliminate tax breaks, even in the face of a consensus that overall taxes need to be lowered or that deficits need to be eliminated. The decision-making behind the design and passage of federal tax reforms in 1986, for example, was closed to the public and interest groups. If the process had been more open, lobby groups would have insisted on maintaining their own tax breaks and reform probably would not have been achieved.

Moreover, no budget can be inclusive and still readable. A budget that presented all relevant information, even for a small government, would be thousands of pages long and would quickly overwhelm the reader with detail. Every budget necessarily involves some selection about what information to present. The question is to what extent the selection process is guided by desires to evade accountability, protect cronyism, hide waste or corruption, and avoid blame. Analyzing what is not in the budget is often as revealing as examining what is included.

Although no budget can be fully open, budgetary secrecy, even well-intentioned secrecy, is a serious problem in a democracy. Secrecy can sever the relationship between the elected officials and the taxpayers if taxpayers ask for or demand particular outcomes and the officials do something different. The budget and the audit reports that go with it are major tools of accountability. A redacted audit report on a government contract, essentially edited by the contractor, raises suspicions about the purposes and success of the contract and the willingness of the government to hold the contractor accountable. For many years, the overall trend in budgeting has been increasing openness and accountability. The movement toward accountability websites that publish details of contracts and contractors, which include budgets and audit reports as well as check ledgers, has accelerated this trend. To avoid overwhelming the reader with telephone directory–like details, these websites allow for overall summaries and the ability to drill down for more details when the reader wishes. The national government and many states publish tax expenditure reports, which, though of varying quality, make the costs and purposes of tax breaks more visible. At the federal level, since the 2008 reforms, inspectors general have their own websites on which they publish their reports, making them available to the public and the press. An increasing number of inspector general offices at all levels of government suggests greater openness.

Despite the overall trends, there have been some important setbacks. Federal IGs have recently complained that some agencies block or delay their access to necessary documents. In a related development, the Department of Justice Office of Legal Counsel issued a sixty-eight-page decision in which it asserted that "all documents" did not mean "all documents," and so the inspector general for the Department of Justice did not have access to all documents as required by law. The association for Inspectors General president feared that this interpretation would affect the access of all inspectors general and was working for a legislative clarification.[1] The independence of inspectors general in state and local governments is often questionable. Some of them do not publish any reports available to the public. Political control over IGs makes it look as if there are some potentially important things that the public is not being allowed to see. Some states have begun charging money for access to public documents, not only for copies, but for the time it takes staff to search for the information. Such fees are likely to reduce public and press access to the documents.

At the national level, the size of the black or secret budget jumped up after September 11, 2001. Many tens of billions of dollars of spending cannot be named, discussed and debated, or compared with other spending priorities. The numbers have begun to come down, and the totals are now published but no details are provided. Although there is nothing like the black budget at the state or local level, legislators do sometimes withhold budget information or release it in such disaggregated form that it takes months of teamwork by the press and many dollars to use the information.

The passage of omnibus legislation—bundling many important decisions together in huge packages and passing them quickly, without giving legislators a chance to read the bill, evaluate it, or object to parts of it—has also created a kind of secrecy. The budget process may be formally open, while the real decisions are made behind closed doors. At the state level, states that use shell bills (that can be amended and replaced by entirely new content late in the legislative session) make it difficult for the public or the press to follow the progress of particular pieces of legislation. Sometimes colorfully called "carcass" or "strike everything" bills, they are used by many states, such as Illinois, Florida, California, Texas, Oklahoma, Arizona,[2] South Dakota, Washington, Connecticut, Colorado, Minnesota, and Arkansas. Sometimes even opposition legislators are kept in the dark in this way.

The openness of public budgets is not a given, determined by the degree of democracy in the society, but rather the reverse: The degree of openness and accountability in the budget frames the amount of democracy in the society. The amount of openness and accountability in the budget can erode.

The tenuousness of the budget's openness and thus of its ability to function as a major tool of accountability, suggests the importance of isolating the factors that seem to increase or decrease the level of secrecy. Based on the observations reported in this book, the following are some hypotheses researchers might want to investigate:

1. The greater the amount of corruption, the greater the amount of secrecy. Highly publicized corruption creates a need to appear to eliminate or reduce corruption—which stimulates the creation or expansion of oversight bodies such as the IGs—while at the same time controlling the overseers and watchdogs so that they do not embarrass elected officials by revealing inefficiencies, fraud, or remaining corruption.

2. The waging of war and the experience of terrorism make it easier to sell secrecy in budgeting as necessary for national defense. The more freedom and flexibility granted to defense agencies to carry out wars, the less the public knows about how money is being spent. Secrecy for convenience and political expedience may be hidden within the folds of the apparently necessary secrecy of war.

3. The New York State model suggests that a budget process that radically disempowers one of the key actors is going to generate informal ways of getting around that process, creating a second, less-visible process that distributes power more fairly. Thus, budget processes that shift too much power to the executive branch may end up generating budget processes that occur behind closed doors.

4. When people or interest groups demand not only different but also contradictory spending and taxing priorities, the amount of secrecy—or at least the amount of obfuscation—is likely to rise. In recent years, there has been major pressure to reduce taxation, while program recipients still demand benefits and taxpayers insist on their services at the same level as before. When elected officials give in to these contradictory demands, deficits result. Those same officials then often try to obscure the resulting deficits and their consequences. Deficits in general tend to result in more budget games and budget manipulation.

5. Fragmentation of the budget and the various tools used to take programs out of the competitive parts of the budget facilitate secrecy. Programs that

supposedly fund themselves may be insulated from public scrutiny, and transfers into or out of them may be obscured. Off-budget entities are necessarily less visible than on-budget entities. They go off budget not only to get out of the competition but also to get out from under the rules, to gain freedom, which includes freedom from oversight and reporting.

6. Spending through tax breaks rather than direct spending contributes to secrecy, because money that is never collected is less visible than money that is collected and then spent. At the local level, a lack of tax expenditure reporting has exacerbated this problem, though the Government Accounting Standards Board is working at fixing this problem. The more a state or local government focuses on taxation through exception rather than reforming the tax structure more broadly, the more complex and less easily seen and understood the spending program becomes. Because the tendency to increase these breaks increases when the economy deteriorates, a failing economy is likely to reduce the information content of the budget.

7. The more the emphasis on contracting out, even with the most careful attention to achieving greater efficiency, the less information there is likely to be on crucial financial decisions. Although reporting on contracts can be improved, the very nature of contracting assumes a black box—that how the contractor does the work is not considered relevant, so long as the work is done as specified in the contract and for the agreed-on price. This perspective suggests the government has no right to knowledge about the number of employees, the costs of production, source of savings, or anything else other than the price and the description of the delivered product or project. If there is more contracting out, we should expect less information in the budget.

8. Increased polarization contributes to a politics of exaggeration or minimization, to make forceful arguments. The greater the polarization, the less reliable estimates become. Thus the cost of pensions may be exaggerated in an effort to force cuts in benefits for current employees and retirees; the costs of wars may be hidden in an effort to make war seem like a more affordable strategy. Those who want public funding for stadiums or airports may exaggerate the economic benefits from them. Those who wish to cut services to the poor or otherwise wish to change policies may obscure the information on which current policies are based, by under-funding the information gathering agencies and eliminating studies or reports. They may exaggerate error rates or cheating, to imply that such spending is wasteful.

Fortunately, there are continuing pressures for maintaining or restoring openness and accountability. One powerful argument for maintaining openness is the need to enforce the budget agreements that were arrived at in public. Budget implementation is generally very close to the budget that passes in full public view; there is little behind-the-scenes redoing of the policy choices in the budget. Actors who need to come to agreement on the next budget do not wish to see the last set of agreements come undone or be remade by someone else during the budget year. To keep the whole decision-making process going, the budget actors need to believe that their previous agreements will be implemented without change.

Environmental changes sometimes reduce the causes of secrecy. The end of the Cold War helped to reduce secrecy in the Department of Defense, just as the wars in Afghanistan and Iraq have increased it. Pressure from the deficit to find and reduce waste and shrink the scope of programs has also contributed to congressional pressure to expand the authority of the IGs. States wrestling with recession-induced deficits created new offices to reduce fraud in government programs such as Medicaid. Improved economic conditions reduce pressure to grant tax breaks to businesses, making spending programs more visible.

While these counterpressures help maintain a level of openness in budgeting, at times they may not be sufficient. In the worst case, the budget loses much of its utility as a tool of accountability.

Increased Polarization

A second theme that runs through the chapters is the increased polarization that has characterized budget politics in recent years, resulting in inflexible and ideological positions, government shutdowns, and symbolic votes. Intractable conflicts are much more apparent than in the past.

Inability to agree was apparent in the failure of the congressional supercommittee to decide on ways to cut spending in 2011, resulting in across-the-board cuts that practically no one wanted. The failure of the supercommittee was widely attributed to partisan deadlock.

Willingness to use the debt ceiling as a way of forcing desired cuts, threatening the credit quality of the country, was a demonstration of a newer force-oriented, as opposed to bargaining-oriented, budget politics. In 2011 and then again in 2013, the debt ceiling was taken hostage; Republicans would not vote to raise the debt ceiling and pay the nation's bills unless spending was reduced by an amount specified by them. One result was a partial government shutdown in 2013. A second result was a reduction in the reported credit quality of U.S. borrowing by several rating agencies.

Failure to pass a budget and prolonged government shutdowns over policy disagreements have also occurred at the state level as a result of partisan stand-offs. Minnesota government was closed for twenty days in 2011. In Illinois, in 2015, the Republican governor threatened to veto any legislative budget proposal unless the Democratically dominated legislature caved in and approved his list of his pro-business, antiunion policy measures. The fiscal year began without a budget, and no compromise occurred during the entire fiscal year, though pieces of the budget had been approved. The state government in this case was not fully shut down; state workers were ordered to continue at their jobs. Nonprofits and Medicaid providers dependent on the state budget were told by the governor to continue to provide services and to wait for reimbursement, but it is not clear how long they could hold out without pay. Some nonprofit service providers closed for lack of funds; many reduced their services. By mid-September, the state had stopped paying the bills for state health care costs of employees covered by the state's self insurance program, affecting 146,000 people. The legislature voted to allow federal pass-through funds to help the social service agencies, but the state budget impasse continued.

In Pennsylvania in 2015, a somewhat similar partisan standoff prevented the passage of a budget. In Pennsylvania, the governor was a Democrat, the legislature Republican. The governor initially vetoed the legislature's entire budget, demanding more funding for public schools to help alleviate huge gaps in funding between richer and poorer districts. The Republican legislature demanded an end to traditional pensions for public employees and wanted tax reductions for malls. Rumors suggested the Republicans might support the school funding increase, even if it meant tax increases, if the governor would support the end of traditional public pensions. While this controversy was going on, agencies were running out of money and public school systems were getting very nervous. It was six months before the governor gave in and signed a budget, but in doing so, he line-item vetoed almost $7 billion of the $30 billion budget passed by the Republicans. He thus released spending for schools, while maintaining some leverage to pressure the legislature into approving his policies.

North Carolina missed its deadline for a budget by a long shot in 2015, but the reason was less a split between Democrats and Republicans than differences between Republicans, who dominated both houses of the legislature and the governorship. The House and Senate battled over policies the Senate included in its budget proposal and over how to allocate spending reductions. Their delay prompted several continuing resolutions, similar to those at the federal level, which kept the government going at last year's levels, while the unknown cuts for the current budget year kept everyone who was dependent on the budget on tenterhooks.

Schools opened without knowing what their staffing was going to be as one proposal cut teaching assistants in order to increase staffing at the primary levels. Tea Party members wanted steeper cuts, and there were advocates for a Colorado-style TABOR, complicating the discussions. The Senate agreed to remove some of its more controversial policy proposals from the budget discussion and consider them separately, if the House would accept deeper cuts in spending.

Rather than bargaining in a timely fashion to find middle ground, increasingly the model seems to be to stake out more extreme positions, which sometimes seem irreconcilable. Some budget actors threaten and actually do great damage to force compliance with preferred policies. This recent pattern could be called a politics of ultimatums. In its most extreme form, it looks like extortion and hostage taking.

Inflexible and/or ideological budgeting was illustrated in the revenue chapter, with the discussion of the Grover Norquist pledge of no new taxes. The pledge became a litmus test for Republicans and for Democrats running in Republican-dominated districts and was monitored and enforced. The policy had some bizarre consequences, such as inability to eliminate some tax breaks and running large deficits when revenue did not keep pace with expenditures that had already been pared back.

The antitax thrust with its accompanying pressure to cut spending has resulted in a politics of ignoring or obscuring the consequences. In Kansas, along with tax reductions, came a refusal to comply with court orders on education spending, because they would cost money and would require tax increases. The governor's response seemed to be, I don't care about the courts, I can defund them and make them approve my decisions. In Illinois, the governor and some of the legislators seemed to ignore the law as they sought to cut the pensions despite the plain language of the constitution that maintained that pensions could not be reduced. Officials argued they were free to ignore the constitution if they invoked their police powers. The New Jersey governor failed to fulfill his end of a bargain with labor when he did not make the required annual contribution into the pension fund. The Louisiana governor pursued a policy of cutting corporate taxes so singlemindedly that it resulted in huge deficits. The governor of Wisconsin shepherded over $2 billion of tax cuts through his legislature, resulting in deficits, spending cuts, and debt "restructuring," which meant delaying payment on short term debt.

The implications of such cases go well beyond annual budgets. What happens when a state cuts or freezes taxes so that it cannot afford to pay its bills and then delays payments on debts to note holders and vendors and fails to contribute to contractually mandated pensions? What is the function of collective bargaining or the meaning of a contract if it can be violated with impunity by one side? What happens to the business of a state (or the broader society) if contracts to pay for services already received are not honored if they become burdensome? What will the outcome be when states that have cut taxes for the wealthy and find themselves deeply in debt add to the tax burden of the poor to balance the budget? Instead of offsetting the increasing gap between the rich and poor generated by the private sector, is government going to broaden the gap through tax policy?

What will happen to the independence of the courts, if governors are determined to use their budget power to control them? Our government is structured around three independent branches that provide checks and balances, assuring the continuation of democracy. What happens if those checks and balances are eroded?

More narrowly, what will happen to credit quality and ability to borrow money if the states can cut taxes and then claim they are too poor to pay whatever bills they choose not to pay? Representatives of business groups have often stood on the sidelines cheering on the states and urging them to cut payments to public employees, with the idea that the result will be lower taxes for them and more profit; but once a governmental body has succeeded in violating a contract that has become burdensome, might it not also decide not to pay vendors for services already rendered? There seems to be a willingness on all sides to not see or discuss the broader implications of the more extreme partisan policies.

Standoffs and inflexible position taking have been particularly in evidence when there is an executive and legislature of opposite parties. At the national level, Republican legislators want to lift the spending caps for defense; the Democratic president and his Democratic allies refuse to lift the caps for defense unless the caps are also lifted for other programs. Democrats are willing to increase taxes to pay for lifting the caps, Republicans oppose such a move. Republicans want to offset increased spending by cutting entitlement programs, not by any new taxation or requiring corporations to bring profits home and to pay U.S. taxes on them. The battle lines are clear and firm: business versus labor, the rich versus the poor.

At the state level, the lines of cleavage sometimes have resulted in constitutional challenges. The legislature in Alaska is suing the governor over the expansion of Medicaid. The governor favors it; the legislature opposes it. The governor decided to go ahead on his own; the legislature claims the governor is violating the separation of powers, that the decision to expand or not expand must be a legislative one.

While some of the issues of contention rise to the level of constitutional conflicts, some seem more like personal battles between Democrats and Republicans in which budgets are used as weapons. Thus, in Maine, some Democrats in the legislature began to support impeachment of the Republican governor when he threatened to withhold funding from a school for at-risk children if the school hired the Democratic House Speaker. A constitutional issue was raised when the bipartisan legislative watchdog agreed to look into the matter, while the governor's legal counsel claimed the legislative committee had no constitutional authority to investigate the governor. As one of the cochairs of the investigative committee described in an effort to smooth over the conflict, "As often happens in partisan politics, it seems like some people immediately go to their corners, getting ready to fight."[3]

One of the key issues dividing Democrats and Republicans is whether to side with business or with labor. In unemployment insurance, when Republicans wanted to keep insurance rates paid by businesses low (too low as it turned out) and reduce the number of weeks that an unemployed person could draw insurance, Democrats wanted a more realistic tax on businesses to help buffer the labor force against recessions. It was a clear case of business versus labor.

One result of increased partisanship has been an increase in symbolic politics, where the losing side on any issue keeps on proposing to roll back the legislation or policies of the winners, again and again. The purpose is to show supporters that they are trying to reverse the policies of which they disapprove. Symbolic politics encourages extreme position taking, playing to the audience rather than to their colleagues in the other party. Such public position taking makes it difficult to back down or compromise.

The increase in polarized politics suggests a number of possible avenues for research.

1. Do Democrats and Republicans use the same, similar, or different budget strategies?
2. What kind of responses occur or have occurred to budgeting by threat? What strategies are likely to work or have worked to defuse such threats?
3. What have been the number and duration of government shutdowns over time, and what have been the prime contributors to those shutdowns? Are there discernible trends, patterns, or differences?
4. Can we trace the shift from deficit hawks to antitaxers? What caused the shift? How durable does it seem? Is the strategy a phased one, to starve the beast first, cutting revenues, and then argue that the need to balance the budget necessitates cuts in particular services and spending programs?
5. What mechanisms show promise of curtailing the extremes? At least a few no-tax-increase pledgers have repudiated their pledges; what happened to them after that? Is there a trend? What happens when the tax cutting states face huge deficits and are forced to either slow the tax reductions or add new revenue sources? Is there a pattern to which ones they add? How far does the fiscal situation have to deteriorate and how deep do the service cuts have to get before the revenue response kicks in?

Action and Reaction

A third theme that appears in multiple decision streams is a kind of pendulum swing, an action taken to extremes promotes a reaction, sometimes equally extreme and likely to generate additional adaptations.

When there was a dramatic increase in the number of legislative earmarks at the federal level and corruption became visible, earmarks were banned completely. Congress and the administration went from one extreme to the other. To get around the ban, some legislators included suggestions or hints in committee reports or required reports on particular products that legislators wanted an agency to buy.

When a governor was granted broad discretion but used it to overrule legislative intent, an angry legislature spearheaded a referendum to deny the governor such broad discretion. The new ban, embodied in the state constitution, is as inflexible as the initial grant of discretion was flexible and will probably stimulate other forms of informal control.

If corruption appears common and embarrassing, offices of the inspector general may be created to win back public support. If the office is granted broad independence, its creation may be followed by efforts to weaken, control, or eliminate it. Such themes play out over a period of years.

When rules are strong or seen as overly constricting, they may be ignored, as the Budget Enforcement Act requirements were toward the end of their life. When not ignored, the rules may generate informal adaptations to get around them. The evasive strategies are typically less public and may have odd consequences. In both Maryland and New York State, where the governor has extreme budget powers, informal rules have emerged that give the legislature some influence. Governors may then try to curtail those legislative adaptations. Thus when the legislature routinely held up the budget in order to force the governor to negotiate over the budget, the governor of New York promoted a legislative loss of control over the budget if the legislature missed its deadlines.

When deficits became too large, they generated pressure to change the budget process to curtail those deficits; when those rules were perceived as too restrictive, they were initially ignored (informal response) and then the rules themselves were changed (formal response).

This pattern of pushing some strategy to extremes, prompting an answering response, which may also be extreme, and sometimes a reaction against that reaction, suggests some possibly fruitful lines of inquiry and methods of research.

1. How many of these chains of action and reaction can we find?
2. What encourages the taking of some strategy to extremes, and what stimulates counter measures? What kind of triggers are there? Does secrecy, once

accepted, become more and more extreme, because it is so convenient and not open to scrutiny? If so, what, short of a whistle blower, can bring the levels of secrecy back down? Is there some intrinsic limit to how much taxes can be reduced and services cut before the effort is slowed down or reversed? Do some of these action and reaction chains reach equilibrium, or do some of the oscillations get larger over time? The mayor and the inspector general in Chicago eventually reached an understanding: How did this happen? Is there a generalizable model here?

3. Do consequences matter? Does it matter if the policy that is taken to extremes achieves its promised goals, or are public arguments in its favor ideological and not subject to proof or disproof or any evaluation at all?

Federalism

A fourth theme that appears in multiple chapters is the importance of federalism in public budgeting. For most purposes, the states are independent, not under the direct control of the national government, but there are a number of joint programs, funded by both, and tailored by the states. The federal government can give grants to the states, to persuade them to do things, such as expand Medicaid. The local governments, by contrast, are creatures of the state governments. On the one hand, the states can order the local governments around; on the other hand, the states are responsible for their local governments.

In the revenue stream, the states can control the local governments' revenues. They can pass home rule laws that allow some local governments to raise taxes on their own authority. On the other hand, they can pass tax and expenditure limitations that apply to their cities, counties, and school districts. They can prohibit local governments from levying particular taxes, reserving those resources for themselves. They can even take local government revenues, as California has done in the past. They can share—or not share—revenue with local governments; they can mandate services levels at the local level and provide—or not provide—money to cover the costs. The states can authorize tax breaks for the local level.

In the expenditure stream, some programs are shared between states and the federal government. One example is the Unemployment Insurance Program. The structure of the Unemployment Insurance Program made it possible for some states to tax their businesses too little, because they could borrow from the federal government if they ran out of money during a long and deep recession. A number of states, rather than increase the burden on businesses to pay a proportion of wages for those thrown out of work during a recession, reduced benefits to the unemployed. They could do this because the program design, the size of benefits, the duration benefits, and eligibility criteria were all left to the states in this shared program.

In the balance chapter, some states tried to balance their own budgets by cutting funding to their local governments, making it harder for the local governments to balance their budgets. In Michigan, such reductions contributed to Detroit's financial meltdown and eventual bankruptcy. Sometimes the states have taken over the financial management of their troubled local governments. Some states allowed their local governments to declare bankruptcy under federal bankruptcy law. The case of Detroit suggests that the state not only permitted or even encouraged but also facilitated and may have forced the city into bankruptcy. The result minimized the state's responsibility to rescue the city. Not only can states divert revenue targeted for local governments, they can also mandate expenditures for their local governments, sometimes providing funding for those mandates and sometimes not. The effort to curtail unfunded mandates has been a more positive state level response to local fiscal distress.

With respect to budget implementation and control, a complicated dual structure of oversight of expensive Medicaid programs grew up in some states as the federal government required oversight of providers and states sought oversight of clients. The example of New York State and the overly nitpicky inspector general for Medicaid occurred because the federal government shared the expense of Medicaid with the state and hence had an interest in discovering and reducing fraud. The federal government loaned the state money to improve its system of controls, money that the inspector general was expected to recover from providers, in order to pay back the loan.

None of these stories would make any sense without understanding the context of federalism, the independence of the states and their local governments from the federal government on the one hand and the shared programs and responsibilities on the other. Nor would these stories make any sense without a clear understanding of the financial authority of states over their local governments.

Reconceptualizing Reform

This description of real-time budgeting and the patterns of change over time is intended to contribute to a descriptive theory of how the politics of budgeting works and what kinds of reforms are likely to be desirable or effective.

The description of budgeting offered here emphasizes that there are multiple actors, with a variety of motivations and with different amounts of power over time. Legislators are interested not only in constituency benefits but also in maintaining their own power and the power of the legislative body. Equally important, at times they are interested in providing for the public good. When their personal or constituent interests clash with the public good, legislators sometimes opt for the public good. Sometimes they do not see a problem coming or they underestimate the severity of the public consequences of their individual actions, but they learn from disasters and are often able to restructure their processes to increase discipline or delegate decision-making to a location that is better buffered from interest groups. Restructuring can be successful with a consensus that it is necessary to avoid a disaster.

This observation-based conclusion suggests a model for reform. Those who want to improve budget decision-making; strengthen the norms of balance; reduce, relatively speaking, the role of narrow interests; or open up the budget process and documents to more public scrutiny might appropriately work at clarifying the consequences of similar actions taken in the past or at documenting the likely future outcomes. Closing down the government? What was the cost of doing that the last time? Shutting down military bases—how much money was actually saved during the last round of base closings? There is much turnover of decision makers and among their staffs; one ought not to assume that past experience is known or likely consequences understood.

The swings in budgetary decision-making suggest that there are some internal mechanisms for balance, but they are not well regulated. They depend on knowledge of outcomes that often is not there. Moreover, responses to problems may get locked in, unable to change with changing conditions. The same solutions may be employed over and over until some extreme and unacceptable outcome is reached. When new constraints are finally devised, they may pay too little attention to possible long-term side effects. For example, historically, when cities ran up huge debts, the states responded by limiting cities' ability to borrow long term. Because there were also taxing limits, cities had no way to legitimately respond to the problems of growth. The consequence was a buildup in short-term debt, which was rolled over from year to year, for operating purposes, resulting in the deterioration of the cities' financial condition and the quality of information in their budgets. More extreme policy responses to problems typically do not take into consideration their secondary effects. When the policy response to problems is extreme and leads to unacceptable long-term problems, then the pressure to change the rules or allow them to lapse eventually takes over, setting the stage for a new round of abuses and controls. If those devising the original set of solutions could better envision the potential consequences over the long term, they might phrase their proposals more moderately, solving the original problem without the kind of side effects that result in evasion or elimination of the rules.

The historical pattern suggests that research and reform should concentrate on identifying the places and times—the mechanisms—that allow balance to swing too widely and the turning points or mechanisms that historically have brought situations back from dangerous extremes. It may be that the size of the swings can be narrowed.

For example, a more careful monitoring of deficits and intense publicity about early warning signs may be helpful in averting the huge accumulation of deficits that sometimes occurs when small deficits are hidden or overlooked. If deficits are not allowed to grow too large, then pressure for rigid and enduring constraints will be less, and the cycle of control and evasion might be broken. A belief that all budgets should balance has left the public sector without a series of fallback positions and triggers for correction. Building a consensus about what kinds of deficits will be acceptable and for how long may be helpful; devising a measure of deficits and monitoring the effects on the economy of deficits of different sizes may also be helpful. It may be that we are willing to accept deficits from some sources but not others, for some periods of time but not longer than a certain number of years. If the conceptual murk can be cleared by a series of definitions, each acceptable to major groups of decision makers, then the level and degree of deficits may be plainer and the efforts to eliminate them more effective.

A second issue in which better warning signs might be helpful is budgetary secrecy. Perhaps warning bells should go off if secrecy in the budget begins to increase—for example, if earmarks are slipped into the black budget, if non war-related expenditures are slipped into the Overseas Contingency Account, if programs are taken "off budget," or if the IGs withhold or edit reports. Maybe an alarm should be raised if budget deliberations are intentionally so rushed that legislators do not have time to read proposals before voting on them. If the budget passed in public is seriously altered during implementation, maybe an openness failure klaxon should be sounded. If budget problems can be flagged earlier, they may not grow so large that the temptation to handcuff government results in poor management, public mistrust, or inability to collectively address public problems.

Some violations of process represent serious threats to democracy and should be flagged and publicized and possibly checked by rules to stop them. Some such measures are in place, but they have weaknesses. For example, at the federal level and in some states, there are laws that prohibit unfunded mandates. The prohibitions kick in when the costs being passed along are of a particular magnitude. However, the federal Unfunded Mandates Law does not prohibit underfunding of programs and is otherwise limited in scope. At the state level as well, there are many loopholes in the anti-mandates laws and constitutional provisions. Similarly, controls on reprogramming and transfers between funds may need some fine-tuning.

Before designing and adopting reforms, we need to replace simple dichotomies—balanced-unbalanced, funded-unfunded, above the line or below the line—with more nuanced definitions that include continua and that focus on serious violations having major policy consequences.

A second theme for reform that emerges from this book has to do with the interchangeability of budget roles. Reforms that simply have given the executive more power have not proven to be long-term solutions to budget discipline or balance. Governors sometimes play restrictive and sometimes expansionary roles; similarly, legislatures are sometimes restrictive and sometimes expansionary. History does not support the position that increasing the executive's power will solve deficits or other budgetary problems.

Reform that shifts the location of budget power changes outcomes in the short run by shifting power to actors who have a particular set of goals. If a state has a reform governor and an unreformed legislature riddled with corruption and eager for pork, then shifting power to the governor may bring about short-term improvement. But endless reinforcement of the governor's powers does not bring continuous budget improvement. Illinois has one of the strongest governorships in terms of budget powers, but years ago Gov. Jim Thompson shifted from more to less fiscally conservative accounting; he routinely hid deficits, and he was oriented to patronage spending for capital projects. Under his leadership, the state ran deficits despite the strong executive budget powers. More recently, Gov. Rod Blagojevich brought the state to a new level of financial mismanagement and deficit financing and ended up in prison.

A balance of power between the executive and the legislature, so that one actor can catch the other in bad practices, is probably sounder over the long run than the weakening of one and the continual strengthening of the other. The arrangements of the mid-1800s, when distrust of government drastically curtailed the powers of both governors and legislatures, were not particularly successful; it is not weak government that is required but fairly balanced powers. This conclusion echoes the debate over the founding of the nation. Over the past decade, supporters of increased presidential power have argued that the president needs more budgetary power to control the deficit. They argue that Congress is profligate and only the president can exercise discipline. But the experience of the states suggests that shifting more power to the president is no long-term improvement, and the George W. Bush administration's increases in presidential power and big tax cuts did not result in a more balanced budget.

While the location of major budget power in the executive or legislative branches does not predict budget outcomes, this book suggests that there is a relationship between budget process and outcomes. However, there is no single ideal process that will guarantee balance and limit taxation over time. Budgetary reform that emphasizes fiscal discipline has to have the serious support of key actors if it is to work; if recognition of the need for discipline erodes or if the case is never well made, the process will not create the desired outcome. Process does not sit out there by itself, exerting discipline on unruly and unwilling actors. The actors create the process and try to abide by it once it exists, but if it is not working for them and for the public, they change the process, formally or informally.

A third theme of reform has to do with the ability of budgeting to help articulate to government what the public wants. At times budgets have been obscure documents, and audit reports have gathered dust. The public has no interest in them because they do not address recognizable policy issues. Moreover, budget hearings are typically held after decisions already have been made. Officials sometimes fear citizen participation in budgeting, lest the process encourage the public to make demands that cannot be met or that violate what the officials feel are priorities. Public participation complicates what is already a complicated process. At the same time, if the budget process does not allow for the articulation of citizen interests, at what point and in what manner can citizens express their approval or disapproval? Citizens may increasingly take policymaking into their own hands, through binding and nonbinding referendums, which often result in simplistic and overly rigid constraints. A better-managed process that allows for dissent and also the articulation of interests is needed in many jurisdictions. Public officials need to solicit public advice in a form that they can act on and then demonstrate that they have heard and followed the advice.

It may be better public policy to allow a controversy to be stated than to use the power of budgeting to prevent it from being discussed and possibly resolved. Budgeting handles controversy all the time; it is designed to cope with the interruptions resulting from unresolved and controversial policy matters.

Avenues for Research

This book suggests many avenues for productive research, for students as well as scholars. It also suggests some lines of inquiry that probably will not be productive. Studies that compare last year's total appropriations to this year's total appropriations are unlikely to contribute much to the understanding of budget processes; they examine the budget over too short a period and ignore government sponsored enterprises, off budget programs, and agencies that bring in their own revenue. Studies of budgetary trade-offs may well produce major insights, if they adopt a realistic view of the way budgeting works. That is, they must assume that revenue constraints are variable, not fixed; that most routine trade-offs occur within departments and within the capital budget rather than across sections of the budget; that major changes in spending priorities occur only over fairly long periods of time; and that budgets are structured so that some expenditures are much more flexible than others. The kind of expenditure makes a difference, because much of the politics of budgeting revolves around the degree of flexibility and the attempt to lock in some expenditures.

The descriptive outline of budgeting presented here needs to be documented and elaborated. Much more research is needed on state and local budgeting and on the links between the decision clusters. One issue only lightly touched on is the tension between discretion and control. This book describes a discretion-and-control cycle for budget implementation but does not deal in any detail with the ways in which administrators recreate discretion within a control budget. More needs to be described about these internal dynamics and the different political value of different resources, depending on the degree of discretion they entail. New money, unencumbered money, and money without strings all have a special value in a tightly controlled budget, so that there may in fact be two budgets, one with less discretion and one with more. Administrators may strive to get more money into the budget with greater discretion. When circumstances reduce the discretionary money, the impact on the politics of budgeting may be very different from a reduction in the more tightly controlled portion of the budget.

A second theme that warrants future investigation is the process of locking and unlocking decisions. Budgeting involves a number of decisions that budget actors at the peak of their power try to make permanent. There are often attempts to unlock decisions, to reverse them, once they are made. Under what circumstances do locking or unlocking strategies work? More study needs to be made of these processes—for example, the efforts to put bans on certain forms of taxation into state and national constitutions or the establishment of trust funds or public enterprises. Efforts to create rights-based entitlements need more explicit study. In each of these cases, more attention should be focused on the processes and circumstances for undoing or reversing them.

A third theme of the book that needs further exploration is the relationship between the technical and political aspects of budgeting. The technical concerns of the budget include accurate estimates of expenditures and revenues, realistic evaluations of the economy, compliance with balance requirements (no matter how formulated), timely completion of decisions, prevention of agency overspending, and the creation of a plan that puts enough resources in the right places to get mandated work accomplished. The political concerns of the budget include establishing and enforcing priorities, holding taxes down or getting sufficient support for taxation to allow expenditures to occur and balance to be achieved, creating a workable budget process, designing and implementing rules of balance, and satisfying perceived needs for constituency benefits. These functions are not neatly divided into those performed by elected officials and those performed by career bureaucrats. Who performs which functions? When does political distortion of economic projections become so severe as to force more neutral estimates? When do technical efforts to achieve balance cause major policy changes? Whose responsibility is it to maintain the informational integrity of the budget and its usefulness as a tool of accountability to the public? How far can that integrity erode before counter pressures are exerted?

More broadly, this book has characterized budgeting changes over time as the pendulum swings. Changes in one direction begin to generate support for the opposite, or flaws in the current system make it obvious that a new system is needed. But more research has to be done on turning points, on the dynamics and timing of shifting from one policy extreme back toward the center or toward the other extreme. In some cases, there may be equilibrium points, at which the forces in one direction offset those pushing the other way, resulting in at least temporary stability. When does such stability occur and with what effect?

These suggested topics are only a preliminary list; there are many more possibilities. Such research could meaningfully be quantitative or qualitative, as long as it covers a sufficiently long time span, views budget constraints as flexible, and is sensitive to the different kinds of resources in a budget and the different streams of budgetary decision making.

Summary and Conclusions

Public budgeting is highly political, but it is not the same thing as politics in general. It occupies a special corner of politics, with many of its own characteristics. The politics of taxation may illustrate broader political desires to avoid unpopular decisions, but the process of turning taxation into distributive politics through the award of tax breaks and the eventual need for reform, the tension between spending and taxing, and the occasional passage of new or increased taxes are unique to the politics of budgeting. Real-time decision-making is peculiar to budget decision-making, with its intense sensitivity to the environment, its interruptibility, its nested options, and its time constraints. Budgeting has a bottom line and a due date, which distinguish it from many other political decisions.

Budgeting carries in itself a way of measuring failure that creates pressures for action and reaction over time.

Budgeting is a particularly important arena of politics, because many policy decisions are meaningless unless they can be implemented through the budget process. When political actors want to enhance their power, they often focus on power over budgeting as a way to achieve it. Consequently, battles over budgeting processes that otherwise might seem dry, technical matters, turn out to be lively contests. Individuals try to get into positions of budgetary power and then try to increase the power of the positions they hold. Budgeting is the setting for major contests over the separation of powers and the balance between the legislature and the executive. At the federal level, legislative committees battle with one another for jurisdiction, budget power becomes fragmented, and coordination becomes problematic.

The budget document itself plays a unique role in the political system. It is a management document designed to help plan expenditures and maintain financial control; it may reflect important policy decisions made during the budget process and thus represent a summary of major government actions; and it presents to taxpayers an explanation of how their money is being spent. The role of the budget in providing public accountability is a crucial one in a democracy. Yet budgets do not always play that role well. Budgets sometimes change during implementation; the figures in the budget are not always accurate; and the information may be displayed in such a way as to obscure rather than elucidate key decisions. Budgets have to remain somewhat flexible, which may reduce their usefulness as tools of public accountability. Secrecy in making decisions may be necessary to buffer decision makers from the pleadings of special interests; and secrecy may be used to do something desired but formally prohibited.

The level of secrecy in budgeting needs to be carefully monitored. When the level of secrecy increases and budget decisions are made out of public view, when politically damaging judgments can be edited out of audits and inspectors general can be selected based on loyalty to the chief executive or department head, democracy receives a body blow. When secrecy is low, citizens can use the budget process and documents to hold government accountable. The coercive power of government may force citizens to pay taxes for programs they do not want, but this is—still—a democracy, and citizens can and do rebel.

Useful Websites

NASBO, the National Association of State Budget Officers (www.nasbo.org), has a publication on **budgeting for winter storms** (www.nasbo.org/publications -data/issue-briefs/analyzing-costs-associated-winter-storms). Winter storms are only one of the many contingencies that budgets need to be able to deal with during the budget year.

Because states generally have to balance their budgets annually, external emergencies may be funded by special reserve funds or require midyear cuts in other programs. States also rely on federal assistance for major disasters, natural or manmade. The Federal Emergency Management Agency, FEMA, is funded annually to cover a ten-year average cost for emergencies. A **recent FEMA budget justification** is available online (www.fema.gov/pdf/about/budget/11f_fema _disaster_relief_ fund_dhs_fy13_cj.pdf).

The level of secrecy in budgeting is difficult to measure directly, but one approach is to monitor the news releases for the **total of the federal black budget for intelligence** (for a recent example, see www.dni.gov/index.php/newsroom/ press-releases/96-press-releases-2012/756-dni-releases-fy-2012-appropriated -budget-figure). These are issued by the Office of the Director of National Intelligence.

Some nonprofits track accountability issues, such as the **Center for Public Integrity** (www.publicintegrity.org), a nonpartisan news organization. They evaluate state budget processes for openness, for example, as well as for possible corruption. A particularly intriguing recent piece was on **Arizona's budget process**, which has become less transparent over the past decade (www.publicinteg rity.org/2012/08/01/10493/transparency-missing-arizonas-legislature). One reason has been the frequent use of "strike-out" amendments, in which the original bill is swapped out for something completely different at the last possible moment, making it impossible for citizens or interest groups to follow legislation. Illinois has a similar process called "shell bills," in which the bill is merely a shell, to be filled in at the last moment. For information on the Illinois process, see Illinois Voices for Reform, **"Shell bills"** (http://ilvoices.com/shell-bills.html).

Notes

Chapter 1

1. Patricia Ingraham and Charles Barrilleaux, "Motivating Government Managers for Retrenchment: Some Possible Lessons from the Senior Executive Service," *Public Administration Review* 43, no. 3 (1983): 393–402. They cite the Office of Personnel Management Federal Employee Attitude Surveys of 1979 and 1980, extracting responses from those in the Senior Executive Service, the upper ranks of the civil service, and appointed administrators. In 1979, 99 percent of the senior executives said that they considered accomplishing something worthwhile very important; 97 percent said the same in 1980. By contrast, in response to the question, "How much would you be motivated by a cash award?" only 45 percent said either to a great extent or to a very great extent.

2. Lance LeLoup and William Moreland, "Agency Strategies and Executive Review: The Hidden Politics of Budgeting," *Public Administration Review* 38, no. 3 (1978): 232–239; 12 percent of LeLoup and Moreland's Department of Agriculture requests between 1946 and 1971 were for decreases. See Lance LeLoup, *Budgetary Politics,* 3rd ed. (Brunswick, Ohio: King's Court, 1986), 83. See also the case study of the Office of Personnel Management, in Irene Rubin, *Shrinking the Federal Government* (New York: Longman, 1985) and Irene Rubin, *Running in the Red: The Political Dynamics of Urban Fiscal Stress* (Albany: State University of New York Press, 1982).

3. For a good discussion of this phenomenon, see Frank Thompson, *The Politics of Personnel in the City* (Berkeley: University of California Press, 1975).

4. See Rubin, *Shrinking the Federal Government,* for examples during the Reagan administration.

5. U.S. Senate, Committee on Governmental Affairs, *Office of Management and Budget: Evolving Roles and Future Issues,* Committee Print 99–134, 99th

Cong., 2d sess., prepared by the Congressional Research Service of the Library of Congress, February 1986. OMB's role changed some in the 1990s, as it was engaged in helping implement the Government Performance and Results Act (GPRA) and various efforts at downsizing to help balance the budget. But it still remains a more top-down agency, implementing presidential policy, doing analysis, and making recommendations to the president. See Shelley Lynn Tomkin, *Inside OMB: Politics and Process in the President's Budget Office* (Armonk, NY: M. E. Sharpe, 1998), for both the history of OMB and its later roles.

6. See, for example, Kenneth Shepsle and Barry Weingast, "Legislative Politics and Budget Outcomes," in *Federal Budget Policy in the 1980s,* ed. Gregory Mills and John Palmer (Washington, DC: Urban Institute Press, 1984), 343–367.

7. Quoted in Rubin, *Running in the Red,* 56.

8. Rachel La Corte, "Legislative Bills Put Spotlight on Cost of Citizens Initiatives," *The Seattle Times,* February 15, 2015, updated June 15, 2015, online at http://www.seattletimes.com/seattle-news/legislative-bills-put-spotlight-on-cost-of-citizens-initiatives/

9. Linda Harriman and Jeffrey Straussman, "Do Judges Determine Budget Decisions? Federal Court Decisions in Prison Reform and State Spending for Corrections," *Public Administration Review* 43, no. 4 (1983): 343–351.

10. John Higgins, "Washington's Pending Showdown on School Funding: Legislature vs. the Supreme Court," *The Seattle Times,* February 14, 2015, http://old.seattletimes.com/html/education/2025702421_mcclearystate comparsionsxml.html; Joseph O'Sullivan and Jim Brunner, "School Funding Back on Table as Court Fines State $100,000 a Day," *The Seattle Times,* August 14, 2015, file:///C:/Users/puss/Documents/ppb15/washstcourtrl.htm

11. Rubin, *Class, Tax, and Power: Municipal Budgeting in the United States* (Chatham, NJ: Chatham House, 1998).

12. For more on budget strategies, see Irene Rubin, "Strategies for the New Budgeting," in *Handbook of Public Administration,* 2nd ed., ed. James Perry (San Francisco: Jossey-Bass, 1996), 279–296.

Chapter 2

1. Alan Meltzer and Scott F. Richard, "Why Government Grows (and Grows) in a Democracy," *The Public Interest* 52 (Summer 1978): 111–118.

2. Tim Mak, "Grover Norquist Defends No-Tax Pledge," *Politico,* October 19, 2011, www.politico.com/news/stories/1011/66359.html.

3. www.atr.org/pledge-database

4. Bruce Bartlett, "Higher Taxes Are Not Politically Impossible," *Tax Notes* 133, no. 9 (November 2011).

5. Margaret Butler, "Oregon Unions Save Services, Tapping Voter Anger to Tax Wealthy," *Labor Notes,* February 18, 2010, http://labornotes.org/2010/02/oregon-unions-save-services-tapping-voter-anger-tax-wealthy.

6. Eric Black, "Grover Norquist Looms Over Minnesota's Budget Impasse," *Minnesota Post,* July 8, 2011, www.minnpost.com/eric-black-ink/2011/07/grover-norquist-looms-over-minnesotas-budget-impasse.

7. John F. Witte, *The Politics and Development of the Federal Income Tax* (Madison: University of Wisconsin Press, 1985), 68.

8. Drew Desilver, "The Biggest U.S. Tax Breaks," PEW Research Center, April 13, 2015, http://www.pewresearch.org/fact-tank/2015/04/13/the-biggest-u-s-tax-breaks/.

9. Institute on Taxation and Economic Policy, "Tax Incentives: Costly for States, Drag on the Nation," 2013, http://itep.org/itep_reports/2013/08/tax-incentives-costly-for-states-drag-on-the-nation.php#.VdyaaCVViko; Kenneth Thomas, *Investment Incentives and the Global Competition for Capital* (New York: Palgrave Macmillan 2010).

10. Louise Story, "As Companies Seek Tax Deals, Governments Pay High Price," *New York Times*, December 1, 2012, http://www.nytimes.com/2012/12/02/us/how-local-taxpayers-bankroll-corporations.html?_r=1.

11. Congressional Budget Office, "The Distribution of Major Tax Expenditures in the Individual Income Tax System," May 29, 2013, http://www.cbo.gov/publication/43768.

12. Alejandra Cancino, "Effort Stalls to Revamp Illinois' Corporate Tax Breaks Program," *Chicago Tribune*, December 19, 2014, http://www.chicagotribune.com/business/ct-tax-breaks-stall-1221-biz-20141219-story.html#page=1.

13. Philip Mattera, Kasia Tarczynska, Leigh McIlvaine, Thomas Cafcas, and Greg LeRoy, "PAYING TAXES TO THE BOSS: How a Growing Number of States Subsidize Companies with the Withholding Taxes of Workers," *Good Jobs First*, April 2012, http://www.goodjobsfirst.org/sites/default/files/docs/pdf/taxestotheboss.pdf; Warren Vieth and Mark Lash, "State Program Diverting Workers' Tax Payments to Businesses," *Oklahoma Watch Data Center*, June 2015, http://oklahomawatch.org/2015/06/09/state-program-diverts-workers-tax-payments-to-businesses/

14. Letter of comment 121, to David Bean, GASB, December 2014, from Zach Schiller, Gordon MacInnes, Elliot Richardson, and Jason Bailey, http://www.gasb.org/cs/BlobServer?blobkey=id&blobnocache=true&blobwhere=1175829984993&blobheader= application%2Fpdf&blobheadername2=Con

tent-Length&blobheadername1=Content-Disposition&blobheadervalue2= 582515&blobheadervalue1=filename%3DTAD_ED_CL121.pdf&blobcol=u rldata&blobtable=MungoBlobs).

15. David Cay Johnston, "Taxed by the Boss," *Reuters,* April 12, 2012, www .reuters.com/article/2012/04/12/us-column-dcjohnston-report-idUSBRE 83B0XQ20120412; and Philip Mattera, Kasia Tarczynska, Leigh McIlvaine, Thomas Cafcas, and Greg LeRoy, "Paying Taxes to the Boss."

16. Pat Kimbrough, "Rethinking Incentives: Recession Brings Changes in Ways Cities Use Economic Development Tool," *High Point Enterprise,* November 29, 2010, www.hpe.com/view/full_story/10478576/article-Rethinking -incentives—Recession-brings-changes-in-ways-cities -use-economic -development-tool?.

17. Tim Bartik and George Erickcek, "The Employment and Fiscal Effects of Michigan's MEGA Tax Credit Program" (Working Paper 10–1064, W.E. Upjohn Institute for Employment Research, Kalamazoo, Mich., 2010, http:// research.upjohn.org/up_workingpapers/164).

18. "Do Tax Incentives Really Create Jobs?" Editorial, *Los Angeles Times,* September 10, 2014, http://www.latimes.com/opinion/editorials/la-ed-tesla -incentives-20140911-story.html.

19. William Luther, *Movie Production Incentives: Blockbuster Support for Lackluster Policies,* Special Report No. 173, Tax Foundation, January 2010, http://taxfoundation.org/sites/taxfoundation.org/files/docs/sr173.pdf.

20. Brian Sala and Maeve Roche, "The Motion Picture Industry in California: A Brief Update," California Research Bureau, March 2011, www.stop-runaway -production.com/wp-content/uploads/2009/07/2011 -CA-research-bureau -update-on-film-industry.pdf.

21. Ibid.

22. Pew Charitable Trusts, "States Make Progress Evaluating Tax Incentives," January 21, 2015, http://www.pewtrusts.org/en/research-and-analysis/fact -sheets/2015/01/tax-incentive-evaluation-law-state-fact-sheets.

23. Philip Mattera, Thomas Cafcas, Leigh McIlvaine, Andrew Seifter, and Kasia Tarczynska, "Money for Something: Job Creation and Job Quality Standards in State Economic Development Subsidy Programs," Good Jobs First, December 2011, www.goodjobsfirst.org/sites/default/files/docs/pdf/money forsomething.pdf.

24. Robert S. McIntyre, Matthew Gardner, Rebecca J. Wilkins, and Richard Phillips, "Corporate Tax Dodging in the Fifty States, 2008–2010," Institute for Taxation and Economic Policy and Citizens for Tax Justice, November 2011, www.ctj.org/corporatetaxdodgers/CorporateTaxDodgersReport.pdf.

25. Robert S. McIntyre. Matthew Gardner, Richard Phillips, "The Sorry State of Corporate Taxes: What Fortune 500 Firms Pay (or Don't Pay) in the USA and What They Pay Abroad—2008 to 2012," Citizens for Tax Justice and the Institute on Taxation & Economic Policy, February 2014, http://www.ctj.org/corporatetaxdodgers/sorrystateofcorptaxes.php.

26. Citizens for Tax Justice, "Who Pays Taxes in America in 2015?" April 9, 2015, http://ctj.org/ctjreports/2015/04/who_pays_taxes_in_america_in_2015 .php#.VYsLMhtVik.

27. Carl Davis, Kelly Davis, Matthew Gardner, Harley Heimovitz, Sebastian Johnson, Robert S. McIntyre, Richard Phillips, Alla Sapozhnikova, and Meg Wiehe, "Who Pays: A Distributional Analysis of the Tax Systems in All Fifty States," ITEP, 5th ed., January 2015, http://www.itep.org/whopays/.

28. Drew DeSilver, "Global Inequality: How the US Compares," PEW Research Center, December 19, 2013, online at http://www.pewresearch.org/fact -tank/2013/12/19/global-inequality-how-the-u-s-compares/.

29. "The Distribution of Household Income and Federal Taxes, 2011," Congressional Budget Office, 2014, https://www.cbo.gov/publication/49440.

30. "Tax Preferences: The Struggle Goes On," September 10, 2013, Washington House Democrats, http://housedemocrats.wa.gov/the-advance/tax-prefer ences-the-struggle-goes-on/.

Chapter 3

1. National Association of State Budget Officers, *Budget Processes in the States, 2015,* http://www.nasbo.org/sites/default/files/2015%20Budget%20 Processes%20-%20S.pdf. In thirty-three states, in 2015, the governor could make reductions in the budget without legislative agreement (Table 7). In the 2002 edition, the number of states where the governor could do this was thirty-seven. In twenty-six states, in 2015, the departments' budget requests appear in the governor's budget proposal, giving the legislature the opportunity to see what the departments asked for and what the governor approved or disapproved and hence the possibility of disagreeing with the governor's recommendation and substituting their own (Table 21). In 2002, the number of states where the department request was included was thirty-two. Thus the governors have increased their control over the departmental budget requests, minimizing the legislature's ability to make end runs around the governor, but at the same time, the governors are increasingly required to consult with the legislature before withholding funds during the year.

2. NASBO's *Budget Process in the States* 2015 edition. http://www.nasbo.org/sites/default/files/2015%20Budget%20Processes%28S%29.pdf. Table 8, Governor's veto powers.

3. Robert Bland and Wes Clarke, "Performance Budgeting in Texas State Government" (paper delivered at the meetings of the Association for Budgeting and Financial Management, Chicago, October 7, 2004).

4. Glenn Abney and Thomas P. Lauth, *The Politics of State and City Administration* (Albany: State University of New York Press, 1986), esp. chap. 9.

5. Allen Schick, *The Capacity to Budget* (Washington, DC: Urban Institute Press, 1990), chap. 6. See also Shelley Tomkin, *Inside OMB* (New York: M. E. Sharpe, 1998).

6. Robert Bland and Wes Clarke, "Performance Budgeting in Texas State Government," in *Budgeting in the States, Institutions, Processes and Politics,* ed. Edward Clynch and Thomas P. Lauth (Westport, CT: Praeger, 2006); and *Budget 101: A Guide to the Budget Process in Texas* (Austin: Senate Research Center, 2011), www.senate.state.tx.us/src/pdf/Budget_101-2011.pdf.

7. Carolyn Bourdeaux, "Legislative Barriers to Budget Reform" (paper presented to the Association for Budgeting and Financial Management meeting, Chicago, October 9, 2004) and personal communication.

8. The Georgia Budget and Policy Institute, *Georgia Budget Primer, 2015* (Atlanta: Georgia Budget and Policy Institute, 2014), http://gbpi.org/wp-content/uploads/2014/08/Budget-Primer-Online-Version.pdf.

9. Jennifer Grooters and Corina Eckl, *Legislative Budget Procedures: A Guide to Appropriations and Budget Processes in the States and Territories* (Denver: National Conference of States, 1999); Kentucky revised statutes 48.050; Florida Office of Public Information, *Florida's Budget Process,* http://www.myflorida house.gov/Handlers/LeagisDocumentRetriever.ashx?Leaf=housecontent/opi/Lists/Announcements/Attachments/45/OPI%20Pulse%20-%20Florida%27s%20Budget%20Process%202-7-12.pdf&Area=House.

10. Nelson C. Dometrius and Deil S. Wright, "Governors, Legislatures, Partisanship, and State Budget Processes" (paper prepared for delivery at the annual meeting of the State Politics and Policy Conference, Kent, Ohio, April 30–May 1, 2004).

Chapter 4

1. Howard Shuman, *Politics and the Budget: The Struggle between the President and the Congress* (Englewood Cliffs, NJ: Prentice Hall, 1984), 27.

2. Ibid., 28.

3. Allen Schick, *Congress and Money* (Washington, DC: Urban Institute Press, 1980), chap. 2.

4. Congressional Budget Office, *The Economic and Fiscal Outlook: Fiscal Years, 1992–1996* (Washington, DC: Government Printing Office, January 1991), chap. 2.

5. Ibid., 57.

6. Allen Schick, *The Federal Budget: Politics, Policy and Process* (Washington, DC: Brookings Institution Press, 1995), 41.

7. Allen Schick, "The Deficit That Didn't Just Happen: A Sober Perspective on the Budget," *Brookings Review* 20, no. 2 (Spring 2002): 45–48.

8. Philip Joyce, "Federal Budgeting after September 11th: A Whole New Ballgame, or Is It Déjà Vu All over Again?" *Public Budgeting and Finance* 25, no. 1 (Winter 2005): 15–31.

9. Megan Lynch, "Provisions in the Bipartisan Budget Act of 2013 as an Alternative to a Traditional Budget Resolution," Congressional Research Service, May 8, 2014, https://crsreports.com/download?hash=247ee90a5809 0b6a27a4c925ad159dfffa3c9f9d5d5efc7fcee5a5796e5b6166.

10. Alexander Bolton and Jonathan E. Kaplan, "Congress Veils Appropriations Spending Totals," TheHill.com, May 28, 2003.

11. Peter Cohn, "Senate Spending Process to Go Forward Even Without Budget Deal," *Government Executive Magazine,* June 8, 2004, http://www.govexec .com/management/2004/06/senate-spending-process-to-go-forward-even -without-budget-deal/16892/.

12. Ken Nakamura, "AFSANET Legislative Up-Date: The FY 05 Omnibus and State and Commerce Funding," December 10, 2004 (circulating e-mail from AFSA, the union for the employees of the State Department). Ken Nakamura was the American Foreign Service Association director of congressional relations.

13. "Improvisational" and "ad hoc budgeting" are terms used by Allen Schick in his book *The Capacity to Budget* (Washington, DC: Urban Institute Press, 1990). He meant by these terms making up or adjusting budget procedures as you go along, instead of using budget rules or routines that are known in advance, agreed to by all parties, and repeated from year to year. He argues that improvisational budgeting is a sign of reduced capacity to budget, which involves reasoned comparisons between possible items of expenditure.

14. Megan Lynch, "Provisions in the Bipartisan Budget Act."

15. Ronald Snell, "The Power of the Purse: Legislatures That Write State Budgets Independently of the Governor," National Conference of State Legislatures, March 2008, www.ncsl.org/issues-research/budget/the-power-of-the-purse -legislatures-that-write-st.aspx.

16. Data come from the NCSL, *Legislative Budget Procedures in the 50 States,* 1983; *Legislative Budget Procedures in the 50 States,* 1988; and Jennifer Grooters and Corina Eckl, *Legislative Budget Procedures: A Guide to Appropriations and Budget Procedures in the States, Commonwealths, and Territories, 1999* (Denver: National Conference of State Legislatures, 1999), chap. 3, n. 6.

17. Nelson C. Dometrius and Deil S. Wright, "Governors, Legislatures, Partisanship, and State Budget Processes" (paper prepared for delivery at the Fourth Annual Meeting of the State Politics and Policy Conference, Kent, Ohio, April 30–May 1, 2004).

18. Interview with deputy county attorney, July 20, 1995. The example is taken from Irene Rubin, *Class, Tax, and Power: Municipal Budgeting in the United States* (Chatham, NJ: Chatham House, 1998).

19. Claude Tharp, *Control of Local Finance Through Taxpayers Associations and Centralized Administration* (Indianapolis: M. Ford Publishing, 1933), p. 16.

20. The federal government also passes on unfunded mandates to both the state and local levels. However, because local governments are legally subordinate to the states, the potential scope of mandates is much greater from the states to the local level. The states could, if they wished, completely preempt local decision-making.

21. David Barron, Gerald Frug, and Rick Su, *Dispelling the Myth of Home Rule: Local Power in Greater Boston* (Cambridge, MA: Rappaport Institute for Greater Boston, Kennedy School of Government, Harvard University, 2004), www.ksg.harvard.edu/rappaport/research/homerule/chaptertwofinance.pdf.

22. Ibid.

23. Martin Schiesl, *The Politics of Efficiency: Municipal Administration and Reform in America* (Berkeley: University of California Press, 1986), 91.

24. Ibid., 92.

25. Charles Glaab and A. Theodore Brown, *A History of Urban America*, 3rd ed. (New York: Macmillan, 1983), 200.

26. Caitlin Rother, "Is Shift in Structure of Power Ahead? Strong Mayor Model Getting Another Look," *San Diego Union Tribune*, March 21, 2004, http://pqasb.pqarchiver.com/sandiego/.

Chapter 5

1. David Willman, "Seventeen Years and $2.7 Billion in, Pentagon's High-Tech Blimps Fail to Deliver on Promise," *The Baltimore Sun*, September 24, 2015, http://www.baltimoresun.com/business/federal-workplace/bs-md-blimps-20150924-story.html.

2. Travis J. Tritten, "Base Closure Proposal Meets Resistance in Senate, *Stars and Stripes*, March 11, 2015, http://www.stripes.com/news/base-closure-proposal-meets-resistance-in-senate-1.333890.

3. Sean Reilly, "2014 Budget Guidance: Cut Another 5%, More for IT," *The Federal Times*, May 21, 2012, www.federaltimes.com/article/20120521/AGENCY01/205210302/1001.

4. Travis Madsen, Benjamin Davis, and Phineas Baxandall, "Road Work Ahead, Holding Government Accountable for Fixing America's Crumbling Roads and Bridges," the U.S. PIRG, April 2010, p. 3, http://www.frontiergroup.org/sites/default/files/reports/Road-Work-Ahead-vUS.pdf.

5. Pamela M. Prah, "Businesses to Bear Cost of State Unemployment Insurance Debt, Employers in 20 States to Pay More in Taxes," *Chicago Tribune,* December 19, 2011, http://articles.chicagotribune.com/2011-12-19/business/ct-biz-1219-unemployment-insurance-20111219_1_unemployment-insurance-unemployment-loans-wayne-vroman.

6. Claire McKenna and George Wentworth, *Unraveling the Unemployment Insurance Lifeline: Responding to Insolvency, States Begin Reducing Benefits and Restricting Eligibility in 2011,* National Employment Law Project, August 2011, http://nelp.3cdn.net/833c7eeb782f18bdb3_a5m6b0wvp.pdf.

7. Government Accountability Office, *Unemployment Insurance Trust Funds: Long-Standing State Financing Policies Have Increased Risk of Insolvency* (Washington, DC: GAO 10–440, April 2010).

8. Testimony regarding [Connecticut] House Bill 5402, National Employment Law Project, www.nelp.org/page/-/UI/2012/CT_UI_testimony_HB5402.pdf?nocdn=1.

9. Congressional Budget Office, "Competition and the Cost of Medicare's Prescription Drug Program," July 2014, https://www.cbo.gov/publication/45552.

10. Margot Sanger-Katz and Kevin Quealy, "Medicare: Not Such a Budget-Buster Anymore," *New York Times,* Aug. 27, 2014, http://www.nytimes.com/2014/08/28/upshot/medicare-not-such-a-budget-buster-anymore.html?_r=0&abt=0002&abg=1.

11. Kaiser Family Foundation, "The Facts on Medicare Spending and Financing: Overview of Medicare Spending," based on CBO data, Jul 28, 2014, http://kff.org/medicare/fact-sheet/medicare-spending-and-financing-fact-sheet/.

12. Organization for Economic Co-operation and Development, *Health at a Glance 2011: OECD Indicators,* www.oecd.org/dataoecd/12/16/49084355.pdf.

Chapter 6

1. National Conference of State Legislatures, *NCSL Fiscal Brief: State Balanced Budget Provisions,* October 2010, www.ncsl.org/documents/fiscal/StateBalancedBudgetProvisions2010.pdf.

2. Ibid.

3. Jason Mercier, "From Near Last to Almost First on State-Balanced Budget Requirement," Washington Policy Center, April 17, 2012, www.washingtonpolicy.org/blog/post/near-last-almost-first-state-balanced-budget-requirement.

4. Reining Petacchi, Anna Costello, and Joseph Weber, "The Unintended Consequences of Balanced Budget Requirements" (working paper, April, 2012), www.hbs.edu/units/am/pdf/Patacchi and Weber_AssetSale_2012 .pdf.

5. OMB, *Historical Tables of the United States Budget* (Washington, DC: Government Printing Office, January 1996), Table 1.1.

6. House Permanent Select Committee on Intelligence, Inquiry into September 11.

7. Federation of American Scientists, "Intelligence Resource Program," www .fas.org/irp/budget/index.html.

8. Neta C. Crawford, "U.S. Costs of Wars Through 2014: $4.4 Trillion and Counting, Summary of Costs for the U.S. Wars in Iraq, Afghanistan and Pakistan," Watson Institute at Brown University, Cost of War project, 25 June 2014. http://costsofwar.org/sites/default/files/articles/20/attach ments/Costs%20of%20War%20Summary%20Crawford%20June%202014 .pdf.

9. Quoted in the U.S. Department of Treasury, Office of Financial Stability, *Troubled Asset Relief Program: Two Year Retrospective,* 2010, www.treasury .gov/presscenter/news/Documents/TARP%20Two%20Year%20 Retrospec tive_10%2005%2010_transmittal%20letter.pdf.

10. CBO, "Report on the Troubled Asset Relief Program—March 2015" (March 18, 2015), https://www.cbo.gov/publication/50034.

11. Jonathan Weisman, "House Bill Offers Aid Cuts to Save Military Spending," *New York Times,* May 7, 2012, www.nytimes.com/2012/05/08/us/house-bill -offers-aid-cuts-to-save-military-spending.html?

12. Quoted in *Brian Faler,* "U.S. Senate Defeats Two Balanced-Budget Amendment Proposals," *Bloomberg Business Week,* December 20, 2011, www .business-week.com/news/2011–12–20/u-s-senate-defeats-two-balanced -budget-amendment-proposals.html.

13. Alan Fram, "Balanced Budget Amendment Injected Into Debt Ceiling Fight," *Huffington Post,* July 14, 2011, www.huffingtonpost.com/2011/07/14/balanced -budget-amendment_n_899301.html#.

14. Quoted in U.S. Congress, House, *Hearings Before the Committee on the Budget,* 102d Cong., 2d sess. (May 12, 1992), 8.

15. Example modified from ibid., 14.

16. Robert Albritton and Ellen Dran, "Balanced Budgets and State Surpluses: The Politics of Budgeting in Illinois," *Public Administration Review* 47, no. 2 (March–April 1987): 135–142.

17. Illinois Economic and Fiscal Commission, *Revenue Estimate and Economic Outlook for FY 1978* (Springfield, IL: June 1977), 17; quoted in Albritton and Dran, "Balanced Budgets," 144.

18. Ron Snell, "State Experiences With Annual and Biennial Budgeting," NCSL, 2011, http://www.ncsl.org/research/fiscal-policy/state-experiences-with -annual-and-biennial-budgeti.aspx.

19. National Association of State Budget Officers, *Budget Process in the States, 2015* (Washington, DC: NASBO, 2015),Table 7, Gubernatorial Budget Authority and Responsibility, http://www.nasbo.org/sites/default/ files/2015%20Budget%20Processes%20-%20S.pdf.

20. State of Wisconsin Legislative Reference Bureau, "Funding Federal and State Mandates," Legislative Reference Bureau Informational Bulletin 96–3, April 1996, 11, www.legis.state.wi.us/lrb/pubs/ib/96ib3.pdf; Joseph Zimmerman, "Trends in State Local Relations," Council of State Governments, 2007 book of the states, http://knowledgecenter.csg.org/kc/system/files/Zimmerman_ Article_3.pdf.

21. King County [Washington] Budget Office, *Review of Legislative Mandates Imposed on King County, 1995–2000* (October 11, 2000).

22. California Legislative Analyst Office, *Overview of Mandates* (January 31, 2011), www.lao.ca.gov/handouts/state_admin/2011/Mandates_1_31_11.pdf.

23. Tim Cromartie, "Understanding State Mandates and Suspended Mandates: Local Government Impacts," Western City, March 2014, online at http:// www.westerncity.com/Western-City/March-2014/Feature-Understanding -State-Mandates/.

24. Ken McLaughlin, "Bid to Halt State's Tax Grab Has Wide Push; Little Opposition to Proposition 1A," *San Jose Mercury News*, October 23, 2004, www.mercurynews.com/mld/mercurynews/.

25. Ballotpedia, "California Proposition 22, Ban on State Borrowing from Local Governments," (2010), http://ballotpedia.org/California_Proposition_22,_ Ban_on_State_Borrowing_from_Local_Governments_(2010).

26. Michael Leachman and Chris Mai, "Most States Still Funding Schools Less Than Before the Recession," Center for Budget and Policy Priorities, October 16, 2014, http://www.cbpp.org/research/most-states-still-funding-schools -less-than-before-the-recession.

27. Tamarine Cornelius and Jon Peacock, "Local Governments Continue to Lose Ground Under 2013–15 Budget," Wisconsin budget project, July 3, 2013, http://www.wisconsinbudgetproject.org/local-governments-continue-to -lose-ground-under-2013–15-budget.

28. Wendy Patton, "Three Blows to Local Government: Loss in State Aid, Estate Tax, Property Tax Rollback," Policy Matters Ohio, July 24, 2013, http://www .policymattersohio.org/wp-content/uploads/2013/07/72313-Tthree-blows -to-local-government.pdf.

29. Michael Cooper, "States Pass Budget Pain to Cities," *New York Times*, March 23, 2011.

30. Jeff Van Wychen, "Problems With Minnesota's State Aid System," Minnesota 2020, December 7, 2008, www.mn2020.org.

31. Julie Liew, "No Increase in Governor's Supplemental Budget," LGA Archives, Coalition of Greater Minnesota Cities, March 20, 2015, http://greatermn cities.org/blog/no-lga-increase-in-governors-supplemental-budget/.

32. Michigan Municipal League, "Revenue Sharing Fact Sheet," http://www.mml .org/advocacy/2014-revenue-sharing-factsheet.html.

33. Jonathan Oostling, "How Michigan's Revenue Sharing 'Raid' Cost Communities Billions for Local Services," MLive.com, March 30, 2014, updated April 13, 2014, http://www.mlive.com/lansing-news/index .ssf/2014/03/michigan_revenue_sharing_strug.html; and Anthony Minghine, "The Great Revenue Sharing Heist," Michigan Municipal League, March April 2014, http://www.mml.org/advocacy/great-revenue-sharing-heist.html.

34. New York State Assembly, Ways and Means Committee, "Graphic Overview of the 2014–2015 Executive Budget," January 2014, online at http://assembly .state.ny.us/Reports/WAM/2014graphic_overview/2014_graphic_overview .pdf

35. Office of Policy Analysis, Department of Legislative Services, Overview of State Aid to Local Governments Fiscal 2014 and 2015 Allowance (two different volumes; Annapolis, MD: Department of Legislative Services Office of Policy Analysis, January 2013 and 2014) http://mgaleg.maryland.gov/Pubs/ BudgetFiscal/2014fy-state-aid-local-governments.pdf.; and http://dls.state .md.us/data/polanasubare/polanasubare_intmatnpubadm/polanasubare_int matnpubadm_staaidrep/Overview-of-State-Aid-to-Local-Governments.pdf.

36. Thanh Tan, "Sine Die Report: What Survived, What Died," *The Texas Tribune*, June 30, 2011, www.texastribune.org/texas-legislature/82nd-legisla tive-session/sine-die-report-what-survived-what-died-/.

37. "Kasich Signs House Bill 30-School Mandate Relief Act" (Press Release, Office of Governor John Kasich, March 30, 2011), www.governor.ohio.gov/ Portals/0/pdf/news/03302011.pdf.

38. Mandate Relief Redesign Team, *2011 Mandate Relief Redesign Team Report: Mandate Relief, Final Report* (report to the Governor of New York, December 2011), www.governor.ny.gov/assets/documents/FInal_Mandate_Relief_ Report.pdf.

39. Pew Charitable Trusts, "The State Role in Local Government Financial Distress, 2013," http://www.pewtrusts.org/~/media/Assets/2013/07/23/Pew_ State_Role_in_Local_Government_Financial_Distress.pdf.

40. "Municipal Bankruptcy, State Laws," Governing Data website, based on 2012 data, http://www.governing.com/gov-data/state-municipal-bankruptcy -laws-policies-map.html.

41. Congressional Budget Office, *Fiscal Stress Faced by Local Governments*, notes omitted.

42. "Municipal Bankruptcies: We're Not Going To Take It Anymore," *Bondview*, November 18, 2011, www.bondview.com/blog/municipal-bankruptcies -were-not-going-to-take-it-anymore/.

43. Charles Levine, Irene Rubin, and George Wolohojian, *The Politics of Retrenchment* (Thousand Oaks, CA: Sage, 1981).

Chapter 7

1. CBO, "CBO Data on Supplemental Appropriations Budget Authority: 2000— Present," 2014, https://www.cbo.gov/sites/default/files/17129-SuppApprops 2000-Present-8–2014.pdf.

2. CRS, "Jessica Tollestrup, Across-the-Board Rescissions in Appropriations Acts: Overview and Recent Practices," September 2, 2015, https://www.fas .org/sgp/crs/misc/R43234.pdf.

3. Allen Schick, *The Capacity to Budget* (Washington, DC: Urban Institute Press, 1990), 113.

4. City of New Haven, Connecticut v. United States of America, slip opinion 86–5319 (D.C. Circuit, 1987). See also Walter Oleszek, *Congressional Procedures and the Policy Process*, 3rd ed. (Washington, DC: CQ Press, 1989), 65.

5. Michael Hirsch, "NYSUT Sues Governor for Withholding State School Funding," United Federation of Teachers, January 11, 2010, http://www.uft .org/news-stories/nysut-sues-governor-withholding-state-school-funding.

6. Bridgeport v. Agostinelli, 163 Conn. 537 (1972), http://law.justia.com/cases/ connecticut/supreme-court/1972/163-conn-537–2.html.

7. Government Accountability Office, Letter to the Honorable Silvio O. Conte, Ranking Minority Member, Committee on Appropriations House of Representatives, B-196854.3, March 19, 1984.

8. Signing statement, December 23, 2011. pl. 112–74, Consolidated Appropriations Act 2012.

9. House Reports included prior permission constraints not only for Transportation and Housing and Urban Development; Interior and Related Agencies; and Defense, described here, but also for Military Construction, Veterans Administration, and related agencies, and Financial Services and General Government. Thus at least five of the twelve appropriations subcommittees continued to require prior approval for reprogramming. The Department of Homeland Security was under a somewhat looser control: it

needed only to provide advanced notification on proposed reprogrammings to the committee; the department did not need advanced permission, but it is not clear what the committee would do if it were informed of a reprogramming of which it disapproved.

10. *Congressional Record,* V. 149, Pt. 3, February 12, 2003, to February 24, 2003.

11. House of Representatives, Departments of Transportation, and Housing and Urban Development, and Related Agencies Appropriations Bill, 2015, report 113, http://appropriations.house.gov/uploadedfiles/hrpt-113-hr-fy2015 -thud.pdf.

12. House Report 112–151—Department of The Interior, Environment, and Related Agencies Appropriation Bill, 2012.

13. Department of Defense Appropriations Bill, 2015 Report of the Committee on Appropriations, 2014.

14. Departments of Transportation, Housing and Urban Development, and Related Agencies Appropriations Bill, 2011, July 26, 2010, 111–564.

15. Report accompanying the 2013 appropriation for Commerce, Justice, Science and Related Agencies, 112–158, April 19, 2012.

16. Chairman Frank Wolf Subcommittee on Commerce, Justice, and Science, and Related Agencies House Appropriations Committee, United States Department of Justice FY 2014 Budget Hearing, April 18, 2013 Opening Statement as Prepared.

17. Charles Levine, Irene Rubin, and George Wolohojian, "Resource Scarcity and the Reform Model: The Management of Reform in Cincinnati and Oakland," *Public Administration Review* 41, no. 6 (November/December 1981): 619–628.

18. See Irene Rubin, *Running in the Red* (Albany: State University of New York Press, 1982), for an example of a general fund borrowing from the water fund and causing deficits in the water fund.

Chapter 8

1. U.S. Congress, Senate, *Joint Hearings Before Committees on Government Operations and on the Judiciary, Impoundment of Appropriated Funds by the President,* 93d Cong., 1st sess., 1973, 411; quoted in Louis Fisher, "The Effect of the Budget Act on Agency Operations," in *The Congressional Budget Process After Five Years,* ed. Rudolph Penner (Washington, DC: AEI Press [American Enterprise Institute], 1981), 173.

2. For a good summary of the tools, offices, and roles of various budget overseers, along with some detailed case studies, see Daniel Feldman and David Eichenthal, *The Art of the Watchdog: Fighting Fraud, Waste, Abuse and Corruption in Government* (Albany, NY: State University of New York Press, 2013).

3. Department of Justice, "Justice Department Announces Criminal Charge Against Toyota Motor Corporation and Deferred Prosecution Agreement with $1.2 Billion Financial Penalty," press release, March 19, 2014, http://www.justice.gov/opa/pr/justice-department-announces-criminal-charge-against-toyota-motor-corporation-and-deferred.

4. Council of the Inspectors General on Integrity and Efficiency, "Inspector General Community Accomplishments Will Receive Recognition," press release, October 2015, https://www.ignet.gov/sites/default/files/files/CIGIE%20awards%20press%20release%20-%200ct%2020.pdf.

5. Office of the Inspector General, Commonwealth of Massachusetts, 2013 Annual Report, April 30, 2014, http://www.mass.gov/ig/about-us/annual-reports/office-of-the-inspector-general-2013-annual-report.pdf.

6. Annual Management and Program Analysis, Fiscal year 2013–2014, http://oig.louisiana.gov/assets/docs/OIG%20Annual%20Management%20and%20Program%20Analysis%20Report%2012-5-14.pdf.

7. D.C. Office of the Inspector General, Report on Activities, 2014, http://app.oig.dc.gov/news/view2.asp?url=release10%2FFY+2014+Annual+Report++-+Electronic.pdf&mode=release&archived=0&month=00000&agency=0.

8. Mark H. Moore and Margaret Jane Gates, *Inspectors General, Junkyard Dogs or Man's Best Friend*, Social Research Perspectives 13 (New York: Russell Sage, 1986).

9. Charles Dempsey, "The Inspector General Concept: Where It's Been, Where It's Going," *Public Budgeting and Finance* 5, no. 2 (Summer 1985): 39.

10. Moore and Gates, "Inspectors General," 11.

11. Al Gore, *The National Performance Review: From Red Tape to Results, Creating a Government That Works Better and Costs Less* (Washington, DC: U.S. Government Printing Office, 1993), Chap. 1.

12. U.S. Congress, House, "25th Anniversary of the Inspector General Act—Where Do We Go from Here?" Hearing before the House Government Reform Committee, Subcommittee on Government Efficiency and Financial Management, 108th Cong., 1st sess., October 8, 2003.

13. *The Historical Tables of the 2005 U.S. Budget* (table 17.1), www.gpoaccess.gov/usbudget/.

14. U.S. Congress, House, *Hearing, 25th Anniversary of the Inspector General Act.*

15. Florence Olsen, "Report Finds Understaffing in DOD IG's Office," *Federal Computer Week,* May 28, 2008, www.fcw.com.

16. GAO testimony, GAO-08-135T, October 31, 2007, www.gao.gov.

17. Government Accountability Office, "HUD Office of Inspector General Resources and Results," 2012, GAO 12–618, http://www.gao.gov/assets/600/591270.pdf.

18. Kearney and Company for the AGA, "Accelerating Change: The 2015 Inspector General Survey," September 2015, http://www.kearneyco.com/pdfs/AGA-IG -Survey-2015.pdf. It is not clear from the survey report how many respondents there were from each IG office or whether all IG offices responded to the survey. The results reported here are therefore suggestive but not definitive.

19. There are many sources for this information. See, for example, the statement of Gaston L. Gianni Jr., July 19, 2000, in *Legislative Proposals and Issues Relevant to the Operations of the Inspectors General, Hearing before the Committee on Governmental Affairs,* U.S. Senate, 106th Cong., 2d sess.; and Senate Report 106–470, *Amending the Inspector General Act of 1978 (5 U.S.C. App.) to Establish Police Powers for Certain Inspector General Agents Engaged in Official Duties and Provide an Oversight Mechanism for the Exercise of Those Powers,* 106th Cong., 2d Session, 2000, the report of the Committee on Governmental Affairs, to accompany S. 3144.

20. Amendment 4893 to Bill S. 2530 in the Senate reflected this change in 2002.

21. Jason Peckenpaugh, "IG Raps NASA's Use of Service Contractors," *Government Executive Magazine* February 20, 2001, www.govexec.com; Paul Light, "Off With Their Heads," reprinted in *Governance,* April 3, 2005 (Brookings Institution publication; originally in *Government Executive,* May 2002).

22. "Bill Improving Inspectors General Independence Passes Congress," OMBwatch, October 7, 2008, www.ombwatch.org. My comments are interspersed with the report from OMBwatch; "IG Reform Sent to the White House," *IEC Journal,* October 1, 2008, www.iecjournal.org/iec/inspectors_ general/; Beverley Lumpkin, "At Long Last Congress Passes IG Reform Act," Project on Government Oversight (POGO) blogpost, September 29, 2008, http://pogoblog.typepad.com/pogo/2008/09/at-long-last-co.html.

23. Government Accountability Office, *Inspectors General: Reporting on Independence, Effectiveness, and Expertise,* September 2011, www.gao.gov/ new.items/d11770.pdf.

24. Government Accountability Office report, ibid.

25. Stephen Power and Ian Talley, "Inspectors General at EPA, OPM Complain About Their Budgets," *Wall Street Journal,* February 1, 2010.

26. S. Report 114–36, May, 2015, Inspectors General Empowerment Act 2015, Homeland Security and Governmental Affairs Committee.

27. "House Committee Approves Legislation to Give IGs More Power," Fierce Government, http://www.fiercegovernment.com/story/house-committee -approves-legislation-give-igs-more-power/2014–09–18.

28. "IG Council Asks Congress to Codify Their Independence," Fierce Government, http://www.fiercegovernment.com/story/ig-council-asks-congress-codify -their-independence/2015–08–05.

29. POGO, "Where Are All the Watchdogs?" Project on Government Oversight, vacancy monitor, http://www.pogo.org/tools-and-data/ig-watchdogs/go-igi-20120208-where-are-all-the-watchdogs-inspector-general-vacancies1.html.

30. Opening Statement of Chairman Ron Johnson: "Improving the Efficiency, Effectiveness, and Independence of Inspectors General" June 3, 2015, http://www.hsgac.senate.gov/media/majority-media/opening-statement-of-chairman-ron-johnson-improving-the-efficiency-effectiveness-and-independence-of-inspectors-general.

31. Thomas Novotny, "The IGs—A Random Walk," *The Bureaucrat* 12, no. 3, (Fall 1983) p., 39.

32. Ibid.

33. Texas Medicaid Fraud Control Unit, https://www.texasattorneygeneral.gov/files/cj/mfcu_pf.pdf.

34. Ryan Hutchins, "N.J. Comptroller Matthew Boxer Not Afraid to Take on the State's Power Brokers," NJ.com, July 28, 2003, http://blog.nj.com/perspective/2013/07/nj_comptroller_matthew_boxer_n.html.

35. Patrick McCraney, "Mission Unaccomplished," *Chicago Tribune*, June 26, 2013, http://articles.chicagotribune.com/2013–06–26/opinion/ct-perspec-0626-inspector-20130626_1_inspector-general-ethics-commission-ethics-act.

36. Joseph M. Ferguson, Inspector General of the City of Chicago v. Stephen R. Patton in the Supreme Court of the State of Illinois, March 21, 2013.

37. Article XIII. Office of Inspector General (OIG), New Orleans City Code.

38. Sec. 2–1120. Office of Inspector General, New Orleans City Code.

39. Quoted in Brian Thevenot, "New Orleans Inspector General Robert Cerasoli Quits Post, Citing Health Issues," nola.com, January 29, 2009, www.nola.com/news/index.ssf/2009/01/ncw_orleans_inspector_general_1.html.

40. Steven Miller, "New City of Houston Inspector General Says There's 'a Place to Come' with Allegations of Wrongdoing," *Texas Watchdog*, December 17, 2010, www.texaswatchdog.org/2010/12/new-city-of-houston-inspector-general-Robert-Hoguim-says-theres-a-place/1292599872.column.

41. Chris Moran, "Houston's Inspector General Resigns," *Houston Chronicle*, January 16, 2012.

42. Steve Miller, "Houston's Inspector General Quits, Says Authority 'Not There,'" *Your Houston News,* February 8, 2012, www.yourhoustonnews.com/news/houston-s-inspector-general-quits-says-authority-not-there/article_e94e4d1e-e42d-5b8e-84c9-a8582f9d7467.html.

43. Status report of the grand jury regarding Palm Beach County governance and public corruption issues, September, 2011.

44. Eliot Kleinberg, Palm Beach County Cities Want Rehearing in Inspector General Suit, *Palm Beach Post*, March 27, 2015, http://www.palmbeach post.com/news/news/local-govt-politics/palm-beach-county-cities-want -rehearing-in-inspect/nkgn6/.

45. The complexity of federal programs and the inevitability of some waste, fraud, and abuse are the central points made by John Young, "Reflections on the Root Causes of Fraud, Abuse, and Waste in Federal Social Programs," *Public Administration Review* 43, no. 4 (July/August 1983): 362–369.

46. Thomas W. Novotny, "The IGs—A Random Walk," *Bureaucrat* 12, no. 3 (Fall 1983): 37.

Chapter 9

1. Letter, from Stephen Street, President of the Association of Inspectors General, to Honorable Chuck Grassley et al., November 19, 2015, http://inspectorsgeneral .org/files/2015/11/Letter-from-AIG-to-Chairmen-and-Ranking-Members-on -IG-Records-Access-11–19–20151.pdf.

2. Arizona posts its "strike everything" amendments on the legislative website, see for example, http://www.azleg.gov/StrikeEverything.asp. Nevertheless, budget legislation may be considered very quickly, without time for citizens or interest groups to follow or comment.

3. Steve Mistler, "Maine Watchdog Agency to Investigate LePage's Funding Threat in Mark Eves Hiring," *Portland Herald Press,* July 2, 2015, http://www .pressherald.com/2015/07/01/lepage-attorney-to-watchdog-agency-you -dont-have-power-to-investigate-governor/.

Author Index

Subject Index

About the Author

Irene Rubin is professor emerita of Public Administration at Northern Illinois University. Her teaching, research, and writing have focused on public budgeting and qualitative research design and methods. Within public budgeting, she has concentrated on the politics and administration of governments in financial trouble and on techniques and implications of contracting out, especially for public enterprises, such as water and wastewater treatment. Recent research has included work on the relationship between executive budgeting and fiscal health and on long-term budgeting for entitlements. Her books on budgeting include *Balancing the Federal Budget: Trimming the Herds or Eating the Seed Corn* and *Class, Tax, and Power: Municipal Budgeting in the United States*. A former editor of *Public Budgeting and Finance* and *Public Administration Review*, she has also done editing projects for GFOA and the American Water Works Association. Her BA is from Barnard College, her MA is from Harvard, and her PhD is from the University of Chicago. As an activist, in recent years she has been advocating for the pension system in her state, and as a practitioner, she sat on the board of the budget review committee for a small city for several years, taking budgets apart and examining them line by line. The awards she is most proud of include the Aaron Wildavsky Award for lifetime achievements in scholarship in public budgeting and a fellowship at the Woodrow Wilson International Center for Scholars in Washington, D.C.